Global Overview of Anti-Bribery Laws

2016

Primera edición, 2016

THOMSON REUTERS PROVIEW™ eBOOKS
Incluye versión en digital

Editorial Aranzadi, SA
Camino de Galar, 15
31190 Cizur Menor (Navarra)
ISBN: 978-84-9135-220-4
Depósito Legal: NA 769/2015
Printed in Spain. Impreso en España
Impresión: Rodona Industria Gráfica, SL
Polígono Agustinos Calle A. Nave D-11
31013 - Pamplona

Foreword

On 11 May 2016, Baker & McKenzie and other leading UK law firms signed a pledge to tackle corruption within the professional services sector ahead of an anti-corruption summit hosted by the UK Prime Minister David Cameron. The signatories promised to increase efforts to tackle corruption and "work together to share experience, promote the codification of good practice, and in dialogue with government, regulators and professional bodies to support their work addressing the practical limitations of the wider system we currently work within."

The pledge added: "We deplore the damage caused to social progress and economic development by corruption."

Through this public statement, and with our continuing work with the B20 Anti-Corruption Taskforce and the Partnering Against Corruption Initiative (PACI) of the World Economic Forum, Baker & McKenzie is committed to do all it can to fight the global scourge of bribery and corruption. We are also proud of our clients who share this commitment, and together we are finding practical ways of conducting business not only compliant with laws but also promoting ethical conduct with robust corporate governance standards.

The threat of exposure is even greater today than yesterday, with increased investigative journalism breaking open corporate scandals and whistleblower activism at an all-time high. In response, we are assisting our multinational clients to use innovative disruption to change old business models and find new solutions that reduce and mitigate bribery and corruption risk in high-risk jurisdictions. These companies are asking the hard questions of their business leaders to ensure that investment in ethics is not just on paper or an afterthought - but that it is a spotlight on their business wherever it is based, whether it is expanding or just about to be launched.

Madame Christine Lagarde, head of the IMF and our ex-chair, penned in her May 2016 essay **Addressing corruption – openly:** "*although corruption is an extraordinarily complex phenomenon, I do not accept the proposition – or the myth – that it is primarily a 'cultural' problem that will always take generations to address. There are examples of countries that have managed to make significant progress in addressing it in a relatively short time.*"

I strongly agree with Madame Lagarde' s view and in the way of countries, we have seen companies also make significant progress in addressing their bribery and corruption challenges, whether that be in Brazil, India, China or sub-Saharan Africa. While there may be additional costs, time and effort involved, these multinationals are leading the way - in some cases creating environments where corrupt governments are toppled as a result.

We are therefore very proud to publish our updated and extremely popular 2016 Global Overview of Anti-Bribery Laws. On behalf of the Global Compliance & Investigations team at Baker & McKenzie, we continue to be confident that this handbook provides the requisite knowledge for the first step towards running your business untainted by corruption. We hope you continue to find it a useful tool.

Mini vandePol
Chair, Global Compliance and Investigations Group

Hong Kong

Editor's note

Baker & McKenzie is very pleased to provide you with the 2016 edition of its publication **Global Overview of Anti-Bribery Laws**. This publication is the result of the collective efforts of close to 100 of our compliance and investigations practitioners, covering 46 jurisdictions where Baker & McKenzie has local teams with extensive expertise advising clients on compliance and investigations as well as on anti-bribery laws.

Bribery, compliance and investigations continue to be some of the main challenges that companies face, both in their domestic markets and abroad.

At a global scale, we see an increasing number of countries promulgating new and more sophisticated anti-bribery legislation as well as more aggressive enforcement by the relevant agencies and courts. We also notice increased cooperation between enforcement agencies of different countries as well as more efficient ways of sharing relevant information, resulting in an increase in high profile global anti-corruption cases. As a legal trend, we see more and more countries introducing criminal liability for legal entities for bribery-related crimes as well as specific legislation encouraging companies to adopt compliance programs by recognizing the adoption and implementation of said programs as a mitigating factor in their defense against corporate criminal liability.

In light of the above, it is critical to develop good understanding of the relevant anti-bribery laws regulating domestic bribery, both private to public and private to private, as well as corruption of foreign public officials. It is also important to adopt adequate business strategies and practices to mitigate the criminal, administrative and reputational risks associated with the infringement of anti-bribery laws. In addition, it is necessary to understand the legal value given to compliance programs as a defense to shape corporate strategies in order to protect the company, its directors and employees from criminal liability.

This 2016 edition of the Global Anti-Bribery Laws has been prepared to provide you with an overview of the anti-bribery laws in 46 jurisdictions, including definitions as well as a fair number of recommended practices. For specific and definite advice, please feel free to contact the authors of each chapter.

I hope that you will find this publication useful.

Rafael Jiménez-Gusi
Partner, EMEA Compliance Group Steering Committee
Co-Chair, Spanish Compliance Group

Global Steering Committee

Mini vandePol, Practice Chair, Partner
Hong Kong
Tel: +852 2846 2562
mini.vandepol@bakermckenzie.com

Richard Dean, Partner
Washington, DC
Tel: +1 202 452 7009
richard.dean@bakermckenzie.com

Esther Flesch
Sao Paulo
Tel: +55 11 3048-6940
esther.flesch@trenchrossi.com

Aurelio Giovannelli, Partner
Rome
Tel: +39 06 44 063 239
aurelio.giovannelli@bakermckenzie.com

David Hackett, Partner
Chicago
Tel: +1 312 861 6640
david.hackett@bakermckenzie.com

Andreas Lohner, Partner
Munich
Tel: +49 89 5 52 38 133
andreas.lohner@bakermckenzie.com

Joanna Ludlam, Partner
London
Tel: +44 20 7919 1822
joanna.ludlam@bakermckenzie.com

Bruno Maeda
Sao Paulo
Tel: +55 11 3048-6838
bruno.maeda@trenchrossi.com

Sunny Mann, Partner
London
Tel: +44 20 7919 1397
sunny.mann@bakermckenzie.com

Andrew Martin, Partner
Singapore
Tel: +65 6434 2507
andrew.martin@bakermckenzie.com

Joan Meyer
Washington, DC
Tel: +1 202 835 6119
joan.meyer@bakermckenzie.com

Table of Contents

Asia Pacific

Australia

Georgie Farrant

Georgie Farrant is part of Baker & McKenzie's Global Compliance Team and Global Anti-Money Laundering and Counter-Terrorism Financing Team.

Georgie practices in commercial disputes, with a particular focus on financial services disputes and regulatory disputes and investigations. This includes civil actions relating to financial services and financial products, insider dealing and market abuse actions, takeover related actions and advice, and disciplinary actions by regulatory bodies. She also advises companies and individuals in relation to a range of compliance and regulatory issues, including anti-money laundering, anti-corruption, whistleblowing and regulator investigations.

Georgie has previously been seconded to the UK Listing Authority, investigating and enforcing breaches of the UK Listing Rules and assisting with the development of the market abuse regime. She has also been seconded to HSBC Investment Bank's Compliance team, advising in relation to information barriers.

georgie.farrant@bakermckenzie.com
Tel: +61 2 8922 5601

Baker & McKenzie
Level 27, A.M.P. Centre
50 Bridge Street
Sydney, NSW 2000
Australia

Angela Sevenson

Angela Sevenson frequently advises clients on cross-jurisdictional legal compliance. She performs inward as well as third-party risk assessments, due diligence and internal investigations. She assists clients in responding to regulators, helping them avoid internal resource drain and manage reputational risk. Angela's knowledge of industry best practice means she can recommend appropriate solutions for her clients' business requirements and budget. She tailors compliance processes and training programs to help protect organizations and support their efforts to operate with integrity in Australia and internationally. Her risk and crisis management matters are typically event-related and extend well beyond compliance. They reflect Angela's adaptability as she applies her investigative and evidentiary skills to the crisis, or her assessment and advisory skills to the risk. Her practice spans a range of commerce, including the resource, energy, food export, hospitality, retail, banking, transport, manufacturing, defense and telecommunication industries.

angela.sevenson@bakermckenzie.com
Tel: +61 3 9617 4486

Ryan Hennessey

Ryan Hennessey has substantial experience in relation to the resolution of commercial disputes involving issues of contract law, environmental liability, insolvency, corporations law, the enforcement of securities, and other complex commercial issues. He has also assisted clients with regulatory investigations and prosecutions concerning issues of fraud and bribery and corruption. Ryan has prepared for, appeared and instructed at both interlocutory and final hearings in the Supreme Court of Victoria and Federal Court of Australia.

ryan.hennessey@bakermckenzie.com
Tel: +61 3 9617 4314

Baker & McKenzie
Level 19, CBW
181 William Street
Melbourne VIC 3000
Australia

1. Domestic bribery (private to public)

1.1 Legal framework

Divisions 141 and 142 of the *Criminal Code Act 1995* (Cth) (the "Australian Criminal Code") make it illegal under Australian law:

- to promise or offer a bribe or corrupting benefit to a Commonwealth public official; or
- to provide or cause to be provided a bribe or corrupting benefit to a Commonwealth public official.

Individuals and corporations may be charged with these criminal offenses and it is not necessary to prove that the defendant, whether that is an individual or corporation, knew that the official was a Commonwealth public official.

Each Australian State and Territory has laws prohibiting bribery and corruption of State or Territory public officials or officers.

Under the new Part 10.9 of the Australian Criminal Code, it is also an offense for an individual or corporation to intentionally or recklessly facilitate, conceal or disguise in their accounting documents an occurrence of bribery, corruption or loss to a person that was not legitimately incurred (the "False Accounting Offences"). Under Section 490.5, proof that a benefit (not legitimately due) was actually received or given by the accused or another person is not required.

1.2 Definition of bribery

Bribery requires intention and conduct. The conduct must be to dishonestly provide or offer a benefit (or cause it to be provided or offered) to a Commonwealth public official. The intention must be to influence the official in the exercise of the official's duties.

The benefit may be intangible, such as the provision of hospitality or entertainment.

There is essentially little difference between a bribe and corrupting benefit other than the offense of providing or offering a corrupting benefit does not require an intention to influence the official. It is sufficient that the receipt or expectation of the receipt of the corrupting benefit would tend to influence a public official in the exercise of the official's duties.

As a result, under the bribery offense, because the defendant must intend to influence the official, the defendant's culpability is greater. So too is the maximum penalty when compared to the offense of offering or providing a corrupting benefit to a Commonwealth public official.

Australian State and Territory laws have a similar focus, though some target different types of public official. One example is specific laws for bribery of elected State officials.

1.3 Definition of Commonwealth public official

The Australian Criminal Code contains a lengthy definition of Commonwealth public official, including categories or classes of individuals. The definition expressly includes Australian (Commonwealth/Federal) public service employees, defense force members, members of the Australian Federal Police, service providers contracted to the Commonwealth, members of statutorily appointed bodies (such as chancellors of universities) or Commonwealth holders of office such as members of Parliament, judicial officers and the Governor-General.

Whether employees of publicly owned companies in Australia will be deemed to be Commonwealth public officials will primarily depend on whether they are considered to be employed by the Commonwealth and whether they exercise powers or perform functions conferred on them by a law of the Commonwealth.

Australian State and Territory laws are usually equally broad, though specific laws apply to different types of State or Territory public officials.

1.4 Consequences of bribery

(a) For individuals

In bribing a Commonwealth public official:

- up to 10 years' imprisonment; and/or
- a fine of up to 10,000 Penalty Units (currently equivalent to AUD1.8 million).

In offering or providing corrupting benefits to a Commonwealth public official:

- up to five years' imprisonment; and/or
- a fine of up to 300 Penalty Units (currently equivalent to AUD54,000).

In respect of the False Accounting Offences:

- if intentional – 10 years' imprisonment and/or a fine of AUD1.8 million; or
- if reckless – five years' imprisonment and/or a fine of AUD900,000.

(b) For corporations

In bribing a Commonwealth public official, the maximum penalty is the greater of:

- 100,000 Penalty Units (currently equivalent to AUD18 million);
- triple the value of the illicit benefit; or

- 10 percent of the annual turnover of the corporation in the year preceding the offense.

In offering or providing corrupting benefits to a Commonwealth public official, the penalty is a fine of up to 1,500 Penalty Units (currently equivalent to AUD270,000).

The Australian Criminal Code provides for corporate liability where the conduct of individuals was within the scope of their employment, and:

- the board of directors or a high managerial agent knowingly or recklessly permitted or carried out the offense;
- a corporate culture existed that tolerated the offense; or
- the organization failed to create a corporate culture that required compliance with the law.

In respect of the False Accounting Offences:

- if intentional – the greater of AUD18 million fine, 3 times the value of the benefit or 10 percent of the annual turnover of the body corporate; or
- if reckless – the greater of AUD9 million fine, 1.5 times the value of the benefit or 5 percent of the annual turnover of the body corporate.

1.5 Political contributions

Contributions to political parties or associated entities are regulated by Part XX of the *Commonwealth Electoral Act 1918* (Cth). In general terms, contributions to political parties are allowed but must be disclosed if exceeding AUD13,000 over the year (effective 1 July 2015 up to 30 June 2016). The threshold is indexed to the official inflation measure so it generally increases each year.

Separate provisions apply for individual States and Territories. These are often far more proscriptive. For example, in New South Wales (NSW), total yearly donations above certain limits are banned. Disclosure is generally required for contributions above AUD1,000.

1.6 Limitation applicable to hospitality expenses (gifts, travel, meals, entertainment, among others)

The Australian Criminal Code does not contain quantitative limitations on hospitality expenses, but these are specifically within the concept of a "benefit" for the purposes of bribery or corrupting benefits.

2. Domestic bribery (private to private)

2.1 Legal framework

There is no Commonwealth private to private bribery offense in Australia. However, private bribery, kickbacks and secret commissions are criminal offenses under some Australian State and Territory laws. For example, in the State of New South Wales (NSW), this is governed by the *Crimes Act* 1900 (NSW) (the "Crimes Act"). The False Accounting Offences described above in Section 1.1 may also be applicable.

2.2 Definition of private bribery

The scope of any private bribery offenses varies between Australian States and Territories but, for example, in the State of NSW, the law prohibiting bribery is called the offense of secret commissions. It is an offense when an agent dishonestly accepts money or benefits from a third party in return for departing from a duty he owes to that agent's principal.

2.3 Consequences of private bribery

The penalties referred to are those for the State of NSW.

For individuals involved

- up to seven years' imprisonment;
- a fine of up to 1,000 Penalty Units (currently equivalent to AUD110,000); and/or
- repayment of the benefit received or given.

Note that penalties are higher in other States. For example, Victorian offenses carry 10-year maximum terms of imprisonment.

2.4 Limitation applicable to hospitality expenses (gifts, travel, meals, entertainment, among others)

The Crimes Act does not establish quantitative nor qualitative limitations on hospitality expenses, but those types of benefits could fall within the scope of the offenses.

3. Corruption of foreign public officials

3.1 Legal framework

Division 70 of the Australian Criminal Code makes it illegal under Australian law to bribe a foreign public official. Limited defenses are included. The facilitation payment defense is one of few such defenses that continue to exist globally, although it has considerable restrictions. The False Accounting Offences described above in Section 1.1 may also be applicable.

3.2 Definition of corruption of foreign public officials

Other than the identity of the target or recipient of the bribe, the elements of the offense of bribing a foreign public official are similar to those of bribing a Commonwealth public official. However, the foreign public official offense contains an additional element, which is stated in italics in the next paragraph.

Bribing a foreign public official under Australian law requires intention and conduct. The conduct must be to dishonestly provide or offer a benefit (or cause it to be provided or offered) to a foreign public official. The intention must be to influence the official in the exercise of the official's duties *in order to obtain or retain a business advantage that is not legitimately due.*

The benefit may be intangible, such as the provision of hospitality or entertainment.

3.3 Definition of foreign public official

Foreign public official is defined broadly and includes employees or officials of foreign government bodies (including military or police service people), contractors to foreign government bodies, intermediaries of foreign public officials, members of the judiciary of a foreign country, employees of public international (inter-governmental) organizations, persons performing duties for an office under a law of that country, and any person in the service of a foreign government body.

3.4 Consequences of corruption of foreign public officials

(a) For the individuals involved

- up to 10 years' imprisonment; and/or
- a fine of up to 10,000 Penalty Units (currently equivalent to AUD1.8 million).

(b) For corporations

The maximum penalty is the greater of:

- 100,000 Penalty Units (currently equivalent to AUD18 million);
- triple the value of the illicit benefit; or
- 10 percent of the annual turnover of the corporation in the year preceding the offense.

The Australian Criminal Code provides for corporate liability where the conduct of individuals was within the scope of their employment, and:

- the board of directors or a high managerial agent knowingly or recklessly permitted or carried out the offense;
- a corporate culture existed that tolerated the offense; or
- the organization failed to create a corporate culture that required compliance with the law.

3.5 Limitation applicable to hospitality expenses (gifts, travel, meals, entertainment, among others)

The Australian Criminal Code does not contain quantitative limitations on hospitality expenses even though these are specifically within the concept of a "benefit" for the purposes of bribery or corrupting benefits.

4. Facilitation payments

The Australian Criminal Code provides that making a facilitation payment can constitute a defense to the charge of bribing a foreign public official. The defense is not available to a charge of bribing a Commonwealth public official. The defense essentially requires that:

- the benefit was of a minor nature;
- the provider of the benefit made a written record of the relevant conduct as soon as practicable; and
- the benefit was offered to expedite or secure the performance of a routine government action of a minor nature.

Somewhat controversially, lawfully made facilitation payments are considered legitimate business expenses for the purposes of reducing a company's taxable income under Australian law.

5. Compliance programs

5.1 Value of a compliance program to mitigate/eliminate the criminal liability for legal entities

Two instances where the Australian Criminal Code imposes criminally liability on a corporation are:

- where it is proven that a corporate culture existed within the corporation that directed, encouraged, tolerated or led to non-compliance with the relevant provision; or
- where the corporation failed to create and maintain a corporate culture that required compliance with anti-corruption law.

Compliance programs are instruments that corporations rely on to discourage and prevent bribery and corruption within their organization and will assist in demonstrating that an appropriate culture exists.

Even if during a criminal prosecution a compliance program is found to be inadequate and does not fully exculpate a corporation, it may be a mitigating factor for the purpose of sentencing.

5.2 Absence of a compliance program as a crime

It is not an offense under the Australian Criminal Code to be without a compliance program; it is only a factor that can be taken into account if a corporation is charged with bribery as a result of an employee's or agent's conduct.

5.3 Elements of compliance program

(a) Legal framework

The Australian Criminal Code does not regulate the elements of any compliance program. There is no Australian legislation, case law or regulatory guidance that sets out the elements to incorporate into a compliance program. Australian Standard AS:8001-2008 Fraud and Corruption Control together with the associated suite of corporate governance Australian Standards are not mandatory in this context but are of some assistance when tailoring compliance programs to suit any organization.

(b) Recommended practice

Baker & McKenzie recommends that corporations adopt a compliance program that is tailored to the corporation's geographical and operational risks, and ensure that it is comprehensively and continually communicated, monitored and enforced. While there is no Australian legislation, case law or regulatory guidance that sets out the elements to incorporate into a compliance program, the UK Ministry of Justice Guidelines and the DOJ/SEC Guidance will provide a starting point in understanding the elements that regulators globally will expect corporations to have considered.

6. Regulator with jurisdiction to prosecute corruption

The Australian Federal Police investigate bribery and corruption allegations at a Commonwealth/Federal level. State and Territory police investigate pursuant to State and Territory laws.

Prosecution under Australian Commonwealth/Federal law is under the auspices of the Commonwealth Director of Public Prosecutions, although the Australian Federal Police may commence the court process (and continue to be involved). At a State and Territory level, the relevant State or Territory department of public prosecutions would be involved in conjunction with the State or Territory police.

The Australian Securities and Investments Commission is the main corporate regulator and can be involved in investigations into corrupt conduct where an Australian corporation is involved.

China

Mini vandePol

Mini vandePol is the chair of the Firm's Global Compliance & Investigations Group. Based in Hong Kong and with more than 24 years' experience, Mini is the trusted advisor of the board, legal, executive and operational personnel of the Firm's most significant global clients assisting them to establish and enhance their risk management programs and credibly investigate transgressions to support a strong commitment to a culture of compliance. As well as leading a global team of 900+ compliance and investigation team members, Mini's work engagements focus on anti-bribery and corruption investigations and risk mitigation in China, India and other parts of Asia in a variety of industries including the ITC and healthcare sectors. Mini has regularly appeared before enforcement bodies in Asia and also the US Department of Justice and SEC in relation to corruption investigations. Moreover, as part of her global outreach activities, Mini is the co-chair of the B20 Anti-Corruption Taskforce.

mini.vandepol@bakermckenzie.com
Tel: +852 2846 2562

Baker & McKenzie
14th Floor, Hutchison House
10 Harcourt Road, Central
Hong Kong, SAR
China

Simon Hui

Simon Hui leads the Firm's Compliance & Investigations team in Shanghai. With more than 20 years of practice experience, his key practice areas include compliance, regulatory and commercial dispute resolution. Simon has in-depth experience in handling compliance/regulatory matters, including anti-bribery/anti-corruption and unfair competition issues. He has conducted complex internal investigations for various multinational companies across a range of industries, including pharmaceutical, life science, automotive, outsourcing and media. Simon has strong on-the-ground experience engaging with China regulators, including the local and state Administration for Industry and Commerce (AIC), the Ministry of Commerce and the People's Procuratorate Office. He has also performed due diligence/risk assessment and provided training to multinational companies, focusing on anti-bribery/anti-corruption as well as anti-trust issues. Simon is admitted to practice in Hong Kong and in England & Wales. He speaks fluent English, Mandarin and Cantonese.

simon.hui@bakermckenzie.com
Tel: +86 21 6105 5996

Baker & McKenzie
Unit 1601, Jin Mao Tower
88 Century Avenue, Pudong
Shanghai 200121, PRC
China

Vivian Wu

Vivian Wu leads the Firm's Compliance & Investigations team in Beijing and her practice focuses on corporate regulatory and compliance matters, such as anti-corruption, anti-trust and environment. She has extensive experience in compliance investigations, risk assessment and compliance training. Vivian regularly assists multinational companies and has represented clients in external investigations initiated by Chinese regulators such as the National Development and Reform Commission (NDRC), local and state AICs, and the Food and Drug Administration. Vivian was seconded to the Firm's Washington DC office in 2014, where she worked closely with the Firm's North American Compliance and Investigations Practice Group on FCPA cases. She is qualified to practice in China and in New York. She speaks fluent English and Mandarin.

vivian.wu@bakermckenzie.com
Tel: +86 10 6535 3860

Baker & McKenzie LLP - Beijing Representative Office
Suite 3401, China World Office 2
China World Trade Center
1 Jianguomenwai Dajie
Beijing 100004, PRC
China

1. Domestic bribery (private to public)

1.1 Legal framework

Bribery of public officials is regulated under the PRC Criminal Code (the "Criminal Code").

1.2 Definition of bribery

Under Articles 389, 390, 390A and 393 of the Criminal Code, bribery means giving money or property to an incumbent or former public official, or the person related to the public official (i.e., a close relative or any other person closely related to the incumbent or former public official) for the purpose of securing illegitimate benefits.

1.3 Definition of public official

The Criminal Code has a broad definition of public official. Public official refers to personnel performing public service in state organs, as well as the following:

- Personnel engaged in public service in state-owned corporations, enterprises, institutions and people's organizations

- Personnel who are assigned to non-state-owned corporations, enterprises, institutions and social organizations by state-owned corporations, enterprises and institutions

- Other working personnel engaged in public service in accordance with law

1.4 Consequences of bribery

The Criminal Code establishes the penalties, as described below, for individuals and companies or legal entities committing bribery.

(a) For the individuals involved

Individuals or persons related to public officials who are found to be guilty of bribery are subject to:

- up to lifetime imprisonment;
- confiscation of property; or
- criminal fine.

Bribe recipients can also be liable. A public official who receives a large amount of bribes can be sentenced to imprisonment or the death penalty. A non-official bribe recipient (e.g., former public official or person related to the public official) can be sentenced to imprisonment.

(b) For the company / legal entity involved

Companies that offer bribes to public officials or persons related to public officials, as well as the responsible persons who are directly in charge of those companies and directly responsible for such offenses, are subject to:

- criminal fine levied on the company; and
- up to five years' imprisonment and a criminal fine for the responsible persons in an official bribery case.

1.5 Political contributions

There is no direct equivalent of the concept of "political contribution" under the Criminal Code.

1.6 Limitation applicable to hospitality expenses (gifts, travel, meals, entertainment, among others)

While the Criminal Code does not establish quantitative nor qualitative limitations on hospitality expenses, there is a threshold amount for the prosecution of official bribery, as follows: RMB10,000 for individual bribe-givers; RMB200,000 for corporate bribe-givers; and RMB5,000 for bribe-recipients. However, within the PRC central government, there is an internal regulation issued in 1995 applicable to public officials of central party and government organs, which provides reference for the limitation of gifts, as follows:

(a) Public officials shall hand over the gift to the government if the value of the gift exceeds RMB200 per person per occasion.

(b) If the cumulative value of all the gifts received by the public officials exceed RMB600 per person per year, the public official shall hand over such gifts to the government.

In other words, if a person or company provides to a public official of central party and government organs a gift or gifts the total value of which exceed the limitations set out as above, the gift(s) may be considered "in violation of state regulations" according to the 1995 internal regulation.

From our experience, due to inflation, RMB200 is no longer considered a sizable gift in the PRC. As a result, the 1995 internal regulation mentioned above has only been loosely followed. Whether a hospitality expense can be considered as bribery will need to be determined on a case-by-case basis, taking into account all the facts and circumstances surrounding the case, and applying 1.6(a) and 1.6(b) referred to above. In practice, most multinationals in China adopt a threshold amount of around RMB200 to RMB500 (approximately USD32 to USD81) for courtesy gifts or entertainment by meal, per occasion, per person. Many companies also provide for a frequency limit; for example, no gifts can be given to the same person over three to four times per year. Some industry associations have set up benchmarking rules on gifts, meals and entertainment, for consideration by the members to level the playing field.

2. Domestic bribery (private to private)

2.1 Legal framework

Private bribery is regulated by the Criminal Code and the PRC Anti-Unfair Competition Law (AUCL).

2.2 Definition of private bribery

Under Article 164 of the Criminal Code, private bribery means giving money or property to any employee of a company, enterprise or other entity for the purpose of seeking improper interests and benefits.

Under Article 8 of the AUCL, private bribery means giving money or property, or secret and off-the-book kickbacks to a business counterparty or its employee, or using other means to bribe a business counterparty or its employee for selling or purchasing goods. The Interim Provisions on Prohibition of Commercial Bribery also describe the forms of private bribery under the AUCL, which include any money or property provided to the business counterparty or its employee for promotion, publicity, sponsorship, scientific research, labor, consultancy, commission, reimbursement, or any other benefits such as trips or visits.

2.3 Consequences of private bribery

2.3.1 Under PRC Criminal Law

The Criminal Code establishes the penalties for the individuals and the company/legal entities committing private bribery when the amount of the bribe is relatively large. The penalties are as follows:

(a) For the individuals involved

- Up to 10 years' imprisonment
- Criminal fine

(b) For the company / legal entity involved

- Criminal fine for the legal entity
- Up to 10 years' imprisonment and a criminal fine for persons who are directly in charge and other persons who are directly responsible for the offense

2.3.2 Under the AUCL

The AUCL establishes administrative penalties for business operators committing private bribery in circumstances where the violations have not constituted criminal offences. The penalties are as follows:

- Administrative fine up to RMB200,000
- Confiscation of illegal gains

2.4 Limitation applicable to hospitality expenses (gifts, travel, meals, entertainment, among others)

The Criminal Code does not establish quantitative nor qualitative limitations on hospitality expenses.

Whether a hospitality expense could be considered as private bribery will need to be determined on a case-by-case basis, taking into account all the facts and circumstances surrounding the case, and applying 1.6(a) and 1.6(b) referred to above.

In the healthcare sector, a donation could be considered as private bribery if it is provided in an inappropriate way for purchasing or selling goods. The Administrative Measures on Accepting Donations for Public Welfare by Healthcare Entities (for Trial Implementation) (the "New Donation Rules") promulgated in 2015 provide specific guidance on donations to healthcare and family planning entities for the non-profit purpose of public welfare such as training, academic or research. The New Donation Rules prohibit donations to these entities if used for any illegal or commercial purpose, or as commercial bribery or an incentive to purchase the goods.

3. Corruption of foreign public officials

3.1 Legal framework

Corruption of foreign public officials is regulated under the Criminal Code.

3.2 Definition of corruption of foreign public officials

Under Article 164 of the Criminal Code, corruption of foreign public officials means the giving of money or property to foreign government functionary or officials of international public organizations for the purpose of seeking improper commercial interests.

3.3 Definition of foreign public official

For the purpose of this offence, a foreign public official means:

- a foreign government functionary; or
- an official of an international public organization.

3.4 Consequences of corruption of foreign public officials

(a) For the individuals involved

- Up to 10 years' imprisonment
- Criminal fine

(b) For the legal entity

- Criminal fine for the legal entity
- Up to 10 years' imprisonment and criminal fine for persons who are directly in charge and other persons who are directly responsible for the offense

3.5 Limitation applicable to hospitality expenses (gifts, travel, meals, entertainment, among others)

The Criminal Code does not establish quantitative nor qualitative limitations on hospitality expenses.

Whether a hospitality expense could be considered bribery will need to be determined on a case-by-case basis, taking into account all the facts and circumstances surrounding the case, and applying 1.6(a) and 1.6(b) referred to above.

4. Facilitation payments

There is no direct equivalent of the concept of "facilitation payments" under the Criminal Code. Facilitation payments may be considered a bribe.

5. Compliance programs

5.1 Value of a compliance program to mitigate/eliminate the liability for legal entities

The Criminal Code and the AUCL do not specifically recognize a compliance program as an instrument to mitigate or eliminate liability for legal entities. However, if a legal entity can prove that it had exercised due control over its employees by means of a compliance program or by any other means, a company can seek leniency or mitigate the risk of liability arising from the corrupt behavior of its employees.

5.2 Absence of a compliance program as a crime

The Criminal Code and the AUCL do not recognize the absence of having a compliance program as a criminal or administrative offense.

5.3 Elements of compliance program

(a) Legal framework

The Criminal Code and the AUCL do not recognize or regulate the elements of a compliance program.

(b) Recommended practice

While having a compliance program does not offer a legal defense for the offense of bribery, it is recommended that legal entities adopt a robust compliance program to prevent internal corruption and bribery. It is also useful to draw a clear line between the legal entities' liability and the employees' individual liability in order to mitigate the potential legal risks of the legal entity.

6. Regulator with jurisdiction to prosecute corruption

The Public Security Bureau (PSB) has jurisdiction to investigate bribery related to non-public officials. The Procuratorate has jurisdiction to investigate and prosecute bribery related to public officials or private bribery. The Administration for Industry and Commerce has the power to investigate and sanction companies for private bribery.

Hong Kong

Mini vandePol

With more than 24 years' experience, Mini vandePol is the trusted advisor of the board, legal, executive and operational personnel of the Firm's most significant global clients, assisting them to establish and enhance their risk management programs and credibly investigate transgressions to support a strong commitment to a culture of compliance. As well as leading a global team of 900+ compliance and investigation team members, Mini's work engagements focus on anti-bribery and corruption investigations and risk mitigation in China, India and other parts of Asia in a variety of industries including the healthcare sector. In addition, as part of her global outreach activities, Mini is a member of the B20 Anti-Corruption Taskforce.

mini.vandepol@bakermckenzie.com
Tel: +852 2846 2562

Gary Seib

Gary Seib is one of the first lawyers to be granted "Solicitor Advocate" status before the Hong Kong courts. He is a commercial litigation specialist with over 30 years' experience in corporate governance, compliance and regulatory matters, including cross-border fraud investigations, asset tracing claims and recovery actions. Gary is currently a member of the Firm's Executive Committee. He also served as the Asia Pacific chair (2006 - 2009) and global chair (2009 - 2014) of the Firm's Dispute Resolution Group, as well as Asia Pacific co-chair of the Compliance Group. He is ranked as Eminent Practitioner and as one of the leading lawyers in his field by top legal directories, including *Chambers Global, Chambers Asia Pacific, Asia Pacific Legal 500 and IFLR1000.*

gary.seib@bakermckenzie.com
Tel: +852 2846 2112

Cynthia Tang

Cynthia Tang heads the Dispute Resolution Group in the Hong Kong office.

She has over 25 years of experience in Hong Kong and Asia and is well-recognized as one of the region's leading contentious regulatory lawyers. Her practice focuses on domestic as well as global regulatory enforcement, and she is an expert in listed company and financial services regulatory enforcement. She regularly advises local and multinational corporations, directors, financial institutions and the financial services industry in regulatory enforcement matters. Cynthia has been acknowledged as a leading lawyer over consecutive years by leading legal publications, including *Chambers Asia Pacific, Asia Pacific Legal 500,* and *IFLR1000.*

cynthia.tang@bakermckenzie.com
Tel: +852 2846 1708

Susan Kendall

Susan Kendall is a disputes lawyer with a particular focus on employment and privacy issues in a compliance and investigations context, commercial fraud and contentious trust matters. She has conducted FCPA investigations for clients in the logistics and technology industries along with numerous internal investigations across a range of compliance issues, including bid rigging, bribery, data breaches, misuse of confidential information and unlawful harassment. With over 28 years' experience in both contentious and non-contentious corporate and commercial law, she has advised on and acted in a number of complex and long running cross-border disputes and numerous international fraud cases. Susan has been consistently recognized as a leading lawyer in her field by various legal publications, including *Chambers Global* and *Chambers Asia Pacific*, *Asia Pacific Legal 500* and *IFLR1000*.

susan.kendall@bakermckenzie.com
Tel: +852 2846 2411

Bryan Ng

Bryan Ng's practice focuses on disputes related to financial services, regulatory investigations, compliance investigations, commercial disputes and insolvency-related matters. He advises and assists multinational corporations in conducting internal compliance investigations and dealing with cross-border regulatory enforcements. He regularly delivers training to clients on compliance and regulatory issues. He is fluent in English, Cantonese and Mandarin. Bryan is admitted as a Solicitor in Hong Kong.

bryan.ng@bakermckenzie.com
Tel: +852 2846 2923

Baker & McKenzie
14th Floor, Hutchison House
10 Harcourt Road, Central
Hong Kong, SAR
China

1. Domestic bribery (private to public)

1.1 Legal framework

In Hong Kong, corruption and bribery constitute the same offense. The offense is governed by the Prevention of Bribery Ordinance (Chapter 201 of the Laws of Hong Kong Special Administrative Region) ("POBO") which, among others, affects three categories of people:

(a) Civil servants of the Hong Kong government[1]

(b) Agents and/or employees of public bodies or private bodies that perform a public function[2]

(c) Agents and/or employees of any company or entity in the private sector

1.2 Definition of bribery

The offense can be committed by both private individuals and public servants. In relation to individuals, bribery is committed when any person, whether in Hong Kong or elsewhere, without lawful authority or reasonable excuse, offers an advantage to a public servant as an inducement to or reward for that public servant:

(a) performing or abstaining from performing an act in the capacity of a public servant;

(b) expediting, delaying, hindering or preventing the performance of an act in the capacity of a public servant; or

(c) assisting, favoring, hindering or delaying any person in the transaction of any business with a public body.[3]

---

[1] S. 2 POBO; see definition for "prescribed officer."
[2] S. 2 POBO; see definitions for "public body" and "public servant" as well as Schedule 1.
[3] S. 4 POBO.

Public servants (which include civil servants, and agents and employees of public bodies) commit the offense when they solicit or accept any advantage in the abovementioned circumstances, whether in Hong Kong or elsewhere. Civil servants who solicit or accept any advantage without the Chief Executive's permission are also guilty of an offense.[4]

The POBO defines an advantage to include:

(a) any gift, loan, fee, reward or commission consisting of money, valuable security or other property of any description;

(b) any office, employment or contract;

(c) any payment release, discharge or liquidation of any loan, obligation or other liability;

(d) any other service or favor (other than entertainment);

(e) the exercise or forbearance from the exercise of any right or power or duty; or

(f) any offer, undertaking or promise, whether conditional or unconditional, of any advantage within the meaning of any of the above paragraphs.

1.3 Definition of public official

The concept of public official is expressed in the POBO as "public servant." A public servant is defined as any prescribed officer or employee of a public body. This definition encompasses employees of the government, the Executive Council, the Legislative Council, any District Council, as well as any board or body appointed by or on behalf of the Chief Executive of Hong Kong. At the date of writing, there are 125 public bodies listed in the POBO.

[4] S. 3 POBO. Note that general permission has been given for certain types of advantages under the Acceptance of Advantages (Chief Executive's Permission) Notice 2010.

1.4 Consequences of bribery

The POBO establishes the same penalties for public servants and individuals who bribe public servants. The penalties include the following:

(a) Up to 10 years in jail and a fine of up to HKD500,000[5]

(b) Payment for value of any advantage received as the court sees fit

(c) Ordering that the convicted person be prohibited from taking employment or becoming a director for up to seven years[7]

1.5 Political contributions

The definition of "advantage" does not include an election donation within the meaning of the Elections (Corrupt and Illegal Conduct) Ordinance (Chapter 554) ("ECICO"), particulars of which are included in an election return in accordance with the ECICO. However, payments or contributions paid to induce officials to perform functions that they are otherwise obligated to perform would still be assessed in terms of whether they constitute an advantage under the POBO.

The ECICO is enforced by the Independent Commission Against Corruption (ICAC) and aims to uphold honesty and prevent corrupt and illegal conduct in public elections. A political candidate engages in corrupt conduct when he uses election donations for any purpose other than meeting his election expenses or to promote his campaign.[8]

---

[5] S. 12 POBO.
[7] S. 33A POBO.
[8] S. 18 ECICO.

When the donation amount exceeds HKD1,000, candidates are required to issue their donors with a receipt,[9] and they are prohibited from using the donation if the donor's name and address are unknown.[10]

1.6 Limitation applicable to hospitality expenses (gifts, travel, meals, entertainment, among others)

The POBO does not establish quantitative limitations on hospitality expenses, which would be assessed as to whether they constitute an advantage under the POBO. Gifts, travel expenses, red packets, tea money and similar favors could all fall within the definition of an advantage.

In relation to gifts, the Chief Executive has granted general permission to civil servants in relation to specific types of advantages.[11] Civil servants can accept (but not solicit) from a close personal friend a gift not exceeding a value of HKD3,000 in total on each occasion when gifts are traditionally exchanged (for example, a wedding or retirement), and not exceeding HKD500 in total on any other occasion. For gifts from persons who are not close personal friends, the limits are HKD1,500 and HKD250, respectively. Further, such gifts can only be given to the civil servant in his private capacity and the giver must not have any official dealings with the department or organization in which the civil servant works. Civil servants can also solicit or accept gifts from relations, and tradesmen and organizations (but only in their private capacity where the advantage applies on equal terms to non-civil servants and the giver has no official dealings with the civil servant). There are no monetary limits attached to such gifts. Civil servants will need permission to accept other types of gifts.

"Entertainment" is specifically excluded from the POBO's definition of an advantage and refers to the provision of food or drink, for consumption on the occasion when it is provided, and of any other

[9] S. 19(1) ECICO.
[10] S. 19(2) ECICO.
[11] Acceptance of Advantages (Chief Executive's Permission) Notice 2010.

entertainment connected with, or provided at the same time as, such provisions.[12] However, civil servants are subject to guidelines that prohibit lavish or unreasonably generous or frequent entertainment that may lead to embarrassment in performing official duties or bring the public service into disrepute.[13]

2. Domestic bribery (private to private)

2.1 Legal framework

Private sector bribery is regulated under Section 9 of the POBO. Section 9 lacks extra-territoriality where the offer, solicitation or acceptance of the advantage does not take place in Hong Kong, even though the planning of the offer might have taken place in Hong Kong.[14]

2.2 Definition of private bribery

Private bribery is committed when any agent who, without lawful authority or reasonable excuse, solicits or accepts any advantage without the permission of his principal as an inducement to, or reward for:

(a) doing or forbearing to do any act in relation to his principal's affairs or business; or

(b) showing or forbearing to show favor or disfavor to any person in relation to his principal's affairs or business.[15]

Likewise, persons who offer any advantage to an agent as an inducement or reward in the abovementioned circumstances commit an offense.

---

[12] S. 2 POBO.
[13] *Civil Servants' Guide to Good Practices*, Civil Service Bureau (2005).
[14] *HKSAR v Lionel John Krieger and Another* (6 August 2014, FAMC1/2014).
[15] S. 9 POBO.

"Agent" includes "a public servant and any person employed by or acting for another."[16] In a 2009 Court of Final Appeal decision,[17] the court considered the question of whether the private bribery provision applied where an advantage is offered in Hong Kong but the offeree is a public official of a place outside Hong Kong, and the act or forbearance concerned his public duties in that place outside Hong Kong. In that case, the chairman of a Hong Kong company had conspired with others to offer in Hong Kong advantages to a public official of a foreign jurisdiction as reward for the public official's assistance in that foreign jurisdiction. The court concluded that the relevant public official was an agent acting in relation to his principal's affairs when conducting his public duties in the foreign jurisdiction.

It is also an offense for any agent who, with intent to deceive his principal, uses any receipt, account or document:

(a) in respect of which the principal is interested;

(b) that contains any statement that is false or erroneous or defective in any material particular; and

(c) to his knowledge is intended to mislead the principal.[18]

2.3 Consequences of private bribery

The POBO establishes the following penalties for private individuals:[19]

(a) Up to 10 years in jail and a fine of up to HKD500,000

(b) Payment for value of any advantage received as the court sees fit

---

[16] S. 2 POBO.
[17] *B v. The Commissioner of the ICAC* (28 January 2010, FACC6/2009)
[18] S. 9(3) POBO.
[19] S. 12 POBO.

(c) Ordering the convicted person to be prohibited from taking employment or becoming a director for up to seven years[21]

2.4 Limitation applicable to hospitality expenses (gifts, travel, meals, entertainment, among others)

The POBO does not set any quantitative or qualitative limitations on hospitality expenses and gifts, which would be assessed as to whether they constitute an advantage under the POBO. A recipient of gifts would need to obtain approval from his principal if the gifts are related to the principal's affairs or business. The defense of having a "reasonable excuse" to accept an advantage was recently tested in a 2015 Court of Appeal decision[22] relating to secret payments for external work engagements. In that case, a prior pattern of receiving secret payments without the principal's approval was not sufficient to constitute a "reasonable excuse." At the date of writing, the Court of Appeal has refused to grant the defendants leave to appeal to the Court of Final Appeal.

As mentioned in paragraph 1.6, "entertainment" is excluded from the definition of "advantage." Nevertheless, this area could be a potential red flag where there is a conflict of interest. The ICAC cautions against lavish or frequent entertainment, and recommends that staff of organizations avoid offers of meals or entertainment that are excessive or frequent.

3. Corruption of foreign public officials

The POBO does not expressly regulate the bribery of foreign public officials. However, foreign public officials may be found to be acting as "agents" in relation to their principals' affairs under the POBO.

---

[21] S. 33A POBO.

[22] *Secretary for Justice v Chan Chi Wan Stephen and Tseng Pei Kun* (26 October 2015, CACC92/2013 and CACC183/2014).

As mentioned in paragraph 2.2, the 2009 Court of Final Appeal decision[23] confirmed that advantages offered in Hong Kong to a foreign public official for acts or forbearance outside Hong Kong fall within the jurisdiction of Hong Kong. Local individuals may still be liable for advantages offered to foreign public officials in relation to their activities outside Hong Kong if the offer, solicitation or acceptance of the advantages takes place in Hong Kong.

4. Facilitation payments

The POBO does not recognize facilitation payments. Unlike the FCPA, there are no provisions or exceptions for facilitation payments in Hong Kong. Any form of advantage would be assessed based on the elements of the offenses under the POBO.

5. Compliance programs

5.1 Value of a compliance program to mitigate/eliminate the criminal liability for legal entities

The POBO does not specifically recognize compliance programs as instruments to mitigate or eliminate liability for legal entities before the crime of corruption has been committed. However, the ICAC recommends the adoption of an effective compliance program to prevent corruption and mitigate the risk of violations.

5.2 Absence of a compliance program as a crime

The POBO does not recognize the absence of a compliance program as a crime.

5.3 Elements of a compliance program

(a) Legal framework

The POBO does not recognize or regulate the elements of a compliance program.

---

[23] *B v The Commissioner of the ICAC* (28 January 2010, FACC6/2009).

(b) Recommended practice

While having a compliance program does not offer a legal defense for an offense, the ICAC nonetheless notes the importance of introducing such programs in the interest of preventing internal corruption and bribery. Recommended mitigation measures include adopting a risk-based approach; due diligence of counterparties, agents and intermediaries; drafting and implementing effective policies and procedures; and effective embedding, monitoring and reviewing of compliance programs. The ICAC also provides free corruption prevention programs for companies in order to educate management staff regarding the relevant law.

6. Regulator with jurisdiction to prosecute corruption

The enforcement body in Hong Kong is the ICAC. The ICAC has powers to investigate, arrest and detain suspects pursuant to the Independent Commission Against Corruption Ordinance (Chapter 204) and the POBO. The POBO grants the ICAC further investigative powers to uncover transactions and assets, including the ability to search bank accounts as well as examine private business documents. With prescribed authorization under the Interception of Communications and Surveillance Ordinance (Chapter 589), the ICAC may also conduct telecommunications interception and covert surveillance for corruption investigations.

For prosecution of a bribery or corruption offense under the POBO, the consent of the Secretary for Justice is required.[24]

[24] S.31 POBO.

Indonesia

Timur Sukirno

Timur Sukirno is head of the Commercial Dispute Resolution Practice Group of Hadiputranto, Hadinoto & Partners in Jakarta. Timur has supervised various cases relating to compliance and anti-bribery. He has assisted a German-based major insurance company in conducting an internal anti-bribery investigation; a major Finland-based telecommunications company in an internal anti-bribery investigation; a UK-based valves manufacturing company in conducting compliance review; along with many other related cases for clients from various local and internationally based industries. He has been awarded as Leading Lawyer and Leading Individual in several publications, such as *IFLR 1000, Asia Pacific Legal 500, Chambers Asia*, and *AsiaLaw Profiles*.

timur.sukirno@bakernet.com
Tel: +62 21 2960 8500

Reno Hirdarisvita

Reno Hirdarisvita is an associate in the Commercial Dispute Resolution Practice Group of Hadiputranto, Hadinoto & Partners in Jakarta. Reno has experience in advising and assisting clients on issues relating to compliance and anti-bribery. She has assisted a major European pharmaceutical company in assessing the potential exposure to anti-bribery legislation of its Indonesian subsidiary's marketing practices; a Canada-based oil and gas company on anti-bribery issues in Indonesia; and a Japan-based pharmaceutical company in conducting an anti-corruption due diligence on its Indonesian subsidiary. She has likewise advised a US-based defense technology company on anti-bribery issues in Indonesia, along with other related cases for various local and internationally based clients.

reno.hirdarisvita@bakernet.com
Tel: +62 21 2960 8571

Hadiputranto, Hadinoto & Partners
The Indonesia Stock Exchange Building
Tower II, 21st Floor
Sudirman Central Business District
Jl. Jendral Sudirman Kav. 52-53
Jakarta 12190
Indonesia

Key Practitioners

Cahyani Endahayu
Jakarta
Tel: +62 21 2960 8515
cahyani.endahayu@BAKERNET.com

Andi Y. Kadir
Jakarta
Tel: +62 21 2960 8511
andi.y.kadir@BAKERNET.com

1. Domestic bribery (private to public)

1.1 Legal framework

Bribery of public officials is regulated under the Indonesian Anti-Bribery Law and Anti-Corruption Law. In practice, however, prosecutions of bribery in Indonesia generally invoke the more recent Anti-Corruption Law.

1.2 Definition of bribery

The Anti-Bribery Law describes bribery as giving or promising something to someone with the intention to persuade the recipient to do or not to do something, which is contrary to the recipient's authority or obligations that relates to public interest. Under the Anti-Bribery Law, the recipient is not restricted to civil servants/public officials. Rather, it applies to anyone holding a position of authority over any matter of public interest, such as a private surveyor entrusted with verifying an applicant's eligibility to receive fiscal facility. Under the Anti-Bribery Law, the giver and the recipient are equally liable. Note that the Anti-Bribery Law does not apply where the Anti-Corruption Law and the Indonesian Criminal Code already apply.

Under the Anti-Corruption Law, bribery is one of the acts defined as corruption. The definition of bribery is provided in Article 5 of the Anti-Corruption Law, that is: (i) giving or promising something to a civil servant or state administrative official with the intention that the recipient do or not do something in his position that is contrary to his obligations; and (ii) giving something to a civil servant or state administrative official because of or in connection with something that is contrary to his obligations, whether or not performed in his position. The central thrust of Article 5 is the corrupt offering of a gift (or gratification) related to a specific action or non-action of the recipient, in contravention of his obligations or duty.

1.3 Definition of public official

The Indonesian Anti-Corruption Law and Anti-Bribery Law have a fairly broad definition of public officials, including employees and officers of corporations financed by or using the facilities of the state or the public. A person who is not on the government payroll (the classic civil servant) may nevertheless be regarded as a civil servant if he or she is employed by a corporation that is financed by the state (i.e., the Republic of Indonesia or a region within the Republic of Indonesia). State administrative officials who carry on executive, legislative and judicial functions also fall under the definition of public official for the purpose of the Anti-Corruption Law (e.g., members of the House of Representatives, ministers, judges and head of a state university).

1.4 Consequences of bribery

Any party who violates Article 5 of the Anti-Corruption Law is subject to imprisonment for a minimum of one year and a maximum of five years, and/or a penalty in a minimum amount of IDR50 million and a maximum amount of IDR250 million.

(a) For the individuals involved

The Indonesian Anti-Corruption Law establishes the same penalties for public officials as for individuals that bribe public officials. The penalties are the following:

- Up to five years in jail
- A penalty in a minimum amount of IDR50 million and a maximum amount of IDR250 million

(b) For the corporation / legal entity involved

The Indonesian Anti-Corruption Law provides that criminal charges may be imposed on the corporation / legal entity or on its management.

- Penalties may be imposed on the corporation's management.
- Fines may be imposed on the corporation itself.

- Imprisonment can be imposed on the corporation's officers if they are proven to have conducted the criminal act of corruption in their duties for the corporation.

1.5 Political contributions

Contribution to political parties is regulated under the Indonesian Political Parties Law. In general terms, the following contributions to political parties are allowed:

(a) For individuals who are not members of the political party, contributions not exceeding IDR1 billion in one financial year

(b) For corporations/legal entities, contributions not exceeding IDR7.5 billion in one financial year

1.6 Limitation applicable to hospitality expenses (gifts, travel, meals, entertainment, among others)

The Indonesian Anti-Corruption Law classifies hospitality expenses such as gifts, travel, meals and entertainment as gratification. Note that under the Indonesian Anti-Corruption Law, every gratification given to a public official is potentially a bribe, but to be an actionable crime it must be given with some connection to the public official's position and involve a *quid pro quo* by the recipient to do or not to do something in contravention of his obligations or duties. The penalty for a public official who receives gratification that is proven to be a bribe is as follows:

- Imprisonment for four years up to 20 years

- Depending on the circumstances, life imprisonment is also possible.

- A fine of IDR200 million up to IDR1 billion

This provision applies to gratification performed both in Indonesia and outside of Indonesia. Article 12 C of the Indonesian Anti-

Corruption Law permits the recipient to avoid any form of prosecution in connection with receiving gratification if he reports the gratification to the Indonesian Corruption Eradication Commission (KPK) in a timely manner. The KPK must then decide if the public official can keep the gratification or if the gratification belongs to the state.

2. Domestic bribery (private to private)

2.1 Legal framework

The Indonesian legal system does not specifically regulate bribery in the private sector. The provision that best captures the act of bribery between private entities is Article 378 on fraudulent acts.

2.2 Definition of private bribery

The Indonesian legal system does not have a specific definition of private bribery.

2.3 Consequences of private bribery

Under Article 378 of the Indonesian Criminal Code, fraudulent acts are punishable with a maximum of four years' imprisonment.

2.4 Limitation applicable to hospitality expenses (gifts, travel, meals, entertainment, among others)

The Indonesian legal system does not recognize the concept of hospitality expenses between private entities.

3. Corruption of foreign public officials

Indonesian law does not regulate specifically the practice of corruption that involves foreign public officials. However, as long as it can be proven that the purpose of the alleged corruption harms the public interest, then the provision of the Indonesian Anti-Corruption Law that applies to the act of corruption of public officials also applies to the party who bribes or commits the corruption act of foreign public officials.

4. Facilitation payments

There is no exception for facilitation payments under Indonesian laws. Under the Indonesian Anti-Corruption Law, facilitation payments may fall under the category of gratification. Article 12 B of the Indonesian Anti-Corruption Law sets out the threshold for determining who carries the burden of proving whether a gratification is a bribe or not:

(a) For amounts of IDR10 million and above, the burden to prove that it is not bribery lies with the recipient.

(b) For amounts below IDR10 million, the burden to prove that it is not bribery lies with the prosecutor.

5. Compliance programs

5.1 Value of a compliance program to mitigate/eliminate criminal liability for legal entities

Indonesian law does not specifically recognize compliance programs as instruments to mitigate or eliminate liability for legal entities before the crime of corruption takes place. For that reason, having a compliance program in place is an application of the principle of good corporate governance. However, depending on the line of the business, some government institutions also initiate compliance programs for corporations / legal entities with business under their supervision.

Indonesian legal entities will only be criminally liable for corruption committed by their employees if it is proven that the employees commit the corruption crime in their duties for the legal entities.

5.2 Absence of a compliance program as a crime

Indonesian law does not recognize the absence of a compliance program as a crime.

5.3 Elements of a compliance program

(a) Legal framework

Indonesian law does not recognize or regulate the elements of a compliance program.

(b) Recommended practice

Legal entities are encouraged to have a compliance program in place as a strategy to mitigate the risk of corruption.

6. Regulator with jurisdiction to prosecute corruption

In general, the police and the prosecutor have the authority to investigate any alleged corruption. In 2002, the government of Indonesia established the KPK to fight corruption more effectively. KPK has the authority to investigate and prosecute corruption that: (i) involves law enforcement officials, state administrative officials or other people that are related to the corruption committed by law enforcement officials or state administrative officials; (ii) attracts the public's attention; and/or (iii) involves state loss of at least IDR1 billion. In carrying out its duty, the commission has the authority to request meetings and reports in the course of its investigation. It can also authorize wiretaps, impose travel bans and request financial information about suspects.

Japan

Kengo Nishigaki

Kengo Nishigaki's practice focuses on international litigation, fraud investigations for Japanese and foreign-listed companies, US FCPA compliance, and compliance of pharmaceutical companies and medical device makers. In addition, he advises on negotiations with authorities regarding issues such as leakage of personal information and product recalls. Kengo also assists major Japanese and foreign-listed companies in international corporate acquisitions, business partnerships and the establishment of joint venture companies.

kengo.nishigaki@bakermckenzie.com
Tel: +81 3 6271 9473

Yoshiaki Muto

Yoshiaki Muto focuses his practice on the areas of domestic and international dispute resolution, including litigation and arbitration, corporate investigation and compliance. He also advises on international trade and general corporate and commercial matters, including those pertaining to corporate law, contract law and competition law. Yoshiaki has acted for clients on a wide range of businesses, including the consumer products, software, electronic devices, finance, construction and aerospace/military industries. He has also particular expertise on the information systems business and the medical and pharmaceutical industries.

yoshiaki.muto@bakermckenzie.com
Tel: +81 3 6271 9451

Baker & McKenzie (Gaikokuho Joint Enterprise)
Ark Hills Sengokuyama Mori Tower, 28th Floor
1-9-10 Roppongi, Minato-ku
Tokyo 106-0032

1. Domestic bribery (private to public)

1.1 Legal framework

Bribery of public officials (*komuin*) is regulated under Articles 197 and 198 of the Japanese Criminal Code.

1.2 Definition of bribery

The giving, offering or promising to give a bribe, including anything that satisfies a person's desire, by a private individual to a public official in connection with the public official's duties constitutes the crime of bribery.

1.3 Definition of public official

A national or local government employee, a member of an assembly or committee or another employee engaged in the performance of public duties in accordance with laws and regulations constitutes a public official. Furthermore, officers and employees of government-related entities, including independent administrative agencies (*dokuritsu gyousei houjin*), local incorporated administrative agencies (*chihou dokuritsu gyousei houjin*), national university corporations (*kokuritsu daigaku houjin*), state-owned enterprises, and public hospitals are treated as public officials (quasi-public officials).

1.4 Consequences of bribery

(a) For the individuals involved

Individuals that corrupt public officials are subject to imprisonment for a maximum of three years or a fine of up to JPY2.5 million.

(b) For the company / legal entity

The Criminal Code does not provide for a penalty to be imposed on the company / legal entity. However, the company / legal entity may be disqualified from public bidding or be subject to other sanctions under the relevant regulatory laws (e.g., revocation of license).

1.5 Political contributions

Political contributions are regulated under Political Funds Control Law. It provides the following rules:

- A company may not give a political activity-related donation to an entity other than a political party or a political funding entity.
- No person may give a monetary donation in connection with any political activity (except for an election campaign) engaged in by a candidate for elected public office.
- The total annual aggregate donations to a particular political party or political funding entity must be: (i) less than JPY20 million when given by an individual person; and (ii) less than JPY7.5 million to JPY100 million (depending on the capital amount of the company) when given by a company.
- The total annual aggregate donations by an individual to all candidates for elected public office must be less than JPY10 million.
- The annual aggregate donations by an individual to a specific candidate for elected public office must be less than JPY1.5 million.
- A non-Japanese citizen or company may not give donations in connection with any political activity.
- Anonymous donations or donations made in the name of another person are prohibited.

1.6 Limitations applicable to hospitality expenses (gifts, travel, meals, entertainment, among others)

The Criminal Code does not establish quantitative or qualitative limitations on hospitality expenses. Anything of value can constitute a bribe under the Criminal Code.

It is worth noting that a national public official who is subject to the National Public Official Ethics Act and the National Public Official Ethics Code must comply with the following rules, among others:

- A public official may not receive a meal from an interested person under any circumstances other than casual box lunches during a conference (usually valued at JPY2,000 to JPY3,000) or a party at which a buffet is provided for a number of attendees (usually more than 20 attendees).
- A public official may not receive entertainment.
- A public official may not receive hospitality. Even when paying their own expenses, they need to obtain approval from their ethics supervisor.

Furthermore, other public officials, including local government and independent administrative agency officials, are usually subject to similar ethics ordinances or ethics rules established by such organizations.

2. Domestic bribery (private to private)

2.1 Legal framework

No Japanese law or regulation specifically restricts bribery of private persons.

However, under the Japanese Criminal Code, a person who is in charge of the affairs of a company, for the purpose of promoting his or her own interest or the interest of a third party, or inflicting damage on the company, commits an act in breach of legal duty and causes financial loss to the company is punished (Breach of Trust). Accordingly, an officer or employee of a private company who receives a bribe may be punished under the Criminal Code.

In addition, under the Japanese Company Act, a director of a company who receives a property benefit based on an unlawful request in connection with his or her duty shall be punished (Bribery by Director).

Furthermore, it is worth noting that some industries have established industry guidelines restricting bribery of private persons, which apply only to companies subject to the guidelines. For example, the pharmaceutical industry and the medical device industry have established fair competition codes that restrict the provision of benefits to physicians, among others, regardless of whether they are public officials. However, these guidelines are industry codes (not statutes) and impose no criminal penalties (they may impose civil penalties up to JPY1 million).

2.2 Definition of private bribery

None

2.3 Consequences of private bribery

(a) For the individuals involved

A person who commits the abovementioned Breach of Trust shall be subject to imprisonment for up to five years or fine of up to JPY500,000 under the Japanese Criminal Code.

A person who commits the abovementioned Bribery by Director shall be subject to imprisonment for up to five years or fine of up to JPY5 million under the Japanese Company Act.

(b) For the company / legal entity

None

2.4 Limitations applicable to hospitality expenses (gifts, travel, meals, entertainment, among others)

None

3. Corruption of foreign public officials

3.1 Legal framework

Corruption of foreign public officials is prohibited under the Japanese Unfair Competition Prevention Act (Article 18).

3.2 Definition of corruption of foreign public officials

Corruption of a foreign public official is defined as giving, offering or promising any pecuniary or other advantage to a foreign public official in order that the official act or refrain from acting in relation to the performance of official duties, or in order that the official, using his or her position, exert upon another foreign official so as to cause him or her to act or refrain from acting in relation to the performance of official duties, in order to obtain or retain improper business advantage in the conduct of international business.

3.3 Definition of foreign public official

For the purpose of this crime, a foreign public official means any of the following persons:

- Any person who engages in public services for national or local foreign governments
- Any person who engages in services for an entity constituted under foreign special laws to carry out specific tasks concerning public interest
- Any person who engages in services for an enterprise of which the number of stocks with the right to vote or the amount of capital subscription directly owned a by national or local foreign government exceeds one-half of that enterprise's

total issued stocks with the right to vote or total subscribed capital, or of which the number of executives (including directors, statutory auditors, trustees, inspectors, liquidators or other persons who engage in management of its business) appointed or named by a national or local foreign government exceeds one-half of that enterprise's executives, and to which special privileges are given by national or local foreign governments to do its business; and such person as defined in the government ordinances as "foreign public official"

- Any person who engages in public services for an international organization (hereinafter, an "international organization" means an international organization that is formed either by governments or by an international organization formed by governments)
- Any person who exercises a public function that falls under the authorized competence of national or local foreign governments or an international organization and is delegated by them

3.4 Consequences of corruption of foreign public officials

(a) For the individuals involved

- Maximum of five years' imprisonment
- Maximum fine of JPY5 million

(b) For the legal entity

- In the case where a representative, an agent or an employee of a legal person or a person has committed violations in relation to the business of the legal person, in addition to the violator being punished, the legal person shall also be liable for a fine not exceeding JPY300 million.

3.5 Limitation applicable to hospitality expenses (gifts, travel, meals, entertainment, among others)

The Unfair Competition Prevention Act does not establish quantitative or qualitative limitations on hospitality expenses. Anything of value may constitute a bribe.

4. Facilitation payments

The Unfair Competition Prevention Act does not recognize so-called facilitation payments.

There is no article literally mentioning small facilitation payments in the Unfair Competition Prevention Law in Japan, and no action is freed of punishment under the title of small facilitation payment exemption. As long as the prerequisite, "to obtain or retain improper business advantage in the conduct of international business," is fulfilled in specific individual cases, it will constitute the offense of bribery of foreign public officials under the Unfair Competition Prevention Law, regardless of whether or not it is small facilitation payment.

5. Compliance programs

5.1 Value of a compliance program in mitigating/eliminating criminal liability for legal entities

The Japanese Criminal Code does not specifically recognize a compliance programs as an instrument to mitigate or eliminate liability for legal entities before the crime of corruption has been committed.

However, in order to prevent a company from incurring liability due to a violation by an employee of the Unfair Competition Prevention Act, the company is likely required to exercise caution as necessary to prevent violations. General and abstract advice is insufficient; proactive and specific instructions, among others, must be given.

In July 2015, the Japanese Ministry of Economy, Trade and Industry updated guidelines describing the framework for a compliance program capable of appropriately preventing bribery of foreign public officials.

5.2 Absence of a compliance program as a crime

Neither the Japanese Criminal Code nor the Unfair Competition Prevention Act recognizes the absence of a Compliance Program as a crime.

5.3 Compliance program elements

(a) Legal framework

Neither the Japanese Criminal Code nor the Unfair Competition Prevention Act recognizes or regulates the elements of a compliance program.

(b) Recommended practice

With respect to the Unfair Competition Prevention Act, the Ministry of Economy, Trade and Industry in July 2015 updated its guidelines describing the framework of a compliance program. According to the guidelines, the compliance program should contain the following mechanisms:

- Establishing and announcing a basic policy
- Establishing internal rules including an approval procedure for high risk activity and disciplinary measure against a violator
- Establishing Organizational Structure, including: (i) involvement of a senior corporate officer; (ii) appointment of a compliance officer or compliance supervisor; (iii) establishment of an internal consultation desk and a reporting

desk, among others; and (iv) development of a follow-up structure after suspicion is brought to light

- Conducting orientation sessions for employees in the company
- Regular audit
- Review by the chief executives

6. Regulator with jurisdiction to prosecute corruption

The Japanese legal system does not have a specific regulator with the exclusive responsibility to prosecute corruption. Any public prosecutor can indict a perpetrator.

Malaysia

Kherk Ying Chew

Kherk Ying Chew heads the Kuala Lumpur office's Dispute Resolution Practice Group, with more than 25 years of practice in the area of civil litigation. She has extensive experience in advising multinational corporations on risk-related issues, and has assisted companies in developing and managing their corporate compliance programs, particularly in internal investigation matters concerning anti-corruption regulations.

She is recognized as a leading individual by *Asia Pacific Legal 500, 2014*, which stated that she is "highly respected for contentious and non-contentious work" and has recently won "an important precedent-setting case for Malaysian software copyright law." *IAM Patent 1000, 2013* ranks her in the first tier of litigation and licensing professionals, acknowledging her "loyal following as 'a hugely valued player.'"

kherkying.chew@wongpartners.com
Tel: +60 3 2298 7933

Eddie Chuah

Eddie Chuah is a senior associate with the Firm's Dispute Resolution Practice Group. He focuses his practice on providing advisory and assistance work to domestic and multinational corporations in a broad range of risk-related issues and in compliance with local authorities, particularly concerning anti-corruption related matters. He has represented clients in developing internal policies and procedures, as well as conducting necessary audits and training in mitigating risks of non-compliance. He is also experienced in advising relevant stakeholders on the necessary investigations and legal remedies upon discovery of fraud or corruption.

eddie.chuah@wongpartners.com
Tel: +60 3 2298 7939

Wong & Partners
Level 21, The Gardens South Tower
Mid Valley City
Lingkaran Syed Putra
59200 Kuala Lumpur
Malaysia

The key anti-corruption legislation in Malaysia is the Malaysian Anti-Corruption Commission Act 2009 (MACCA), which came into force on 1 January 2009. The relevant authority in charge of the MACCA is the Malaysian Anti-Corruption Commission (MACC). The MACCA applies to both the private sector and to public bodies / officers of a public body. The MACCA does not make a distinction between private sector bribery and bribery of public officials.

1.1 Definition of bribery

Instead of the word "bribe," the MACCA Act defines the word "gratification," which includes both pecuniary and non-pecuniary bribes. Generally, gratification is defined as money, donation, gift, any valuable thing of any kind, any forbearance to demand any money or money's worth or valuable thing, any other service or favor of any kind or any offer, undertaking or promise of any such gratifications.

The MACCA makes it an offense when "any person who by himself, or by or in conjunction with any other person corruptly solicits or receives or agrees to receive for himself or for any other person; or corruptly gives, promises or offers to any person whether for the benefit of that person or of another person, any gratification as an inducement to or a reward for, or otherwise on account of any person doing or forbearing to do anything in respect of any matter or transaction, actual or proposed or likely to take place; or any officer of a public body doing or forbearing to do anything in respect of any matter or transaction, actual or proposed or likely to take place, in which the public body is concerned."

There is an additional offense under the Act for any person to offer to an officer of any public body, or being an officer of any public body, to solicit or accept any gratification as an inducement or a reward for:

- the officer voting or abstaining from voting at any meeting of the public body in favor of or against any measure, resolution or question submitted to the public body;

- the officer performing or abstaining from performing or aiding in procuring, expediting, delaying, hindering or preventing the performance of any official act;
- the officer aiding in procuring or preventing the passing of any vote or the granting of any contract or advantage in favor of any person; or
- the officer showing or forbearing to show any favor or disfavor in his or her capacity as such officer.

An offense would be committed even if the officer did not have the power, right or opportunity to do so, show or forbear, or accepted the gratification without intending to do so, show or forbear, or did not in fact so do, show or forbear, or that the inducement or reward was not in relation to the affairs of the public body.

Attempting to commit, conspiring to commit or abetting the commission of any of the abovementioned offenses is also prohibited, as is dealing with, using, holding, receiving or concealing any property that was the subject matter of an abovementioned offense.

1.2 Definition of public official

Under the MACCA, "officer of a public body" is defined as any person who is a member, an officer, an employee or a servant of a public body. This includes a member of the administration; a member of Parliament; a member of a State Legislative Assembly; a judge of the High Court, Court of Appeal or Federal Court; and any person receiving any remuneration from public funds, and where the public body is a corporation sole, includes the person who is incorporated as such. The courts have adopted a broad approach in defining and determining who falls within such definition. A public body includes the federal government, state government, local authorities, and their departments, services and undertakings. Also included are companies or subsidiaries over which a public body has controlling power or interest, and various registered societies and trade unions.

1.3 Consequences of bribery

(a) For the individuals involved

For more serious bribery, imprisonment of up to 20 years and a fine of not less than five times the sum/value of the gratification where it is capable of being valued or is of a pecuniary nature, or MYR10,000, whichever is higher

There is also a general penalty of a fine of up to MYR10,000 or imprisonment of up to two years, or both.

(b) For the company/legal entity

There is no additional penalty specific to companies.

1.4 Political contributions

There are no specific laws governing political contributions. Though political donations are not specifically covered by any law in Malaysia, particular care must be taken in ensuring that such donations are not construed as an inducement or a reward for doing or forbearing to do any act as this would fall within the general prohibitions of the MACCA. Further, kindly note that the MACCA deems a corrupt intent in the giving or receiving of gratification unless the contrary is proven.

1.5 Limitation applicable to hospitality expenses (gifts, travel, meals, entertainment, among others)

Under the MACCA, offering and accepting gifts, services and hospitality will be a corruption offense if there is the requisite intention for such an offer/acceptance to be a bribe. The MACCA does not contain any provision for a *de minimis* threshold.

The Malaysian government has issued the Guidelines on Giving and Receiving of Gifts in the Public Service / Service Circular No. 3 of 1998 (the "Circular"), which sets out the parameters concerning the giving and receiving of gifts. The Circular provides that, as a general rule, the amount/value of a gift is considered not commensurate with the purpose of the gift if the value of the gift exceeds one-fourth of the officer's monthly remuneration or MYR500, whichever is lower.

Accordingly, public officials are generally not allowed to receive or give gifts, or allow their spouse or any other person to receive or give on their behalf any gift, whether in tangible form or otherwise, from or to any person, association, body or group of persons if the receipt or giving of such present is in any way connected, either directly or indirectly, with his or her official duties. However, there are exceptions for certain personal celebrations such as retirement, assignment transfer or marriage. There is also an exception if the circumstances make it difficult for the officer to refuse the gift. For example, the Guidelines provide that an officer would be allowed to receive a gift given to him when carrying out public duties at a seminar, symposium, workshop or any official event, and the public officer was not informed of the presentation of the gift beforehand. However, the officer is required to submit a written report in such cases.

2. Domestic bribery (private to private)

2.1 Legal framework

The MACCA prohibits both public and private bribery. The MACCA does not make a distinction between private sector bribery and bribery of public officials. For example, the provision dealing with the offense of accepting gratification, as referred to in Paragraph 1.2, has general application and so it applies to any person regardless of whether the bribery was between two private individuals or whether a public officer was involved.

2.2 Definition of private bribery

Malaysia does not distinguish between bribes paid to a public official and those paid in the private sector. See Paragraph 1.2.

2.3 Consequences of private bribery

Malaysia's anti-corruption legislation does not distinguish between bribes paid to a public official and those paid in the private sector. See Paragraph 1.4.

2.4 Limitation applicable to hospitality expenses (gifts, travel, meals, entertainment, among others)

Under the MACCA, offering and accepting gifts, services and hospitality will be a corruption offense if there is the requisite intention for such an offer/acceptance to be a bribe. MACCA does not contain any provision for a *de minimis* threshold. Nevertheless, MACC encourages corporations to adopt a "no-gift" policy to prevent bribery.

3. Corruption of foreign public officials

3.1 Legal framework

The MACCA includes a specific offense of "bribery of foreign public officials."

3.2 Definition of corruption of foreign public officials

An offense will be committed where foreign a public official solicits, accepts, obtains, agrees to accept or attempts to obtain the gratification as an inducement or reward. Active and passive foreign bribery are covered under the MACCA. Therefore, bribery through intermediaries and bribery that benefits third parties are covered as well. The offense is not limited to foreign bribery in international business transactions.

3.3 Definition of foreign public official

For the purpose of this crime, a foreign public official means:

- any person who, whether appointed or elected, holds a legislative, executive, administrative or judicial office of a foreign country;

- any person who exercises a public function for a foreign country, including a person employed by a board, commission, corporation, or other body or authority that is established to perform a duty or function on behalf of the foreign country; and

- any person who is authorized by a public international organization to act on behalf of that organization.

3.4 Consequences of corruption of foreign public officials

(a) For the individuals involved

Imprisonment for a term not exceeding 20 years

A fine of not less than five times the sum or value of the gratification that is the subject matter of the offense, where such gratification is capable of being valued or is of a pecuniary nature, or MYR10,000, whichever is higher

(b) For the legal entity

There is no additional penalty specific to companies.

3.5 Limitation applicable to hospitality expenses (gifts, travel, meals, entertainment, among others)

Under the MACCA, offering and accepting gifts, services and hospitality will be a corruption offense if there is the requisite intention for such an offer/acceptance to be a bribe. The MACCA does not contain any provision for a *de minimis* threshold.

4. Facilitation payments

"Facilitation payments" fall within the interpretation of "gratification" under MACCA and are therefore generally prohibited in Malaysia.

5. Compliance programs

5.1 Value of a compliance program to mitigate/eliminate the criminal liability for legal entities

Malaysian laws do not regulate compliance programs, though this position is likely to change with the introduction of corporate liability, where defense mechanisms are available for companies taking appropriate steps to prevent corruption.

5.2 Absence of a compliance program as a crime

N/A

5.3 Elements of compliance program

(a) Legal framework

Malaysian laws are silent on compliance programs, though this will change with the introduction of corporate liability offenses in Malaysia.

(b) Recommended practice

Compliance programs are not commonly adopted by corporations, though this will change with the introduction of corporate liability offenses in Malaysia.

6. Regulator with jurisdiction to prosecute corruption

The MACC has jurisdiction to investigate bribery offenses under the MACCA and PC. Other Malaysian law enforcement authorities may also investigate bribery offenses under both statutes, though they may not be able to use the investigative tools provided by the MACCA. The MACC may also prosecute MACCA and PC bribery offenses since the MACC chief commissioner has the status of a deputy public prosecutor. However, the prosecution of all bribery offenses can be instituted only with the consent of the public prosecutor, which is the attorney general of Malaysia.

Myanmar

John W. Hancock

John Hancock is the managing director of the Yangon office of Baker & McKenzie. John has a long history with Baker & McKenzie, as a former Baker & McKenzie principal, chairman of the Bangkok office, chairman of Baker & McKenzie in Asia Pacific, and as member of the Firm's Global Executive Committee. He was involved in the establishment of several Baker & McKenzie offices in the Asia Pacific region, and the establishment of the Baker & McKenzie Myanmar Centre in Bangkok in 2012, which evolved into the Yangon office.

john.hancock@bakermckenzie.com
Tel: +95 1 255 057

Ross Taylor

Ross Taylor re-joined Baker & McKenzie in 2013, and is a senior member in the Corporate Practice Group, advising multinational clients in a wide range of industries on investment, project development and ongoing business operations in Myanmar. Ross began his legal career as a barrister in London in 1984, followed by 15 years of common law practice. Ross first became consultant to Baker & McKenzie in Bangkok in 2002, where he was involved in numerous aircraft-related and M&A transactions.

ross.taylor@bakermckenzie.com
Tel: +95 1 255056 ext. 833

Baker & McKenzie Yangon
1203 12th Floor Sakura Tower
339 Bogyoke Aung San Road
Kyauktada Township
Yangon
Myanmar

Key Practitioners

Ola Nicolai Borge
Yangon
Tel: +95 1 255 056 # 8 845
olanicolai.borge@bakermckenzie.com

1. Domestic bribery (private to public)

1.1 Legal framework

Bribery of public officials is primarily regulated by the Myanmar Penal Code, Chapters IX and XIA, and the Anti-Corruption Law 2013 (the "Anti-Corruption Law"). Other corruption-related offenses and penalty clauses are contained in numerous laws, such as in taxation, banking and financial laws; the Myanmar Official Secrets Act 1923; the Defence Services Act 1959; the Fire Services Law 1997; and the Civil Service Law 2013.

1.2 Definition of bribery

Several offenses related to bribery are created by the Penal Code. The general offense is:

> Whoever, being or expecting to be a public servant, accepts or obtains or agrees to accept, or attempts to obtain from any person, for himself or for any other person, any gratification whatever, other than legal remuneration, as a motive or reward for doing or forbearing to do any official act or for showing or forbearing to show, in the exercise of his official functions, favour or disfavour to any person, or for rendering or attempting to render any service or disservice to any person with the Union Parliament or the Government or with any public servant, as such, shall be punished.

All offenses under the Penal Code (except those relating to bribery in connection with elections) can only be committed by public servants. In theory, however, the person offering the gratification could be convicted of abetting the public servant in the crime.

Under the Anti-Corruption Law, "corruption" is defined as follows:

> Corruption means doing directly or indirectly of an authoritative person by abusing his authoritative position, such as giving, accepting, receiving, attempting to receive, offering, pledging, or discussing in any way of a consideration from a person concerned for himself or any other or any organization in order to do anything, refrain from doing any lawful act, give a person his legitimate right, or prohibit a person wrongfully from his legitimate right.

1.3 Definition of public official

The Myanmar Penal Code has a broad definition of public servants, ranging from government servants, armed forces personnel, judges and court officials, to the police and inland revenue officials.

Under the Anti-Corruption Law, an "authoritative person" means a public servant who holds authoritative power either by his tenure or by jurisdictional or administrative authority, a public servant abroad, an existing holder of a political post, a high official, or an administrator or representative of any public organization.

1.4 Consequences of bribery

(a) For the individuals involved

If an offense is committed under the Penal Code, an abettor could be punished with the same punishment as that for the public official. For the offense relating to public servants under the Penal Code used as an example above, this could be a fine, or imprisonment of up to three years, or both.

Under the Anti-Corruption Law, any "political post holder" convicted of corruption is liable to a fine and up to 15 years' imprisonment; any other authorized person is liable to a fine and up to 10 years' imprisonment; anyone else is liable to a fine and up to seven years' imprisonment.

(b) For the company / legal entity

No separate penalties for companies or legal entities are provided under either the Penal Code or the Anti-Corruption Law. However, under the Myanmar Interpretation of Expressions Law 1973, the word "person" includes any company, and therefore the same penalties theoretically apply to companies as to private individuals. The same position applies under the Penal Code.

1.5 Political contributions

Under the Political Party Registration Law (2010), there is no limit placed on contributions to political parties. However, contributions can only be made from domestic as opposed to foreign sources.

1.6 Limitation applicable to hospitality expenses (gifts, travel, meals, entertainment, among others)

In an effort to reduce corruption, the new Myanmar government issued on 4 April 2016, guidelines to government officials regarding gifts that can be accepted. These guidelines also provide an extremely important guide for foreign investors in an area where there has previously been very little guidance. In the guidelines, the basic principle is that a government officer, member of any commission or committee formed by the government, or member of the public service may not accept any gift given by virtue of their official position. There are, however, important exceptions which will be of interest: (i) gifts not exceeding the value of MMK25,000 (approximately USD25) may be accepted; (ii) gifts given due to a family or personal relationship (what "personal relationship" means is not specified) are allowed; and (iii) gifts not exceeding the value of MMK100,000 (approximately USD100) may be given on religious occasions such as Christmas and Thadingyut (end of Buddhist lent festival). The position is slightly different where the gift is from a foreign government. In this case: (i) gifts not exceeding the value of MMK400,000 (approximately USD400) may be accepted; (ii) travel allowances for official trips may be accepted; (iii) scholarships and medical expenses may be accepted; and (iv) other gifts in certain circumstances may also be accepted.

These guidelines provide a welcome degree of clarity in an area where it has previously been extremely difficult to gauge what is acceptable gift-giving to government officials and what is not. Although the guidelines do not have any clear legal status, they are bound to be extremely influential. We can only wait if they will have any effect on the application of the Anti-Corruption Law.

The entertainment of public officials is not allowed, unless this is in the context of a seminar, workshop or other similar event. It also has to be remembered that context is particularly important where public officials are concerned - a gift by a CEO to a minister would be expected to be of higher value than that given to lower-ranking officials.

2. Domestic bribery (private to private)

2.1 Legal framework

Domestic bribery is regulated under the Anti-Corruption Law.

2.2 Definition of private bribery

There is no separate definition of private bribery. At face value, the Anti-Corruption Law appears intended to apply primarily to public officials. However, on a broad interpretation, it could encompass what might be termed as private corruption. The definition of corruption would therefore be the same as set out in section 1.2.

Authoritative persons who would fall under this category are defined in the Anti-Corruption Law as a director general or managing director of a state and private joint venture company, board, corporation or other organization. However, on wider interpretation, authoritative persons could include other high-level officials or managers.

There have not been any cases that would aid in the interpretation of this provision. However, we would advise that a cautious approach be taken under the circumstances. It should be noted that the intention of the legislature at the time of passing the Anti-Corruption Law was to implement the obligations of Myanmar under the UN Convention Against Corruption, which clearly deals with bribery in the private sector. In addition, the Myanmar legislature have amended the Anti-Corruption Law to include a wider definition of "corruption," which implies that private-private corruption is included.

2.3 Consequences of private bribery

(a) For the individuals involved

Any authorized person is liable to a fine and up to 10 years' imprisonment; anyone else is liable to a fine and up to seven years' imprisonment.

(b) For the company / legal entity

No separate penalties for companies or legal entities are provided under the Anti-Corruption Law. However, under the Myanmar Interpretation of Expressions Law 1973, the word "person" includes any company, and therefore the same penalties theoretically apply to companies as to private individuals. The same position applies under the Penal Code.

2.4 Limitation applicable to hospitality expenses (gifts, travel, meals, entertainment, among others)

There are no specific limitations applied to hospitality expenses and therefore to a large extent, what is socially acceptable in the commercial context has to be relied on as a guide.

The usual value of gift and entertainment expenses would be up to USD75 for gifts, and the same amount per head for entertainment. Obviously, what is acceptable can depend on the context and the status of the individuals involved. As we have indicated, the government have just released guidelines on gifts that may and may not be accepted by government officials, which are of considerably lower value than was previously thought. It is not known how this guidance might influence the treatment of norms of private-to-private gift-giving. Because of the newness of the Anti-Corruption Law and the lack of precedents in this area, we advise prudence.

3. Corruption of foreign public officials

3.1 Legal framework

The Anti-Corruption Law

3.2 Definition of corruption of foreign public officials

There is no separate definition of corruption of foreign public officials. The offense is corruption of authorized persons, and a foreign public official is an authorized person. The offense of corruption is defined in section 1.2.

3.3 Definition of foreign public official

Under the Anti-Corruption Law, a "foreign public service man" is defined as "a person who is appointed or selected by any foreign country legislation, administration or judiciary officer, a person who works in a board, commission, corporation or other organization formed to carry out the duties of a foreign country and an authorized person who works on behalf of an international organization."

3.4 Consequences of corruption of foreign public officials

(a) For the individuals involved

A foreign public service man is liable to a fine and up to 10 years' imprisonment; anyone else is liable to a fine and up to seven years' imprisonment.

(b) For the company / legal entity

No separate penalties for companies or legal entities are provided under the Anti-Corruption Law. However, under the Myanmar Interpretation of Expressions Law 1973, the word "person" includes any company, and therefore the same penalties theoretically apply to companies as to private individuals. The same position applies under the Penal Code.

3.5 Limitation applicable to hospitality expenses (gifts, travel, meals, entertainment, among others)

As we have advised in Section 1.6 above, new government guidelines severely limit the value of gifts that may be given to Myanmar government officials. The new guidelines are, however, silent in relation to foreign government officials. However, as corruption of foreign government officials is covered by the Anti-Corruption Law, we would suggest that, given the lack of clarity in this area, the prudent course is to follow the same guidelines in relation to foreign public officials and limit gift-giving accordingly. Entertainment should also be limited in the same manner, and only to that connected with seminars and workshops.

4. Facilitation payments

Neither the Penal Code nor the Anti-Corruption Law recognizes facilitation payments. Facilitation payments could be interpreted as a "gratification" under the Penal Code, or more likely, as corruption within the wide definition of corruption under the Anti-Corruption Law.

5. Compliance programs

5.1 Value of a compliance program to mitigate/eliminate the criminal liability for legal entities

Under Myanmar law, because of the lack of clarity on liability of corporate bodies, it is advisable to have a compliance program in the event that the company was found liable under the Penal Code or Anti-Corruption Law. However, many foreign companies operating in Myanmar have compliance programs for a number of other reasons, primarily for governance, or because they are potentially liable under anti-corruption legislation within their respective jurisdictions (e.g.,

FCPA, UK Bribery Act), where the existence of a compliance program may at least mitigate the offense.

5.2 Absence of a compliance program as a crime

The absence of a compliance program is not recognized as a crime in Myanmar.

5.3 Elements of compliance program

(1) Clear policies and procedures should be established to ensure compliance.

(2) Employees should undergo training explaining:

  (i) relevant legislation;

  (ii) company policies and procedures developed in (1) above; and

  (iii) situations in which difficulties could occur.

(3) The effectiveness of the program should be monitored and adjustments be made where necessary.

(4) Employee training should be repeated at least annually.

(5) There should be whistleblowing procedures and protection.

(6) Individuals and companies that you intend to conduct business with should be checked against the Specially Designated Nationals (SDN) list.

(7) Consideration should be given to having compliance provisions in all material contracts affecting the business, such as compliance with the Anti-Corruption Law, the FCPA and the UK Bribery Act.

6. Regulator with jurisdiction to prosecute corruption

The police investigate any alleged offense under the Penal Code, which would then be prosecuted by the Prosecution Department of the Attorney General's Office.

Offenses under the Anti-Corruption Law are investigated by a team under a special "Bribery Eradication Commission" established by the Anti-Corruption Law.

Qualifications

Our advice above is qualified by the following:

(1) Myanmar has had a number of different governments/administrations that have had a different approach to the promulgation and maintenance of its basic laws. This, together with the mixed use of English and the Myanmar language in the writing of these laws, as well as their style and coverage, has meant that they are not always complete or consistent. Thus, there are many areas that are not adequately dealt with and have not been the subject of judicial determination. Furthermore, there are a number of new laws and regulations being introduced for which there is no prior point of reference. This provides significant limitation on the ability to give definitive advice.

(2) Our advice is based upon the laws, decrees, rules, regulations and official notifications of Myanmar that are available to the public as of the date of publication. There may be new or amended laws, decrees, rules, regulations or official notifications, or unofficial or internal guidelines, which exist but which are not published or which are not generally available to the public, and the existence of the same may affect the advice herein.

(3) Only a limited number of court judgments are published or made available to the public, and the judicial interpretation of the laws of Myanmar is uncertain. Thus, there may be unpublished opinions or decisions of the courts of Myanmar that may affect the advice expressed herein.

(4) Our advice is only based upon the laws of Myanmar and we have not considered the laws of any other jurisdiction in rendering our advice.

(5) While we may refer to policies, practices and customs policies in our advice, these are only in relation to prevailing policies, customs and practices of which we are aware. It is possible that there are other policies, practices and customs or changes than those known to us, and which may affect the advice expressed herein.

(6) Administrative interpretation or implementation of the laws of Myanmar is not always consistent or certain and may vary from case to case or with respect to the same facts.

Philippines

Rodrigo Quimbo

Rodrigo Quimbo's practice includes administrative and civil litigation, alternative dispute resolution, and transportation, public utilities and aviation matters. He regularly advises clients on the review of confidentiality and restrictive agreements, compliance and government reporting requirements, and antitrust and competition regulatory requirements.

rodrigo.quimbo@quisumbingtorres.com
Tel: +63 2 819 4910

Miguel Galvez

Miguel Galvez's practice includes commercial, civil, criminal and administrative litigation; arbitration; anti-bribery and anti-corruption compliance; and immigration. He has conducted several audits, lectures and trainings on the subject of anti-bribery and anti-corruption compliance, and he regularly represents and advises various global and local clients in these areas.

miguel.galvez@quisumbingtorres.com
Tel: +63 2 819 4950

Camille Bianca M. Gatmaitan

Camille Bianca Gatmaitan is an associate in the Dispute Resolution Practice Group. She has five years of experience in commercial and criminal litigation, as well as arbitration. She is an accredited arbitrator of the Wholesale Electricity Spot Market. Her practice focuses on general dispute resolution involving criminal, civil and commercial disputes, as well as anti-bribery and anti-corruption matters. She has advised various clients engaged in the energy, aviation, outsourcing, pharmaceutical, mining, engineering and manufacturing industries.

camillebianca.gatmaitan@quisumbingtorres.com
Tel: +63 2 819 4914

Quisumbing Torres
12th Floor, Net One Center
26th Street corner 3rd Avenue
Crescent Park West
Bonifacio Global City
Taguig, Metro Manila 1634
Philippines

Key Practitioners

Mia Imperial
Manila
Tel: +63 2 819 4956
miacarmela.imperial@quisumbingtorres.com

1. Domestic bribery (private to public)

1.1 Legal framework

Bribery of public officials is penalized under Articles 210 to 212 of the Revised Penal Code.

There are other laws that penalize corrupt acts/practices and prohibit the giving of gifts to public officers under certain circumstances.

Republic Act No. 3019 (The Anti-Graft and Corrupt Practices Act) is the main anti-corruption law. It enumerates certain acts of public officers that constitute graft or corrupt practices, or which may lead thereto, as follows:

- Persuading, inducing or influencing another public officer to perform an act constituting a violation of rules, or an offense in connection with official duties

- Requesting or receiving any gift, present, share, percentage or benefit, for himself or for any other person, in connection with any contract or transaction between the government and any other party, wherein the public officer in his official capacity has to intervene under the law

- Requesting or receiving any gift, present or other pecuniary or material benefit, from any person for whom the public officer has secured or obtained, or will secure or obtain, any government permit or license

- Accepting or having any member of his family accept employment in a private enterprise that has pending official business with him, during the pendency thereof or within one year after its termination

- Causing any undue injury to any party, including the government, or giving any private party any unwarranted benefits, advantage or preference in the discharge of his functions through manifest partiality, evident bad faith or gross inexcusable negligence

- Neglecting or refusing to act within a reasonable time on any matter pending before him for the purpose of obtaining some pecuniary or material benefit or advantage, or for the purpose of favoring his own interest or giving undue advantage in favor of or discriminating against any other interested party

- Entering, on behalf of the government, into any contract or transaction manifestly and grossly disadvantageous to the same, whether or not the public officer profited or will profit thereby

- Having financial or pecuniary interest in any business, contract or transaction in connection with which he intervenes or takes part in his official capacity, or in which he is prohibited from having any interest

- Becoming interested, for personal gain, or having a material interest in any transaction or act requiring the approval of a board, panel or group of which he is a member, even if he votes against the same or does not participate in the action of the board, committee, panel or group

- Knowingly approving or granting any license, permit, privilege or benefit in favor of any person not qualified

- Divulging valuable information of a confidential character acquired by his office or by him on account of his official position to unauthorized persons, or releasing such information in advance of its authorized release date

Republic Act 6713 (The Code of Conduct and Ethical Standards for Public Officials and Employees) prohibits public officials and employees from soliciting or accepting, directly or indirectly, any gift, gratuity, favor, entertainment, loan or anything of monetary value from any person (a) in the course of their official duties; or (b) in connection with any operation being regulated by, or any transaction which may be affected by the functions of their office.

Presidential Decree No. 46 (Giving of Gifts on any Occasion) punishes the act of giving, or offering to give, to a public official or employee, a gift, present or other valuable thing on any occasion, including Christmas, when such gift, present or other valuable thing is given by reason of the public official/employee's position, regardless of whether or not the same is for past favor or the giver hopes or expects to receive a favor or better treatment in the future from the public official or employee concerned in the discharge of his official functions. Included within the prohibition is the throwing of parties or entertainment in honor of the public official or employee or of his immediate relatives.

Republic Act 7080 (Plunder) penalizes a public officer who acquires ill-gotten wealth in the total of at least PHP50 million through overt or criminal acts.

1.2 Definition of bribery

The Revised Penal Code penalizes three kinds of bribery: (a) direct bribery; (b) indirect bribery; and (c) qualified bribery.

Direct bribery is committed by a public officer who accepts an offer or promise or receives a gift or present, by himself or through another, with a view to committing a crime, or in consideration of the execution of an act that does not constitute a crime but is unjust, or to refrain from doing something that it is his official duty to do.

Indirect bribery is committed by a public officer who accepts a gift offered to him by reason of his office.

Qualified bribery is committed by a public officer entrusted with law enforcement, who refrains from arresting or prosecuting an offender who has committed a crime punishable by *reclusion perpetua* (imprisonment of 20 years to 40 years) and/or death, in consideration of any offer, promise, gift or present.

Corruption of public officials is the crime committed by the private person who shall have made the offers or promises or given the gifts or presents to the public officers, as described in the abovementioned crimes of bribery.

1.3 Definition of public official

The Revised Penal Code defines the term "public officer" as any person who, by direct provision of law, popular election or appointment by competent authority, shall take part in the performance of public functions in the government of the Philippine Islands, or shall perform in said government or in any of its branches public duties as an employee, agent or subordinate official, of any rank or class.

1.4 Consequences of bribery

(a) For the individuals involved

Direct Bribery

The penalty for direct bribery is determined by the manner in which it is committed.

Manner of commission	**Penalties**
1) With a view to committing a crime	• *Prision mayor* in its medium and maximum periods (8 years and 1 day to 12 years' imprisonment) • Fine of not less than three times the value of the gift • The penalty corresponding to the crime agreed upon, if the crime shall have been committed

Manner of commission	Penalties
2) In consideration of the execution of an act that does not constitute a crime, but is unjust	If the public officer executed the act: • Same penalties as above If the act was not accomplished • *Prision correccional* in its medium period (2 years, 4 months and 1 day to 4 years and 2 months' imprisonment) • Fine of not less than two times the value of the gift
3) To refrain from doing something that is his official duty to do	• *Prision correccional* in its maximum period to *prision mayor* in its minimum period (4 years, 2 months and 1 day to 10 years' imprisonment) • Fine of not less than three times the value of the gift

Indirect Bribery

The penalties for indirect bribery are as follows:

- *Prision correccional* in its medium and maximum periods (2 years, 4 months and 1 day to 6 years' imprisonment)
- Suspension
- Public censure

Qualified Bribery

The penalty for qualified bribery is the penalty for the offense that was not prosecuted.

Corruption of public officials

The same penalties imposed upon the officer corrupted, except those of disqualification and suspension, shall be imposed upon the private person who shall have made the offers or promises or given the gifts or presents to the public officers under the different forms of bribery.

(b) For the company/legal entity

The laws that penalize bribery do not apply to juridical/legal entities. The penalties are imposed against the individual corporate officers / employees who authorized or performed the prohibited acts.

Note, however, that the primary registration or license to do business of a Philippine corporation or a foreign corporation doing business in the Philippines may be revoked if it is shown that such corporation committed serious violations of Philippine law or otherwise performed acts that would render it unfit to transact business in the Philippines.

1.5 Political contributions

Batas Pambansa Bilang 881 (The Omnibus Election Code of the Philippines) regulates political contributions. It prohibits the following contributions for purposes of partisan political activity, directly or indirectly, by any of the following:

(a) Public or private financial institutions (except loans to a candidate or political party)

(b) Persons operating a public utility or in possession of or exploiting any natural resources of the nation

(c) Persons who hold contracts or sub-contracts to supply the government with goods or services, or to perform construction or other works

(d) Persons who have been granted franchises, incentives, exemptions, allocations or similar privileges or concessions by the government

(e) Persons who, within one year prior to the date of the election, have been granted loans or other accommodations in excess of PHP100,000 by the government

(f) Educational institutions that have received grants of public funds amounting to no less than PHP100,000

(g) Officials or employees in the Civil Service, or members of the Armed Forces of the Philippines

(h) Foreigners and foreign corporations

The Omnibus Election Code also makes it unlawful for any person, including a political party or public or private entity, to solicit or receive any aid or contribution of whatever form or nature from any foreign national, government or entity for the purpose of influencing the results of an election.

1.6 Limitation applicable to hospitality expenses (gifts, travel, meals, entertainment, among others)

Philippine bribery laws do not provide quantitative limitations.

Republic Act 3019 and Republic Act 6713 provide exceptions for unsolicited gifts of "small or insignificant value" under certain circumstances. However, such exceptions are not recognized under other laws and may not be invoked as a defense in a prosecution under such cases.

It must also be noted that in a prosecution for violation of special laws on anti-corruption, the motive or intent of the person committing the crime is generally not considered. The mere performance of the prohibited act is considered a violation of the law.

2. Domestic bribery (private to private)

Philippine laws currently do not regulate/penalize private bribery.

3. Corruption of foreign public officials

Philippine laws currently do not penalize the corruption of foreign public officials.

4. Facilitation payments

Facilitation payments are prohibited under Republic Act 9485 (The Anti-Red Tape Act of 2007). Among the acts constituting a violation of the Anti-Red Tape Act is fixing and/or collusion with fixers in consideration of economic and/or other gain or advantage.

The term "fixer" refers to any individual, whether or not officially involved in the operation of a government office, who has access to people working therein and facilitates the speedy completion of transactions for any advantage or consideration.

The Anti-Red Tape Act applies to all government offices and agencies, including local government units and government-owned or -controlled corporations that provide frontline services. Excluded from the coverage are those performing judicial, quasi-judicial and legislative functions.

"Frontline service" refers to transactions between clients and government offices involving applications for any privilege, right, permit, reward, license, concession, or for any modification, renewal or extension of the enumerated applications and/or requests that are acted upon in the ordinary course of business of the office concerned.

5. Compliance programs

5.1 Value of a compliance program to mitigate/eliminate the criminal liability for legal entities

Generally, Philippine laws do not require persons or companies to adopt a compliance program. The presence of a compliance program does not mitigate or eliminate a person's criminal liability.

As an exception, prescription pharmaceutical products and medical devices (PPMD) companies are required to establish a written compliance program, approved and signed by the company head, to ensure compliance with Department of Health Administrative Order No. 2015-0053 ("DOH AO 2015-0053"), or the Implementing Guidelines on the Promotion and Marketing of Prescription Pharmaceutical Products and Medical Devices, which regulates, among others, the promotion to and sponsorship of, healthcare professionals of prescription pharmaceutical products and medical devices.

5.2 Absence of a compliance program as a crime

Philippine law does not penalize the absence of a compliance program as a crime.

Although DOH-AO 2015-0053 requires a compliance program to be in place for PPMD companies, no specific sanction or penalty is provided for its absence. The Food and Drug Administration is, however, given the authority to recommend the filing of appropriate charges with the concerned government agency or appropriate court for violations of DOH-AO 2015-0053, including the absence of a compliance program.

5.3 Elements of compliance program

(a) Legal framework

DOH-AO 2015-0053 requires PPMD companies to observe the seven elements of effective compliance programs:

- Implementing written policies and procedures
- Designating compliance offices and compliance committee
- Conducting effective training and education
- Developing effective lines of communication
- Conducting internal monitoring and auditing
- Enforcing standards through well-publicized disciplinary guidelines
- Responding promptly to detected problems and undertaking corrective action

(b) Recommended practice

1. Formation of compliance team - It is recommended that companies form a compliance team to monitor observance of the company's compliance policies, code of conduct, etc.; answer questions and provide guidance to employees; and investigate and impose sanctions on erring employees.

2. Education of employees - It is important to educate company employees regarding the prohibited activities that may result to liability for themselves and others. The adoption of a company code of conduct for compliance purposes is also recommended to provide guidance to the employees.

3. Reporting mechanism - The company should have mechanisms through which employees may report acts of bribery and corruption (i.e., anonymous hotline, drop-box, etc.).

4. Enforcement - The company must impose appropriate sanctions on employees who commit bribery and corruption in violation of compliance policies and the code of conduct, to serve as a lesson and deterrent to other employees.

6. Regulator with jurisdiction to prosecute corruption

The Office of the Ombudsman is tasked with the investigation and prosecution of any act or omission of any public officer or employee, office or agency, when such act or omission appears to be illegal, unjust, improper or inefficient. Bribery and corruption cases fall under the prosecutorial jurisdiction of the Office of the Ombudsman.

The Philippine Department of Justice (**DOJ**), which serves as the government's prosecution arm, leads the investigation and prosecution of all criminal cases, including anti-bribery and anti-corruption laws. For public officials, the Office of the Ombudsman has concurrent jurisdiction with the DOJ to investigate and prosecute cases against public officials.

Singapore

Andrew Martin

Andrew Martin is a corporate and commercial lawyer with a particular focus on cross-border M&A and joint ventures, including post-acquisition integration and restructuring. He also advises extensively on compliance and governance matters, especially anti-bribery issues where he supports clients on their internal investigation and compliance programs. His practice covers and contacts span the wider ASEAN region, giving him a sound understanding of operating in Southeast Asia. He advises both multinational companies and private equity houses from Asia, the US and Europe on their investments and business conduct in the region.

andrew.martin@bakermckenzie.com
Tel: +65 6434 2507

Yi Lin Seng

Yi Lin Seng's practice covers matters involving IT, telecommunications, trade compliance and competition law. She has also worked in our Firm's Hong Kong office. She routinely advises multi-national corporations on regulatory and compliance matters, including anti-bribery, export controls and data privacy issues. In addition to regularly advising on anti-bribery matters, Yi Lin also assists clients with drafting of anti-bribery compliance policies. She likewise advises on various commercial agreements, including supply chain, IT and telecommunications, licensing and outsourcing agreements. She has also worked on secondment with various clients, including a major UK telecommunications network operator, a global consumer electronics manufacturer and a top-tier management consultancy firm.

yilin.seng@bakermckenzie.com
Tel: +65 6434 2713

Key Practitioners

Celeste Ang
Singapore
Tel: +65 6434 2753
celeste.ang@bakermckenzie.com

1. Domestic bribery (private to public)

1.1 Legal framework

The primary legislation regulating corruption/bribery in Singapore is the Prevention of Corruption Act, Chapter 241 of Singapore (the "PCA"), which applies to both private sector bribery and bribery of public officials. Other bribery legislation includes the Penal Code, Chapter 224 of Singapore (the "Penal Code"), which contains provisions directed at public officials. The Corruption, Drug Trafficking and other Serious Crimes (Confiscation of Benefits) Act, Chapter 65A of Singapore (the "CDTSA") is a related statute that provides for the confiscation of benefits derived from, *inter alia*, corruption offenses.

As the corruption/bribery offenses relating to public officials under the Penal Code largely overlap with those in the PCA, and the punishment meted out under the Penal Code is lesser than the prescribed punishments under the PCA, it is very rare for a prosecution to be brought under the Penal Code for the receiving or taking of illegal gratification.

1.2 Definition of bribery

PCA

The key offense is set out in Section 5 of the PCA[1]:

A person is guilty of a corruption offense when he, by himself, or in conjunction with any other person:

(a) corruptly solicits or receives, or agrees to receive for himself, or for any other person; or

(b) corruptly gives, promises, or offers to any person whether for the benefit of that person or of another person,

any gratification as an inducement to or reward for, or otherwise on account of any person to do or forbear to do anything in respect of any matter or transaction whatsoever, actual or proposed.

Therefore, the two core elements are that: (a) the transaction was corrupt; and (b) gratification was given/received.

There must first be a corrupt element in the transaction according to the ordinary and objective standard, followed by the accused's guilty knowledge that what he was doing was, by that standard, corrupt. Both limbs must be fulfilled beyond reasonable doubt. The question of

---

[1] Separately, Section 6 of the PCA specifically provides for corrupt transactions involving agents. In this regard, a person commits an offense by giving, and an agent commits an offense by receiving, gratification as an inducement or reward for doing or forbearing to do any act in relation to the principal's affairs or business. A recent decision by the High Court established that the lack of an agreement or discussion prior to the event does not prevent a finding of corruption from being made. The crucial inquiry is whether the agent, in carrying out his duties, showed favor to the third party or was tainted by the contemplation of a reward. To prove corruption in cases where gratification was received after the allegedly corrupt conduct had occurred, the evidence must at least lead the court to infer that the idea of gratification was already operating in the accused's mind at the time the allegedly corrupt conduct occurred.

'corrupt' would therefore be determined on the facts of the individual case.

In particular, please note that there is a presumption of corruption where it is proved that gratification has been given to Singapore public officials.

The definition of "gratification" under the PCA is very broad and includes monies, gifts, loans, fees, rewards, commissions, valuable security and properties, and can also cover "any other service, favour or advantage of any description whatsoever."

Penal Code

The Penal Code contains provisions that prohibit, among others, any public servant from taking any gratification as a motive or reward for doing or forbearing to do any official act, or the taking of any gratification by any person as a motive or reward for inducing, by the exercise of personal influence, any public servant to do or forbear to do any official act.

1.3 Definition of public official

The definition of a public person under the PCA and the Penal Code are both very broad.

The PCA defines a public body as "any corporation, board, council, commissioners or other body which has power to act under and for the purposes of any written law relating to public health or to undertakings or public utility or otherwise to administer money levied or raised by rates or charges in pursuance of any written law." This has been held by a Singapore court to include the National University of Singapore, an autonomous university that is open to the public for tertiary education.

Under the Penal Code, the definition of a public servant includes, among others, officers in the Singapore Armed Forces, judges, officers of a court of justice, assessors assisting a court of justice or public servant, and officers of and acting on behalf of the Singapore government.

1.4 Consequences of bribery

PCA

A person guilty of bribery of a public official under the key provisions of the PCA (Section 5 or Section 6) shall be liable on conviction to a fine not exceeding SGD100,000, or to imprisonment for a term not exceeding five years, or both. There are also certain offenses relating to government contracts or bribery of a member of a public body under certain circumstances, which may result in a fine not exceeding SGD100,000, or to imprisonment for a term not exceeding seven years, or both. If a person is convicted for accepting any gratification in contravention of the PCA, the court may also order him to pay a penalty equivalent to the amount of bribes he received as a fine.

In this regard, please note that the Singapore High Court has clarified that there are no sentencing presumptions in respect of private sector and public sector corruption, both of which can attract custodial sentences.

The term "person" includes any company or association or body of persons, and as such, a company could accordingly face the consequences of bribery. Although the prosecutions for bribery offenses in Singapore to date have been at an individual level, there is no legal impediment barring companies from being prosecuted for a bribery offense.

CDTSA

"Criminal conduct," as defined in the CDTSA, covers a range of serious offenses, including bribery under the PCA. Where a defendant is convicted of one or more serious offenses, the court shall, on the application of the public prosecutor, make a confiscation order against the defendant in respect of benefits derived by him from criminal conduct if the court is satisfied that such benefits have been so derived.

Penal Code

A bribery offense under the Penal Code shall be punishable by imprisonment of up to three years and/or a fine.

1.5 Political contributions

Political contributions that are not provided for a corrupt purpose or intent or for the purposes of influencing a public servant to do or forbear to do any official act, are acceptable. However, as previously mentioned, under the PCA there is a presumption of corruption where it is proved that gratification has been given to public officials in Singapore.

1.6 Limitation applicable to hospitality expenses (gifts, travel, meals, entertainment, among others)

Neither the Penal Code nor the PCA provides any "safe harbor" monetary guidelines for gifts, hospitality expenses or other entertainment, nor are there favorable presumptions under the statutes if such gifts are below a certain monetary value. Generally, and only as a rule of thumb, any arrangements that may be considered as lavish, extravagant or excessive so as to invite an inference to be drawn that the arrangements were intended as a form of corruption, should be avoided.

Based on anecdotal evidence, we understand that no public official may receive any gifts in a personal capacity. Gifts should only be officially made to the relevant government department, and the giver should write to the relevant Permanent Secretary (or at least the official's superior or head of department) to offer the gift.

2. Domestic bribery (private to private)

2.1 Legal framework

Private bribery is regulated under the PCA.

2.2 Definition of private bribery

Paragraph 1.2. Section 5 (and Section 6) of the PCA applies to private bribery as well.

2.3 Consequences of private bribery

As mentioned in paragraph 1.4, a person guilty of bribery shall be liable on conviction to a fine not exceeding SGD100,000, or to imprisonment for a term not exceeding five years, or both. If a person is convicted for accepting any gratification in contravention of the PCA, the court may also order him to pay a penalty equivalent to the amount of bribes he received as a fine. Under the CDTSA, the Singapore courts can also make a confiscation order against a defendant in respect of benefits derived by him from the bribery offense (as mentioned in paragraph 1.4).

Also, as mentioned in paragraph 1.4, there are no sentencing presumptions in respect of private sector and public sector corruption, both of which can attract custodial sentences.

2.4 Limitation applicable to hospitality expenses (gifts, travel, meals, entertainment, among others)

As mentioned in paragraph 1.6, the PCA does not provide any safe harbor monetary guidelines for gifts, hospitality expenses or other entertainment, nor are there favorable presumptions under the statute if such gifts are below a certain monetary value.

3. Corruption of foreign public officials

3.1 Legal framework

There is no specific legislation regulating corruption in relation to foreign public officials. However, Section 37(1) of the PCA provides that the provisions of the PCA have effect, in relation to Singapore citizens, outside as well as within Singapore, where an offense under the PCA is committed by a citizen of Singapore in any place outside Singapore. Accordingly, the corruption of foreign public officials by a Singapore citizen outside of Singapore will be an offense under the PCA. Where the corruption takes place outside of Singapore, it will be an offense only if the person committing such offense is a Singapore citizen.

It has also been announced that there will be a legislative review of the PCA, and there may be a change to the PCA to strengthen its extraterritorial scope.

Notwithstanding the above, if the corruption takes place within Singapore and involves a foreign public official, Section 5 (or possibly Section 6) of the PCA will apply to any Singapore citizen who gives the bribe to, or receives the bribe from that foreign public official.

3.2 Definition of corruption of foreign public officials

Please see paragraph 1.2, which will apply to the corruption of foreign public officials.

3.3 Definition of foreign public official

There is no definition of a foreign public official in the PCA. However, the PCA does apply widely to all natural persons as well as companies or association or body of persons (corporate or incorporate), which includes foreign public officials.

3.4 Consequences of Corruption of foreign public officials

As mentioned in paragraph 1.4, a person guilty of bribery shall be liable on conviction to a fine not exceeding SGD100,000, or to imprisonment for a term not exceeding five years, or both.

3.5 Limitation applicable to hospitality expenses (gifts, travel, meals, entertainment, among others)

As mentioned in paragraph 1.6 above, the PCA does not provide any safe harbor monetary guidelines for gifts, hospitality expenses or other entertainment, nor are there favorable presumptions under the statute if such gifts are below a certain monetary value.

4. Facilitation payments

As explained in paragraph 1.2, the definition of "gratification" under the PCA is very broad and will include facilitation payments. Accordingly, the provisions of the PCA will likely apply to any facilitation payments if such facilitation payments have been given or received corruptly.

5. Compliance programs

5.1 Value of a compliance program to mitigate/eliminate the criminal liability for legal entities

The PCA does not specifically recognize compliance programs as a mitigating factor that will eliminate liability for companies. However, in the event that an entity is prosecuted for a bribery offense, the fact that such entity has a compliance program in place may mitigate any punishment imposed in respect of such offense, although the degree of mitigation is not clear and will likely turn on the particular facts.

5.2 Absence of a compliance program as a crime

The absence of a compliance program is not an offense.

5.3 Elements of compliance program

The PCA does not provide for elements that must be present in a compliance program. However, we would recommend that the compliance program include the following:

- Processes for assessing compliance risks, including due diligence on third party business partners
- Company anti-bribery policies / codes of conduct
- Compliance training and appropriate messaging from the board and senior management
- Compliance audits, reporting and monitoring procedures
- Whistleblowing procedures

6. Regulator with Jurisdiction to prosecute corruption

The regulator responsible for the investigation and prevention of corruption in Singapore is the Corrupt Practices Investigation Bureau (CPIB).

The functions of the CPIB are:

- to receive and investigate complaints alleging corrupt practices;
- to investigate malpractices and misconduct by public officers with an undertone of corruption; and
- to prevent corruption by examining the practices and procedures in the public service to minimize opportunities for corrupt practices.

The CPIB does not have prosecution functions. The CPIB will hand any such potential cases over to the public prosecutor, who has prosecutorial discretion to initiate criminal proceedings.

South Korea

Nam Paik (CLF: Shin & Kim)

Nam Paik primarily advises multinational corporations and financial institutions on a wide variety of legal issues, including corporate, commercial, cross-border, employment, distributorship, litigation and foreign investment matters. Nam has worked on a variety of transactions, including mergers, acquisitions, joint ventures, divestitures, restructuring projects, financings, leases, reorganizations, strategic alliances, and other business combinations and separations.

nam.paik@bakermckenzie.com
Tel: +82 2 6137 6802

Baker & McKenzie LLP Foreign Legal
Consultant Office
17/F, Two IFC
10 Gukjegeumyung-ro
Yeongdeungpo-gu
Seoul 150-945
Korea

Seong-Jin Choi

Seong-Jin Choi's main areas of practice are anti-corruption, financial crime, anti-money laundering and high-tech crime. As a public prosecutor for over 17 years, he handled a number of investigations and litigations in the areas of fraud, financial crime, high-tech crime and money laundering, as well as anti-corruption. He joined Shin & Kim in 2014.

sjinchoi@shinkim.com
Tel: +82 2 316 4405
Mobile: +82 10 4612 2798

Tak-Kyun Hong

Tak-Kyun Hong's main areas of practice are anti-corruption and white-collar criminal defense. He has handled a number of investigations and litigations in the areas of fraud, embezzlement, securities-related crimes, technology theft, criminal cartels and criminal extradition, as well as anti-corruption, both as a public prosecutor and as a defense attorney.

tkhong@shinkim.com
Tel: +82 2 316 4085
Mobile: +82 10 5451 0819

SHIN & KIM
8th Floor, State Tower Namsan
100 Toegye-ro, Jung-gu
Seoul 100-052, South Korea

1. Domestic bribery (private to public)

1.1 Legal framework

Both the giving and taking of a bribe is regulated under Articles 129 to 133 of the Criminal Act, covering the anti-bribery statutes.

In addition, there are laws that categorically prevent public officials from taking bribes. For example, Articles 7 and 8 of the Act on the Prevention of Corruption and the Establishment and Management of the Anti-Corruption and Civil Right Commission (the "Act on Prevention of Corruption") and the Public Officials' Code of Conduct for Maintenance of Integrity act as regulations to prevent the taking of bribes. To discourage the giving of bribes to public officials during bids for government contracts, the Act on Contracts to Which the State is a Party excludes an entity found guilty of giving a bribe to a bid committee member from participation in a government procurement contract for up to two years.

1.2 Definition of bribery

There has been no explicit definition of bribery in the statutes that regulate bribery in Korea. However, the term has been interpreted broadly, and bribery can be any tangible or intangible benefit. Past cases involving prosecution of bribery included bribes that ranged from cash gifts, to expensive meals, complimentary products, travel and entertainment.

For a benefit to become a bribe, it should be given or received "in connection with" the performance of duty of the official. Courts interpret the "in connection with" requirement broadly. From 28 September 2016, however, a benefit need not be given or received "in connection with" the performance of duty of the official when the amount exceeds KRW1 million at a time, or KRW3 million in aggregate per year (Article 8.1 of Act on Prevention of Illegal Solicitation or Exchange of Benefits).

In contrast to private or commercial bribery, the public official does not have to receive an economic benefit "in response to an improper request" concerning his or her duty in order for him or her to be found guilty of taking a bribe.

1.3 Definition of public official

The Criminal Act does not include a definition of a public official. Thus, the definition of who is a public official may vary depending on the statute regulating the specific act, and can be determined by core precedents. There are many statutes that specify the officers, directors or representatives of certain state-owned or state-controlled entities as public officials.

A representative statute is the Act Concerning Aggravated Punishment of Specific Crimes (the "Specific Crimes Act"). The Specific Crimes Act extends the definition to officers of organizations prescribed by Presidential Decree. Qualifying organizations include those in which government funds constitute 50 percent or more of their capital investments directly or indirectly, and organizations over which any level of government exercises significant control, including appointment and dismissal of officers or making material decisions due to the impact of the organization on the national economy. In addition, the Enforcement Decree of the Specific Crimes Act sets out an exhaustive list of state-controlled entities that are considered to be public officials.

The Ministry of Strategy and Finance also issues annually a list of state owned, controlled or subsidized entities. The corporate entities constitute public corporations and quasi-government entities pursuant to the Act on Administration of Public Entities (AAPE). The directors and officers of the public corporations and government-controlled entities are considered to be public officials.

In addition, the State Public Officials Act and the Local Public Officials Act give basic definitions of public officials and those employed by state and local governments.

1.4 Consequences of bribery

Depending on the methods a bribe was given or extracted by the public official, punishments to public officials range from suspension of qualifications for up to 10 years, to prison sentences for up to five years. A suspension of qualifications is described in Article 43 of the Criminal Act as a deprivation of: (i) the qualifications to be a public official; (ii) voting rights and eligibility to run in public elections; (iii) qualifications to conduct necessary business prescribed by the Public Act; and (iv) qualifications to be a director, auditor or manager of a company or an inspector or custodian of a company's business. If the amount of the bribe is KRW30 million or more, the prison sentence may be increased up to life imprisonment, based on the amount of bribery. If there are multiple counts of violations, the prison sentence or fines can be increased by up to 150 percent.

Article 134 of the Criminal Act also prescribes confiscation of the bribes or the disgorgement of the monetary equivalent from the recipient.

The party that is found guilty of giving a bribe to a public official may be sentenced to a maximum of five years' imprisonment or a fine of up to KRW20 million. In multiple counts of violations, prison sentences and fines can be increased by up to 150 percent.

1.5 Political contributions

The Political Funds Act sets specific procedures of political contributions and sets limits on the amount. If anyone contributes political funds of more than KRW3 million over a year (more than KRW5 million, when donated to presidential candidates), the amount donated and his or her personal details shall be reported to National Election Commission, and shall be open to the public (Article 40, 41 of National Election Commission Rule on Management of Political Fund). Article 31 of the Political Funds Act prevents companies or foreign nationals from making political contributions.

1.6 Limitation applicable to hospitality expenses (gifts, travel, meals, entertainment, among others)

There are no specific limitations to hospitality expenses; this would be determined on a case-by-case basis, depending on the circumstances and the benefits conferred in exchange for the bribes.

2. Domestic bribery (private to private)

2.1 Legal framework

Article 357 of the Criminal Act describes *Baeim*, a criminal breach of duties, which makes both the giving and taking of bribes punishable by fines and imprisonment. Article 357(1) states that a person entrusted to administer another's business and who receives an economic benefit from a third person in response to an improper request concerning his or her duty is to be punished. Article 357(2) states that the third person who provides the economic benefit is also to be punished.

Industry-specific regulations exist to target those industries that have higher instances of bribe-giving and bribe-taking. For instance, the medical and pharmaceutical industry is regulated by Article 23(2) of the Medical Service Act, Article 18 of the Medical Device Act and Article 47 of the Pharmaceutical Affairs Act. The construction industry is regulated by Article 38(2) of the Framework Act on the Construction Industry.

2.2 Definition of private bribery

The Criminal Act defines private bribery as the receipt of economic benefits by an agent or fiduciary where the benefits are related to an improper request regarding the duty of the recipient of the bribe.

A key element of private bribery under the Korean Criminal Act is the requirement of an improper request with regard to the duty of the recipient of the bribe. The Korean courts have been fairly lax in requiring prosecutors to make a satisfactory showing of an improper request. However, the courts will consider factors such as the circumstances surrounding a potential request for a bribe, as well as the type and amount of the bribe sought to determine whether an improper request had been made.

2.3 Consequences of private bribery

The consequence of taking private or commercial bribery as codified in the Criminal Act is prison sentence of up to five years or a fine of up to KRW10 million. The consequence for giving private or commercial bribery is prison sentence up to two years or a fine of up to KRW5 million. The bribe itself is confiscated, or if a physical confiscation is not possible, the recipient of the bribe will be disgorged of the monetary equivalent of the bribe.

2.4 Limitation applicable to hospitality expenses (gifts, travel, meals, entertainment, among others)

There are no specific limitations to hospitality expenses; this would be determined on a case-by-case basis depending on the circumstances and the benefits conferred in exchange for the bribes.

3. Corruption of foreign public officials

3.1 Legal framework

Korea has signed and ratified the OECD Convention on Combatting Bribery of Foreign Public Officials in International Business Transactions and the UN Convention against corruption.

Bribery of foreign officials is regulated under the Act on Preventing Bribery of Foreign Public Officials in International Business Transactions (FBPA), enacted in 1999 pursuant to the OECD Convention. The FBPA is a Korean statute that functions as the Korean law equivalent of the Foreign Corrupt Practices Act of the United States.

Article 357 of the Criminal Act, covering *Baeim* (a concept of criminal breach of fiduciary duties), may also apply for bribery of foreign officials.

3.2 Definition of corruption of foreign public officials

Article 3.1 of the FBPA defines corruption of foreign public officials as the giving, offering or promising to give a bribe to a foreign public official in connection with the performance of his or her official duties in exchange for an improper advantage in an international business transaction. The bribe may be in the form of money, goods and other pecuniary or intangible benefits that satisfies the wishes of the recipient.

The FBPA provides for an exception in Article 3.2, where certain gifts to foreign public officials are allowed if the laws of the foreign public official's country allow receiving or giving of such benefits.

3.3 Definition of foreign public official

Article 2 of the FPBA provides a broad definition of a foreign public official, including not only government officials but also individuals performing public functions on behalf of foreign governments and agencies. The definition of foreign public officials extends to employees of public agencies, international organizations and companies controlled by foreign governments.

3.4 Consequences of corruption of foreign public officials

The consequence for individuals found in violation of the FBPA is a prison sentence of up to five years or a fine of up to KRW20 million. However, if the profit gained through bribery exceeds KRW10 million, the fine may be increased up to double the value of the profit gained.

Consequences for corporate or legal entities found in violation of the FBPA may include a fine of up to KRW1 billion in addition to the sanctions imposed on the individual offender. If the profits gained in the commission of the violation exceed a total of KRW500 million, the fine imposed on the corporate or legal entity may be increased up to double the value of the total profit gained.

3.5 Limitation applicable to hospitality expenses (gifts, travel, meals, entertainment, among others)

There are no specific limitations to hospitality expenses; this would be determined on a case-by-case basis depending on the circumstances and the benefits conferred in exchange for the bribes.

4. Facilitation payments

The Criminal Act does not officially recognize the concept of facilitation payments.

There had been a facilitation payment exception in the FBPA, but this exception was repealed in October 2014. Prior to October 2014, Article 3.2(2) of the FBPA had provided for an instance "[w]here any person promises, gives, or expresses his/her intent to give a small amount of money or any other advantage to a foreign public official, who performs daily routine duties, with intent to encourage the official to perform his/her duties in a fair manner."

Currently, the prevailing practice of the Prosecutors' Office and case law recognizes an exception for "socially acceptable" gifts, as long as the amount is small and the gift was provided in normal personal or business relationships.

5. Compliance programs

5.1 Value of a compliance program to mitigate/eliminate the criminal liability for legal entities

For statutes that have a vicarious criminal liability provision (e.g., the FBPA), if a company can satisfactorily show that it had discharged its duty to adequately supervise its employees, it may be exempt from liability for the improper actions of its employees. Even if the company fails to satisfactorily show that it had discharged its duty to adequately supervise its employees, vigorous implementation of compliance programs may act as mitigating circumstance of the corporate's criminal liability in such case.

5.2 Absence of a compliance program as a crime

Since corporate criminal liability is not recognized according to the Criminal Act, the absence of a compliance program itself is not a crime under the Criminal Act. There are some anti-corruption regulations that require specific types of companies to establish compliance programs and impose sanctions for failing to maintain compliance programs.

5.3 Elements of compliance program

(a) Legal framework

The Korean Criminal Act does not establish a framework for internal compliance programs. However, specific anti-corruption regulations require certain types of established compliance programs.

For example, Article 5 of the Act on Reporting and Using Specified Financial Transaction Information provides that a certain type of financial company or entity is to take prescribed measures to facilitate reporting to prevent money laundering and financing of terrorism through the financial company or entity. The measures may include the appointment of a person to be in charge of reporting duties such as preparation and operation of the procedure and guidelines to be followed, and to be in charge of educating and training the employees.

(b) Recommended practice

Corporate entities should follow the legal framework if specifically applicable regulations exist. In addition to complying with the legal requirements, companies should educate its employees on anti-corruption laws and the consequences of breaking the laws. Companies should make it a priority to stress on a regular basis the importance of preventing corrupt practices. Companies should also keep records of educational programs that are geared towards preventing corrupt practices and maintain logs of such programs' attendees.

6. Regulator with jurisdiction to prosecute corruption

The Prosecutors' Office and the police are the two main agencies that prosecute corruption. They have special investigative departments that perform criminal investigation for corruption. The Anti-Corruption and Civil Rights Commission (ACRC) receives information or complaints filed by whistleblowers and members of the public. For the financial sector, the Financial Supervisory Service (FSS) and the Financial Services Commission (FSC) conduct investigations as administrative agencies, and depending on the findings, may render administrative sanctions on a corporate entity. For rebates in the medical sector, the Korean Fair Trade Commission (KFTC) conducts investigations and may render administrative sanctions on a corporate entity. These agencies may also hand over their findings to the Prosecutors' Office for criminal prosecution by prosecutors specialized in cases involving bribery and other applicable corruption-related crimes.

Taiwan

H. Henry Chang

Focusing on the areas of corporate compliance and technology, media and telecom (TMT), H. Henry Chang has acted for both domestic and multinational corporations in their cross-border work for over 20 years. He sits on the steering committee of the Firm's Asia Pacific Information, Technology and Communications (ITC) Practice Group.

henry.chang@bakermckenzie.com
Tel: +886 2 2715 7259

Baker & McKenzie
15th Floor, Hung Tai Center
No. 168, Tun Hwa North Road
Taipei 105
Taiwan

1. Domestic bribery (private to public)

1.1 Legal framework

Bribery of public officials is regulated under Taiwan's Anti-Corruption Act, Articles 4, 5, 6, 11; and Criminal Code, Articles 121, 122, 123, 131. The provisions in the Criminal Code dealing with anti-corruption and the defenses thereof are similar to those contained in the Anti-Corruption Act. However, bribing a public official to perform his official duties is not punished under the Criminal Code. When both the Anti-Corruption Act and the Criminal Code apply, the former, being a specialized law, shall govern.

1.2 Definition of bribery

Bribery can be committed both by public officials receiving and by private individuals who try to bribe a public official.

Bribery: " . . . to offer, promise or give a bribe or other unjust benefits to a public official to perform his official duties or to procure a breach of his official duties." Article 11 of the Anti-Corruption Act

1.3 Definition of public official

The Taiwan Criminal Code has a broad definition of public official, and it includes those who serve an organization of the state or a local autonomous body with legal function and authority and others engaged in public affairs with legal function and authority, and those who, entrusted by an organization of the state or a local autonomous body, are engaged in the public affairs within the authority of the entrusting organization.

1.4 Consequences of bribery

(a) For the individuals involved

The Anti-Corruption Act and the Criminal Code establishes different penalties for the public officials receiving and the individuals that bribe public officials. The penalties are as follows:

- Public official who:

    (1) breaches his official duties – imprisonment for life or a period of no less than 10 years and/or a fine of up to TWD100 million; or

    (2) performs official duties – imprisonment for a period of no less than seven years and/or a fine of up to TWD60 million.

- Individuals that corrupt public official to:

    (1) breach his official duties – imprisonment for a period between one and seven years and/or a fine of up to TWD3 million; or

    (2) perform official duties – imprisonment for up to three years, detention and/or a fine of up to TWD500,000.

(b) For the company / legal entity

The Anti-Corruption Act and the Criminal Code do not provide for any corporate offense against the legal entity.

1.5 Political contributions

Contributions to political parties are regulated under the Political Donations Act. In general terms, contributions to political parties are allowed if they do not exceed a certain amount per year:

(a) For individual donators – TWD300,000 per political party and TWD600,000 in aggregate

(b) For corporate donators – TWD3 million per political party and TWD6 million in aggregate

1.6 Limitation applicable to hospitality expenses (gifts, travel, meals, entertainment, among others)

Hospitality accepted by a public official may only be allowed in the limited circumstances stipulated in the Integrity and Ethics Guidelines for Public Officials (公務員廉政倫理規範) (the "Guidelines"). Pursuant to the Guidelines, generally, the value of each gift should not exceed TWD500. For certain special occasions, such as an engagement, wedding, promotion, retirement and other specified occasions, the value of each gift should not exceed TWD3,000. The total value of gifts received from the same source in one year shall not exceed TWD10,000.

2. Domestic bribery (private to private)

2.1 Legal framework

Private bribery is regulated under the Taiwan Criminal Code, Article *342*, and the Securities and Exchange Act, Article 171, paragraphs 1 and 2.

2.2 Definition of private bribery

<u>Private bribery</u>: "A person who manages the affairs of another, with intent to procure an illegal benefit for himself or for a third person or to harm the interests of his principal, acts contrary to his duties and

thereby causes damage to the property or other interest of the principal." Article 342 of the Criminal Code

2.3 Consequences of private bribery

(a) For the individuals involved

- Damage of less than TWD5 million – imprisonment for up to five years, detention and/or a fine of up to TWD500,000
- Damage of TWD5 million or more (applicable to a director, supervisor or officer of a public company) – imprisonment for between three years and 10 years and/or a fine between TWD10 million and TWD200 million
- Amount gained TWD100 million or more (applicable to a director, supervisor or officer of a public company) – imprisonment for not less than seven years and/or a fine between TWD25 million and TWD500 million

(b) For the company/legal entity

- The Criminal Code and the Securities and Exchange Act do not provide for any corporate offense.

2.4 Limitation applicable to hospitality expenses (gifts, travel, meals, entertainment, among others)

The Criminal Code and the Securities and Exchange Act do not establish quantitative nor qualitative limitations on hospitality expenses. Whether a hospitality expense could be considered bribery will need to be determined on a case-by-case basis, taking into account the facts and circumstances surrounding the case.

3. Corruption of foreign public officials

3.1 Legal framework

Corruption of foreign public officials is regulated under the Taiwan Anti-Corruption Act, paragraph 3, Article 11.

3.2 Definition of corruption of foreign public officials

Corruption of foreign public officials means to offer, promise or give a bribe or other unjust benefits to a foreign public official to perform his official duties or to procure a breach of his official duties in relation to international trade, investment or other business activities.

3.3 Definition of foreign public official

A foreign public official means a public official (as defined in the Criminal Code) in a foreign country, PRC, Hong Kong or Macau.

3.4 Consequences of Corruption of foreign public officials

(a) For the individuals involved

- Individuals that corrupt foreign public officials to:

  (1) breach his official duties – imprisonment for a period between one year and seven years and/or a fine of up to TWD3 million; or

  (2) perform official duties – imprisonment for up to three years, detention and/or a fine of up to TWD500,000.

(b) For the legal entity

The Anti-Corruption Act does not provide for any corporate offense.

3.5 Limitation applicable to hospitality expenses (gifts, travel, meals, entertainment, among others)

The Anti-Corruption Act does not establish quantitative nor qualitative limitations on hospitality expenses. Whether a hospitality expense could be considered bribery will need to be determined on a case-by-case basis, taking into account the facts and circumstances surrounding the case.

4. Facilitation payments

The Anti-Corruption Act, the Criminal Code and the Securities and Exchange Act do not make exceptions for so called facilitation payments.

5. Compliance programs

5.1 Value of a compliance program to mitigate/eliminate the criminal liability for legal entities

The Anti-Corruption Act and the Criminal Code do not provide for any corporate offense relating to compliance programs.

5.2 Absence of a compliance program as a crime

The Taiwan Anti-Corruption Act and Criminal Code do not recognize the absence of having a compliance program as a crime.

5.3 Elements of Compliance Program

(a) Legal framework

The Taiwan Anti-Corruption Act and Criminal Code do not recognize or regulate the elements of a Compliance Program.

(b) Recommended practice

N/A

6. Regulator with jurisdiction to prosecute corruption

The Ministry of Justice, which has established the following supporting offices, has jurisdiction to prosecute corruption:

(a) Agency against Corruption (廉政署)

(b) Investigation Bureau (調查局)

(c) Prosecutors Office (檢察署)

(d) Special Investigation Division of the Supreme Court Prosecutors Office (最高法院檢察署特別偵查組)

Thailand

Timothy Breier

Timothy Breier is a partner in the Dispute Resolution Practice Group in Baker & McKenzie's Bangkok office and works closely on a variety of projects and cases for international clientele, primarily involving international arbitration, compliance and anti-corruption, construction matters, bankruptcy and contractual disputes. Timothy regularly advises clients regarding compliance with Thai anti-corruption legislation, provides training on compliance with international anti-corruption laws, and assists clients in conducting internal investigations and compliance program reviews.

timothy.breier@bakermckenzie.com
Tel +66 2 6362000 X3223

Baker & McKenzie Limited
25th Floor, Abdulrahim Place
990 Rama IV Road
Bangkok 10500
Thailand

Key Practitioners

Wynn Pakdeejit
Bangkok
Tel: +66 2636 2000 p 3010
wynn.pakdeejit@bakermckenzie.com

Chaiporn Supvoranid
Bangkok
Tel: +66 2636 2000 p 3067
chaiporn.supvoranid@bakermckenzie.com

Peerappan Tungsuwan
Bangkok
Tel: +662 636 2000 p 4333
peerapan.tungsuwan@bakermckenzie.com

1. Domestic bribery (private to public)

1.1 Legal framework

The Penal Code of Thailand generally criminalizes: (i) the offering of property or other benefits by a private party to an official for the purpose of inducing the official to act or omit to act, or to delay acting, contrary to the official's functions; or (ii) the acceptance of, or demand for, property or other benefits by an official, for the purpose of inducing the official to act in accordance with the official's functions or to omit to act, or to delay acting, contrary to the official's functions. The Penal Code specifically criminalizes: (i) bribery of public officials, legislators, public prosecutors, judges and inquiry officials; (ii) soliciting or accepting gifts by public servants, public prosecutors and judges; (iii) malfeasance of public officials to obtain property or benefits; and (iv) malfeasance of public prosecutors and judges for property or benefits.

1.2 Definition of bribery

The Penal Code of Thailand does not provide a clear definition of bribery, but the meaning thereof can be inferred from relevant legal provisions.

> Bribery: to give or promise to give property or any other benefit to an official, member of a state legislative assembly, member of a state legislative assembly or provincial assembly or member of a municipal assembly, official holding a judicial post, public prosecutor, or an official responsible for conducting cases or inquiries, so as to induce such person to do or not to do any act, or to delay the doing of any act, contrary to their duty.[1]

Under the Penal Code of Thailand, bribery can be committed both by public officials and by private individuals who attempt to bribe any public official, members of the state legislative assembly, members of

[1] Sections 144 and 167 of the Penal Code of Thailand.

a provincial or municipal assembly, public prosecutors, inquiry officials, judges or execution officers.

1.3 Definition of public official

Pursuant to the Penal Code of Thailand, "public officials" include not only public servants but also members of the state legislative assembly, members of provincial and municipal assemblies, public prosecutors, inquiry officials, judges and execution officers.

Supreme Court precedent has established two criteria providing a broad definition of a public official under the Thai Penal Code, as follows:[2]

1. A person appointed by the Kingdom of Thailand

2. To assume public duties for the Kingdom of Thailand

Note that the definition of "public official" will also vary depending on the relevant Act governing the related crime.

Under the Act Supplementing the Constitution Relating to the Prevention and Suppression of Corruption B.E. 2542, "State Official" is defined as a person in a political position; a government official or local government official or employee holding a position or having a regular salary; an employee or person who carries out work in a state enterprise or state agency; a local administrative officer or member of a local council who is not a person holding a political position; a competent official under the law on local administration, including a committee member, sub-committee member, and employee of an authority, state enterprise or state agency; or a person or party who exercises or who has been authorized to exercise authority in the administration of the state in carrying out the state's power, regardless of whether the administrative function is established under

---

[2] Supreme Court Decision No. 700/2490.

governmental bureaucratic channels, state enterprise or other activity of the state.[3]

Under the Act on Offenses by Officers in State Organizations or Agencies B.E. 2502, the term "Officer" is defined to include a board chairman, president, board member or person who performs work in an organization, limited company, registered partnership or agency, or a work unit otherwise named, where all the capital or more than 50 percent of it belongs to the state, and who receives a monthly salary or other benefits in return from the organization, limited company, registered partnership or agency, but excluding those persons who are already officials under the law.[4]

Under the Act on Offenses Relating to the Submission of Bids to Government Agencies B.E. 2542, "Government Agency" is defined as ministries, bureaus, departments, provincial administration authorities, local administration authorities, state enterprises, or other governmental agencies or agencies that perform public duties under the law and receive financial aid or capital from the state.[5]

1.4 Consequences of bribery

Penalties differ depending on whether the person committing the crime is a private party bribing a public official or a public official accepting a bribe under the Penal Code (Titles II and III) or other relevant legislation.

---

[3] Section 4 of the Act Supplementing the Constitution Relating to the Prevention and Suppression of Corruption B.E. 2542 (also known as "The Organic Act on Counter Corruption").

[4] Section 3 of the Act on Offenses by Officers in State Organizations or Agencies B.E. 2502.

[5] Section 3 of the Act on Offenses Relating to the Submission of Bids to Government Agencies B.E. 2542.

(a) Penalties for a private party bribing public officials

(i) For the private individual involved

- Imprisonment not exceeding five years or a fine not exceeding THB10,000, or both imprisonment and a fine, for bribing a public official, member of the state legislative assembly or member of a provincial or municipal assembly to act or refrain from acting or to delay acting[6]

- Imprisonment not exceeding seven years and a fine not exceeding THB14,000 for agreeing to give a benefit to an official holding a judicial post, a public prosecutor, inquiry official, judge or execution officer so that such person will wrongly do or not do any act or will delay in acting[7]

- Imprisonment for one year to three years, or a fine equal to 50 percent of the highest bid by offenders or the value of the contract, whichever is higher, for collaborating in the submission of bids to provide a benefit by avoiding fair competition, or preventing the offer of other goods or services, or taking advantage of government agencies[8]

- Imprisonment for one year to five years and a fine equal to 50 percent of the highest bid by offenders or the value of the contract, whichever is higher, for providing money or benefits to induce a person to

---

[6] Section 144 of the Penal Code of Thailand.
[7] Section 167 of the Penal Code of Thailand.
[8] Section 4 of the Act on Offenses Relating to the Submission of Bids to Government Agencies B.E. 2542.

submit a bid at a high or low level, or to refrain from bidding or to withdraw a bid[9]

- Imprisonment for five years to 10 years and a fine equal to 50 percent of the highest bid by the offenders or the value of the contract, whichever is higher, for compelling a person, including by force or violence, to involuntarily participate or not participate in the submission of bids or to withdraw bids[10]

- Imprisonment for one year to five years and a fine equal to 50 percent of the highest bid by the offenders or the value of the contract, whichever is higher, for using deceitful means to deprive others of an opportunity to make fair submissions or to cause a mistaken submission of bids[11]

- Imprisonment for one year to five years or a fine equal to 50 percent of the highest bid by the offenders for dishonestly submitting a low or high bid[12]

(ii) For the private company or legal entity involved

- A fine not exceeding THB10,000 for bribing a public official to act or refrain from acting[13]

- A fine not exceeding THB14,000 for agreeing to give a benefit to an official to wrongly do or not do any act[14]

---

[9] Section 5 of the Act on Offenses Relating to the Submission of Bids to Government Agencies B.E. 2542.
[10] Section 6 of the Act on Offenses Relating to the Submission of Bids to Government Agencies B.E. 2542.
[11] Section 7 of the Act on Offenses Relating to the Submission of Bids to Government Agencies B.E. 2542.
[12] Section 8 of the Act on Offenses Relating to the Submission of Bids to Government Agencies B.E. 2542.
[13] Section 144 of the Penal Code of Thailand.

(b) Penalties for public officials demanding or accepting bribes

- Imprisonment for five years to 20 years, or imprisonment for life, and a fine of THB2,000 to THB40,000, or death, for abuse of public power through coercion, or for accepting an inducement to act or not act before or after appointment[15]

- Imprisonment for one year to 10 years or a fine of THB2,000 to THB20,000, or both imprisonment and a fine, for an officer with a duty of managing business who takes an interest in the business for his or others' benefit; or for an officer with a duty related to disbursement who makes a disbursement to himself or to others; or for an officer who unlawfully performs or fails to perform a duty, thereby causing injury to others[16]

- Imprisonment for five years to 20 years, or for life, and a fine of THB2,000 to THB40,000 for an officer guilty of misappropriation; or for an officer a with duty related to procurement who unlawfully acts in a manner that damages business[17]

- Imprisonment for five years to 20 years, or for life, and a fine of THB2,000 to THB40,000 for an officer who acts or refrains from acting based on benefits he consented to receive prior to appointment or procurement; or for an officer who unlawfully exercises his power, causing damage to the organization[18]

---

[14] Section 167 of the Penal Code of Thailand.
[15] Section 148, 149, 150 of the Penal Code of Thailand.
[16] Section 9 -11 of the Act on Offenses by Officers in State Organizations or Agencies.
[17] Section 4 of the Act on Offenses by Officers in State Organizations or Agencies.
[18] Sections 7 and 8 of the Act on Offenses by Officers in State Organizations or Agencies.

- Imprisonment for five years to 20 years, or for life, or the death penalty, and fine of THB2,000 to THB40,000 for an officer who uses coercion to obtain property; or for an officer who unlawfully asks to receive benefits[19]

- Imprisonment for one year to 10 years and a fine of THB20,000 to THB200,000 for malfeasance by an officer with power to approve or consider bids[20]

- Imprisonment for five years to 20 years, or for life, and a fine of THB100,000 to THB400,000 for an official who dishonestly designs price specifications, conditions or kickbacks in order to prevent fair competition; or for an official who prevents fair competition during bidding[21]

- Imprisonment for seven years to 20 years, or for life, and a fine of THB140,000 to THB400,000 for a political officer, holder of political office, local administrator, member of a local administrative council or committee or sub-committee member who violates the Act on Offenses Relating to the Submission of Bids to Government Agencies B.E. 2542, or commits any act against officials in relation to the submission of bids in order to induce or influence the acceptance of certain bids[22]

1.5 Political contributions

Contributions to political parties are regulated under the Act Supplementing the Constitution Concerning Political Parties B.E. 2550. In general terms, a party leader, members of the party's

---

[19] Sections 5 and 6 of the Act on Offenses by Officers in State Organizations or Agencies.
[20] Section 10 of the Act on Offenses Relating to the Submission of Bids to Government Agencies B.E. 2542.
[21] Sections 11 and 12 of the Act on Offenses Relating to the Submission of Bids to Government Agencies B.E. 2542.
[22] Section 13 of the Act on Offenses Relating to the Submission of Bids to Government Agencies B.E. 2542.

administrative committee and sub-administrative committee, and general party members are prohibited from personally receiving any contributions or benefits from an anonymous source. The law applies different measures regarding disclosure of information with respect to the granting of political contributions depending on the value of such contributions, as follows:

- For any political contribution with a value higher than THB1,000, the name of the contributor must be disclosed and made accessible for scrutiny.

- For any political contribution with a value higher than THB5,000, the name of the contributor must be disclosed to the public.

- For any political contribution with a value higher than THB20,000, the contribution must be made in the form of a bill of exchange or a crossed check.

- For any political contribution with a value higher than THB5 million, the contributing company or legal entity must receive prior approval or endorsement from the board of directors or the shareholders or members of such juristic person.

However, individuals and legal entities are prohibited from making political contributions to a political party in excess of THB10 million per annum.

Political contributions are tax deductible, and it is possible for individuals to deduct up to THB5,000 per annum and for companies and legal entities to deduct up to THB20,000 per annum for political contributions.

Any individual taxpayer who holds Thai nationality is entitled to make contributions of THB100 to one political party by indicating such in the annual income tax form as prescribed by the regulations of the

Revenue Department (No. 176) concerning standards and processes of political contribution, dated 17 February 2009.[23]

1.6 Limitations applicable to hospitality expenses (gifts, travel, meals, entertainment, among others)

The Act Supplementing the Constitution on Anti-Corruption B.E. 2542 prohibits public officials from receiving gifts, either in the form of tangible assets or other benefits, from other individuals, except for those they are legally entitled to receive and those received per moral obligation.[24]

The regulations of the National Anti-Corruption Commission concerning criteria for a public official's receipt of gifts or other benefits by moral obligation B.E. 2543 further establish a quantitative limitation on hospitality expenses. In essence, hospitality expenses would not be considered bribery provided they fall under any of the following scenarios:[25]

(a) The hospitality is received from a relative of the receiver and the hospitality has proper value corresponding to the social status of the receiver.

(b) The hospitality is received from another person who is not a relative of the receiver and the value of the hospitality does not exceed THB3,000 per occasion and per person.

(c) The hospitality is received in the manner that such hospitality is given to many undesignated persons.

---

[23] Section 58.
[24] Section 103.
[25] Section 5.

2. Domestic bribery (private to private)

2.1 Legal framework

Bribery laws do not generally extend to promises or gifts requested or accepted and offered or made among persons in the private sector. Unlike the case of public officials, there is no specific law governing private bribery committed by non-governmental persons or entities. However, commercial bribery, as one kind of corporate fraud, may be considered a crime under the Penal Code of Thailand.

2.2 Definition of private bribery

There is no specific definition of "private bribery" under Thai law. However, bribery schemes in Thailand generally fall under two broad categories:

(a) Kickbacks – undisclosed payments made by a vendor to an employee of the purchasing company

(b) Bid-rigging – where the employees of a customer fraudulently assist a vendor in winning a contract through a competitive bidding process

2.3 Consequences of private bribery

Penalties for private bribery vary according to the nature of the crime and the type of legal organization for which the perpetrator works.

- Imprisonment not exceeding three years or a fine not exceeding THB6,000, or both imprisonment and a fine, for an employee who is entrusted to manage another person's property or property co-owned by another person and who dishonestly acts contrary to his duty and jeopardizes the benefits of such other person[26]

[26] Section 353 of the Penal Code of Thailand.

- A fine not exceeding THB50,000 for a person responsible for the operation of a partnership or limited partnership limited or limited company who dishonestly acts or omits to act in order to illegally gain benefits for himself or other persons[27]

- A fine not exceeding THB50,000 for a person responsible for the operation of the business of a public company limited who dishonestly acts or omits to act in order to illegally gain benefits for himself or other persons, thus causing damages to such company[28]

- Imprisonment for five years to 10 years and a fine of THB500,000 to THB1 million for a director or manager or any person responsible for the operation of a company who dishonestly acts or omits to act in order to illegally gain benefits for himself or other persons, thereby causing damages to such company[29]

- Imprisonment for five years to 10 years and a fine of THB500,000 to THB1 million for a director or manager or any person responsible for the operation of a company who is entrusted to manage property that the company owns or co-owns and who dishonestly acts or omits to act in order to illegally gain benefits for himself or other persons, thus causing damages to such company[30]

2.4 Limitation applicable to hospitality expenses (gifts, travel, meals, entertainment, among others)

The Thai Penal Code does not establish quantitative or qualitative limitations on hospitality expenses that may be deemed as private bribery. However, illegal gratuities are prohibited by most private

---

[27] Section 41 of the Act on Penalties Concerning Partnerships, Limited Partnerships, Limited Companies, Associations, and Foundations B.E. 2499.
[28] Section 215 of the Public Company Limited Act B.E. 2535.
[29] Section 311 of the Security Exchange Act B.E. 2535.
[30] Section 307 of the Security Exchange Act B.E. 2535.

company codes of ethics, work rules, regulations or orders. A violation of these rules or regulations may result in termination of employment without severance pay, provided that the employer has already given a written warning, except in serious situations where the employer is not required to give a warning.[31]

In the absence of specific legal provisions governing private bribery, whether a hospitality expense could be considered bribery will need to be determined on a case-by-case basis, taking into account all the facts and circumstances surrounding the case and applying the two previously referenced criteria.

3. Corruption of foreign public officials

3.1 Legal framework

Recent amendments to existing legislation have expanded the scope of Thai anti-corruption laws to cover private bribery involving State Officials, Foreign State Officials and International Organization Officials.[32] The new legislation covers: (1) an official who demands or accepts a bribe; (2) a private party who accepts property or benefits to act as a middleman to induce an official to act improperly; and (3) a private party making a bribe, as well as a juristic entity with which the private party is related and for whose benefit a bribe has been made, if the juristic entity does not have appropriate internal control measures to prevent the offense.

3.2 Definition of corruption of foreign public officials

With respect to bribery of an official by a private party, "Any person who gives, requests to give, or agrees to give property or any other benefits to a State Official, Foreign State Official, or International Organization Official to induce the official to act or omit any act, or delay any act in violation of their duties."

---

[31] Section 119 of the Labour Protection Act B.E. 2541.

[32] Amendment No. 3 (B,E. 2558) to the Act Supplementing the Constitution Relating to the Prevention and Suppression of Corruption B.E. 2542 (also known as "The Organic Act on Counter Corruption").

3.3 Definition of foreign public official

"State Official" has the same meaning ascribed to it in Paragraph 1.3.2, above.

"Foreign State Official" means a person with legislative, executive, administrative or judicial positions of a foreign state, and any person who performs government works for a foreign state and performs duties for government agencies or state enterprises, regardless of whether such person has been appointed or elected, holds a permanent or temporary position, or receives salary or other remuneration.

"International Organization Official" means a person who works in an international organization or a person assigned by an international organization to perform work on behalf of the international organization.

3.4 Consequences of corruption of foreign public officials

With respect to bribery of an official by a private party, the penalty is imprisonment not exceeding five years, or fine not exceeding THB100,000, or both.

With respect to bribery of an official by a private party who is related to, and has acted for the benefit of, a juristic entity that does not have appropriate internal control measures to prevent the offense, the penalty is a fine equal to one, but not exceeding two times, the damages incurred or the benefits obtained.

The court is also empowered to order the forfeiture of: (1) property used or possessed for use in the commission of an offense; (2) property or other tangible benefits obtained from commission of an offense or from acting as instigator, supporter, or person advertising or offering to the general public to commit the offense; (3) property or other tangible benefits obtained from the sale or disposal of property or benefit under (1) or (2); or (4) any other benefits arising from the benefit or property under (1), (2) or (3).

3.5 Limitation applicable to hospitality expenses (gifts, travel, meals, entertainment, among others)

N/A

4. Facilitation payments

There are no exceptions for or limitations on "facilitation expenses" that exclude them from the definition of bribery, whether in the public or private arena. Each such expense must be evaluated on its own and with consideration to the surrounding facts in order to determine whether it is likely to be considered a bribe.

5. Compliance programs

5.1 Value of a compliance program to mitigate/eliminate the criminal liability for legal entities

Other than the newly implemented legislation examined in Section 3.1 above, which suggests a juristic entity can limit or avoid liability by having appropriate internal control measures to prevent bribery of officials, there are no compliance program defenses to liability that otherwise might be attached to acts of bribery in Thailand. However, it is possible that the court might take into account the existence and operation of such programs in considering the liability of, or penalties to be assessed against, a violator, such as a corporate body whose employee engaged in an act of bribery without authorization. The absence of such a compliance program is not in itself an offense and Thai law does not prescribe which elements must be included in a compliance program.

5.2 Absence of a compliance program as a crime

The Thai Penal Code does not recognize the failure to implement a compliance program as a crime.

5.3 Elements of Compliance Program

(a) Legal framework

N/A

(b) Recommended practice

N/A

6. Regulator with jurisdiction to prosecute corruption

There are a number of enforcement agencies under Thai legislation empowered to prosecute corruption, including the various police bodies; the National Counter Corruption Commission (NCCC or NACC); the Anti-money Laundering Office (AMLO); the Department of Special Investigation (DSI); the Election Commission of Thailand; the Assets Examination Committee (AEC); the National Counter Corruption Commission (NCCC); the Office of the Civil Service Commission; the Office of the Council of State (responsible for interpreting legislation); the Office of the Ombudsman; the Public Prosecutor; the Office of the Auditor General; and the Office of the Public Sector Anti-Corruption Commission (PACC).

Vietnam

Frederick Burke

Frederick Burke is highly regarded for his work on foreign investment projects in Vietnam and China for key players in the property development, trade, IT/C and project finance areas. He provides practical advice on the related issues of securities, finance, tax, labor, regulatory compliance and dispute resolution. Frederick also has extensive experience in working closely with Vietnamese legislators and law drafters on the many new laws and decrees that have been introduced to integrate Vietnam into the global economy.

frederick.burke@bakermckenzie.com
Tel: +84 8 3520 2628

Chi Anh Tran

Chi Anh's practice encompasses corporate compliance, arbitration and competition (advisory and contentious). She has advised and assisted multinational companies in compliance reviews and audits in Vietnam, as well as in developing and implementing compliance policies of Vietnam subsidiaries. In addition to corporate compliance, Chi Anh also practices dispute resolution and competition law.

chianh.tran@bakermckenzie.com
Tel: +84 8 35202625

Thuy Duong Van

Thuy Duong Van's principal practice areas include corporate compliance, dispute resolution and competition. She is also involved in corporate compliance audits and investigations in relation to the Foreign Corrupt Practices Act (FCPA) and Vietnam's Anti-Corruption Law, as well as in providing clients with legal advice on anti-corruption, criminalization of offenses, anti-trust compliance and bankruptcy under Vietnamese law.

thuyduong.van@bakermckenzie.com
Tel: + 84 8 3520 2696

Baker & McKenzie (Vietnam) Ltd.
12th Floor, Saigon Tower
29 Le Duan Blvd.
District 1, Ho Chi Minh City
Socialist Republic of Vietnam

Key Practitioners

Yee Chung Seck
Ho Chi Minh City
Tel: +84 8 3520 2633
yeechung.seck@bakermckenzie.com

1. Domestic bribery (private to public)

1.1 Legal framework

The subject of anti-corruption or anti-bribery is governed mainly by the Anti-Corruption Law[1] and the Penal Code.[2]

The Anti-Corruption Law is considered as a "code of conduct" for persons who hold positions of responsibility and power, including state officials, public employees and other persons entrusted with state power in performing their official state duties. The Anti-Corruption Law forms the basis for the application of the Penal Code with respect to bribery offenses. It does not address the act of giving bribes nor does it provide specific sanctions for non-compliance. For non-compliant acts, the Anti-Corruption Law refers to the Penal Code, the Law on Cadres and State Officials[3] and the Law on Public Employees[4] for sanctions, depending on the seriousness of the violation.

The Penal Code addresses both (i) the persons holding "public" positions of responsibility and power; and (ii) those giving bribes or acting as intermediaries for bribery. The Penal Code sets out elements of corruption-related crimes and relevant criminal liabilities and punishments. Specifically, the corruption-related crimes are mainly regulated under the Penal Code, Chapter XXI (Articles 277-291). From 1 July 2016 onwards, the Penal Code will be replaced by the 2015 Penal Code,[5] which extends its application to private bribery and

---

[1] Law No. 55/2005/QH11 on Anti-Corruption, passed by the National Assembly on 29 November 2005, effective on 1 June 2006 as amended in 2007 and 2012 ("Anti-Corruption Law").
[2] Penal Code (the Law No. 15/1999/QH10), passed by the National Assembly on 21 December 1999, effective on 1 July 2000 as amended in 2009 ("Penal Code").
[3] Law No. 22/2008/QH12 on Cadres and Civil Servants, passed by the National Assembly on 13 November 2008, effective on 1 January 2010 ("Law on Cadres and State Officials").
[4] Law No. 58/2010/QH12 on Public Employees, passed by the National Assembly on 29 November 2010, effective on 1 January 2012 ("Law on Public Employees").
[5] Penal Code (the Law No. 100/2015/QH13), passed by the National Assembly on 27 November 2015, effective on 1 July 2016 ("2015 Penal Code").

bribery to foreign public officials and officials of public international organizations.

1.2 Definition of bribery

The Penal Code distinguishes between giving bribes from receiving bribes in relation to persons holding positions of responsibility and power.

(a) Receiving bribes

Under Article 279 of the Penal Code, those who abuse their positions and/or powers, and have accepted or will accept directly or through intermediaries money, property or other material interests in any form worth VND2 million (approximately USD95) or more in order to perform or not to perform certain jobs for the benefit, or at the request of the bribe givers, shall be subject to criminal liability for the crime of "receiving a bribe." They may also be considered to have received a bribe even if the value in question is less than VND2 million if any of the following aggravating circumstances is present:

- Serious consequences are caused.
- The offender has been previously disciplined for similar acts.
- The offender has been previously sentenced for corruption crimes contained in Section A of Chapter XXI of the Penal Code.

Under Article 354 of the 2015 Penal Code, which will be effective on 1 July 2016, those who abuse their positions and/or powers, and have accepted or will accept directly or through intermediaries any of following interests for themselves or other organizations in order to perform or not to perform certain jobs for the benefit, or at the request of the bribe givers, shall be subject to criminal liability for the crime of "receiving a bribe":

- Money, property or other material interests worth VND2 million (approximately USD95) or more, or even less than VND2 million, but wherein other conditions are met, including where (i) the offender has been previously disciplined for similar acts; or (ii) the offender has been previously sentenced for corruption crimes contained in Section 1 of Chapter XXIII of the 2015 Penal Code

- Any non-material interest

(b) Giving bribes

Under Article 289 of the Penal Code, those who give a bribe worth VND2 million or more, or give a bribe worth less than VND2 million but in doing so (i) causes serious consequences; or (ii) the offense is committed more than once, are criminally liable for "giving a bribe" under the provisions of the Penal Code.

The four elements of giving a bribe that must be proven are:

(i) The receiver of the bribe has official state powers.

(ii) The money, property or material interest must be given to the recipient (the act of giving a bribe).

(iii) The material interest must have been given to induce the bribe receiver to do or not do some official task for the benefit, or at the request, of the bribe giver.

(iv) As previously stated, the value of the bribe (if any) must meet the threshold for criminal liability (VND2 million). Otherwise, the Penal Code requires proof that either serious consequence will result, or that the act has been repeated.

Under Article 364 of the 2015 Penal Code which will be effective on 1 July 2016, those who, directly or through intermediaries, have given or will give money, property or other material interests worth VND2 million or more, or any nonmaterial interest in order to induce the bribe receiver to do or not do some official task for the benefit, or at the request, of the bribe giver are criminally liable for "giving a bribe."

Under the Penal Code, a bribe may be in the form of "money, property or other material interests in any form." Please note that, from 1 July 2016 onwards, a bribe may also include "any non-material interest."

1.3 Definition of public official

Under Article 1.3 of the Anti-Corruption Law, officials (or persons holding positions and powers) are broadly defined to include the following:

- Cadres, state officials, public employees
- Officers, professional soldiers, defense workers in agencies or units of the People's Army; officers and non-commissioned officers, professional-technical officers and non-commissioned officers in agencies or units of the Public Security
- Leading, managerial officers in state-owned enterprises (SOEs); leading, managerial officers being representatives of the state's contributed capital portions at enterprises
- Persons assigned tasks or official duties who, through the completion of such tasks or the fulfillment of such duties, have certain authoritative powers

The two main types of officials are: (i) state officials; and (ii) public employees. The relevant definitions of state officials and public employees are as follows:

- State officials are defined as Vietnamese citizens who are recruited; appointed to a rank, a post, or a title in public bodies; under the payroll of these public bodies; and receive salary from the state budget or from the salary fund of the public non-business unit if a state official is in the leading and managerial apparatuses of the non-business unit (Article 4, Law on Cadres and State Officials).

- Public employees are defined as Vietnamese citizens who are recruited through examination or through selection in a public non-business unit, working under a labor contract signed with the head of the public non-business unit, and receive salary from the salary fund of the public non-business unit (Article 2, Law on Public Employees).

1.4 Consequences of bribery

The Penal Code only provides for individual, not corporate, criminal liability. Therefore, only natural persons who have committed an offense or are found responsible may be held culpable for crimes involving a company.

An official who commits a corrupt act, depending on the nature and seriousness of the breach, shall be subject to disciplinary action, or prosecution for criminal liability, in accordance with the Penal Code. In cases where he or she is sentenced for a corrupt act and the decision is legally enforceable, he or she will be dismissed. Those who receive bribes may be subject to criminal liability, up to and including the death penalty. Any properties, funds or other valuables used for corruption or bribery may be expropriated, in accordance with the applicable laws.

Those who give bribes or act as intermediaries for bribery under the Vietnam Penal Code will be subject to criminal liability, including fines and/or prison terms ranging from one year to 20 years or even life imprisonment. However, those who are coerced into giving bribes, but who take the initiative to report their actions before being detected, will be regarded as not guilty and are entitled to receive back any property they were coerced into giving as bribes. Bribe givers who, although not coerced, take the initiative to report their actions before being detected, may be exempted from criminal liability and may receive back at least some of the property they have given as bribes.

Under the 2015 Penal Code, a commercial legal entity is subject to criminal liability for committing certain crimes, which does not include corruption-related crimes, such as receiving bribes, giving bribes and acting as intermediaries for bribery. Individuals who receive bribes may be subject to criminal liability, up to and including the death penalty, and those who give bribes may be subject to criminal liability, including fines and/or prison terms ranging from six months to 20 years.

1.5 Political contributions

Contributions to political parties are not specifically regulated by Vietnamese law. The Constitution of the Socialist Republic of Vietnam provides for just one political party – the Communist Party of Vietnam, but independent candidates can and do run for elected positions.

1.6 Limitation applicable to hospitality expenses (gifts, travel, meals, entertainment, among others)

The Anti-Corruption Law establishes the following limitations on the giving and receipt of gifts:

- Agencies, organizations and units must not use state budget funds or properties as gifts, except in certain exceptional cases provided under the law.

- Cadres, state officials and public employees must not receive money, properties or other material interests of agencies, organizations, units and/or individuals involved in affairs that they are responsible for settling, or ones that fall under their respective management.

- It is strictly forbidden to give or receive gifts as bribes, or to perform other acts meant to serve self-seeking interests.[6]

Please note that Decision No. 64[7] allows individuals who exercise state power or hold positions of public responsibility to accept gifts under certain limited circumstances.[8] Specifically, they may receive gifts:

- from relatives who themselves, in return, receive **no benefits related** to the public duties of the gift recipient (no specific limit on the value of the gift);
- from individuals or entities **unrelated** to the public duties/activities of the gift recipient (no specific limit on the value of the gift); and
- from individuals or entities if such recipient is ill or suffering from an accident, in mourning or celebrating a marriage, or if the gift is in connection with traditional festivals or the lunar new year (Tet). In these situations, please note that the gift value must be less than VND500,000 (approximately USD24) and not given in connection with an official duty of the gift recipient, any benefits, purposes, or acts of corruption prohibited under the Anti-Corruption Law or the Penal Code.

Other than in the abovementioned circumstances, a public official must report all gifts that he or she may receive to his or her immediate supervisor(s), and give the gifts to the supervisor(s) within five working days from the date of receipt.[9] Because this reporting obligation is an internal one, there is no publicly available means of

---

[6] Article 40, Anti-Corruption Law.
[7] Decision No. 64/2007/QD-TT dated 10 May 2007 of the Prime Minister promulgating the regulation on giving, receipt and hand-over of gifts by state budget-funded agencies, state officers ("Decision No. 64").
[8] Article 11 and Article 12.4 of the Regulations on Gifts attached to Decision No. 64.
[9] Article 12 of the Regulations on Gifts attached to Decision No. 64.

verifying the degree to which public officials comply with this requirement.

2. Domestic bribery (private to private)

2.1 Legal framework

Private bribery is currently not regulated under the Penal Code. As discussed in Section 1.3, leading officers and managers of SOEs, who are referred to as "persons holding positions and power," are subject to the Anti-Corruption Law and the Penal Code in relation to corruption-related crimes. Furthermore, if an employee of an SOE is individually assigned official tasks or duties and has certain authoritative powers through the completion of such tasks or the fulfillment of such duties, such employee is also subject to the Anti-Corruption Law and the Penal Code, similarly to state officials.

However, from 1 July 2016 onwards, private bribery will be subject to criminal liability under the provisions of the 2015 Penal Code (Articles 354 and 364).

2.2 Definition of private bribery

Before 1 July 2016, private bribery was not addressed by the Penal Code. From 1 July 2016 onwards, the definition of bribery under the provisions of the 2015 Penal Code (Articles 354 and 364) will also apply for private bribery. (See Section 1.2 above.)

2.3 Consequences of private bribery

From 1 July 2016 onwards, persons holding position in non-state-owned companies and organizations who receive bribes may be subject to criminal liability, up to and including the death penalty. Those who give bribes to persons holding positions in non-state-owned companies and organizations may be subject to criminal liability, including fines and/or prison terms ranging from six months to 20 years.

2.4 Limitation applicable to hospitality expenses (gifts, travel, meals, entertainment, among others)

N/A

3. Corruption of foreign public officials

3.1 Legal framework

Bribery of foreign public officials is currently not specifically regulated under the Penal Code. However, foreign individuals, Vietnamese nationals or companies overseas bribing Vietnamese officials, regardless of where the act is committed, may be subject to criminal liability under the Penal Code.

From 1 July 2016 onwards, giving bribes to foreign public officials and officials of public international organizations will be subject to criminal liability under the provisions of the 2015 Penal Code.

3.2 Definition of corruption of foreign public officials

Before 1 July 2016, corruption of foreign public officials was not addressed under the Vietnamese Penal Code. From 1 July 2016 onwards, the definition of bribery under the provisions of the 2015 Penal Code (Article 364) will also apply to bribery to foreign public officials and officials of public international organizations.

3.3 Definition of foreign public official

The 2015 Penal Code does not provide a definition of foreign public official or official of public international organizations.

3.4 Consequences of corruption of foreign public officials

From 1 July 2016 onwards, individuals who give bribes to foreign public officials and officials of public international organizations may be subject to criminal liability, including fines and/or prison terms ranging from six months to 20 years.

3.5 Limitation applicable to hospitality expenses (gifts, travel, meals, entertainment, among others)

N/A

4. Facilitation payments

Vietnamese law does not recognize facilitation payments. However, such payments could qualify as bribes if meeting the definition of bribery under the Penal Code, and thus, are prohibited by law.

5. Compliance programs

5.1 Value of a compliance program to mitigate/eliminate the criminal liability for legal entities

Commercial legal entities are not subject to criminal liability for corruption-related offenses under Vietnamese law. However, companies are encouraged to implement anti-corruption measures for compliance purposes.

5.2 Absence of a compliance program as a crime

The absence of a compliance program would not be considered a crime under the Penal Code.

5.3 Elements of compliance program

(a) Legal framework

Vietnamese law does not provide for requirements or criteria of a compliance program.

(b) Recommended practice

Although there is no explicit legal requirement for compliance programs, the adoption of a compliance program is a recommended measure to limit a company's exposure to bribery.

6. Regulator with jurisdiction to prosecute corruption

Public prosecutors are eligible to prosecute all criminal cases, including corruption cases.

EMEA

Austria

Georg Krakow

Georg Krakow advises corporate clients on compliance matters and on the consequences of penal law. He focuses on criminal cases, risk analysis and on the development, implementation and control of compliance systems. Georg also counsels on internal investigations for business enterprises.

georg.krakow@bakermckenzie.com
Tel: +43 1 2 42 50 244

Baker & McKenzie
Diwok Hermann Petsche Rechtsanwälte
LLP & Co KG
Schottenring 25
1010 Vienna

Elisabeth Götz

Elisabeth Götz advises clients in corporate criminal law matters and represents clients in criminal proceedings. She also counsels clients regarding internal investigations and compliance systems with a focus on criminal law and anti-corruption issues.

elisabeth.goetz@bakermckenzie.com
Tel: +43 1 2 42 50 283

Baker & McKenzie
Diwok Hermann Petsche Rechtsanwälte
LLP & Co KG
Schottenring 25
1010 Vienna

Key Practitioners

Alexander Petsche
Vienna
Tel: +43 1 2 42 50 510
alexander.petsche@bakermckenzie.com

1. Domestic bribery (private to public)

1.1 Legal framework

Bribery of public officials is regulated by law, specifically under Section 304 to Section 308 of the Austrian Criminal Law Code (*Strafgesetzbuch* or StGB).

1.2 Definition of bribery

Under Austrian Law, both the party granting a benefit (active bribery) and the party accepting such a benefit (passive bribery) may be liable.

Bribery is defined as offering, promising or granting a benefit to a public official or a third party for the purpose of influencing the public functions of the public official. The law is clear on the fact that granting of benefits as compensation for an action or omission that *thwarts* official duties is bribery. If benefits are granted for an action or omission *in line with* official duties or with an intent to gradually influence a public official in the future, then the granting of "improper" benefits (see definition below) is considered bribery.

Austrian Law distinguishes between: (a) active/passive bribery (Sections 304, 307 StGB); (b) accepting/granting of benefits (Sections 305, 307a StGB); (c) accepting/granting of benefits to influence (Sections 306, 307b StGB); and (d) forbidden intervention (Section 308 StGB) (see Chapter 1.4 for more detailed discussion).

1.3 Definition of public official

The definition of a public official is set out in Section 74 Paragraph 1 item 4 of the StGB:

- A public official is any legislative, administrative or judicial public official or person who has been appointed or elected with official duties in any other way (for instance, a park sheriff), including body corporates instituted by public law (for instance, a university), for the Republic of Austria or for any other state or for an international organization.

- With the latest amendment to the StGB that became effective at the beginning of 2013, the definition of a public official was substantially broadened; delegates to the National Assembly and the Federal Assembly as well as the Municipal Council are now fully included.

- Further, since the beginning of 2013, organs or employees of government-owned or controlled companies are now public officials (for instance, national railway company ÖBB, the public road maintenance company ASFINAG, or the national post Post AG). An institution or company is regarded as government-owned or -controlled if it is (i) at least 50 percent (directly or indirectly) owned; or (ii) otherwise factually dominated by domestic or foreign authorities. Furthermore organs or employees of companies subject to auditing by a Court of Auditors are considered public officials.

Note: The definition of public officials as set out in the StGB encompasses many individuals who would not be considered public officials in other jurisdictions. A careful case-by-case analysis is therefore required.

1.4 Consequences of bribery

(a) For the public official involved

Section 304 of the StGB (passive bribery, *Bestechlichkeit*) provides that a public official who demands, takes or accepts another person's promise of any benefit for himself or a third party as compensation for the undutiful performance or omission of his official duties shall be punished with:

- imprisonment for up to three years;

- imprisonment for up to five years if the value of the benefit exceeds EUR3,000; or

- imprisonment for up to 10 years if the value of the benefit exceeds EUR50,000.

Section 305 of the StGB (acceptance of a benefit, *Vorteilsannahme*) provides that a public official who for himself or a third party demands any kind of benefit or who takes or accepts another person's promise of an undue benefit as compensation for an action or omission that is in line with his official duties shall be punished with:

- imprisonment for up to two years;

- imprisonment for up to three years if the value of the benefit exceeds EUR3,000; or

- imprisonment for up to five years if the value of the benefit exceeds EUR50,000.

The same punishment is applicable for Section 306 of the StGB (acceptance of a benefit to be influenced, *Vorteilsannahme zur Beeinflussung*), which provides that a public official who (for himself or a third party) demands any benefit or who takes or accepts another's person promise of an undue benefit with the intent to let himself be influenced without a connection to a concrete official act shall be held criminally liable.

(b) For the private individual involved

Section 307 of the StGB (active bribery, *Bestechung*) provides that a person who offers, promises or grants any benefit to a public official for himself or for a third party for the undutiful performance or omission of the public official's duties, shall be punished with:

- imprisonment for up to three years;

- Imprisonment for up to five years if the value of the benefit exceeds EUR3,000; or

- Imprisonment for up to 10 years if the value of the benefit exceeds EUR50,000.

Section 307a of the StGB (granting of a benefit, *Vorteilszuwendung*) provides that a person who offers, promises or grants an undue benefit to a public official for himself or a third party as compensation for an action or omission in line with the public official's duties (dutiful performance or omission) shall be punished with:

- imprisonment for up to two years;

- imprisonment for up to three years if the value of the benefit exceeds EUR3,000; or

- imprisonment for up to five years if the value of the benefit exceeds EUR50,000.

The same punishment is applicable for Section 307b of the StGB (granting of a benefit to influence, *Vorteilszuwendung zur Beeinflussung*), which provides that a person who offers, promises or grants an undue benefit to a public official (for himself or a third party) in order to influence the exercise of public office without a connection to a concrete official act shall be held criminally liable.

Furthermore Section 308 of the StGB (forbidden intervention, *Verbotene Intervention*) sets out that it is a criminal offense to demand, accept or allow oneself to be promised a benefit for oneself or a third party in return for undue exercise of influence on the decision-making of a public official. Also, the person offering, promising or granting the benefit is criminally liable. Both shall be punished with:

- imprisonment for up to two years;

- imprisonment for up to three years if the value of the benefit exceeds EUR3,000; or

- imprisonment for up to five years if the value of the benefit exceeds EUR50,000.

(c) For the company / legal entity involved

The liability of legal entities and other business associations is regulated under the Act on the Criminal Liability of Associations (*Verbandsverantwortlichkeitsgesetz* or VbVG), specifically in Sections 3 and 4. Section 3 provides that the association shall be held responsible for a criminal offense if the offense was committed for its benefit, or if the commission of the offense violated legal obligations of the association.

- Association fines (Section 4 of the VbVG) will be determined based on a conversion key translating the sentences for natural persons as foreseen in the StGB into daily rates for legal entities.

- The maximum fine for bribery is 130 daily rates. The judge will determine the daily penalty, taking into account the financial strength of the legal entity, from EUR50 per day to a maximum of EUR10,000 per day, and will multiply it by the number of days imposed as penalty.

- The maximum penalty for bribery, therefore, is EUR1.3 million.

1.5 Political contributions

Contributions to political parties are allowed under certain conditions and are regulated under Section 6 of the Austrian Act of Parties (*Parteiengesetz, PartG*).

Parties have to disclose the name and address of a donor whose contributions exceed EUR3,500 within a year. Singular contributions that are higher than EUR50,000 should be reported promptly to the Austrian Court of Audit, which has the obligation to publish on its website the amount of the contribution under the name and address of the contributor.

Moreover, political parties are not allowed to accept political contributions from companies that are at least 25 percent owned by the state. Furthermore, Section 6 Paragraph 6 n 8 and 9 of the Austrian Act of Parties governs the proscription of anonymous political contributions that are higher than EUR1,000 and political contributions higher than EUR2,500, when paid in cash.

1.6 Limitation applicable to hospitality expenses (gifts, travel, meals, entertainment, among others)

Austrian criminal law only allows benefit if NOT granted to unduly influence the public official.

Three criteria are used to determine if a hospitality expense could be considered as a sign of corruption on the part of a public official:

(a) If the public official demands actively a certain hospitality expense, it is punishable as such any time.

(b) However, the exception rule of "hospitality expenses of low value and in accordance with local customs" has been established recently. Expenses are not construed as an improper or not-insignificant benefit if they are below a certain value (case law considers benefits of a value of up to EUR100 to be insignificant for public officials) and in accordance with local customs.

Examples of such expenses are for Christmas presents, flowers for birthdays and meals after lectures. This rule is never applicable to money, because of its value per se.

(c) Finally, a further limitation on hospitality expenses is applicable to benefits that are granted within the scope of a professional event, where there is an official and objective justifiable interest for the participation (see also Section 305

Paragraph 4 n 1 StGB). Whether an official and objective interest can be justified will be assessed on a case-by-case examination. Case law on the matter is non-existent so far. For instance, an invitation to a white collar crime symposium - even if the ticket price is EUR500 - including lunch and dinner may be justifiable for a public official working at the Department of Criminal Law at the Ministry of Justice. In practice, a key point of distinction is whether personal interest might outweigh professional interest, which can be the case if entertainment or accommodation is excessive or luxurious.

2. Domestic bribery (private to private)

2.1 Legal framework

Private bribery is regulated by law in Sections 309 and 153a of the StGB.

2.2 Definition of private bribery

Private bribery may be defined as offering, promising or granting any benefit to an employee or agent of a legal entity, for the employee or agent himself or for a third party, within the course of business as compensation for the undutiful performance or omission of a legal act (Section 309 para 2 of the StGB).

Pursuant to Section 309 Paragraph 1 of the StGB, employees or agents of a business face criminal responsibility if they demand, allow themselves to be promised or accept (for themselves or a third party) any benefit for the undutiful performance or omission of a legal act within the course of business.

Furthermore, persons with legal power to bind their company or to dispose over their company's assets are liable if they accept a not-insignificant benefit (valued at more than EUR100) and contrary to their duties fail to hand it over to the employer (acceptance of gifts by agents, *Geschenkannahme durch Machthaber*, Section 153a of the

StGB). If acceptance is permitted by the employer, in advance or retrospect, there is no liability.

Under Austrian Law, both the party granting the benefit and the party accepting such a benefit may be liable.

2.3 Consequences of private bribery

(a) For the individuals involved

In the case of Section 309 of the StGB, the employee or agent of a legal entity or the individual may be punished with:

- imprisonment for up to two years;
- imprisonment for up to three years if the value of the benefit exceeds EUR3,000; or
- imprisonment for up to five years if the value of the benefit exceeds EUR50,000.

In the case of Section 153a of the StGB (acceptance of gifts by agents, *Geschenkannahme durch Machthaber*), the person who accepts a not-insignificant benefit and fails to pay it over may be punished with imprisonment for up to a year.

(b) For the company / legal entity

- Association fines (Section 4 of the VbVG) must be determined accordingly, to be calculated based on a conversion key of penalties for natural persons in line with the StGB to daily rates for legal entities.
- Bribery fines, according to Section 309 of the StGB, range within 100 daily rates (*per diem*), from wherein the judge will determine the daily penalty, taking into account the financial strength of the legal entity, from EUR50 to EUR10,000 per

day, and which will be multiplied by the number of days imposed.

- The maximum penalty for private bribery, therefore, is EUR1 million.

2.4 Limitation applicable to hospitality expenses (gifts, travel, meals, entertainment, among others)

Private corruption is only punishable in the event of action or omission thwarting professional duties. There are no limitations applicable to private corruption. However, the type and the value of the invitation or hospitality expense may be considered an indication of whether or not there is an intent for the undutiful performance.

For the provision in Section 153a of the StGB, acceptance of gifts by agents, Austrian jurisprudence limits criminal liability to gifts of a not-insignificant value. Generally the limit will be considered at EUR100; however, depending on the specific circumstances, it can be lower.

3. Corruption of foreign public officials

3.1 Legal framework

The provisions governing corruption of Austrian public officials are also applicable in cases involving foreign public officials.

3.2 Definition of corruption of foreign public officials

See Chapter 1.2; no special regulations for foreign public officials apply.

3.3 Definition of foreign public official

See Chapter 1.3; no special regulations apply.

3.4 Consequences of corruption of foreign public officials

See Chapter 1.4; no special regulations apply.

Note: The provisions governing corruption of public officials are also applicable in cases involving foreign public officials. Austrian citizens and Austrian businesses may be prosecuted in Austria even though the act may not be punishable in a foreign country, according to the foreign law. A corruption offense is furthermore punishable in Austria when committed at least in part in Austria or by or against an Austrian citizen.

3.5 Limitation applicable to hospitality expenses (gifts, travel, meals, entertainment, among others)

See Chapter 1.6; no special regulations apply.

4. Facilitation payments

The exception rule of "hospitality expenses of low value and customary in a certain place" does not apply to facilitation payments. Thus, these are illegal, regardless of the amount of money or action "facilitated". In addition, facilitation payments will likely lead to embezzlement proceedings based on Section 153 of the StGB.

5. Compliance programs

5.1 Value of a compliance program in mitigating/eliminating the criminal liability of legal entities

Legal entities may be held responsible for a criminal offense committed by a decision maker (*Entscheidungsträger*) or by an employee if the offense was committed for the benefit of the company or the commission of the offense violated legal obligations of the association.

It is in the event that a criminal offense is committed by an employee that compliance programs may help mitigate or eliminate criminal liability. The law states that companies may only be held liable for criminal offenses committed by their employees if the commission of the offense was made possible (or essentially facilitated) due to the fact that the decision makers disregarded reasonable and necessary diligence. This is possible through a flaw in the implementation of essential technical, organizational or staff-related measures for the prevention of such crimes. These measures include, for example, guidelines, trainings and controls. Which measures are considered necessary has to be assessed on a case-by-case basis, depending on the size, structure, sector, etc. However, an effective compliance program may constitute a mitigating/eliminating factor.

Pursuant to the VbVG, the prosecution also has discretion on whether or not to prosecute associations or conditionally withdraw from the prosecution. In deciding whether to apply these measures, the prosecution will take into account, *inter alia*, the conduct of the entity after the offense and will factor in the taking of preventive measures. The adoption of a compliance system will be considered as such a preventive measure.

5.2 Absence of a compliance program as a crime

The absence of a compliance program is not considered a criminal offense in the StGB.

5.3 Elements of a compliance program

(a) Legal framework

Until now, the StGB does not provide a legal framework for compliance programs, and there are no legal provisions establishing the type of compliance model that has to be adopted in Austrian law. At present, there is also no jurisprudence that sets out criteria. However, recourse can be made to the requirements being set out in ONR 192050, a compliance management system standard published by Austrian Standards in 2013.

Furthermore, a special compliance program is mandatory for banks, according to Paragraph 18 of the Supervision of Securities Act (*Wertpapieraufsichtsgesetz*). The absence of a compliance program leads to regulatory penalties or even to the revocation of the banking license.

(b) Recommended practice

Since the absence of implemented compliance programs can lead to criminal responsibility in the legal entity's part, the effective implementation of a compliance program is highly recommended.

Moreover, the diversified goals of compliance programs include the following: the fulfilling of and compliance with statutes; prevention of dangerous, illegal corporate methods; and prevention of damages to the company through thievery, disloyalty and fraud. Furthermore, the defense against bribery and the increase in the company's value and its heightened reputation make compliance programs indispensable.

Also, it is within corporate decision-makers' responsibility to provide for appropriate systems of control and risk prevention according to the "specific needs of the company" (Section 70 Paragraph 1, 84 Paragraph 1, 99 corporate law *Aktiengesetz*). In this sense, in case of risks of compliance breaches, organs of corporations can be obliged by corporate and thus civil law to implement compliance programs. Failure to do so may lead to liability.

6. Regulator with jurisdiction to prosecute corruption

In September 2011, a central department of public prosecution (*Zentrale Staatsanwaltschaft zur Verfolgung von Wirtschaftsstrafsachen und Korruption* or WKStA) was established solely for the prosecution of economic offenses and corruption. Pursuant to Section 20a n 5 of the Austrian Code of Criminal Procedure (StPO), offenses against Section 304 to 309 of the StGB (when the value of the benefit exceeds EUR3,000) are governed by the WKStA.

Even if the value of the benefit for a corruption offense does not exceed EUR3,000, the WKStA can claim competence for the case if it is in the public's best interest (according to Section 20b, Paragraph 1 StPO).

Azerbaijan

Gunduz Karimov

Gunduz Karimov focuses his practice on dispute resolution, intellectual property law, pharmaceuticals and healthcare, and compliance matters. In particular, he represents clients in commercial disputes, international disputes and tax litigation. He also advises on trademark prosecution, patent and trademark enforcement, antitrust, and regulatory matters.

gunduz.karimov@bakermckenzie.com
Tel: +994 12 497-18-01

Jamil Alizada

Jamil Alizada regularly advises on corporate and commercial transactions, intellectual property, and banking and finance matters

jamil.alizada@bakermckenzie.com
Tel: +994 12 4971801

Baker & McKenzie - CIS, Limited
The Landmark Building
90A Nizami Street
Baku AZ1010
Azerbaijan

1. Domestic bribery (private to public)

1.1 Legal framework

The Law of the Republic of Azerbaijan, On Combatting Corruption, dated 13 January 2004 (the "Anti-Corruption Law"), and the Criminal Code of the Republic of Azerbaijan, effective on 1 September 2000 (the "Criminal Code"), are the principal laws in Azerbaijan intended to prevent and detect offenses related to corruption.

Recently, the Azerbaijani government promulgated new legislation aimed at combating corruption and creating a better legal environment. The National Strategy on Increasing Transparency and Combating Corruption, approved by Presidential Decree, dated 28 July 2007, is an example of the evolution of Azerbaijani anti-corruption legislation.

Under the Anti-Corruption Law, corruption is defined as the illicit obtaining by officials of material and other benefits, privileges, and advantages, through the use of their position, the status of the body they represent, their official powers, or the opportunities deriving from those statuses and powers. Corruption also includes the engagement of those officials by individuals or entities through the illicit offering, promising or giving of the said material and other benefits, privileges and advantages.

The Anti-Corruption Law lists the acts that are considered corruption as well as those that lead to corruption (literally, "create grounds for corruption"). The Anti-Corruption Law also governs other issues, such as the circumstances in which an official is authorized to accept gifts, financial disclosure by officials, and the like.

Both active and passive bribery are criminal offenses in Azerbaijan. It is noteworthy that Azerbaijani law does not distinguish between public sector and commercial bribery; offering a benefit to officers of commercial entities or their acceptance of a benefit in exchange for the performance or non- performance of official duties may constitute active or passive bribery.

Further, the Law on Ethical Standards of Public Officials, dated 31 May 2007 (the "Ethical Standards Law"), is an act that aims to establish ethical and moral rules of behavior for public officials. The Ethical Standards Law requires government officials to be impartial and respect the rule of law. In addition, the Ethical Standards Law requires that officials refrain from accepting any undue or unlawful benefit or advantage, except for gifts whose value is within the legal limits and those that may be construed as expressions of simple hospitality, provided that the gifts or hospitality do not affect their impartiality.

1.2 Definition of bribery

The Criminal Code defines "passive bribery" as the solicitation or acceptance, directly or indirectly, by a public official of a material or other benefit, privilege or undue advantage for himself/herself or others, in consideration for acting or refraining from acting, or providing patronage when exercising official duties.

"Active bribery" is defined in the Criminal Code as an offer, assurance or gift of a material or other benefit, privilege or undue advantage for himself/herself or others, directly or indirectly, to a public official for himself/herself or others, in consideration for acting or refraining from acting when exercising official duties.

1.3 Definition of public official

The Anti-Corruption Law lists individuals who could be "subjects" of corruption offenses, that is, public officials. In particular, Section 2 lists the following types of public officials for the purposes of the Anti-Corruption Law:

- Persons elected or appointed to a government position in accordance with the Azerbaijani Constitution or Azerbaijani laws
- Persons representing state bodies based on special authorities

- Civil servants occupying administrative positions
- Persons occupying managerial or administrative positions in government agencies, government entities and other commercial legal entities in which the state owns the majority of shares
- Registered candidates for elected governmental positions
- Persons elected to a local government
- Persons holding managerial and administrative positions in a local government
- Any person holding managerial or administrative functions in non-state entities, who perform official duties delegated by the state

Although the Criminal Code generally restates the persons listed in Section 2 of the Anti-Corruption Law, it also includes the following in the category of public officials:

- Certain military servicemen
- Members of municipalities and municipal servants
- Managers and persons occupying managerial or administrative positions based on special authorities in state and municipal enterprises, institutions and organizations, and other commercial and non-commercial organizations
- Persons engaged in business without establishing an entity
- Officials of foreign state agencies; members of elected state bodies of foreign states; officials and other servants of international organizations; and members of international parliamentary organizations

- Judges and other officials of international courts; foreign and local arbiters of arbitration tribunals; and foreign and local members of jury

- Managers and employees of state and municipal enterprises; institutions and organizations; and other commercial and non-commercial organizations

1.4 Consequences of bribery

(a) For the individuals involved:

Prison sentence		Active (offering) bribes:	Passive (accepting) bribes:
Public sector	Domestic	up to 8 years of imprisonment	up to 12 years of imprisonment

- Disqualification for up to three years for passive (accepting) bribery

- Fines on individuals of up to AZN4,000 (approximately USD2,500)

Fines can be imposed only for active bribery and may be used as an alternative to imprisonment.

Factors aggravating liability include the following:

- The commission by officials of illegal acts in exchange for a bribe

- The category of the bribe

- A criminal act committed by a group of persons in a preliminary conspiracy, or by "an organized group, or accompanied with the extortion"

(b) For the company / legal entity:

Today, Azerbaijani criminal law does not apply to legal entities. Although articles contemplating corporate criminal liability have been drafted and incorporated into the Criminal Code, they have not yet entered into legal force. Thus, some amendments of the Criminal Code envisage the potential liability of legal entities for bribery (both active and passive) committed for the benefit of the legal entity or in its interests.

Legal entities may be: subject to fines; prohibited from engaging in certain activities; and dissolved and made subject to special confiscation. Section 11.2 of the Anti-Corruption Law further provides that legal persons may likewise be fined if they are found guilty of corruption.

1.5 Political contributions

Contributions to political parties are governed by the Law on Political Parties, dated 3 June 1992. Generally, the law prohibits financing of political parties, including by means of donation, from, *inter alia*: individuals who did not disclose or indicate the details of their identity cards; foreigners; local and foreign legal entities; and foreign states.

1.6 Limitation applicable to hospitality expenses (gifts, travel, meals, entertainment, amongst others)

Under Azerbaijani law, a public officer is allowed to accept small gifts and acts of simple courtesy (or hospitality). The value of such gifts may not exceed AZN55 (approximately USD35) within one year. Any gift exceeding that value belongs to the agency employing the official.

Laws do not define acts of simple courtesy (or hospitality). Persons providing such courtesy or hospitality should assess whether an act would be considered reasonable and not affect the official's impartiality, under the circumstances.

With respect to covering meals and travel expenses, pursuant to Section 20.1.5 of the Law on State Service, dated 21 July 2000, public officials may visit foreign countries at the expense of such countries only with the permission of higher officials of the state bodies in which the employees work. Under Azerbaijani law, when a government employee travels abroad to attend an event or function in his or her capacity as a public official, the visit is considered a "secondment." Pursuant to Order No. Q-01 of the Minister of Finance, On the Rules of the Secondment of Employees, dated 18 January 2012, Azerbaijani government institutions may second their employees at their own expense or at the expense of a hosting party.

Secondment expenses may include reasonable travel, meal and accommodation costs and should not be treated separately from simple courtesies in the context of the Anti-Corruption Law. Daily allowances approved by Resolution No. 14 of the Azerbaijani Cabinet of Ministers, On Approval of the Rates of Travel Allowances, dated 25 January 2008, might help determine the reasonableness of secondment expenses.

2. Domestic bribery (private to private)

2.1 Legal framework

As discussed in Section 1.1 above, the Criminal Code is the one of the principal laws intended to prevent and detect bribery offenses. There is no distinction in Azerbaijan between bribery in the public and private sectors.

2.2 Definition of private bribery

Azerbaijani law does not have a separate definition of private bribery, and the definition of active and passive bribery found in the Criminal Code applies.

Additionally, as stated in the list in the Criminal Code (see Section 1.3), the definition of "public officials" includes, *inter alia*, managerial and other decision-making personnel of commercial entities. Thus, for the purposes of bribery offenses, managers (and other decision-making personnel) of commercial entities are considered "public officers."

2.3 Consequences of private bribery

(a) For the individuals involved:

Prison sentence	Active (offering) bribes:	Passive (accepting) bribes:
Private sector:	up to 8 years of imprisonment	up to 12 years of imprisonment

- Disqualification for up to three years for passive (accepting) bribery
- Fines on individuals of up to AZN4,000 (approximately USD2,500)

Fine can be imposed only for active bribery and may be used as an alternative to imprisonment.

Factors aggravating liability include the following:

- The commission by officials of illegal acts in exchange for a bribe
- The category of the bribe
- A criminal act committed by a group of persons in a preliminary conspiracy, or by "an organized group, or accompanied with the extortion"

(b) For the company / legal entity:

Please see Section 1.4 (b).

2.4 Limitation applicable to hospitality expenses (gifts, travel, meals, entertainment, amongst others)

It is not clear whether the rules applicable to government officials, as discussed in Section 1.6, apply to officers of private entities. As a matter of practice, prosecuting authorities do not closely scrutinize gifts and hospitality to officers of private entities.

3. Corruption of foreign public officials

3.1 Legal framework

Corruption of foreign public officials is regulated by the same provisions, as provided above, of the Criminal Code.

3.2 Definition of corruption of foreign public officials

Azerbaijani law does not define the corruption of foreign public officials. The definitions of corruption and bribery per the Anti-Corruption Law and the Criminal Code apply in this case.

3.3 Definition of foreign public official

Azerbaijani law does not define foreign public official; however, the definition of "public official" in the Criminal Code includes the following:

- Officials of foreign state agencies
- Members of elected state bodies of foreign states
- Officials and other servants of international organizations
- Members of international parliamentary organizations
- Judges and other officials of international courts
- Foreign arbiters
- Foreign members of juries

3.4 Consequences of corruption of foreign public officials

(a) For the individuals involved:

Prison sentence		Active (offering) bribes:	Passive (accepting) bribes:
Public sector	Foreign	up to 8 years of	up to 12 years of

- Disqualification for up to three years for passive (accepting) bribery
- Fines on individuals of up to AZN4,000 (approximately USD2,500)

Fines can be imposed only for active bribery and may be used as an alternative to imprisonment.

Factors aggravating liability include the following:

- The commission by officials of illegal acts in exchange for a bribe
- The category of the bribe
- A criminal act committed by a group of persons in a preliminary conspiracy, or by an organized group, or accompanied with the extortion

(b) For the company / legal entity: Please see Section 1.4(b).

3.5 Limitation applicable to hospitality expenses (gifts, travel, meals, entertainment, amongst others)

It is unlikely that the rules applicable to Azerbaijani government officials, as discussed in Section 1.6, will apply to foreign public officials.

4. Facilitation payments

A facilitation payment is considered a bribe under Azerbaijani law.

5. Compliance programs

5.1 Value of the compliance program in mitigating/eliminating the criminal liability of legal entities

Azerbaijani law does not recognize a compliance program as an instrument to mitigate or eliminate the liability of legal entities.

5.2 Lack of a compliance program as a crime

Azerbaijani law does not recognize the absence of a compliance program as a crime.

5.3 Elements of a compliance program

N/A

6. Regulator with jurisdiction to prosecute corruption

The Anti-Corruption Commission of the Republic of Azerbaijan is vested with powers to participate in state anti-corruption policy, oversee the implementation of national anti-corruption action plans, gather information relating to corruption, and put forward proposals regarding the same.

The Anti-Corruption Department under the General Prosecutor of the Republic of Azerbaijan, established by the president of the Republic of Azerbaijan on 3 March 2004 (the "Anti-Corruption Department"), is authorized to conduct criminal investigations of corruption crimes. In addition, the Anti-Corruption Department conducts investigations of embezzlement crimes.

Belgium

Elisabeth Dehareng

Elisabeth Dehareng mainly advises and assists Belgian, European and multinational companies on all aspects of data protection laws, in particular the setting up of European and global data protection compliance projects, including cross-border data transfers, cloud computing arrangements, whistleblowing hotlines and monitoring activities.

Elisabeth has also assisted a number of companies in carrying out compliance trainings, reviews and internal compliance investigations, including those that relate to anti-bribery and privacy issues.

elisabeth.dehareng@bakermckenzie.com
Tel: +32 2 639 36 11

Baker & McKenzie CVBA/SCRL
Louizalaan 149 Avenue Louise
Eleventh Floor
Brussels 1050
Belgium

1. Domestic bribery (private to public)

1.1 Legal framework

Bribery of public officials is regulated under Articles 246 to 252 of the Belgian Criminal Code (the "Public Bribery Statute").

1.2 Definition of bribery

The Public Bribery Statute distinguishes between passive bribery and active bribery:

Passive bribery is the act by a public official, directly or indirectly, of requesting or accepting an offer, promise or benefit for himself or for a third party, in exchange for performing, or refraining from performing, any act falling within the scope of his responsibilities.

Active bribery is the act of offering, promising or giving a benefit, directly or indirectly, to a public official, to his own benefit or that of a third party, in order to induce him to perform or refrain from performing any act falling within the scope of his responsibilities.

Both active and passive bribery are prohibited when aimed at:

- having a public official perform a lawful act, within the scope of his office, which is otherwise not subject to payment;
- having a public official perform an unfair act in the exercise of his office or refraining from performing an act falling within the scope of his office;
- having a public official commit a crime or misdemeanor in the exercise of his office; or
- the use by a public official of the real or supposed influence that he wields as a result of his function, to obtain an act of a public authority or administration, or the omission of this act (so-called influence peddling).

The key element of bribery is that the action or inaction of the public official must have been conducted, or have been intended to be conducted, in connection with a gift, an offer, or other benefit or the promise of a gift, or an offer of the foregoing. The terms gift, offer, promise and other benefit permit a broad interpretation of the subject matter of the Public Bribery Statute. Bribery does not depend upon the number or value of the gifts or offers. A gift of little value is sufficient to constitute a bribe in the appropriate circumstances. In addition, a simple offer or solicitation of a bribe is illegal, even if it is not accepted.

In order to establish bribery, it is not necessary to prove that a corrupt agreement between the corrupter and the corrupted person exists. However, a corrupt agreement is an aggravating circumstance.

1.3 Definition of public official

The provisions of the Pubic Bribery Statute apply to "any person who holds a public office," that is, a person employed by the Belgian federal or regional governments or any Belgian governmental agency, department or subdivision, or any local or regional body as well as persons elected in public elections or any other person, even a private person, entrusted with a "public service mission." The Public Bribery Statute does not define the concept of "public service mission." According to the definition given by the courts, "public service" must be understood as "an activity of general interest." A case-by-case analysis must be made in order to determine whether a particular company is entrusted with a public service mission.

The Belgian Supreme Court recently ruled that passive public bribery (in a case of influence peddling) requires that the person whose influence is solicited be a person who "holds a public office." It is, however, not the status of such person that is the determining factor in that respect, but the function that such person exercises and that must itself have a 'public character.'

In addition, the Public Bribery Statute also covers the following:

(i) Any public official of a foreign state (the status of the person is determined by reference to the legislation of the foreign state)

(ii) Any official working for an organization of public international law (e.g., the European Commission and the European Parliament), except for non-governmental and sports organizations (e.g., the International Olympic Committee or the International Association Football Federation [FIFA])

(iii) Anyone who is a candidate for public office

(iv) Anyone who, through false pretenses, leads someone to believe that he will hold or that he holds a public office

1.4 Consequences of bribery

Persons committing active or passive bribery are subject to sanctions under Belgian law. The mere requesting or the mere offering can also give rise to sanctions.

Penalties are higher if the request for bribery is eventually followed by a payment, or if the offer of a bribe is accepted. It is worth noting that although the value of the gift, whatever its nature may be, is irrelevant in the event of bribery as the mere intention to bribe matters; the higher the value of the gift, the more likely it is that "intent to bribe" will be presumed.

(a) For the individuals involved

(i) Principal sanctions

- Imprisonment from six months up to 15 years

- Criminal fines ranging from EUR600 up to EUR600,000

The gradation of the sanctions depends on criteria that are found in Articles 246 to 249 of the Criminal Code.

It is also worth noting that if the public official is a police officer or a member of the Public Prosecutor's Office, all penalties are doubled.

If the bribed public official is an arbitrator, a judge-assessor, a juror or a judge, imprisonment is raised up to 15 years and the fine up to EUR600,000.

Entering into a corrupt pact (i.e., an agreement between the donor and the public official), whether in writing or orally, is also considered as an aggravating circumstance.

(ii) Accessory sanctions

The following accessory sanctions may notably apply:

- Prohibition on performing any public function for a certain period of time
- Dispossession of civil and political rights for a certain period of time
- Special confiscation
- Exclusion from exercising certain functions, professions or activities in the commercial sector
- Disciplinary sanctions for state agents
- Tax consequences

(iii) Obligations of public officials

Pursuant to Article 29 of the Code of Criminal Procedure, any public official who, within the scope of his functions, is aware of the existence of a criminal offense (including bribery), is obliged to directly inform the Public Prosecutor thereof and to transmit to the latter any and all information, reports and acts related thereto.

(b) For the company / legal entity

(i) Principal sanctions

- Imprisonment sanction is converted into fines from EUR18,000 up to EUR2.16 million
- Criminal fines ranging from EUR600 up to EUR600,000

(ii) Accessory sanctions

- Exclusion from public procurement procedures
- Exclusion from the list of authorized companies for public procurement
- Dissolution of the company
- Tax consequences
- Reputational damages following publication of the circumstances surrounding the offense in the press

1.5 Political contributions

Any financial support or donation, including in-kind donations, to political parties by legal entities are strictly prohibited under Belgian law (see Article 16 *bis* of the Act of 4 July 1989, on the limitation and supervision over electoral expenses and the financing and transparent accounts of political parties). Only individuals (natural persons) may give gifts, including donations, to political parties and to their components, to electoral lists, to politicians or even to candidates for a political mandate. According to the Act of 4 July 1989, political parties and members thereof are not permitted to receive from a same individual a contribution in excess of EUR500 or equivalent per year. In addition, an individual may not contribute more than EUR2,000 or equivalent per year to political parties and politicians. Any contribution made by an individual to a political party in the amount of EUR125 or above must be registered by the political party.

Please note that the Act of 4 July 1989 also prohibits donations by a natural person who actually acts as an intermediary for a legal entity.

Should a company offer or make such a donation, both the company (and, as the case may arise, the individual who would, in fact, act as an intermediary for such a company) and the politician or candidate who accepts the gift may be subject to criminal fines of up to EUR600,000.

The prohibition is quite broad and will apply even in the absence of a "*quid pro quo*" situation.

Since 1 January 2015, the Act of 4 July 1989 includes a limitation on cash payments to political parties and/or their members (donations of EUR125 or more have to be transmitted by electronic means) as well as a possibility for legal entities, under certain conditions, to sponsor political parties and/or their members. Such sponsoring must notably be in exchange of advertising and must correspond to market price. Sponsoring above EUR 125 must be duly recorded and amounts are limited during periods preceding elections. Anyone who would grant sponsorship in violation of the aforementioned rules may be subject to criminal fines of up to EUR600,000.

1.6 Limitation applicable to hospitality expenses (gifts, travel, meals, entertainment, among others)

Belgian law does not impose mandatory thresholds regarding the offering or receiving of gifts and hospitality.

It is worth noting that normal business entertainment, such as occasional reasonably priced business breakfasts, lunches and dinners, and other business-related entertainment, are generally acceptable if there is no intention to obtain something in return from the public official, and it clearly has a business purpose and provided the expenses are reasonable. Unusual business entertainment and expensive gifts and offers could give rise to a "presumption of bribery."

Generally speaking, small gifts/hospitality acts of modest value may be given (e.g., small promotional items with the company's logo) if they: (i) fall within the bounds of propriety, a normal expression of courtesy or within the normal standards of hospitality; (ii) are not such as to bring suspicion on the recipient's objectivity and impartiality; and (iii) would not compromise the integrity of the recipient.

In practice, although there is no official guidance in that respect from Belgian authorities, as a rule of thumb, the value of such gifts should not exceed, on a cumulative basis, EUR30 to EUR50 per year and per recipient. Acts of hospitality offered should always remain reasonable. Meals in the amount of EUR35 to EUR40 would usually be considered as acceptable, with a calendar year limit of EUR125.

It is worth noting that specific rules and expenses limitations for hospitality apply in determined sectors, in particular in the pharmaceutical / life sciences industry. These rules and limitations are notably set in professional codes of conduct such as the Code of Deontology (Articles 29*bis* and 31, 2*bis*) of the Medicines Association Industry (pharma.be) and the Code of Ethics (Article 5) of the Health Deontological Platform (Mdeon), as well as in their respective guidelines.

2. Domestic bribery (private to private)

2.1 Legal framework

Private (or commercial) bribery is regulated under Article 504 *bis* and 504 *ter* of the Private Bribery Statute.

2.2 Definition of private bribery

The Private Bribery Statute applies to all persons not covered by the public bribery provisions, that is, private persons (both legal entities and individuals).

The Private Bribery Statute defines private bribery as occurring when any person who, in his capacity as director, manager, proxy holder or employee of a legal entity, or proxy holder or employee of a natural person, requests or accepts an offer, promise or benefit, on his own or on behalf of a third party, in exchange for adopting a particular position within the scope of his responsibilities without the authorization and knowledge of the board of directors, the shareholders, the principal or the employer. Any person offering a bribe to a private person may commit private bribery, provided that the former is acting without the authorization or knowledge of his superior.

The Private Bribery Statute makes the same distinction as the Public Bribery Statute between passive bribery and active bribery:

Passive bribery is the act of a private person requesting or accepting an offer, promise or benefit, directly or indirectly, on his own behalf or on behalf of a third party, in order to induce him to perform or refrain from performing an act falling within the scope of his responsibilities, or made easier by his position, without the authorization of and without informing his board of directors, general shareholders' meeting, principal or employer.

Active bribery is the act of making an offer or promise, or offering a benefit to a third party, directly or indirectly, on his own behalf or on behalf of a third party, in order to induce the third party to perform or refrain from performing an act falling within the scope of his responsibilities, or made easier by his position, without the authorization of and without informing his board of directors, general shareholders' meeting, principal or employer.

The Private Bribery Statute's provisions cover employees and representatives of all forms of legal entities, including limited liability companies, public limited corporations and non-profit associations, among others.

Under Belgian law, a request is punishable even if not followed by a proposal to pay by the prospective payor, or if the proposal is not accepted. In order to establish bribery, it is not necessary to prove that a corrupt pact between the corrupter and the corrupted person exists, although a corrupt agreement is an aggravating circumstance. In order for the request or offer to be punishable, the public prosecutor will have to prove that the intent of the donor, when he made the request or offer, was to influence the private person.

2.3 Consequences of private bribery

Private bribery is punishable only if the person acted without the knowledge and without the authorization of his or her superior (the board of directors, the general meeting, the principal or the employer, as the case may be).

(a) For the individuals involved

(i) Principal sanctions

- Imprisonment from six months to three years
- A criminal fine ranging from EUR600 to EUR300,000

The gradation of the sanctions depends on whether the proposal for passive bribery is followed by a proposal for active bribery, as well as whether the proposal for active bribery has been accepted.

(ii) Accessory sanctions

Additional sanctions (e.g., exclusion from exercising certain functions, professions or activities in the commercial sector) may be applicable.

(b) For the company / legal entity

(i) Principal sanctions

- Imprisonment sanction converted into fines from EUR18,000 to EUR600,000
- A criminal fine ranging from EUR600 to EUR300,000

(ii) Accessory sanctions

Additional sanctions (e.g., exclusion from public procurement procedures) may apply.

Entering into a corrupt pact (i.e., an agreement between the donor and the private person) whether in writing or orally is an aggravating circumstance.

2.4 Limitation applicable to hospitality expenses (gifts, travel, meals, entertainment, among others)

Please refer to Section 1.6., it being noted that the decisive criterion for private bribery is the absence of knowledge of, and authorization from, the concerned person (i.e., board of directors or general assembly or principal or employer) to adopt a particular attitude.

3. Corruption of foreign public officials

3.1 Legal framework

Corruption of foreign public officials is regulated under Article 250 of the Public Bribery Statute, which refers to Articles 246 to 249 of the same statute. This is, however, without prejudice to the applicability of applicable foreign laws, such as the UK Bribery Act or the US Foreign Corrupt Practices Act, where relevant.

3.2 Definition of corruption of foreign public officials

Please refer to Section 1.2., as the same definition applies to both Belgian and foreign public officials.

3.3 Definition of foreign public official

Please refer to Section 1.3.

3.4 Consequences of corruption of foreign public officials

The same penalties that apply to public bribery also apply when the bribery concerns a person holding a public office in a foreign state or in a public international organization (please refer to Section 1.4).

Moreover, such offenses can, in most cases, be prosecuted in Belgium regardless of foreign elements, pursuant to Article 10 *quater* of the Belgian Criminal Instruction Code. This section notably recognizes the jurisdiction of Belgian authorities to prosecute any individual who infringed, even outside the Belgian territory, Article 250 of the Public Bribery Statute, where: (i) the official is a Belgian citizen working in a foreign state or in an international public sector organization or where the international public sector organization the official is working for has its seat in Belgium; and (ii) any Belgian citizen or any person having its main residence in Belgium, provided that the deed is sanctioned by the laws of the state where it has been committed.

3.5 Limitation applicable to hospitality expenses (gifts, travel, meals, entertainment, among others)

Please refer to Section 1.6.

4. Facilitation payments

Belgian law prohibits facilitation payments (i.e., making payments to a government official to facilitate or expedite the performance of a routine governmental action, such as obtaining permits, licenses or other official documents and processing of governmental papers). Such facilitation payments will indeed be considered as a benefit granted to a government official for the performance (or the omission) of his duties and therefore fall under the prohibition of the anti-bribery provisions of the Public Bribery Statute.

In addition to the public and private bribery provisions, the following legal provisions must be mentioned:

- Article 311 of the Public Bribery Statute sanctions anyone who, by any fraudulent means, increases or reduces the price of public goods, furniture's and papers.

- Article 314 of the Public Bribery Statute sanctions those who, in public tenders, perturb the freedom of auctions and/or submissions by way of violence, force, gifts, promises or any other fraudulent means. The commission of such offense may lead to the annulment of the relevant contracts.

5. Compliance programs

5.1 Value of a compliance program in mitigating/eliminating the criminal liability of legal entities

The Public Bribery Statute does not recognize a compliance program as an instrument to mitigate or eliminate the liability of legal entities before corruption has been committed.

Please note, however, that foreign legislation, such as the UK Bribery Act, could expose a legal entity's liability for the mere absence of sufficient measures to prevent its employees or authorized representative from committing bribery.

5.2 Absence of a compliance program as a crime

The Public Bribery Statute does not treat the absence of a compliance program as a crime.

5.3 Elements of a compliance program

(a) Legal framework

The Public Bribery Statute does not regulate the elements of a compliance program.

(b) Recommended practice

It is strongly recommended that legal entities adopt a robust compliance program. Such a compliance program should notably encompass a sufficiently broad definition of public sector and public officials, as well as indicate a suitable threshold for the value of permitted gifts and hospitality according to best practices (see Section 1.6 above).

It is worth noting that almost all governmental bodies and enterprises entrusted with public service missions have anti-bribery provisions, either in the statute establishing the body or enterprise, or in the internal rules or codes of conduct.

Over the last few years, more and more emphasis has been put on corporate responsibility, amongst others, with respect to anti-bribery practices. Initiatives have been implemented at the Belgian Federal and local levels to encourage companies to voluntarily implement corporate responsibility plans.

6. Regulator with jurisdiction to prosecute corruption

The Belgian legal system does not have a specific court with exclusive jurisdiction to prosecute corruption. Any public prosecutor could request that a judge start a corruption investigation. However, in practice, the Belgian system has a group of judicial prosecutors called the Central Office for the Repression of Corruption, which specializes in prosecuting corruption.

Czech Republic

Milena Hoffmanova

Milena Hoffmanová's practice focuses mainly on ensuring compliance with legal regulations as well as ethical standards relating to medicinal products and medical devices, including assisting with drafting of internal company guidelines and policies and labeling/packaging requirements. She also advises on anti-corruption compliance matters, including the extraterritorial application of US law, such as application of the Foreign Corrupt Practices Act and foreign bribery laws. She has experience in a broad range of compliance matters, including corporate and regulatory investigations, FCPA and global anti-corruption compliance, compliance program development and anti-corruption due diligence, including data privacy issues such as cross-border data flows, data security, whistle-blower hotlines, e-monitoring and other privacy-related issues.

milena.hoffmanova@bakermckenzie.com
Tel: +420 236 045 001

Baker & McKenzie s.r.o., advokátní kancelář
Klimentská 46
110 02 Prague 1
Czech Republic

1. Domestic bribery (private to public)

1.1 Legal framework

Bribery of public officials is regulated under the Czech Criminal Code, Article 331, *et seq.*

1.2 Definition of bribery crimes

Bribery crimes can be committed by public officials, private individuals, as well as legal entities. However, a legal entity may be relieved of criminal liability.

Acceptance of a bribe – A person who, in connection with procuring a matter of public interest, for himself or herself or for another person, accepts a promise of a or an actual bribe, for himself or herself or for another person, or in connection with the conduct of his or her business or business of another person, for himself or herself, accepts a promise of or an actual bribe, shall be punished by imprisonment of up to four years or exclusion from the performance of an activity.

Request for a bribe – A person who requests a bribe from another person under the circumstances of acceptance of a bribe as discussed above shall be punished by imprisonment of at least six months up to five years.

Offering of a bribe – A person who, in connection with procuring a matter of public interest, provides, offers or promises a bribe for another person, or whomever, or in connection with the conduct of his or her business or business of another person, provides, offers or promises a bribe shall be punished by imprisonment of up to two years or a fine.

Indirect bribery – A person who requests, has someone promise or accepts a bribe for affecting the performance of a power of a government official by his or her influence, or through a third party, or because he or she has already done so, shall be punished by imprisonment of up to three years.

Definition of a bribe – A bribe is an unjust benefit consisting of direct material enrichment or another advantage being provided, or to be provided, to a person being bribed or, with such person's consent, to another person, to which that person is not entitled.

1.3 Definition of public official

The Czech Criminal Code has a broad definition of a public official. It includes those who perform the activities of government officials as well as those who perform activities of private persons in the sphere of matters of public interest (e.g., provision of healthcare, funeral services and bankrupt assets management).

1.4 Consequences of bribery

The Czech Criminal Code and the Act on Criminal Liability of Legal Entities establish higher penalties for public officials and for those who intend to benefit from bribery or cause damage exceeding approximately EUR180,000.

(a) For the individuals involved

- Up to 12 years in prison
- Monetary penalty

(b) For a company / legal entity

- Termination of the legal entity
- Forfeiture of property
- Monetary penalty
- Forfeiture of a thing
- Ban on activities

- Ban on the performance of a public procurement, or participation in concession proceedings or a public competition

- Ban on the acceptance of a subsidy or subvention

- Publication of a judgment

1.5 Political contributions

Contributions to political parties are generally allowed.

1.6 Limitation applicable to hospitality expenses (gifts, travel, meals, entertainment, among others)

The Czech Criminal Code does not establish quantitative or qualitative limitations on hospitality expenses. However, a bribe may consist of a gift of any value. Hospitality is not allowed if it is provided unjustly, with the intent to illegally influence decision making.

Whether a hospitality expense could be considered bribery needs to be determined on a case-by-case basis, taking into account all the facts and circumstances surrounding the case.

2. Domestic bribery (private to private)

2.1 Legal framework

Private bribery is regulated under the Czech Criminal Code as well as the Czech Civil Code.

2.2 Definition of private bribery

Criminal Code: Please see Section 1.2.

Civil Code:

Offering of a bribe occurs when a competitor offers, promises or provides, directly or indirectly, benefits to an individual who is a member of another competitor's statutory body or a similar body, or a competitor's employee, or an individual of a similar status, in order to gain, by means of unfair conduct, an advantage for himself or herself, or for another person, to the detriment of another competitor, or an illegal advantage in competition.

Acceptance or request of a bribe occurs when an individual who is a member of a competitor's statutory body or a similar body, or a competitor's employee, or an individual of a similar status, requests, accepts a promise of or accepts actual benefits from another competitor, directly or indirectly, in order that such another competitor may gain, by means of unfair conduct, an advantage for himself or herself, or for another person, to the detriment of the former said competitor, or an illegal advantage in competition.

2.3 Consequences of private bribery

Criminal Code: Please see Section 1.4.

Civil Code: A person whose rights were, through private bribery, endangered or breached, may require the offending party to: (i) refrain from such activities; or (ii) rectify its consequences. Such person may also require adequate satisfaction and damage compensation; he or she is also entitled to receive unjust enrichment from the offending party.

2.4 Limitation applicable to hospitality expenses (gifts, travel, meals, entertainment, among others)

For the criminal aspects of private bribery, please see Section 1.6.

The Civil Code does not establish quantitative or qualitative limitations on hospitality expenses. However, a bribe may consist of a gift of any amount. Hospitality is not allowed if it is provided to a member of a competitor's statutory body or a similar body, or a competitor's employee, or an individual of a similar status, in order to gain, by means of unfair conduct, an advantage for himself or herself, or for another person, to the detriment of another competitor, or an illegal advantage in competition.

3. Corruption of foreign public officials

3.1 Legal framework

Corruption of foreign public officials is regulated by the Czech Criminal Code, Section 331, *et seq*.

3.2 Definition of corruption of foreign public officials

Please see Section 1.2.

3.3 Definition of foreign public official

In the context of corruption crimes, a foreign public official means any person who:

- has a legislative, judicial or another function in a foreign state body;
- performs functions or works in an international judicial body;
- performs functions or works in an international or multinational organization formed by countries or other subjects of international public law, in its body or institution; or
- performs functions in a business company in which the Czech Republic or another country exercises a decisive influence,

if the performance of such a function, employment or work is connected to the procurement of a matter of public interest, and the crime was committed in connection with such competence.

3.4 Consequences of corruption of foreign public officials

Please see Section 1.4.

3.5 Limitation applicable to hospitality expenses (gifts, travel, meals, entertainment, among others)

Please see Section 1.6.

4. Facilitation payments

The Criminal Code does not recognize so-called facilitation payments. Facilitation payments may not be made if they fall under the definition of a bribe. Please see Section 1.2.

5. Compliance programs

5.1 Value of a compliance program in mitigating/eliminating the criminal liability of legal entities

The Act on Criminal Liability of Legal Entities does not specifically recognize a compliance program as an instrument to mitigate or eliminate the liability of legal entities before the crime of corruption has been committed. However, one of the many requirements to establish the criminal liability of a legal entity is that it must be proved that the legal entity failed to take precautions that should have been taken, pursuant to any law, or which could be justly required. Such precautions include, in particular: (i) conclusion of any obligatory or necessary inspection of employees or other persons who are superior to the employees; or (ii) taking necessary measures to prevent or avert the consequences of the committed crime. If such precautions are taken, the legal entities complying with such requirements would be exempt from criminal liability.

5.2 Absence of a compliance program as a crime

Neither the Czech Criminal Code nor the Act on Criminal Liability of Legal Entities recognizes the absence of a compliance program as a crime.

5.3 Elements of a compliance program

(a) Legal framework

The Czech Criminal Code and the Act on Criminal Liability of Legal Entities do not recognize or regulate the elements of a compliance program.

(b) Recommended practice

It is recommended that all precautions be taken, as described in Section 5.1. Regular audits, codes of conduct, education, standard operating procedures and similar precautions should mitigate or even exclude a legal entity's criminal liability for crimes of corruption.

6. Regulator with jurisdiction to prosecute corruption

The Czech legal system does not have a specific regulator with exclusive responsibilities to prosecute corruption. Any public prosecutor could request that a judge start a corruption investigation.

However, there are discussions regarding the creation of a group of specialized prosecutors who would be responsible for handling large or complicated corruption cases. This group should be constituted by the new Act on Public Prosecutor's Office, which is expected to be adopted and come into effect in 2017.

Egypt

Mohamad Talaat

Mohamad Talaat concentrates on securities and capital markets, corporate, anti-trust, arbitration, commercial, tax, labor, administrative and Islamic law, and project finance. His transactional work focuses on initial public offerings, private placements, mergers and acquisitions and major projects. He regularly acts as the lead lawyer in deals he is involved in. Mohamad has experience advising leading real estate and finance companies execute large, cross-border transactions.

mohamad.talaat@bakermckenzie.com
Tel: +20 2 2 461 9301

Helmy, Hamza and Partners
Nile City Building, North Tower
21st Floor 2005C, Cornich El Nil
Ramlet Beaulac
Cairo
Egypt

1. Domestic bribery (private to public)

1.1 Legal framework

The Egyptian Anti-Bribery Law (the "Law") is contained in the Penal Code. Articles 103 to 111 address bribery.

The Law punishes any questionable activity or a payment or promise of payment or benefit to a public official (i.e., public or government employees).

In the light of the Egyptian law, the foundation of an act of bribery requires the following three elements to be present:

(i) The recipient must be a public official (subject to some exceptions set out below).

(ii) There must be a "gift," a "benefit" or a "promise" that will constitute the material/physical element of the crime.

(iii) There must be requisite criminal intent (*mens rea*).

1.2 Definition of bribery

Articles 103 to 106 of the Law prohibit a public official from "requesting," "accepting" or "taking for him/herself or another," a "promise," a "gift" or a "benefit," whether material or non-material, for "performing" or "abstaining from performing" an inherent function of his or her position, even if he or she mistakenly believes such a function falls within the scope of his or her "official duties." Furthermore, the Law provides that a public official who violates or abuses the duties of his or her position with the intent of being rewarded for his or her behavior shall be subject to imprisonment.

In light of the foregoing, the Law addresses the "trading" or "peddling" a public official in his capacity as such. In this regard, the Law punishes the offeror of the bribe, the recipient and any intermediary, if there is any, (between the briber and the recipient) with the same punishment.

Article 107 states that "any benefit, of whatever value, obtained by the recipient of the bribe or by the person either designated by him for receipt of such (or knowing and agreeing to his or her appointment), shall be considered a promise or a gift."

It thus appears that the benefit constituting the "bribe" may be the promise or payment of money (or any tangible benefit) received or requested by an official or the briber's agreement to discharge a debt of the recipient of the bribe.

Furthermore, the Law does not distinguish between the benefit an official obtains for himself or herself and the benefit requested or accepted for another person. The crime of bribery is in the request itself and is not contingent upon the recipient, whoever he or she was.

The provisions of the Law are so broad that they encompass almost all forms of trading on a position or its duties (or an attempt to do so), regardless of what might be called the "timing" of the benefit. An official may be deemed a recipient of a bribe, even though he did not actually accept a payment, and bribery may exist even in the absence of an agreement for such between the official and the other party. As mentioned above, the Law considers the official's mere request a complete crime, even if such a request was not accepted by the other party. This is so because an official who offers his position "for sale" is no less of a criminal than the one actually completing the bribery transaction.

According to the general principles of criminal intent, the crime of bribery is not deemed to have occurred unless the recipient of the bribe realizes, at the time of the request or acceptance of a promise, or the taking of a gift, that such is the reward for performance, or abstention therefrom, of a duty within the scope of his authority or that he claims or erroneously believes is part thereof.

It should be noted, as well, that it does not matter if the receipt of the benefit was before or after the Act. If an official accepts a gift from a person, believing that it was presented innocently, then the official has not committed bribery. By the same token, if he pretends acceptance of the offer in order to facilitate the offeror's apprehension, the foundation for the crime of bribery is not met.

1.3 Definition of public official

According to Article 111 of the Law, "public officials" (for purposes of the Bribery provisions) are considered to include the following:

(i) Employees of government entities or employees working in departments affiliated with the government or those under its supervision

(ii) Members of the general or local legislative assemblies, whether elected or appointed

(iii) Arbitrators and experts, debtors' trustees, liquidators and judicial receivers

(iv) Any person entrusted with public service

(v) Members of the board of directors, as well as managers and employees of associations, companies, societies, foundations or establishments if the state or one of its public authorities contributes to its funding at any level and in any form whatsoever

(vi) The Egyptian courts have also decided that certain organizations, as indicated in their articles of association and the like, are "public" and, therefore, workers in such organizations are considered public officials

Under the Egyptian rules on bribery, trading on one's position is not deemed to occur unless the relevant act was within the authority of the official. "Duties of the position" are understood as any act within the legal scope of the position assumed by the official. This element of the crime of bribery is satisfied even if the official mistakenly believes or claims that the requested/promised act is within the official's duties (i.e., "illusory competency").

1.4 Consequences of bribery

(a) For the individuals involved

- Imprisonment, up to restrictive imprisonment depending on the crime attributed to the accused
- In addition to a fine not less than EGP1,000, depending on the crime attributed to the accused
- In all cases, the ruling shall order confiscating whatever is paid by the briber or mediator by way of a bribe.
- The accused shall be subject to Ancillary Penalties, which are:

  (A) Depriving the accused of the rights and privileges prescribed in Article 25 of the Penal Code, which are:

  1) Acceptance in any service with the government, whether direct, or in the quality of an entrepreneur or concessionaire, whatever the importance of the service

  2) Decoration with a rank or medal

  3) Testifying before the courts for the period of penalty, unless it is for evidentiary fact-finding

  4) Managing his works concerning his funds and property during the period of his arrest

  5) Remaining, from the day of the final ruling against him, as a member of the probate councils, the councils of the Directorates, the

municipality or local councils, or any general committee

6) His or her eligibility to be, ever, a member of one of the bodies indicated in the fifth clause, or an expert or witness on contracts, if a rigid imprisonment penalty is ruled finally against him or her

(B) Removal from governmental positions

(C) Being placed under surveillance by the police

(D) Confiscation of the substance of the bribe.

In addition to the above, in pursuance of Article 89 of the Companies Law No. 159 of 1981, he or she shall not be eligible to be a board member in a joint stock company or a manager of a limited liability company.

(b) For the company/legal entity

The Law does not adopt the principle of criminal responsibility of legal entities such as corporations, except with respect to specific financial crimes that are not relevant to the crime of bribery. The Egyptian Court of Cassation has traditionally ruled that, "Legal entities are not criminally responsible for crimes committed by their representatives; the persons who commit the crime are the ones who are personally responsible."

1.5 Political contributions

Pursuant to Article 111 of the Law, "public officials" (for purposes of the bribery provisions) include members of the general or local legislative assemblies, whether elected or appointed.

In addition, Law No. 40 of 1977 regulates the incorporation of political parties and their financial resources. To this end, the said law provides that such resources are formed out of the subscriptions, donations and investment in non-trading activities.

Furthermore, the said law provides that the funds of the political parties are considered particularly public funds in pursuance of the same meaning provided under the Law and the managers of the party and its employees are considered public officials as provided in the definition of a "public official" in Article 111 of the Law.

1.6 Limitation applicable to hospitality expenses (gifts, travel, meals, entertainment, among others)

In principal, the Law does not distinguish if the value of a gift is small or large. Any amount, however small, is subject to the Law. Therefore, "grease" or facilitation payments are strictly regarded as bribes.

However, entertainment expenses and small gifts given in certain occasions may be received, provided that they are not given or received for the purpose of corrupting a government official.

By and large, the amount spent on business entertainment should be reasonable in light of what is customary and appropriate in the context in which the entertainment takes place. A customary business lunch or dinner that is neither lavish nor frequent in nature would be unlikely to give rise to any inference of an improper purpose or corrupt intent.

However, it is not appropriate, and thus not recommended, to invite public officials for meals at restaurants that are not frequented by ordinary businessmen or, after a review of the facts and circumstances, to a restaurant that is considered extravagant in light of the public official's ordinary practices.

In general, inexpensive gifts, such as calendars, pens, notebooks, cigarette lighters and samples of the company's products bearing the company's logos are not typically regarded as prohibited under the anti-bribery provisions, especially when given on occasions such as the New Year or *Bayram*.

The foregoing limits apply to both public and private officials. It should be highlighted that the Prime Ministerial Decree No. 1883 of 1993 sets out the conditions for any governmental agency to receive any gifts, grants or donations. Such conditions provide that any such entity must obtain the approval of the relevant Minister before accepting any in-kind or monetary gift from foreign or international entities that has a value of more than EGP10,000 up to EGP150,000. If such a gift's value exceeds EGP150,000, then the approval of the Prime Minister must be obtained.

Kindly note also that if such business courtesy is unrelated to the business of the governmental agency, then its nature might raise suspicion.

Based on the foregoing, if any of the gifts is to fall within the above scope, then the governmental agency must obtain approval.

2. Domestic bribery (private to private)

2.1 Legal framework

The Law also regulates bribes offered to employees in the private sector, in addition to those offered to the board members, directors or employees of joint stock companies in Egypt.

2.2 Definition of private bribery

The wording of Article 106 of the Egyptian Penal Code provides that the definition of bribery has been expanded to include bribes given to private corporate officials to obtain an interest or other advantages, which are against company policy and which are without the knowledge of the employer or his consent. The wording of the said article clearly states in relevant part that, "any EMPLOYEE (The Code usually uses the word Public Official) who requests for himself or herself, or any third person, or accepts a payment or a promise of payment without his or her employer's consent or knowledge in consideration of performing any act that is considered part of his or her job should be guilty of bribery."

In light of the above, it is our belief that Article 106 prohibits commercial bribery. Aside from that, the wording of Article 106 *bis* applies the bribery rules also to board members, directors or employees of joint stock companies in Egypt.

2.3 Consequences of private bribery

(a) For the individuals involved

- Any employee who demands for himself or herself, or for a third party, or accepts or takes a promise or donation without the knowledge or consent of his master (employer), in order to perform or refrain from performing work or the duties he or she is charged with to fulfil, shall be considered a bribe-taker and shall be punished with imprisonment for a period not exceeding two years and a fine of not less than EGP200 and not exceeding EGP500, or either penalty.

- Any board member of a joint stock company, a cooperative association or a union established according to the rules prescribed legally, or of any establishment or association that is legally considered a public utility, and any director or employee of these bodies who demands for himself or herself, or for a third party, accepts or takes a promise or donation to perform or refrain from performing work or duties inherent to his or her position, or which he or she erroneously believes or alleges to be part of the duties of his or her position, or to default on the duties of the position shall be considered a bribe-taker and shall be liable to imprisonment for a period not exceeding seven years and a fine of not less than EGP500 and not exceeding what he or she was given or promised to be given, even if the felon has in mind not to effect the work, or not to refrain from it, or not to default on the duties of his or her position. In this event, it should be noted that he or she shall not be eligible to be a board member in a joint stock company or a manager of a limited liability company.

- In all cases, the ruling shall order confiscating whatever is paid by the briber or mediator by way of a bribe, according to the previous articles.

(b) For the company/legal entity

The Law does not adopt the principle of criminal responsibility of legal entities such as corporations, except with respect to specific financial crimes that are not relevant to the bribery crime. The Egyptian Court of Cassation has traditionally ruled that, "legal entities are not criminally responsible for crimes committed by their representatives; the persons who commit the crime are the ones who are personally responsible."

2.4 Limitation applicable to hospitality expenses (gifts, travel, meals, entertainment, among others)

Although there are no specific, similar guidelines for private employees, we recommend that the gift or business courtesy fall within the above-mentioned ranges in Section 1.6. This is so since, as previously mentioned, the language of Article 106 provides that any employee who requests or receives any unlawful payments of promises of payments shall be guilty of bribery. In light of that, it is our belief, from an interpretive perspective, that the general rules of bribery apply to both public and private officials.

3. Corruption of foreign public officials

3.1 Legal framework

The Egyptian Penal Code does not explicitly recognize nor regulate the corruption of foreign public officials. However, it recognizes the concept of extraterritoriality.

According to Article 2(1) of the Law, the Egyptian Penal Code applies to "any person who commits, outside the country, an act that makes him a principal or an accessory in a crime committed wholly or partially in Egypt."

Therefore, where the elements of the crime were perpetrated, as defined in the Egyptian Penal Code, will not have any impact on its qualification as bribery.

3.2 Definition of corruption of foreign public officials

N/A

3.3 Definition of foreign public official

N/A

3.4 Consequences of corruption of foreign public officials

N/A

3.5 For the individuals involved

N/A

3.6 For the legal entity

N/A

3.7 Limitation applicable to hospitality expenses (gifts, travel, meals, entertainment, among others)

N/A

4. Facilitation payments

In principal, the Law does not distinguish if the value of a gift is small or large. Any amount, however small, is subject to the Law. Therefore, "grease" or facilitation payments are strictly regarded as bribes.

However, pursuant to customary practice, facilitation payments should not be regarded as bribery in light of what is customary and appropriate, as long as they are not given or received for purposes of corrupting a public official, otherwise, such payments shall fall within the definition of bribery under the Law.

In accordance therewith, a gift payment to public employees, according to the courts, is not deemed bribery, so long as it does not meet the parameters of bribery under criminal law.

5. Compliance programs

5.1 Value of a compliance program in mitigating/eliminating the criminal liability of companies

As previously provided, the Law does not adopt the principle of criminal responsibility of legal entities such as corporations, except with respect to specific financial crimes that are not relevant to the bribery crime. The Egyptian Court of Cassation has traditionally ruled that: "Legal entities are not criminally responsible for crimes committed by their representatives; the persons who commit the crime are the ones who are personally responsible."

Thus, the Egyptian Penal Code does not require compliance programs as instruments to mitigate or eliminate the liability of legal entities before the crime of corruption has been committed.

5.2 Absence of a compliance program as a criminal offense

A compliance program is not required by the law.

5.3 Elements of a compliance program

A compliance program is not required by the law.

6. Regulator with jurisdiction to prosecute corruption

The general provisions of the Criminal Procedures Code do not indicate a specific regulator with exclusive responsibilities to prosecute corruption cases. Yet, in pursuance of the General Instructions issued by the General Prosecutor, a division named State Prosecution was established, which specializes - among other crimes- on prosecuting bribery cases.

In this respect, it is worth noting that in practice, any prosecutor may handle the interrogation on bribery cases in the event that such cases are of less importance in terms of the amount of the bribe, the parties, and the governmental authority for which the public officer works. Yet, once a prosecutor finalizes the interrogations, all cases shall be mandatory referred to the State Prosecution, which will issue a decision on the case. In other words, the State Prosecutor will decide whether to shelve the case or refer it to the criminal court.

France

Eric Lasry

Eric Lasry practices in the Mergers & Acquisitions Group of Baker & McKenzie in Paris, as well as in the area of corporate compliance.

Eric was instrumental in the development of the Firm's M&A practice and is founder and co-lead of the Compliance and Risk Management practice in Paris. He has held several management positions within Baker & McKenzie. He has served as managing partner of the Paris office and was a member of the Firm's Global Executive Committee. He also served as chairman of the European Regional Council and of the Policy Committee.

Eric is exceptionally fluent in cross-border transactions. His extensive experience includes advising American and French Companies on their strategic corporate transactions. His wide client base includes companies in the information technology, luxury, pharmaceuticals, food and services industries. Within his Compliance and Risk Management practice, Eric advises French and international groups in the context of risk assessments, coordination of internal investigations and implementation of compliance programs both in France and abroad.

eric.lasry@bakermckenzie.com
Tel: +33 1 44 17 53 65

Sara Koski

Sara Koski joined the Corporate and Mergers & Acquisitions Group at Baker & McKenzie SCP in 2012 and is also a member of the Compliance & Risk Management Group. She specializes in corporate law, transactions and compliance, and she intervenes principally in due diligence, drafting of acquisition contracts, internal restructuring within corporate groups and anti-bribery (compliance due diligence, risk assessment, implementation of compliance programs and internal investigations).

Sara holds a post-graduate degree in Anglo-American Business Law and in International Business Law from the University of Paris I – Panthéon-Sorbonne.

sara.koski@bakermckenzie.com
Tel: +33 1 44 17 6451

Baker & McKenzie SCP
1 rue Paul Baudry
75008 Paris
France

Key Practitioners

Emanuel Guillaume
Paris
Tel: +33 1 44 17 53 90
emmanuel.guillaume@bakermckenzie.com

1. Domestic bribery (private to public)

1.1 Legal framework

Bribery of French public officials is regulated under the French Criminal Code, Articles 433-1, 1 (active bribery, i.e., committed by the person bribing a public official) and 432-11, 1 (passive bribery, i.e., committed by the public official who is bribed).

1.2 Definition of bribery

Bribery may be committed by both public officials who solicit or accept a bribe and private individuals who try to corrupt a public official.

Bribery refers to proffering, without any right, at any moment, directly or indirectly, offers, promises, gifts, presents or any advantages, to induce a public official to perform or not to perform (or to reward a public official for having performed or for not having performed) any act within his or her occupation, position or office, or facilitated by his or her occupation, position or office. The person receiving or requesting the bribe is liable for passive bribery, whereas the person offering the bribe is liable for active bribery.

1.3 Definition of public official

A public official means any person (i) holding a public elected office; (ii) vested with public authority; or (iii) discharging a public service mission. A "person discharging a public service mission" refers to a person who, although not entrusted with public authority, discharges a public service mission on either a temporary or permanent basis. This may notably, but not exclusively, include anyone working for a state-controlled company or who, although working in a private sector company, carries out a public service mission.

1.4 Consequences of bribery

(a) For individuals involved in cases of active or passive bribery

The French Criminal Code establishes the same penalties for public officials and for individuals who corrupt public officials (Articles 433-1, 1; 433-22 and 433-23; 432-11, 1; and 432-17) The penalties are the following:

- Up to 10 years in jail
- Fine of up to EUR1 million (alternatively, the amount of the fine may also be set at twice the proceeds of the offense)
- Prohibition (for up to five years) from exercising civil, civic and family rights
- Prohibition (for up to 10 years or permanently) from exercising public functions or from exercising the activity within which the offense was committed
- Prohibition (for up to 15 years or permanently) from exercising a commercial or industrial profession, or to direct or control, directly or indirectly, an industrial or commercial company
- Confiscation of the amount or the object received by the offender
- Publication of the decision

The custodial sentence may be reduced by half if the offender informs the administrative and judicial authority of the offense and in doing so causes the offense to be discontinued or the other offenders or accomplices to be identified (Articles 433-2-1 and 432-11-1 of the French Criminal Code).

(b) For the company/legal entity in case of active bribery

The French Criminal Code establishes the following penalties (Article 433-25):

- Fines of up to EUR5 million (alternatively, the amount of the fine may also be set at twice the proceeds of the offense)
- Prohibition (for up to five years) from operating, directly or indirectly, one or several professional or social activities within which the offense was committed
- Being placed under judicial supervision (for up to five years)
- Closing down (for up to five years) the legal entity's facilities used to commit the offense
- Debarment from public procurement (for up to five years)
- Prohibition (for up to five years) from proceeding with a public tender offer or from making an initial public offering
- Prohibition (for up to five years) from issuing a check or using a payment card
- Confiscation of the object that has been used in or intended for use in committing the offense, or the proceeds of the offense
- Publication of the decision

A bill of law relating to transparency, fight against bribery and modernization of economy (the "Bill of Law"), published on 30 March 2016, was expected to introduce a new criminal settlement procedure, inspired by FCPA-type deferred prosecution agreements. This measure that was initially included in the Bill of Law has now been removed from the latest published version, further to an unfavorable opinion of the French Council of State on 26 March 2016. It is currently anticipated that this measure could, however, be reintroduced during a debate before the French parliament.[1]

1.5 Political contributions

Contributions to political parties are regulated by Law No. 88-227, of 11 March 1988, as amended. In general terms, contributions to political parties are only allowed for natural persons and may not exceed EUR7,500 per year. Contributions by legal entities to political parties have been prohibited since 1995.

1.6 Limitations applicable to hospitality expenses (gifts, travel, meals, entertainment, among others)

The French Criminal Code does not establish quantitative or qualitative limitations on hospitality expenses.

It should be noted that there are no *de minimis* amounts, no safe harbors and no official rulings available that establish when or under which circumstances an act of hospitality might be deemed a bribe. Any advantage given with a corrupt intent is considered a bribe under French law. Even small payments may be considered bribes if circumstances reveal improper intent. Also, the repeated offering of gifts of small value may indicate a corrupt intent.

Any advantages, irrespective of the context in which they are given, ought to be reasonable and proportionate, consistent with customary practices, for the sole benefit of the intended beneficiary (i.e., not extended to persons other than the business person directly concerned), not meant to obtain anything in return, justified by a valid business reason and legally acceptable for the beneficiary. In practice, what matters to the courts is whether the advantage has been offered

---

[1] The Bill of Law was approved by the French Council of Ministers on 30 March 2016, and is currently being reviewed before the National Assembly. The Bill of Law is still being discussed at the time of publication and is subject to changes, which may be significant by the time of actual adoption. Therefore, the provisions contemplated under the Bill of Law should not be relied upon until final adoption.

in order to induce the public official to accomplish (or refrain from accomplishing) or to reward him for accomplishing (or for having refrained from accomplishing) an act of his or her function. Otherwise stated, a *quid pro quo* arrangement is prohibited.

Whether a hospitality expense could be considered a bribe will need to be determined on a case-by-case basis, taking into account all the facts and circumstances surrounding the case.

2. Domestic bribery (private to private)

2.1 Legal framework

Bribery is regulated under the French Criminal Code, Articles 445-1 (active bribery, i.e., committed by the person bribing a public official) and 445-2 (passive bribery, i.e., committed by the person who is bribed).

2.2 Definition of private bribery

Bribery pertains to proffering, without any right, at any moment, directly or indirectly, offers, promises, gifts, presents or any other advantage, to a person who is not a public official and who, within a professional or social activity, occupies a management position or works for any person or organization, to get such private party to perform or not perform (or for having performed or not performed) an act within his or her activity or occupation, or facilitated by his or her activity or occupation, in violation of his or her legal, contractual or professional obligations. Requesting or accepting such advantages is further constitutive of the criminal offense of passive corruption of a private party, whereas the person offering the bribe is liable for active bribery of a private party.

2.3 Consequences of private bribery

(a) For individuals involved in cases of active or passive bribery (Articles 445-1, 445-2 and 445-3 of the French Criminal Code):

- Up to five years in jail
- Fines of up to EUR500,000 (alternatively, the amount of the fine may also be set at twice the proceeds of the offense)
- Prohibition (for up to five years) from exercising civic, civil and family rights
- Prohibition (for up to five years or permanently) from exercising public functions or from exercising the activity within which the offense was committed
- Prohibition (for up to 15 years or permanently) from exercising a commercial or industrial profession, from directing or controlling, directly or indirectly, an industrial or commercial company
- Confiscation of the object that has been used in or intended for use in committing the offense, or the proceeds of the offense
- Publication of the decision

(b) For the company / legal entity in cases of active or passive bribery (Article 445-4 of the French Criminal Code):

- Fines of up to EUR2.5 million (alternatively, the amount of the fine may also be set at twice the proceeds of the offense)
- Prohibition (for up to five years) from operating, directly or indirectly, one or several professional or social activities within which the offense was committed

- Being placed under judicial supervision (for up to five years)
- Closing (for up to five years) the establishment that was used to commit the offense
- Debarment from public procurement (for up to five years)
- Prohibition (for up to five years) from proceeding with a public tender offer or from making an initial public offering
- Prohibition (for up to five years) from issuing a check or using a payment card
- Confiscation of the object that has been used in or intended for use in committing the offense, or the proceeds of the offense
- Publication of the decision

2.4 Limitations applicable to hospitality expenses (gifts, travel, meals, entertainment, among others)

The Criminal Code does not establish quantitative or qualitative limitations on hospitality expenses.

It should be noted that there are no *de minimis* amounts, no safe harbors and no official rulings available that define as to when or under which circumstances an act of hospitality might be deemed to constitute a bribe. Any advantage given with a corrupt intent is considered a bribe under French law. Even small payments may be considered bribes if circumstances reveal improper intent. Also, the repeated offering of gifts of small value may indicate a corrupt intent.

Any advantages, irrespective of the context in which they are given, ought to be reasonable and proportionate, consistent with customary practices, for the sole benefit of the intended beneficiary (i.e., not extended to persons other than the business person directly concerned), not meant to obtain anything in return, justified by a valid business reason and legally acceptable for the beneficiary. In practice, what matters to the courts is whether the advantage has been offered in order to induce the private party to accomplish (or refrain from accomplishing) or to reward him for accomplishing (or for having refrained from accomplishing) an act of his or her function. Otherwise stated, a *quid pro quo* arrangement is prohibited.

Whether a hospitality expense could be considered a bribe will need to be determined on a case-by-case basis, taking into account all the facts and circumstances surrounding the case.

3. Corruption of foreign public officials and officials of international public organizations

3.1 Legal framework

Bribery of foreign public officials and officials of international public organizations is regulated under the French Criminal Code, Articles 435-1 (passive bribery, i.e., committed by the public official who is bribed) and 435-3 (active bribery, i.e., committed by the person bribing a public official).[2]

3.2 Definition of corruption of foreign public officials and officials of international public organizations

Bribery pertains to proffering, without any right, at any moment, directly or indirectly, offers, promises, gifts, presents or any other advantage, to a person who is a public official (i) in a foreign country; or (ii) in an international public organization, to perform or not perform (or for having performed or not performed) any act within his or her occupation or position, or office, or facilitated by his or her occupation, position or office. Requesting or accepting such advantages is further constitutive of a criminal offense of passive corruption of a foreign public official or an official of an international public organization.

---

[2] The Bill of Law also contains measures aiming at facilitating prosecution of bribery of foreign public officials.

3.3 Definition of foreign public official and officials of international public organizations

For the purposes of this offense, a foreign public official means:

- any person who has a legislative, administrative or judicial function in a foreign country, whether by appointment or by election;
- any person who works in a public company or public body; or
- any public servant or officer of a public international organization.

More specifically, a foreign public official refers to any person: (i) holding a public elected office; (ii) vested with public authority; or (iii) discharging a public service mission in a foreign country or in a public international organization.

3.4 Consequences of bribery of foreign public officials and officials of international public organizations

(a) For the individuals involved in cases of active or passive bribery (Articles 435-1, 435-3 and 435-14 of the French Criminal Code):

- Up to 10 years in jail
- Fines of up to EUR1 million (alternatively, the amount of the fine may also be set at twice the proceeds of the offense)
- Prohibition (for up to five years) from exercising civic, civil and family rights
- Prohibition (for up to five years) from exercising a public function or from exercising a professional or social activity within which the offense was committed

- Publication of the decision
- Confiscation of the object that was used in or intended for use in committing the offense, or the proceeds of the offense
- For foreigners, prohibition (for up to 10 years or permanently) from staying on French territory

The custodial sentence may be reduced by half if the offender informs the administrative and judicial authority of the offense and in doing so causes the offense to be discontinued or the other offenders or accomplices to be identified (Articles 435-6-1 of the French Criminal Code).

(b) For the company / legal entity in the event of active bribery (Article 435-15 of the French Criminal Code):

- Fines of up to EUR5 million (alternatively, the amount of the fine may also be set at double of the proceeds of the offense)
- Prohibition (for up to five years) from operating, directly or indirectly, one or several professional or social activities within which the offense was committed
- Being placed under judicial supervision (for up to five years)
- Closing (for up to five years) of the establishment that was used to commit the offense
- Debarment from public procurement (for up to five years)
- Prohibition (for up to five years) from proceeding to with a public tender offer or from making an initial public offering
- Prohibition (for up to five years) from issuing a check or using a payment card

- Confiscation of the object that has been used in or intended for use in committing the offense, or the proceeds of the offense

- Publication of the decision

3.5 Limitations applicable to hospitality expenses (gifts, travel, meals, entertainment, among others)

The French Criminal Code does not establish quantitative or qualitative limitations on hospitality expenses.

It should be noted that there are no *de minimis* amounts, no safe harbors and no official rulings available that define when or under which circumstances an act of hospitality might be deemed to constitute a bribe. Any advantage given with a corrupt intent is considered a bribe under French law. Even small payments may be considered bribes if circumstances reveal improper intent. Also, the repeated offering of gifts of small value may indicate a corrupt intent.

Any advantages, irrespective of the context in which they are given, ought to be reasonable and proportionate, consistent with customary practices, for the sole benefit of the intended beneficiary (i.e., not extended to persons other than the business person directly concerned), not meant to obtain anything in return, justified by a valid business reason and legally acceptable for the beneficiary. In practice, what matters to the courts is whether the advantage has been offered in order to induce the public official to accomplish (or refrain from accomplishing) or to reward him or her for accomplishing (or for having refrained from accomplishing) an act of his or her function. Otherwise stated, a *quid pro quo* arrangement is prohibited.

Whether a hospitality expense could be considered bribery will need to be determined on a case-by-case basis, taking into account all the facts and circumstances surrounding the case.

4. Facilitation payments

The French Criminal Code does not recognize so-called facilitation payments. Facilitation payments must therefore be analyzed on a case-by-case basis, as previously described, following the general guidelines for assessing any other hospitality acts or advantages granted to public officials. Any person may be held liable for bribery in the event of facilitation payments since these are generally intended to influence the beneficiary.

5. Compliance programs

5.1 Value of a compliance program in mitigating/eliminating the criminal liability of legal entities

The French Criminal Code does not specifically recognize a compliance program as an instruments to mitigate or eliminate the liability of legal entities. That being said, based on French market practice, it appears that many companies implement compliance programs. Moreover, the existence or efficiency of a compliance program may be taken into account before initiating legal proceedings or when deciding whether the legal entity was liable for the relevant offense.

5.2 Absence of a compliance program as a crime

Absence of a compliance program as such does not give rise, under French law, to either civil or criminal liability. Indeed, French law does not require that companies set up compliance programs.

The Bill of Law is expected to introduce a new duty to prevent bribery, which would apply to: (i) companies having more than 500 employees; and (ii) to companies belonging to a group having more than 500 employees with a turnover of more than EUR100 million per year. These companies would be required to adopt a robust compliance program to prevent bribery. Violation of this obligation would give rise to financial sanctions (from EUR200,000 for individuals to EUR1 million for legal persons) and would be decided by a new anti-corruption authority, the National Service for

Prevention and Assisting with Detection of Corruption (the "Agency"), which would also be created under the Bill of Law.

It is also contemplated that companies found guilty of bribery could be required to set up a similar compliance program as the companies subject to duty to prevent bribery. The compliance program would be supervised by the new Agency, under a format inspired by the US concept of corporate monitor.

Finally, another bill of law relating to the creation of a so-called duty of vigilance of parent companies ("Bill of Law II"), which requires setting up measures to counter bribery, is also currently pending. The Bill of Law II was already adopted by the French National Assembly in March 2015, rejected by the Senate at the end of 2015, and again adopted by the National Assembly on March 23, 2016.

The Bill of Law II, if adopted, would create an obligation for certain companies to implement and publish a vigilance program (*plan de vigilance*) aimed at controlling the activities of their subsidiaries, subcontractors and suppliers. The vigilance program would, in particular, include reasonable vigilance measures to prevent active or passive corruption in the company and in the companies controlled by it. Measures would also be required to be adopted to identify and prevent the occurrence of violations of human rights and fundamental freedoms, severe physical or environmental damage, or health risks resulting from the company's activities and from the activities of the companies it controls directly or indirectly, as well as the activities of the subcontractors or suppliers with which it has established business relationships.

Pursuant to the Bill of Law II, the failure to comply with such obligations would give rise to a civil fine of up to EUR10 million. However, the parent company could further be required to compensate losses under the general French law principles of tortious liability referred to in Articles 1382 and 1383 of the French Civil Code.

5.3 Elements of a compliance program

(a) Legal framework

The French Criminal Code, or more generally French law, does not currently recognize nor regulate the elements of a compliance program.

As set out in section 5.2 here above, the Bill of Law is expected to introduce a new duty to prevent bribery, which would require certain companies to adopt a compliance program, the elements of which would be set out by law. The required measures would include, *inter alia*, adopting a code of conduct and a whistleblowing mechanism, carrying out risk mapping exercises and internal or external accounting controls, setting up procedures to assess third parties, disciplinary sanctions, as well as training of managers and other staff exposed to risks of bribery. The new Agency that is contemplated to be created by the Bill of Law is expected to issue recommendations relating to the new duty to prevent bribery, including best practice recommendations as to the compliance program required to be adopted.

(b) Recommended practice

In the absence of case law, French legal commentators recommend that legal entities adopt a robust compliance program as a defense strategy to try to mitigate, or eliminate the legal entity's criminal liability, subject to comments regarding the value of compliance programs in mitigating criminal liability.

In March 2015, the French Central Service for the Prevention of Bribery ("SCPC") issued guidelines, including notably, guidance on the implementation of anti-bribery compliance programs. The SCPC recommends that compliance systems be based on six key principles: (i) management commitment at the highest level; (ii) risk assessment; (iii) setting up a compliance program; (iv) control mechanism; (v) communication, training and follow-up of the anti-corruption compliance program; and (vi) setting up appropriate sanctions in case of violations of the policy.

6. Regulator with jurisdiction to prosecute corruption

The French legal system does not currently have a specific regulator with exclusive responsibilities to prosecute corruption cases.

However, Law No. 2013-1117 of 6 December 2013, relating to the fight against tax fraud and large economic and financial crime, introduced a new prosecuting authority, the Financial Public Prosecutor, which coordinates the enforcement activities in relation to financial crime at a national level. As regards bribery-related offenses, the Financial Public Prosecutor shares its jurisdiction with the financial section of the Paris Prosecutor's Office and specialized inter-regional courts. This new prosecuting authority has a fully dedicated team of specialized assistants and judges and has the authority over a new specialized investigation office, the Central Office for the Fight Against Corruption and Financial and Tax Offenses ("OCLCIFF").

The Bill of Law provides for the creation of the new national Agency for the prevention and detection of corruption, which would be placed under the authority of the Minister of Finance and the Minister of Justice. The Agency would have authority to carry out investigations and mete out sanctions. This new Agency would notably: (i) issue recommendations regarding the duty to prevent bribery and monitor compliance with such duty; (ii) issue recommendations regarding compliance measures adopted by public sector actors, and control quality and efficiency of such measures; (iii) control respect of the French blocking statue in the context of performance of remedial actions required by foreign authorities; and (iv) assume specific monitorship missions in companies found guilty of bribery-related offenses required to set up compliance programs.

Germany

Dr. Andreas Lohner

Andreas Lohner advises and represents companies in corporate governance and compliance-related issues. Over the last years, he has conducted a number of multijurisdictional compliance projects and compliance investigations.

andreas.lohner@bakermckenzie.com
Tel: + 49 89 5 52 38 263

Dr. Thomas Gruetzner

Thomas Gruetzner advises and represents companies in compliance-related disputes and compliance and white-collar crime issues in general. He is a visiting lecturer on criminal law at the Freie Universität Berlin. Thomas has managed numerous investigations for multinational corporations and multinational compliance projects.

thomas.gruetzner@bakermckenzie.com
Tel: + 49 89 5 52 38 243

Dr. Nicolai Behr

Nicolai Behr assists clients in a broad range of compliance and dispute resolution matters, including internal investigations, anti-corruption due diligence, corporate compliance, risk minimization strategies and related civil litigation. He also focuses on corporate litigation and commercial litigation and arbitration.

nicolai.behr@bakermckenzie.com
Tel: + 49 89 5 52 38 243

Baker & McKenzie Partnerschaft von
Rechtsanwälten, Wirtschaftsprüfern und
Steuerberatern mbB
Theatinerstrasse 23
80333 Munich
Germany

1. Domestic bribery (private to public)

1.1 Legal framework

Bribery of public officials (*Vorteilsannahme, Bestechlichkeit, Vorteilsgewährung* and *Bestechung*) is regulated under the German Criminal Code, Sections 331 to 338.

1.2 Definition of bribery

Bribery is committed by anyone who tries to corrupt a public official. German law distinguishes between: (i) giving/taking a bribe; and (ii) giving/taking a bribe as an incentive to perform an act in violation of one's official duties. Whereas the former "broader" form of bribery involves the *discharge* of a duty, the latter form of bribery requires performance of an official act in *violation of an official duty.*

(a) Giving/taking a bribe

Giving bribes (Section 333 German Criminal Code) – This refers to offering, promising or granting a benefit to a public official, for that person or a third person for the discharge of a duty.

Taking bribes (Section 331 German Criminal Code) – This refers to demanding, allowing oneself to be promised, or accepting a benefit for oneself or for a third person for the discharge of a duty.

Under sections (331, 333 German Criminal Code), as long as the public official's duties are not violated, granting or receiving benefits is not punishable if the public official's principal has authorized the benefit before or immediately after its receipt.

(b) Giving/taking a bribe as an incentive to perform an act in violation of one's official duties

Giving bribes as an incentive to the recipient violating his or her official duties (Section 334 German Criminal Code) – This pertains to offering, promising or granting a benefit to a public official for that person or a third person, in return for the fact that he or she performed, or, will, in the future, perform an official act and thereby violated or will violate his or her official duties.

Taking bribes as an incentive to violating one's official duties (Section 332 German Criminal Code) – This constitutes demanding, allowing oneself to be promised, or accepting a benefit for oneself or for a third person in return for the fact that one performed or, will, in the future, perform an official act and thereby violated or will violate one's official duties.

(c) Bribery of a delegate / member of parliament

It is a criminal offense to offer, promise or grant any delegate or member of parliament an undue benefit for that member or a third party as a consideration for an act or omission of an act in relation to that member's or delegate's mandate (Section 108e para. 2 German Criminal Code). In the same token, the delegate / member of parliament can be held criminally liable if he demands or accepts the promise of such an undue benefit (Section 108e para. 1 German Criminal Code).

The term "member of parliament" comprises members of the two federal legislative chambers *Bundestag* and *Bundesrat*, the parliaments of the German Federal States, the European Parliament, elected members of municipal or regional associations, members of a parliamentary assembly of an international organization, and members of a legislative body of a foreign state (Section 108e para. 3 German Criminal Code).

1.3 Definition of public official

The German Criminal Code defines "public official" in Section 11 as anyone who: (1) serves as civil servant or judge; (2) otherwise carries out public official functions; or (3) has otherwise been appointed to serve with a public authority or another agency, or has been commissioned to perform public administrative services regardless of the organizational form chosen to fulfil such duties. The definition of public official is very broad and includes virtually any individual who exercises public functions. In particular, the definition is not limited to individuals in government functions. It also encompasses individuals employed by universities or public hospitals (i.e., all employees of public sector entities). The definition by the German Criminal Code, however, only comprises public officials under German law. For the extension of the Criminal Code to European and international public officials, see Section 3.

1.4 Consequences of bribery

(a) For the individuals involved

- Imprisonment not exceeding three years or a fine (giving and taking bribes; Sections 331 and 333 German Criminal Code)
- Imprisonment from three months (six months for public officials) to five years (giving and taking bribes as an incentive to the recipient's violating his official duties; Sections 332 and 334 German Criminal Code; Bribery of a member of parliament; Section 108e German Criminal Code)
- In aggravated cases, imprisonment for up to 10 years (Section 335 German Criminal Code)
- Fines: Under German criminal law, the fine is sanctioned through a number of daily penalties (up to 24 months); the amount to be paid per daily penalty is determined by the court and depends on the offender's income.

(b) For the company / legal entity

Companies cannot be held criminally liable under German law. However, administrative monetary fines may be imposed directly on companies if a company representative or representative body (e.g., member of the board of directors, general manager) commits a criminal or administrative offense, and the company hereby breaches a company duty or profits in an illegal manner (Section 30 of the German Administrative Offence Act). If a company representative violates his or her supervisory duties, that is, if for example no adequate safeguards to prevent corruption have been implemented, the company representative can be held liable. At the same time, the violation of a supervisory duty by the company representative can be attributed to the company and a monetary fine can be imposed on the company (Section 130 of the German Administrative Offence Act). The fines for a company can be up to EUR10 million per offense.

Moreover, if an employee or company representative commits an administrative or criminal offense, a court can order the forfeiture "of the acquired something" (see Sections 73, 73a of the German Criminal Code, and Section 29a of the German Administrative Offence Act) against the company, meaning that the company may have to release all assets resulting from the commission of the unlawful act. Forfeiture may not be ordered if the company has already been fined (Section 30 para 5 of the German Administrative Offence Act).

In 2014, a discussion around implementing criminal liability for companies emerged. Discussion is ongoing and the outcome is not foreseeable yet.

1.5 Political contributions

Contributions to political parties are regulated by the *Parteispendengesetz*. In general terms, contributions to political parties are unrestricted. However, political parties are subject to a transparency mechanism, requiring the immediate publication of any contribution exceeding EUR50,000 and the corresponding benefactor. Contributions exceeding EUR10,000 (but amounting to less than EUR50,000) will be published approximately 12 to 18 months from the contribution.

1.6 Limitation applicable to hospitality expenses (gifts, travel, meals, entertainment, among others)

The German Criminal Code does not establish quantitative or qualitative limitations on hospitality expenses. However, German courts consider "small" favors permissible and use a very strict approach in determining what is or is not legal. Even inexpensive presents, such as pens or promotional free gifts, may be (but are not necessarily) considered impermissible. Whether a hospitality expense could be considered bribery needs to be assessed on a case-by-case basis, taking into account all available facts. Some public bodies have issued guidelines that provide for a threshold of EUR25. This threshold may serve as a guideline for companies. However, in general, it is advisable not to provide any benefits to public officials.

2. Domestic bribery (private to private)

2.1 Legal framework

Private bribery is regulated under the German Criminal Code, Sections 299 to 301. It is applicable to all employees or agents of a business.

The main section on private bribery has been amended in November 2015.

2.2 Definition of private bribery

Taking bribes in commercial practice – Whosoever as an employee or agent of a company (including the management of a company):

(a) demands, allows himself to be promised or accepts a benefit for himself or third person in a business transaction as consideration for according an unfair preference to third person in the competitive (domestic or foreign) purchase of goods or commercial services; or

(b) without the prior approval of the company demands, allows himself to be promised or accepts a benefit for himself or third person as consideration for an act or omission of an act that violates the duties towards the company shall be held criminally liable (Section 299 para 1 German Criminal Code).

Giving bribes in commercial practice – Whosoever:

1. for competitive purposes offers, promises or grants an employee or agent of a business a benefit for himself or for a third person in a business transaction as consideration for such employee's or agent's according him or another person an unfair preference in the purchase of goods or commercial services;

2. without the prior approval of the company offers, promises or grants an employee or agent of a business a benefit for himself or for a third person as consideration for an act or omission of an act that violates the duties towards the company shall be held criminally liable (Section 299 para 2 German Criminal Code).

2.3 Consequences of private bribery

(a) For the individuals involved

- Imprisonment not exceeding three years or a fine

- In aggravated cases, imprisonment for up to five years

(b) For the company / legal entity

See Section 1.4 (b).

2.4 Limitation applicable to hospitality expenses (gifts, travel, meals, entertainment, among others)

The German Criminal Code does not establish quantitative or qualitative limitations on hospitality expenses. Usually, it is permissible to offer private sector business associates a favor to enhance the goodwill of the (future) business partner or to reward him or her for past actions. This behavior becomes impermissible when a court sees it as an attempt to influence future business decisions. Presents of low value or an invitation to a middle-class restaurant are generally socially acceptable. To determine social acceptability, courts take into account the particular circumstances of the case and decide whether granting a specific favor could have led to favorable treatment in an unfair manner or to a violation of the recipient's duties towards the company. In particular, a court would consider the benefit, the personal background of the acting persons, the financial value of the favor and the business relationship between the giver and the recipient's employer. Even though the courts do not state which favors are socially acceptable, general opinion contends that favors granted to employees or agents of private entities are less likely to be considered socially unacceptable than comparable favors granted to public officials.

3. Corruption of foreign public officials

3.1 Legal framework

Bribery of foreign public officials usually takes place abroad (i.e., outside Germany). German criminal law applies extraterritorially if there is a connection to Germany (i.e., if one of the participants was a German citizen or if one of the actions in connection with the bribing of a public official took place in Germany). Action in this sense could be the approval of a bribe payment via email or via phone and the granting of funds for the bribe payments abroad, among others.

German Criminal law distinguishes between:

(i) public officials of the European Union;

(ii) public officials of foreign countries (including member states of the European Union) and international organizations; and

(iii) foreign delegates / members of parliament.

3.2 Bribery of public officials of the European Union

Public officials of the European Union are to be treated as German public officials. Therefore, Section 2 above applies.

3.3 Bribery of public officials of foreign countries and international organizations

The new Section 335a German Criminal Code extends in particular the scope of Section 334 of the German Criminal Code, that is, offering, promising or giving bribes as an incentive to the recipient's future violation of his official duties (see Section 1.2) to foreign public officials. Foreign public officials are equally liable if they demand, allow themselves to be promised or accept a bribe as incentive for the future violation of their official duties.

Foreign public officials include public officials of a foreign state (including public officials of a member state of the European Union) or international organization, any person entrusted to exercise a public function with or for an authority of a foreign state or international organization, or soldiers of a foreign state or international organization.

3.4 Bribery of foreign delegates / members of parliament

Bribery of foreign delegates / members of parliament may be covered by two sections. The first one is Section 108e German Criminal Code (see above Section 1.2 (c)). Similarly, under Section 2 of the Law against International Bribery, it is prohibited to offer, promise or give a benefit to a member of a legislative body of a foreign state or a parliamentary assembly of an international organization as consideration for an action or omission in connection with his mandate or tasks, with the intent to obtain or secure for oneself or a third party an undue advantage in the international competition.

3.5 Consequences of corruption of foreign public officials

(a) For the individuals involved

- Imprisonment from three months (six months for public officials) to five years (giving and taking bribes as an incentive for the recipient's violation of his or her official duties)

- In aggravated cases, imprisonment for up to 10 years
- Daily fine for up to 24 months (a judge will ultimately determine the daily penalty, taking the financial situation of the individual into account)

(b) For the legal entity

See Section 1.4 (b).

3.6 Limitation applicable to hospitality expenses (gifts, travel, meals, entertainment, among others)

See Section 2.4.

4. Facilitation payments

The German Criminal Code does not distinguish between facilitation payments and other payments. No facilitation payment exception applies under German law. Therefore, it is advisable to refrain from facilitation payments.

5. Compliance programs

5.1 Value of a compliance program in mitigating/eliminating the criminal liability of legal entities

The German Criminal Code neither imposes criminal liability on legal entities nor expressly allows for compliance programs to mitigate or eliminate liability. However, legal entities may mitigate the risk of being exposed to fines under the German Administrative Offence Act (see 5.3.).

5.2 Absence of a compliance program as a crime

The German Criminal Code does not recognize the absence of a compliance program as a crime. However, failure to implement adequate measures to supervise the company and its employees and to prevent illegal conduct may constitute an administrative offense by the company and the company representatives (see Section 1.4). If misconduct known to the management continues, there is a risk that failure to stop the misconduct can be viewed as aiding and abetting by the management and thus, could cause its criminal liability.

5.3 Elements of a compliance program

(a) Legal framework

The German Criminal Code does not recognize nor regulate the elements of a compliance program. There are some special regulations that apply to, for example, financial institutions. Provisions in the German Administrative Offence Act, the German Stock Corporation Act and the German Corporate Governance Codex require companies on an abstract basis to implement a compliance program.

(b) Recommended practice

German civil courts are in the process of establishing a best practice. The District Court in Munich recently handed down a decision that defines the compliance-related duties of the board of directors of a German stock corporation. The key points of the decision are the following:

(a) As a consequence of his duty of legality, each board member is obliged to organize and monitor the company in a way that no violations of law such as bribe payments to foreign public officials or foreign private persons occur. A board member violates his duties if he implements a deficient compliance system and if he does not sufficiently monitor the compliance system.

(b) In case of a respective risk exposure, a board member only complies with his organizational duty if he implements a compliance organization aiming at damage prevention and risk control. Decisive factors for the extent of the compliance organization are type, size and organization of the company, applicable laws, geographical presence and previous compliance incidents.

(c) The adherence to the duty of legality and therefore the implementation of an effective compliance system are joint obligations of all board members. The board is obliged to obtain on a continuous basis comprehensive information about known compliance incidents. The board must assess whether the implemented compliance system is adequate to prevent violations against compulsory laws.

(d) Cross-border bribe payments constitute violations of the law and may not be justified by arguing that economic success in corrupt markets would otherwise not be possible. Strict rules apply to the implementation of a compliance system to prevent bribe payments.

6. Regulator with jurisdiction to prosecute corruption

There is no specific office or institution that exercises exclusive responsibility to prosecute corruption cases. Provided an initial suspicion of corruption persists, any public prosecutor may begin to investigate facts he becomes aware of. However, within the public prosecutor's service, certain prosecutors specialize in white collar crimes such as corruption.

Hungary

Zoltan Barakonyi

Zoltan Hegymegi-Barakonyi is highly experienced in competition law and compliance matters, including litigation work in these areas. He represents companies in unfair competition, cartel, dominant position and merger control cases, and advises on antitrust and other corporate compliance programs. Zoltan represents clients before Hungarian and EU authorities in various antitrust and anti-corruption cases. He works for major international and Hungarian companies in a number of sectors, including the banking, energy, telecommunications, automotive and pharmaceutical industries. He practices law in Hungary as well as at EU level, including the European Commission and the Court of Justice of the European Union.

zoltan.barakonyi@bakermckenzie.com
Tel: +36 1 302 3330 316

Janos Puskas

Janos Puskas specializes in compliance and investigations, government enforcement and litigation. As an investigation practitioner, he assists clients with internal and government investigations, anti-corruption due diligence, compliance and ethics inquiries, risk assessment, risk minimization strategies, and creating and implementing compliance programs. He also focuses on disclosure issues and represents clients in civil and criminal procedures initiated in relation to violations. Janos has a proven track record in government enforcement cases, in which he represented several multinational companies in administrative litigation against the regulator, including extraordinary judicial review procedures before the Supreme Court.

janos.puskas@bakermckenzie.com
Tel: + 36 1 302 3330 367

Kajtár Takács Hegymegi-Barakonyi Baker & McKenzie Ügyvédi Iroda
Dorottya utca 6.
1051 Budapest
Hungary

1. Domestic bribery (private to public)

1.1 Legal framework

Bribery of public officials is regulated under Articles 293-294 and 298-300 of Act C of 2012 on Hungarian Criminal Code. Additionally, Act CIV of 2001 on Measures Applicable to Legal Entities under Criminal Law contains relevant provisions.

1.2 Definition of bribery

Individuals can commit bribery, but the acts of public officials in this regard also constitute a crime. In addition, under the given circumstances, legal entities may be criminally punished for bribery of public officials.

(a) By an individual

This refers to any person who attempts to influence a public official in connection with his or her actions in an official capacity by giving or promising an (unlawful) advantage to such person or to another person on account of such person (active corruption).

(b) By a public official

This refers to any public official who requests or accepts an (unlawful) advantage in connection with his or her actions in an official capacity, for himself or herself, or for a third party, or accepts a promise of such an advantage, or is in league with the person requesting or accepting the advantage for himself or herself, or for a third party on his or her behest (passive corruption).

1.3 Definition of public official

The Hungarian Criminal Code has a broad definition of public official, and includes any individual that exercises public functions. This concept includes not only public servants, but also members of parliament, persons working at public authorities (if such activity is attached to the public function of such authority), notaries and bailiffs, among others.

1.4 Consequences of bribery

In most cases, punishment may be reduced without limitation (or dismissed in special cases) if, before authorities discover the bribe, a voluntary disclosure is made revealing the circumstances of the bribe, and the (unlawful) advantage is surrendered.

(a) For the individuals involved

The Hungarian Criminal Code provides for more stringent penalties for public officials than for individuals that corrupt public officials. Company executives may be criminally punished if they fail to exercise proper oversight and such failure results in public bribery. The penalties are the following:

- For individuals corrupting public officials
  - Up to two years in jail for negligent criminal offense if a company executive or anyone being in an oversight function at a company (e.g., a compliance officer) fails to exercise proper oversight in connection with the prevention of such crime
  - Up to three years in jail for corruption; also if committed by an executive officer/person entitled to supervise the economic operator
  - Up to five years in jail if the advantage is to induce the public official to breach his or her official duty, to exceed his or her competence, or abuse his or her position of authority

- For corrupted public officials
  - Up to three years in jail for failure to report a bribery known by him
  - Up to five years in jail for the basic scenario (see above as passive corruption)
  - Up to eight years in jail if committed by a high-ranking public official; if the public official breaches his or her official duty, exceeds his or her competence or abuses his or her position of authority to gain the unlawful advantage; also, if it's committed in criminal association or on a commercial scale
  - Up to ten years if more serious circumstances are present

(b) For the company / legal entity (if the legal entity benefited from an intentional crime that was caused by its executive, employee or board member)

- A fine of an amount three times the required advantage (but at least HUF500,000, or approximately EUR1,625)
- Dissolution of the legal entity
- Prohibition from carrying out certain activities (as determined by the court)
- Debarment from public contracting and state/EU subsidies

1.5 Political contributions

Contributions to political parties are regulated under Act XXXIII of 1989 of the Operation and Financial Management of Political Parties. In general terms, contributions to political parties are allowed only by natural persons and, with narrow exceptions, prohibited by legal entities.

1.6 Limitation applicable to hospitality expenses (gifts, travel, meals, entertainment, among others)

The Criminal Code does not establish quantitative or qualitative limitations on hospitality expenses. Case law has established the following two criteria to determine when a hospitality expense could be considered bribery:

(a) The hospitality offered or received is not "socially acceptable."

(b) The hospitality offered or received may presumably affect the acts of the receiver in connection with his or her official function.

Whether a hospitality expense could be considered bribery will need to be determined on a case-by-case basis, taking into account all the facts and circumstances surrounding the case and applying the two criteria referred to previously. Also, the Code of Ethics for Government Officials has established that the value of an acceptable general gift may not be more than 10 percent of the remuneration base (approximately EUR12).

More stringent hospitality expense limitations may apply in the pharmaceutical / life sciences industry.

It is important to mention that Act XXXVI of 2012 on the Hungarian Parliament provides that members of the Parliament (MPs) may accept a gift or benefit of value that is equal to or less than the base amount of their monthly remuneration (approximately EUR800), which is related to their mandate.

This specific provision does not give MPs any exemption from the anti-bribery rules of the Hungarian Criminal Code.

2. Domestic bribery (private to private)

2.1 Legal framework

Private bribery is regulated under Articles 290-291, 295-296, 298-300 of Act C of 2012 on Hungarian Criminal Code; and Act CIV of 2001 on Measures Applicable to Legal Entities under Criminal Law.

2.2 Definition of private bribery

(a) General

Any person who gives or promises unlawful advantage to a person working for or on behalf of an economic operator, or to another person on account of such employee, to induce him or her to breach his or her duties commits active corruption.

Any person who requests or accepts an unlawful advantage in connection with his or her activities performed for or on behalf of an economic operator, for himself or herself or for a third party, or accepts a promise of such an advantage, or is in league with the person requesting or accepting the advantage for a third party on his or her behest commits passive corruption.

(b) In judicial proceedings

Any person who promises or gives an unlawful advantage to another person for himself or herself or for a third party for him or her to refrain from acting in accordance with his or her duty or in the exercise of his or her rights in court, arbitration or other judicial proceedings or proceedings of an international criminal court installed under international convention promulgated by an act, or under a statutory resolution adopted by the United Nations Security Council, or by the Court of Justice of the European Union commits active corruption in the context of a judicial proceeding.

Any person who requests or accepts an unlawful advantage to refrain from acting in accordance with his or her duty or in the exercise of his or her rights in a court, arbitration or other judicial proceedings, or proceedings of an international criminal court installed under international convention promulgated by an act, or under a statutory resolution adopted by the United Nations Security Council, or by the Court of Justice of the European Union, for himself or herself or for a third party, or accepts a promise of such an advantage, or is in league with the person requesting or accepting the advantage for a third party on his or her behest commits passive corruption in the context of a judicial proceeding.

2.3 Consequences of private bribery

In most of the cases, punishment may be reduced without limitation (or dismissed in special cases) in the case of a voluntary disclosure, including revealing the circumstances and surrendering the (unlawful) advantage before authorities come to know about the case.

(a) For the individuals involved

- For corrupting individuals
  - Up to three years in jail for basic commercial bribery
  - Up to five years in jail if corruption is committed against a person entitled to act individually on behalf of the economic operator, committed in criminal association, or on a commercial scale
  - Up to eight years in jail if more serious circumstances are present
- For corrupted individuals
  - Up to three years in jail for being corrupted
  - Up to five years in jail if breach of duty for the unlawful advantage by a person entitled to act individually on behalf of the economic operator

- o Up to 10 years in jail if committed in criminal association or on a commercial scale, or if more serious circumstances are present

(b) For the company / legal entity

- As defined in Section 1.4 (b)

2.4 Limitation applicable to private/commercial hospitality expenses (gifts, travel, meals, entertainment, among others)

The Criminal Code does not establish quantitative or qualitative limitations on private/commercial hospitality expenses. Case law has established two criteria to determine whether a hospitality payment could be considered private/commercial bribery:

(a) The hospitality offered or received is not "socially acceptable."

(b) The hospitality offered or received could affect the acts of the receiver in connection with his or her function.

Whether a hospitality expense could be considered bribery will need to be determined on a case-by-case basis, taking into account all the facts and circumstances surrounding the case and applying the two criteria referred to previously. In general, hospitality expenses are socially more acceptable in the private sector.

3. Corruption of foreign public officials

3.1 Legal framework

Corruption of foreign public officials is regulated under Articles 293(3) and 294(4) of Act C of 2012 on Hungarian Criminal Code and by Act CIV of 2001 on Measures Applicable to Legal Entities under Criminal Law.

3.2 Definition of corruption of foreign public officials

Please see the definition in Sections 1.2 and 2.2.

3.3 Definition of foreign public official

With regard to this crime, a foreign public official means:

- Any person that has a legislative, judicial, administrative or law enforcement function in a foreign country
- Any person serving in an international organization created under an international treaty, whose activities form part of the organization's activities
- Any person elected to serve in the general assembly or body of an international organization created under an international treaty (including members of the European Parliament elected abroad)
- Any member of an international court that is vested with jurisdiction over the territory or over the citizens of Hungary, and any person serving in such international court, whose activities form part of the court's activities

3.4 Consequences of corruption of foreign public officials

(a) For the individuals involved

- Please see the definition in Section 1.4 (a).

(b) For the legal entity

- Please see the definition in Section 1.4 (b).

3.5 Limitation applicable to hospitality expenses (gifts, travel, meals, entertainment, among others)

As defined in Section 1.6.

4. Facilitation payments

The Criminal Code does not recognize so-called facilitation payments. However, case law has established two criteria to determine whether a payment could be considered as a corrupt payment:

(a) The payment offered or received is not "socially acceptable."

(b) The payment offered or received may affect the act of the receiver in connection with his or her function.

As Hungarian anti-corruption rules are rather strict, even if such facilitation payment is lawful in the country of the person involved, it may still constitute a crime under Hungarian law.

5. Compliance programs

5.1 Value of a compliance program in mitigating/eliminating the criminal liability of legal entities

As to corporate criminal liability, the Hungarian Criminal Code does not recognize a compliance programs as an instrument to mitigate or eliminate the liability of legal entities before the crime of corruption has been committed.

As to personal criminal liability of corporate executives or employees being in an oversight function (e.g., a compliance officer), an existing and proactively managed compliance program may provide immunity from personal criminal liability in connection with negligent criminal offense for the failure to exercise proper oversight.

5.2 Absence of a compliance program as a crime

Under the Hungarian Criminal Code, the absence of a compliance program itself is not a crime. However, the absence of a compliance program can be effectively used by the public prosecutor in the case of charging corporate executives or employees being in an oversight function (e.g., a compliance officer), in connection with negligent criminal offense for the failure to exercise proper oversight.

5.3 Elements of a compliance program

(a) Legal framework

Act CLXV of 2013 on Complaints and Whistleblowing prescribes certain data protection, as well as procedural and other legal requirements for whistleblowing systems operated by employers or their parent companies in the context of their compliance program. Mandatory criminal reporting obligation has also been introduced in order to fight white-collar crime, which is an unusually stringent regulation within the Hungarian legal system.

(b) Recommended practice

Employees, contracting parties and third parties who have legitimate interest to remedy the infringement may file a report by submitting their information and a declaration that they are acting as whistleblowers in good faith. The operation of a whistleblowing system is optional for the companies; however, if they have any whistleblowing system (including a global whistleblowing system available to the employees of a local subsidiary), it must comply with the new law. The whistleblowing rules shall be published on the website of the company in Hungarian; even if the information mostly concerns employees, the company must submit an application to the Hungarian Authority of Data Protection and Freedom of Information for registration into the data protection register to be able to process such data.

Failure to meet this requirement may lead to an investigation by the Hungarian Authority for Data Protection and Freedom of Information and may affect the validity of an employer's actions based on such codes of conduct.

Pursuant to the Act on Complaints and Whistleblowing, if the internal investigation carried out on the basis of the whistleblowing establishes that a criminal offense (not limited to bribery, but also including corporate fraud or any criminal offense) was committed, disclosure to the criminal authorities is mandatory.

6. Regulator with jurisdiction to prosecute corruption

All corruption activity is subject to public prosecution, but investigating authorities may differ, according to the crime concerned. Pursuant to Act XIX of 1998 on Criminal Proceedings, most crimes of bribery are investigated by the police but in some cases (e.g., corruption in connection with a high-ranking public official, failure to report a bribery and influence peddling in connection with foreign public official), the public prosecutor's office has jurisdiction to conduct the investigation.

Italy

Aurelio Giovannelli

International partner of Baker & McKenzie since 1989, Aurelio Giovannelli assists Italian and foreign clients in various industries in organizing and managing internal investigations, setting up compliance programs, and developing and implementing risk assessment functions, codes of conduct and whistle blowing tools. Aurelio is former chair of the Firm's EMEA Compliance Steering Committee and is a current member of its Global and EMEA Compliance Steering Committees.

aurelio.giovannelli@bakermckenzie.com
Tel: +39 06 44 063 239

Studio Professionale Associato a
Baker & McKenzie
Viale di Villa Massimo 57
00161 Rome
Italy

Roberto Cursano

Roberto Cursano regularly advises on pharmaceutical and healthcare law, administrative and public procurement law, and litigation before the administrative courts. Over the course of his practice, he has successfully assisted several multinational companies in regulatory and compliance matters and in setting up internal compliance programs in line with Italian anti-corruption law (Legislative Decree 231/2001).

roberto.cursano@bakermckenzie.com
Tel: +39 06 44 06 3241

Enrico Maria Mancuso

Enrico Maria Mancuso's practice focuses on the area of dispute resolution in criminal matters. He also regularly assists domestic and foreign clients on various aspects of corporate criminal law, compliance issues, bribery and corruption. Enrico has experience in tax crimes, health and safety issues related to criminal proceedings, bankruptcy, and environmental compliance and offenses. Throughout his career, he has defended several companies and individuals in major litigation cases.

enricomaria.mancuso@bakermckenzie.com
Tel: +39 02 76231 461

Studio Professionale Associato a
Baker & McKenzie
Piazza Meda, 3
Milan 20121
Italy

1. Domestic bribery (private to public)

1.1 Legal framework

Private-to-public bribery offenses are governed by Sections 317, 318, 319, 319-*quarter*, 320, 321 and 322 of the Italian Criminal Code (ICC).

1.2 Definition of bribery

Italian law criminalizes both "active bribery," namely the conduct of a person who corrupts or tries to corrupt a public official, and "passive bribery," namely the conduct of the corrupted public official.

Bribery is defined as offering, promising, requesting or receiving, or accepting a promise to receive money or other advantages for the public official to perform his or her functions (Section 318 of the ICC) or for the public official to omit or delay, or having omitted or delayed, an act relating to his or her office, or to act or having acted in breach of his or her official duties ("proper bribery" - see Section 319 of the ICC).

The meaning of "advantages" with respect to bribery offenses is very broad and includes any advantage for the recipient of any kind, material or moral, pecuniary or not.

The Supreme Court, in a series of judgments, has affirmed that in order to constitute corruption, the offer or the commitment to offer money or other advantages must be suitable to achieve the purpose of the crime, that is, suitable to improperly influence the performance of the public official's duties. This must be evaluated having regard to objective and subjective situations, such as the type or amount of the compensation paid and the economic position of the beneficiary of the payment, which must be such as to determine the likely possibility that the beneficiary is influenced by the offer and is induced to accept it to perform his or her duties.

In case the private party is forced by the public official to give or promise a bribe, this conduct constitutes the offense of "extortion by a public official" (*concussion* - see Section 317 of the ICC), for which only the public official is held criminally liable, with the private party being the victim of the crime.

However, following the recent reform of Italian anti-corruption legislation, a new offense has been introduced, that of "unlawful inducement to give or promise money or other benefits" (see Section 319-*quarter* of the ICC), which punishes the public official who, by abusing his or her position or authority, induces a person to give or promise unduly to him or her or a third person money or other benefits. In such a case, the private party who gives or promises money or other benefits is punished as well (although the penalty applicable to the private party is less severe than the one for the public official).

Finally, the less serious offense of "inducement to bribery" (see Section 322 of the ICC) occurs when a private party offers or promises undue money or other advantages to a public official and the offer or promise is not accepted, or when the public official solicits an undue promise or giving of money or other advantages that is not carried out by the private party.

1.3 Definition of public official

The definition of "public official" under the ICC is quite broad and includes any individual who performs a public function, "either legislative, judicial or administrative" (see Section 357, Paragraph 1 of the ICC). For the same criminal purposes, "an administrative function is public if it is regulated by public law provisions and by acts of a public authority, and is characterized by the forming and manifestation of the public administration's will or by a procedure involving an authority's powers or powers to certify" (see Section 357, Paragraph 2 of the ICC). Examples of "public officials" are members of the Parliament, regional councillors, judges and their consultants, public notaries and police officers.

Under Italian Criminal law, bribery offenses apply to public officials as well as to persons in charge of a public service (*incaricato di pubblico servizio*), which are those who, under any title, perform a public service, namely, "an activity governed by the same forms as the public function, but characterized by the lack of its typical powers, and with the exclusion of simple ordinary tasks and merely material work" (see Section 358 of the ICC). Examples of "persons in charge of a public service" are state and public administration employees lacking the typical powers of a public authority, such as electricity and gas men, security guards and the manager of a public landfill.

1.4 Consequences of bribery

(a) For the individuals involved

A public official may be punished with imprisonment from one year to six years in the case of bribery for the exercise of his or her functions (see Section 318 of the ICC) and with imprisonment from six years to 10 years in the case of proper bribery (see Section 319 of the ICC).

The penalties described are reduced by not more than one-third in the case of bribery of persons in charge of a public service.

The briber faces the same criminal consequences as the public official or the person in charge of a public service to whom he or she gives, offers or promises money or any other undue advantage.

(b) For the company / legal entity

Under Section 25 of Legislative Decree No. 231, dated 8 June 2001 ("Decree 231"), the company is punishable with the following:

- A fine of up to 200 quotas in the case of bribery of a public official for the exercise of his or her functions under Section 318 of the ICC

- A fine from 200 to 600 quotas in the case of proper bribery under Section 319 of the ICC

The amount of a quota ranges from a minimum of EUR 258 to a maximum of EUR 1,549.

The following restraining measures may also be applied to the company:

- Temporary suspension from conducting business

- Suspension or revocation of any authorizations, licenses or permits held by the legal entity with respect to the business unit connected with the crime

- Prohibition from negotiating and entering into contracts with public administration entities, except for contracts relating to public services

- Exclusion from subsidies and contributions, or revocation of any subsidy and contribution already granted to the company

- Prohibition from advertising the company's goods and/or services

Restraining measures may also be applied to the company as a pre-judgment remedy under certain circumstances.

1.5 Political contributions

The regulation concerning private contributions to political parties has been recently amended by Law Decree No. 149/2013.

According to this decree, private contributions to political parties are allowed under the following restrictions:

- A natural person cannot donate money or contribute goods or services in favor of a single political party, in any form and in any way provided, even through a third person or controlled companies for a total amount exceeding EUR100,000 per year. Such limits do not apply to legacies to political parties.

- A legal entity / company cannot donate money or contribute goods or services, in any form and in any way provided, in favor of political parties for an amount exceeding EUR100,000 per year. Such restriction does not apply to transfers of money or of capital in general between political parties.

Donations have to be made through a bank or post office or by any method that ensures their traceability.

Violations of the regulation concerning limits and modalities of private contributions to political parties are sanctioned with administrative fines.

Additionally, under Section 7 of Law No. 195, dated 2 May 1974, as recently amended by Law No. 96, dated 6 July 2012, private companies cannot, in any manner, directly or indirectly, finance or give contributions to any politician and political party, including their political-organizational structures and parliamentary groups, unless such financing/contributions have been deliberated on by the relevant managing body and duly registered in the balance sheet. The violation of this provision is punishable with imprisonment from six months up to four years and a fine of up to three times the amounts paid in breach of the law.

1.6 Limitation applicable to hospitality expenses (gifts, travel, meals, entertainment, among others)

Italian criminal law does not expressly prohibit or restrict the giving of gifts, travel expenses, meals or entertainment to public officials or persons in charge of a public service. However, those expenses may represent "undue advantage," the giving/offering/promising or receiving/accepting of which is forbidden by the ICC.

Italian law also does not expressly provide for currency limits generally applicable to gifts and hospitality. However, according to case law, gifts of small value (*modico valore*) are not *per se* prohibited as they do not fall within the scope of anti-bribery offenses. Small-value gifts may be relevant under anti-bribery law in cases where they are offered and/or received repeatedly and in certain specific circumstances (for example, there is a pending negotiation between the parties, or a business decision is imminent).

The amount of this "small value" is not expressly set by law. Some guidance on this aspect may be found in Italian case law. Additionally, the Italian government recently enacted a regulation with a code of conduct for public employees (Presidential Decree no. 62 of 16 April 2013), which provides that a public employee shall not accept, for himself or herself or for others, gifts or other advantages. However, an exception exists for public officials where the following conditions are met:

(a) The gratuities do not exceed the value of EUR150. Lower limits to gratuities may be provided by the internal code of ethics of each public entity.

(b) Such gratuities present no inducement and are given only for courtesy purposes.

As general principles, the following seem worth noting:

- The repeated offering/receiving of gifts and hospitality (i.e., to the benefit of the same person or provided on a regular basis) should generally be discouraged, irrespective of their value.

- Gifts and hospitality, even of small value, should be discouraged in the context of pending negotiations, tenders or imminent business decisions between the parties and in general, in the event that under concrete circumstances, they may be capable of persuading the beneficiary to do or not do something in breach of the latter's duties.

2. Domestic bribery (private to private)

2.1 Legal framework

The offense of private-to-private bribery is provided for under Section 2635 of the Italian Civil Code.

2.2 Definition of private bribery

Section 2635 of the Italian Civil Code, as recently amended, introduces the offense of "corruption between private parties," which punishes the directors, general managers, executives entrusted with the preparation of the company's accounting documents, statutory auditors, liquidators or anyone subjected to their direction or supervision who, as a consequence of the giving or promising of money or other advantage, for their own or others' benefit, perform or omit to perform actions in violation of the obligations pertaining to their office or of their duty of loyalty, causing harm to their company.

In such a case, the person who gives or promises money or other advantages to the subjects indicated above is also punished.

2.3 Consequences of private-to-private bribery

(a) For the individuals involved

Pursuant to Section 2635 of the Italian Civil Code, directors, general managers and executives entrusted with the preparation of the company's accounting documents, as well as statutory auditors and liquidators, may be charged with imprisonment from one year to three years.

The penalty for offenses committed by anyone subject to the direction or supervision of the above individuals is imprisonment for up to one year and six months.

The person who gives or promises money or other advantages to the subjects indicated above faces the same criminal consequences as the corrupted individual.

(b) For the company / legal entity

The company/entity that the person who gives or promises money or other advantages to the subjects set forth in Section 2635 of the Italian Civil Code belongs to may be held liable, pursuant to Decree 231.

Under Section 25-*ter* of Decree 231, the company/entity is punishable with a fine from 200 to 400 quotas.

In case the company/entity obtained a considerable profit as a result of the commission of the crime, the pecuniary sanction is increased by one-third.

2.4 Limitation applicable to hospitality expenses (gifts, travel, meals, entertainment, among others)

Italian criminal law does not expressly prohibit or restrict the giving of gifts, travel expenses, meals or entertainment to private persons. However, those expenses may represent undue advantage, the giving/offering/promising or receiving/accepting of which is forbidden by the ICC.

Italian law also does not expressly provide for currency limits generally applicable to gifts and hospitality. However, according to case law, gifts of small value (*modico valore*) are not *per se* prohibited as they do not fall within the scope of anti-bribery offenses. Small-value gifts may be relevant under the anti-bribery law in cases where they are offered and/or received repeatedly and in certain specific circumstances (for example, there is a pending negotiation between the parties or a business decision is imminent).

The amount of this small value is not expressly set by law. Some guidance on this aspect may be found in Italian case law. Additionally, the Italian government recently enacted a regulation with a code of conduct for public employees (Presidential Decree no. 62 of 16 April 2013), which provides that a public employee shall not accept, for himself or herself or for others, gifts or other advantages.

However, as an exception, public officials are allowed to accept gifts or other advantages provided that the following conditions are met:

(a) The gratuities do not exceed the value of EUR150.

(b) Such gratuities present no inducement and are given only for courtesy purposes.

As general principles, the following seem worth noting:

- The repeated offering/receiving of gifts and hospitality (i.e., to the benefit of the same person or provided on a regular basis) should generally be discouraged, irrespective of their value.

- Gifts and hospitality, even of small value, should be discouraged in the context of pending negotiations, tenders or imminent business decisions between the parties and in general, in the event that, under concrete circumstances, they may be capable of persuading the beneficiary to do or not do something in breach of the latter's duties.

3. Corruption of foreign public officials

3.1 Legal framework

Corruption of foreign officials is regulated under Section 322-*bis* of the ICC.

3.2 Definition of corruption of foreign public officials

Section 322-*bis* of the ICC extends the scope of (domestic) bribery offenses to include bribery of public officials in EU institutions or EU member states. Therefore, with respect to EU public officials, the general definition of corruption of a public official, as follows, remains valid:

Bribery: This refers to the offer, promise, request or receipt, or acceptance of the promise to receive money or other advantages for the public official to perform his or her functions (see Section 318 of the ICC), or for the public official to omit or delay, or having omitted or delayed, an act relating to his or her office, or to act or having acted in breach of his or her official duties (proper bribery - see Section 319 of the ICC).

Italian law also criminalizes the bribery of non-EU foreign public officials, that is, public officials not working in EU institutions or bodies, or not performing a public function in an EU member state.

However, with respect to non-EU foreign public officials, only active bribery is punished, namely the offering or promising of money or other advantages for the foreign public official to perform his or her functions (see Section 318 of the ICC) or for the foreign public official to omit or delay, or having omitted or delayed, an act relating to his or her office or to act or having acted in breach of his or her official duties (proper bribery - see Section 319 of the ICC), provided that:

1. the offense is committed in order to obtain an undue advantage in the framework of an international business transaction; or

2. the offense is perpetrated for the purpose of obtaining or maintaining a business or financial activity.

In this case, the non-EU foreign public official is not punished under Italian law.

3.3 Definition of foreign public official

Pursuant to Section 322-*bis* of the ICC, bribery offenses apply to the following categories:

- Members of the European Commission, of the European Parliament, of the European Court of Justice and of the European Court of Auditors

- Officials and agents hired by contract pursuant to the Staff Regulations of European Officials or to the Conditions of Employment regarding European agents

- Persons delegated by the member states or by any public or private entity at the European Union, who perform functions equivalent to those performed by officials and agents of the European Union

- Members and employees of entities instituted pursuant to the Treaties establishing the European Union

- Those who, in the context of the other member states of the European Union, perform functions or activities equivalent to those performed by Italian public officials and persons in charge of a public service

- Judges, prosecutors, deputy prosecutors, officials and agents of the International Criminal Court; the persons delegated by the States Parties to the Treaty establishing the International Criminal Court who perform functions equivalent to those performed by the officers or agents of the Court itself, and members and employees of entities instituted pursuant to the Treaty establishing the International Criminal Court

All the above subjects are considered "public officials" if they perform functions corresponding to those performed by (domestic) public officials, or "persons in charge of public services" in all the other cases.

"Non-EU foreign public officials" are all persons performing functions or activities corresponding to those performed by (domestic) public officials and persons in charge of a public service in non-EU states or public international organizations.

For the definition of "public official" and "person in charge of a public service" under Italian law, see Section 1.3.

3.4 Consequences of corruption of foreign public officials

(a) For the individuals involved

As far as bribery relating to EU foreign public officials is concerned, the official may be punished with imprisonment from one year to six years in the case of bribery for the exercise of his or her functions (see Section 318 of the ICC), and with imprisonment from six years to 10 years in the case of proper bribery.

The abovementioned sanctions are reduced by not more than one-third when the corrupted individual performs functions and activities corresponding to those performed by persons in charge of a public service under Italian law.

The briber faces the same criminal consequences as the EU foreign public official/person in charge of a public service to whom he or she gives, offers or promises money or any other undue advantage.

As to bribery of non-EU foreign public officials, only the briber may be punished, with imprisonment from one year to six years in the case of bribery for the exercise of his or her functions (see Section 318 of the ICC), and with imprisonment from six years to 10 years in the case of proper bribery.

The abovementioned sanctions are reduced by not more than one-third when the corrupt individual performs functions and activities corresponding to those performed by persons in charge of a public service under Italian law.

In this case, the non-EU foreign public official/person in charge of a public service may not be punished under Italian law.

(b) For the legal entity

Under Section 25 of Decree 231, the company may be punished with any of the following:

- A fine of up to 200 quotas in the case of bribery of a foreign public official for the exercise of his or her functions under Section 318 of the ICC
- A fine from 200 to 600 quotas, when proper bribery is committed

The following restraining measures may be also applied to the company:

- Temporary suspension from conducting business
- Suspension or revocation of any authorizations, licenses or permits held by the legal entity with respect to the business unit connected with the crime
- Prohibition from negotiating and entering into contracts with public administration entities, except for contracts relating to public services
- Exclusion from subsidies and contributions, or revocation of any subsidy and contribution already granted to the company
- Prohibition from advertising the company's goods and/or services

Restraining measures could be applied to the company even as a pre-judgment remedy under certain circumstances.

3.5 Limitation applicable to hospitality expenses (gifts, travel, meals, entertainment, among others)

Italian criminal law does not expressly prohibit or restrict the giving of gifts, travel expenses, meals or entertainment to foreign public officials or foreign persons in charge of a public service. However, those expenses may represent undue advantage, the giving/offering/promising or receiving/accepting of which is forbidden by the ICC.

Italian law also does not expressly provide for currency limits generally applicable to gifts and hospitality. However, according to case law, gifts of small value (*modico valore*) are not *per se* prohibited as they do not fall within the scope of anti-bribery offenses. Small-value gifts may be relevant under the anti-bribery law in cases where they are offered and/or received repeatedly and in certain specific circumstances (for example, there is a pending negotiation between the parties or a business decision is imminent).

The amount of this small value is not expressly set by law. Some guidance on this aspect may be found in Italian case law. Additionally, the Italian government recently enacted a regulation with a code of conduct for public employees (Presidential Decree no. 62 of 16 April 2013), which provides that a public employee shall not accept, for himself or herself or others, gifts or other advantages. However, the public official is, as an exception, allowed to accept gifts or other advantages, provided the following conditions are met:

(a) The gratuities do not exceed the value of EUR150.

(b) Such gratuities present no inducement and are given only for courtesy purposes.

As general principles, the following seem worth noting:

- The repeated offering/receiving of gifts and hospitality (i.e., to the benefit of the same person or provided on a regular basis) should generally be discouraged, irrespective of their value.

- Gifts and hospitality, even of small value, should be discouraged in the context of pending negotiations, tenders or imminent business decisions between the parties and in general, in the event that, under concrete circumstances, they may be capable of persuading the beneficiary to do or not do something in breach of the latter's duties.

4. Facilitation payments

The ICC does not recognize so-called facilitation payments. Therefore, cash payments or offers/promises of other economic advantages to public officials are very likely to be considered acts of corruption.

5. Compliance programs

5.1 Value of a compliance program to mitigate/eliminate the criminal liability of legal entities

Under Decree 231, companies may be held directly liable for certain crimes listed in Decree 231 that are committed on behalf of, or for the benefit of, the company by individuals who have operational and/or representative authority. This category includes: (i) individuals who represent or manage the company or any relevant autonomous business unit or *de facto* manage and control the company ("Representatives"); and (ii) individuals who are subject to the direction and supervision of the Representatives.

A company's liability under Decree 231 is assessed by the criminal judge in the same trial for the prosecution of the individual who allegedly committed the crime, and the sanctions set forth by Decree 231 are usually applied to the company by the same criminal court's decision upon the request of the public prosecutor.

The relevant courts may apply, among others, the following relevant sanctions:

- Temporary suspension from conducting business

- Suspension or revocation of any authorizations, licenses or permits held by the legal entity with respect to the business unit connected with the crime

- Prohibition from negotiating and entering into contracts with public administration entities, except for contracts relating to public services

- Pecuniary fines quantified as quotas and ranging from a minimum of 100 quotas to a maximum of 1,000 quotas; since the amount of each quota ranges from a minimum of EUR258 to a maximum of EUR 1,549, pursuant to Decree 231, the relevant Courts may therefore apply pecuniary fines ranging from a minimum of EUR 25,800 to a maximum of EUR 1,549,000

Companies may avoid the risk of incurring liability pursuant to Decree 231, provided they adopt an effective compliance program, that is, a Model of Organisation, Management and Control that is able to prevent and detect the commission of crimes (the "Model"), and ensure that the Model and related internal procedures are actually implemented. Therefore, the Model, if correctly implemented and constantly updated, would have the effect of exempting the company from liability arising from crimes committed by its Representatives.

5.2 Absence of a compliance program as a crime

The Italian Criminal Code does not treat the absence of a compliance program (i.e., the Model) as a crime. However, companies that have not implemented a Model will not be able to benefit from the mentioned exemption from liability.

5.3 Elements of a compliance program

According to the relevant case law, industry codes and best practices, an effective Model must: (i) identify the risk activities or areas of activities within the company's business; (ii) identify the modalities for handling financial resources suitable to prevent the commission of crimes; (iii) provide for specific protocols (policies) aimed at the formation and implementation of the company's decisions with respect to the prevention of potential crimes; (iv) provide for the appointment of a monitoring body (*Organo di Vigilanza e Controllo*), with autonomous powers of control, in charge of monitoring the implementation of the Model and updating the Model; and (v) provide for mandatory notices and informational obligations to the monitoring body. Moreover, after the adoption of the Model, the latter must be provided to each company manager, employee and representative, and the monitoring body must constantly oversee the proper application of the Model.

Provided that the above conditions are met, the company can benefit from the exemption from liability by demonstrating that whoever perpetrated a corruption-related crime did so by fraudulently violating or circumventing the company's Model.

6. Regulator with jurisdiction to prosecute corruption

The Italian legal system does not have a specific regulator with exclusive jurisdiction to prosecute corruption cases. Any public prosecutor may start a corruption investigation.

Kazakhstan

Azamat Kuatbekov

Azamat Kuatbekov is a partner of the Almaty office of Baker & McKenzie, heading the natural resources and dispute resolution practices. He also advises clients on local corporate, antimonopoly, compliance and general regulatory matters. He has authored numerous articles on oil and gas, corporate law, bankruptcy and litigation in Kazakhstan and has acted for many multinational companies operating in Kazakhstan.

azamat.kuatbekov@bakermckenzie.com
Tel: +7 727 330 0502

Gulnur Bekmukhanbetova

Gulnur Bekmukhanbetova is an associate of the Almaty office of Baker & McKenzie, specializing in banking and finance, mergers and acquisitions, as well as corporate practice. Her experience includes representing clients on a number of cross-border finance transactions. Gulnur frequently advises various international companies across multiple industries in connection with compliance issues in Kazakhstan.

gulnur.bekmukhanbetova@bakermckenzie.com
Tel: +7 727 330 0523

Baker & McKenzie - CIS, Limited
Samal Towers, 8th Floor.
97 Zholdasbekov Street
Almaty Samal-2, 050051
Kazakhstan

1. Domestic bribery (private to public)

1.1 Legal framework

Bribery of public officials is regulated under Articles 366 to 368 of the Kazakhstani Criminal Code[1]; Articles 676 to 681 of the Code of Administrative Offences[2]; the Law on State Service of the Republic of Kazakhstan[3]; and the Law on Countering Corruption.[4]

1.2 Definition of bribery

Under the law, bribery may be committed by either public officials or private individuals who try to corrupt a public official.

Bribery is indirectly defined in Articles 366 and 367 of the Criminal Code as a grant to or receipt by a public official, directly or through an intermediary, of money, securities, other property, proprietary rights or benefits for an act or non-act in the interests of the bribe giver or persons he or she represents, if the act or non-act is part of the public official's duties under the law, what the public official can do by virtue of his or her authority, or the bribe is given in exchange for general informal protection or advancement.

1.3 Definition of a public official

With regard to corruption, the Criminal Code lists a number of categories of persons who are considered public officials. These categories include the following:

(a) State servants

(b) Persons elected for municipal positions

---

[1] Criminal Code of the Republic of Kazakhstan dated 3 July 2014, as amended.
[2] Code of the Republic of Kazakhstan On Administrative Offences dated 5 July 2014, as amended.
[3] Law on State Service of the Republic of Kazakhstan dated 23 November 2015.
[4] Law on Countering Corruption dated 18 November 2015, as amended.

(c) Persons registered as candidates for president, Parliament or municipal elections

(d) Servants employed by municipalities who are paid out of the state budget

(e) Persons involved in managing state organizations or legal entities in which the state owns more than 50 percent of the shares, as well as their direct and indirect subsidiaries (defined as state organizations or legal entities owning more than 50 percent of the shares)

(f) Employees of the National Bank of Kazakhstan and its divisions

(g) Persons who perform organizational or administrative functions in state authorities, municipalities or Kazakhstan's military forces

(h) Persons who hold positions prescribed by the Constitution or other laws to perform state functions and exercise state authority, as well persons holding political office

1.4 Consequences of bribery

(a) For individuals involved

The Criminal Code establishes a range of penalties for individuals who corrupt public officials, as follows:

- Up to 15 years in jail, with or without the confiscation of property
- Fine of up to 50 times the amount of bribe
- Lifetime prohibition on holding certain positions or performing certain activities

(b) For a company or legal entity

Legal entities that corrupt public officials may be subject to administrative liability in the form of a fine of up to 750 times the monthly calculation index (MCI) (approximately USD4,300; for repeated breaches, a fine of up to 1,500 MCI or approximately USD8,600).

1.5 Political contributions

Contributions to political parties are regulated under Article 18 of the Law on Political Parties.[5] There are no quantitative restrictions on contributions. However, the law does identify persons and entities that are not allowed to make contributions, namely:

(a) Foreign states, foreign legal entities and international organizations

(b) Foreign citizens and persons without citizenship

(c) Legal entities with participation of foreign interest

(d) State authorities and state organizations

(e) Religious and charity organizations

(f) Anonymous contributors

(g) Citizens and legal entities of Kazakhstan that received grants or donations from international non-governmental institutions

1.6 Limitation applicable to hospitality expenses (gifts, travel, meals, entertainment, among others)

Under Kazakhstani law, the provision of any benefits to public officials is generally prohibited, and could amount to criminal or

---

[5] Law on Political Parties dated 15 July 2002, as amended.

administrative liability if the benefits were provided in exchange for an official's state functions.

However, under the Civil Code, certain symbolic gifts with a value not exceeding 10 MCI (approximately USD57) may be provided to government officials, taking into consideration the definition of bribery, as discussed in Section 1.2, that such gifts are legal only if not made in exchange for the official performing his or her official functions. Otherwise, there is a risk of criminal and/or administrative liability.

In addition, government officials may in certain cases be allowed to accept invitations to participate in international science, professional and other similar forums at the expense of organizations, and during the forums, the officials may be permitted to accept certain limited gifts or benefits.

2. Domestic bribery (private to private)

2.1 Legal framework

Private bribery is regulated by Article 253 of the Criminal Code.

2.2 Definition of private bribery

Private bribery is defined as an unlawful grant to or receipt by a person involved in the management of a commercial or other organization, of money, securities or other property, or an illegal performance of services in exchange for that person using his or her position in the interest of the bribe-giver or providing to the bribe-giver general informal protection or advancement.

2.3 Consequences of private bribery

(a) The Criminal Code provides a range of consequences for individuals involved in private bribery, namely:

- Up to 12 years in jail with or without the confiscation of his or her property

- Penalty of up to 5,000 MCI (approximately USD28,700) or correction works in the same amount
- Restriction of freedom for up to five years

(b) For a company or legal entity, no liability is specified.

2.4 Limitation on hospitality expenses (gifts, travel, meals, entertainment, among others)

Generally, Kazakhstani legislation does not establish quantitative or qualitative limitations on paying for hospitality expenses for managers in the private sector.

3. Corruption of foreign public officials

3.1 Legal framework

Corruption of foreign public officials is regulated under Articles 366 and 367 of the Criminal Code. These are the same articles that apply to bribing domestic public officials.

Unlike in other countries such as the United States or the United Kingdom, Kazakhstan's prohibition against bribing foreign public officials does not extend beyond its borders except in very specific cases.

The Criminal Code only views bribing foreign officials as a crime in the following cases:

(a) If the bribery of a foreign public official was committed outside of Kazakhstan by a Kazakhstani citizen and was not prosecuted in the state in which it was committed

(b) If the bribery of a foreign public official was committed outside of Kazakhstan by a non-Kazakhstani citizen directly against the interest of Kazakhstan, and was not prosecuted in the state in which it was committed

(c) If the bribery of a foreign public official was committed outside of Kazakhstan by a non-Kazakhstani citizen and was not prosecuted in the state it was committed, and bribery is subject to an international treaty to which Kazakhstan and this state are parties

3.2 Definition of corruption of foreign public officials

The Criminal Code provides just one definition for corruption of both domestic and foreign public officials.

3.3 Definition of foreign public officials

The Criminal Code does not define a "foreign public official." In practice, this may raise issues of interpretation and application of the relevant provisions of the Criminal Code.

3.4 Consequences of corruption of foreign public officials

Since Kazakhstani legislation does not differentiate between bribery of foreign and domestic officials, the consequences are the same as those mentioned in Section 1.4.

3.5 Limitations on hospitality expenses (gifts, travel, meals, entertainment, among others)

The limitations on hospitality expenses of domestic officials do not apply to hospitality of foreign public officials because the Law On State Service of the Republic of Kazakhstan and Law On Countering Corruption only apply to Kazakhstani public officials.

4. Facilitation payments

Kazakhstani anti-corruption laws do not regulate facilitating payments (e.g., modest payments to a public official to encourage him or her to perform an act he or she is legally required to perform) or gifts provided in accordance with generally accepted norms of courtesy and hospitality.

Thus, as a general rule, the provision of facilitating payments could lead to liability under the Criminal Code or the Administrative Code.

5. Compliance programs

5.1 Value of a compliance program in mitigating/eliminating the criminal liability of legal entities

While Kazakhstani legislation provides for the administrative (not criminal) liability of legal entities, compliance programs within the company do not help to either mitigate or eliminate the company's liability for corruption.

5.2 Absence of a compliance program as a crime

Kazakhstani legislation does not recognize the absence of a compliance program as a crime.

5.3 Elements of a compliance program

(a) Legal framework

Article 16 of the Law On Countering Corruption requires organizations to adopt certain anti-corruption measures. Such measures include, among others, the development and compliance with an internal code of business ethics, prevention of conflict of interest, development of mechanisms to ensure accountability, control and transparency of decision-making processes within the organization, and formation of anticorruption culture. The law does not provide for any penalties or other consequences for organizations that do not comply with the aforementioned requirement. Because this is a new requirement, it remains to be seen how it will be implemented and enforced in practice. Further, Kazakhstani legislation at present does not provide for the criminal liability of legal entities (legal entities could only be subjected to administrative liability – mainly fines). Nevertheless, compliance programs proved to be an effective tool in increasing local companies' and their employees' general awareness of the applicable regulatory regime as well as of potential risks.

(b) Recommended practice

Pursuant to Article 16 of the Law On Countering Corruption, it is recommended that Kazakh companies undertake measures to prevent corruption, including adopting compliance programs.

6. Regulator with jurisdiction to prosecute corruption

Under Kazakhstani legislation, the only agency tasked with prosecuting corruption is the Agency of the Republic of Kazakhstan for Public Service Affairs and Countering Corruption. This agency reports directly to the president of Kazakhstan.

Luxembourg

Andrea Sabine Schmid

Andrea Sabine Schmid has 14-years of international work experience. She has significant experience in insurance law, notably on cross-border business of insurers and insurance intermediaries, on contractual matters (review of life and group insurance policies to comply with the applicable law) and regulatory matters (license, passporting, prudential rules); drafting of investment management and intermediation agreement, run-off operations and outsourcing.

andrea.schmid@bakermckenzie.com
Tel: +352 26 18 44 262

Baker & McKenzie
10 - 12 Boulevard Roosevelt
2450 Luxembourg
Luxembourg

1. Domestic bribery (private to public)

1.1 Legal framework

Articles 240 *et seq.* of the Luxembourg Criminal Code provide the legal framework relating to bribery.

1.2 Definition of bribery

This criminal offense can be committed both by public officials and by private individuals or legal entities trying to corrupt a public official.

Bribery is broadly understood as the fact of offering, promising, giving or granting advantages either to accomplish or to not accomplish an act linked to a public function, duties, mission or mandate or facilitated by such function, duties, mission or mandate, or to abuse a true or assumed influence in order to obtain from a public authority or public administration rewards, employment, business or any other favorable decision.

Both natural and legal person are subject to criminal liability. When a criminal offense is committed in the name of, or in the interest of a natural person by its bodies or by one or several of its legal or *de facto* managers, the legal person may be held liable in addition to the criminal liability of the individuals who committed the offenses. It shall be noted that the maximum fine a legal person can be condemned to is EUR750,000. However, for certain particular offenses such as money laundering or bribery (either public or private), the amount can be multiplied by five times.

1.3 Definition of public official

The definition of public official includes any natural person that exercises public function, duties, mission or mandate. This definition includes civil servants, judges, members of parliament, employees of public bodies (not being civil servants) as well as employees of public companies or companies vested with public concessions.

1.4 Consequences of bribery

(a) For the natural persons involved

The Luxembourg Criminal Code establishes the same penalties for public officials as for individuals who corrupt public officials. The penalties are as follows:

- Imprisonment between five and 10 years
- Fine between EUR500 and EUR187,500
- Destitution (for life, under certain conditions) of certain political rights or to exercise public functions
- Destitution of certain civil rights for a term between five and 10 years.

(b) For the legal persons involved

- Fine up to 3.75 million
- Exclusion from any public bid
- Under certain conditions, dissolution of the legal person

1.5 Political contributions

Contributions to political parties are regulated by the law of 21 December 2007. In general terms, contributions to political parties are allowed provided that they are not anonymous, and are not made by legal persons or by charities or associations or any groups not having a legal personality. Any donation that exceeds EUR250 shall be reflected in the annual accounts of the political party that received it.

1.6 Limitation applicable to hospitality expenses (gifts, travel, meals, entertainment, among others)

The Luxembourg Criminal Code does not establish quantitative or qualitative limitations on such expenses. The analysis regarding a qualification as bribery shall be made on a case-by-case basis.

2. Domestic bribery (private to private)

2.1 Legal framework

Articles 310 *et seq.* of the Luxembourg Criminal Code provide the legal framework relating to private bribery.

2.2 Definition of private bribery

Bribery is broadly understood as proposing to a person who is a director or a manager or having representative powers on behalf of a legal or natural person or by the fact of such director or manager or representative of soliciting or accepting to receive, directly or through another person, an offer, promise or advantage of whatever nature, for himself or herself or for a third person, in order to perform or to not perform his or her duties or to perform or to not perform an act facilitated by the position, without the approval and knowledge of the board of directors or of the general meeting or the employer or the principal.

2.3 Consequences of private bribery

(a) For the individuals involved

- Imprisonment between one month and five years
- Fine between EUR251 and EUR30,000
- Destitution of certain political rights or to exercise public functions between five and 10 years

- Destitution of certain civil rights for a term between five and 10 years.

(b) For the legal persons involved

- Fine up to EUR300,000

Exclusion from any public bid Under certain conditions, dissolution of the legal person

2.4 Limitation applicable to hospitality expenses (gifts, travel, meals, entertainment among others)

The Luxembourg Criminal Code does not establish quantitative or qualitative limitations on such expenses. The analysis regarding a qualification as bribery shall be made on a case-by-case basis.

3. Corruption of foreign public officials

3.1 Legal framework

Article 252 of the Luxembourg Criminal Code provides the framework for bribery of foreign public officials.

3.2 Definition of corruption of foreign public officials

The legal provisions applicable to Luxembourg public officials also apply to foreign public officials.

3.3 Definition of foreign public official

Considered as foreign public officials are civil servants of a foreign state, foreign judges or arbitral judges, to European civil servants and members of the European Commission, of the European Parliament, of the European Court of Justice, of the European Accounting Court, subject to the provisions of European law, civil servants and employees of public or judicial international organizations, members of foreign parliaments, or international Courts.

3.4 Consequences of corruption of foreign public officials

(a) For the natural persons involved

The Luxembourg Criminal Code establishes the same penalties for public officials as for individuals who corrupt public officials. The penalties are as follows:

- Imprisonment between five and 10 years
- Fine between EUR500 to EUR187,500
- Destitution (for life, under certain conditions) of certain political rights or to exercise public functions
- Destitution of certain civil rights between five and 10 years

(b) For the legal persons involved

- Fine up to EUR3.75 million
- Exclusion from any public bid
- Under certain conditions, dissolution of the legal person

3.5 Limitation applicable to hospitality expenses (gifts, travel, meals, entertainment, among others)

The Luxembourg Criminal Code does not establish quantitative or qualitative limitations on such expenses. The analysis regarding a qualification as bribery shall be made on a case-by-case basis.

4. Facilitation payments

The Luxembourg Criminal Code does not establish quantitative or qualitative limitations on such payments. The analysis regarding a qualification as bribery shall be made on a case-by-case basis.

5. Compliance programs

5.1 Value of a compliance program in mitigating/eliminating the criminal liability of legal persons

Compliance programs are not foreseen by the Luxembourg Criminal Code and cannot be understood as such as being an element for mitigating or eliminating risks of liability for legal persons. However, such programs may help in practice to limit such risk by informing employees and agents on good practices.

5.2 Absence of a compliance program as a crime

The Luxembourg Criminal Code does not view the absence of compliance program as a crime.

5.3 Elements of a compliance program

(a) Legal framework

The Luxembourg Criminal Code does not recognize nor regulate the elements of a compliance program.

(b) Recommended practice

In the absence of case law and relevant doctrine, it is generally understood that legal persons shall have such compliance program and inform their employees of the risks related to corruption.

6. Regulator with jurisdiction to prosecute corruption

The Luxembourg legal framework does not have a specific regulator with exclusive jurisdiction to prosecute corruption cases. Any public prosecutor could request that a judge start a corruption investigation. However, the Luxembourg system has a group of public prosecutors who specialize in prosecuting these cases.

Morocco

Kamal Nasrollah

Kamal Nasrollah advises international clients on cross-boarder mergers and acquisitions, energy and project finance contracts, as well as international litigation/arbitration. He collaborates closely with Baker & McKenzie's Paris office and practice groups. Drawing from his experience in diverse business cultures, Kamal has become an adviser of choice for leading companies in the Middle East and North Africa. He works with major companies to identify investment opportunities in Morocco, North Africa and West Africa.

kamal.nasrollah@bakermckenzie.com
Tel: +212 52 2 77 95 95

Keltoum Boudribila

Keltoum Boudribila joined Baker & McKenzie in 2012. She advises leading companies in the Middle East and North Africa in the field of business law, in particular with M&A and financing transactions. Prior to joining Baker & McKenzie, Keltoum worked as an associate of the French law firm August & Debouzy.

keltoum.boudribila@bakermckenzie.com
Tel: +212 5 22 77 95 95

Baker & McKenzie Maroc SARL
Ghandi Mall - Immeuble 9
Boulevard Ghandi
20380 Casablanca
Morocco

1. Domestic bribery (private to public)

1.1 Legal framework

Bribery is governed by Articles 248 to 256 of the Moroccan Criminal Code (the "Code").

1.2 Definition of bribery

Bribery consists of the offer or solicitation made towards or receipt or acceptance on the part of any magistrate, arbitrator, public official or electoral office holder of a gift, donation or other advantage in exchange for performance or taking of any act, favor or decision or abstention from any act or decision (Code, Article 248).

The crime can be committed by any public official and by private individuals who try to corrupt a public official.

1.3 Definition of public official

"Public official" is defined in Article 224 of the Code as any person who exercises a function or assignment, even temporary, on behalf of the state, public administration, municipality or public establishment or public interest service. The law applies broadly, however, to include magistrates and arbitrators appointed by a public or judicial authority or by a private party.

1.4 Consequences of bribery

(a) For the individuals involved

The punishment for public bribery is imprisonment from two years to five years and a fine of MAD2,000 to MAD50,000.

When the amount involved exceeds MAD100,000, the imprisonment sentence is increased to a period of five years to 10 years and the fine to MAD5,000 to MAD100,000.

Under Article 256 of the Code, a person convicted may be deprived of certain civil rights and be barred from public office or employment for a period of up to 10 years.

According to Article 251 of the Code, the same penalties apply to any person committing assault or battery or offering promises, gifts or other advantages or accepting solicitations that facilitate corruption, even if such person has not initiated such acts and whether or not they were effective.

(b) For the company / legal entity

Pursuant to Article 127 of the Code, legal entities are subject only to monetary fines as well as confiscation of assets and forced dissolution, as provided for in Article 36 of the Code.

1.5 Political contributions

Contributions to political parties are regulated under Article 31 of the Law N° 29-11 relating to political parties. In general terms, contributions to political parties are allowed if they do not exceed MAD300,000 per year and per contributor.

Any person having granted or accepted donations or bequests in cash or in kind on behalf of a political party in violation of the MAD300,000 limit is subject to a fine of between MAD20,000 and MAD100,000.

1.6 Limitations applicable to hospitality expenses (gifts, travel, meals, entertainment, among others)

Moroccan Law does not contain any specific *de minimis* or other exemptions with respect to payment or acceptance of hospitality expenses incurred on behalf of public officials. Similarly, there are no statutory or regulatory guidelines with respect to inviting government officials to events that are sponsored by a company or partially sponsored by a company where the company defrays or reimburses the cost of air travel, food, lodging or entertainment expenses.

Whether a hospitality expense would be considered bribery would depend on the specific facts, including any intention of the parties concerned that any payment of expenses or provision of any item of value was carried out with the intent of obtaining performance of an act or other favor.

2. Domestic bribery (private to private)

2.1 Legal framework

Private bribery is regulated under the Moroccan Criminal Code, Article 249.

2.2 Definition of private bribery

Article 249 applies to any paid employee or subordinate who, directly or through an intermediary, without the knowledge or consent of his employer, requests or approves offers, promises, gifts, commissions, discounts or bonuses in order to perform or abstain from performing any act within the scope of employment or which may be facilitated by such employment.

Article 249 does not specifically provide for liability of persons soliciting such acts from an employee or subordinate. However, the provisions of Article 251 cited earlier – providing that the same penalties apply to persons offering or soliciting gifts or other advantages facilitating corruption – includes corrupt offers or solicitations made to employees or subordinates within the scope of Article 249.

2.3 Consequences of private bribery

(a) For the individuals involved

Pursuant to Article 249 of the Code, private bribery is punishable by imprisonment for a period of one year to three years and a fine of between MAD5,000 and MAD50,000.

(b) For the company / legal entity

Pursuant to Article 127 of the Code, legal entities are subject only to monetary fines as well as confiscation of assets and forced dissolution, as provided for in Article 36 of the Code.

2.4 Limitations applicable to hospitality expenses (gifts, travel, meals, entertainment, among others)

As in the case of corruption of a public official, Moroccan law does not provide any specific *de minimis* or other exemptions with respect to hospitality expenses. Accordingly, any determination would depend on the intention of the parties and other specific facts of the case.

3. Corruption of foreign public officials

There are no specific provisions in the Code relating to the corruption of foreign public officials.

4. Facilitation payments

There are no specific provisions under Moroccan law defining or distinguishing facilitation payments. Accordingly, the legality of any such payments would be determined by the general provisions of the law relating to corruption.

As there is no exemption in the Code that would allow the making of facilitation payments, such payments would likely be considered as falling within the scope of Articles 248 to 250, to the extent that the expediting or handling of any matter constituted the performance of an act within the scope of the official duties of the recipient in exchange for payment.

5. Compliance programs

5.1 Value of a compliance program in mitigating/eliminating the criminal liability of legal entities

The Moroccan Code does not specifically recognize compliance programs as instruments to mitigate or eliminate the liability of legal entities before the crime of corruption has been committed.

Legal entities could mitigate their criminal liability if they adopt an effective compliance program after corruption has been committed and before the trial begins.

5.2 Absence of compliance program

The Moroccan Code does not impose any requirement with respect to a compliance program and thus, the absence of implementation of any such program does not give rise to liability.

(a) Legal framework

As mentioned, there is no Moroccan legislation or regulations in relation to compliance programs.

(b) Recommended practice

In the absence of statutory, regulatory or judicial guidance, it is recommended that legal entities adopt strict compliance programs in order to raise the awareness of management and staff, and potentially as a strategy to counter a finding of or to mitigate liability in case of prosecution. However, there are no legal provisions stating that the existence of such programs can limit or exclude liability in a given case.

6. Regulator with jurisdiction to prosecute corruption

There is no special regulatory body with authority to prosecute corruption. Corruption investigations and prosecutions are carried out by the public prosecutor and the criminal courts.

Morocco has, however, recently adopted the law n° 113-12 related to the National Agency for Probity, Prevention and Anti-Corruption dated 20 August 2015, which replaced the Central Agency for Bribery Prevention (*Instance Centrale de Prévention de la Corruption*) by the National Agency for Probity, Prevention and Anti-Corruption (*Instance Nationale de la Probité, de la Prévention et de la lutte contre la Corruption*).

This new law has extended the powers of the agency, granting it the authority to carry out pre-trial investigations; coordinate, supervise and ensure the application of the regulations on corruption; and to collect and disseminate information in relation thereto. The agency does not have jurisdiction to prosecute, but it can alert the public prosecutor, who in turn can apply to a judge for the initiation of a corruption investigation.

The Netherlands

Jasper Helder

Jasper Helder specializes in international trade (economic sanctions, export controls and customs) and corporate compliance (anti-bribery, AML). He frequently assists US clients with their EU compliance and advises a range of multinationals on EU and UN sanctions compliance for countries such as Iran, Russia, Syria and interaction with US sanctions, as well as on the interaction between EU and US export controls rules (e.g., ITAR and EAR). He also advises on other aspects of trade regulation, such as trade remedies, free trade agreements and rules of origin, and he has extensive experience with the EU common agricultural policy and related import/export issues and EU customs compliance, notably customs classification (including Binding Tariff Information) and customs valuation/ transfer pricing.

Jasper further advises clients on anti-bribery and AML compliance, including compliance aspects of third party contracts (e.g., with agents, distributors, intermediaries) and related third party compliance reviews. He has particular experience with regard to Russia and the Middle East and anti-bribery/AML aspects of humanitarian (food/medicine) distribution in sanctioned countries.

Both in the international trade and anti-bribery/AML areas, Jasper works with clients on drafting and maintaining compliance programs and internal training as well as internal investigations and external (government) audits and other government investigations. He represents clients before European national (customs, export and other) administrations and courts as well as before the EU Commission, its advisory committees and the European Court of Justice.

jasper.helder@bakermckenzie.com
Tel: +31 20 551 7579

Chiara Klaui

Chiara Klaui, an attorney practicing in the area of EU international trade, is proficient in economic sanctions, export controls, customs, and product and food regulation. She advises clients on restrictions such as export controls (dual-use and military) and economic sanctions imposed against countries like Iran, Syria, Russia and Ukraine, as well as their implementation in different EU member states. She focuses on the commodities, IT, offshore, and oil and gas sectors.

Her practice includes advice and litigation, and she represents clients before national (customs, export and other) administrations and courts and the European Commission.

In addition, Chiara advises on compliance with anti-bribery and anti-money laundering legislation, and regularly conducts internal investigations. She is also experienced in drafting and reviewing internal compliance programs.

chiara.klaui@bakermckenzie.com
Tel: +31 6 4617 8558

Baker & McKenzie Amsterdam N.V.
Claude Debussylaan 54
1082 MD Amsterdam
P.O. Box 2720
1000 CS Amsterdam
The Netherlands

1. Domestic bribery (private to public)

1.1 Legal framework

Bribery of public officials (*ambtenaren*) is regulated under the Dutch Criminal Code. Article 177 penalizes active bribery (i.e., the bribing of public officials) while Article 363 penalizes passive bribery (i.e., the public officials who are bribed).

1.2 Definition of bribery

Bribery can be committed both by public officials and by companies / private individuals who (try to) bribe a public official.

Under the Dutch Criminal Code, bribery is defined very broadly:

> Public bribe may refer to any pecuniary or non-pecuniary gift, promise (even if not realized), or service to a former, current or future public official, either directly or indirectly/through an intermediary, in order to induce him or her to commit any act, or refrain from acting, in the performance of his or her public duties, whether contrary or in accordance with his or her official duties.

Please note that it is also punishable to offer a gift, benefit or promise after the public servant has already acted contrary to his or her duties. Also, the Dutch anti-corruption provisions do not require that the public official personally gain from the bribe. Moreover, causality between a specific gratuity and a specific performance or non-performance is not required.

As indicated earlier, in addition to direct bribery, indirect bribery is also illegal. If local agents, representatives or consultants are used to bribe a public official, this can lead to criminal liability of the legal entity using the intermediary. Legal entities are therefore expected to have a critical attitude towards the nature and scope of the activities to be performed by such third parties as well as perform a due diligence/risk analysis on their third parties.

1.3 Definition of public official

The Dutch Criminal Code does not define "public official." It only indicates that public officials include any member of a general representative body, arbitrators and persons who form part of the armed forces. The Dutch Criminal Code also determines who should additionally be considered public officials for purposes of anti-bribery legislation, namely, persons with a public function in a foreign state or an international institution, as well as former public officials.

In established case law, the term public official has been interpreted as anyone who is appointed by the public authority in relation to a public function, in order to perform part of the tasks of the Dutch state and its bodies. The person involved must be employed as a public official by a competent body, or its employer must perform government tasks and fall under the supervision and control of the government. In any event, the definition of public official is interpreted broadly.

1.4 Consequences of bribery

(a) For the individuals involved

The Dutch Criminal Code establishes the same range of penalties for public officials and for individuals that bribe public officials.

- Fines of up to EUR82,000 or imprisonment for up to six years
- Exclusion from certain professions
- Confiscation of illegally obtained assets/proceeds of the crime

(b) For the company / legal entity

- Fine of up to 10 percent of the annual turnover of the company if the fine of up to EUR82,000 is considered insufficient punishment
- Confiscation of illegally obtained assets/proceeds of the crime

1.5 Political contributions

Contributions to political parties are regulated under the Political Parties Funding Act (*Wet financiering politieke partijen*). Political parties may accept anonymous contributions up to EUR1,000. Contributions between EUR1,000 and EUR4,500 should be registered (including name and place of residence of the giver, the amount and date of contribution). Contributions exceeding EUR4,500 must be made public. Presently, only national political parties are covered by these rules.[1]

1.6 Limitation applicable to hospitality expenses (gifts, travel, meals, entertainment, among others)

The Dutch Criminal Code does not establish quantitative or qualitative limitations on hospitality expenses. In order to assess whether a hospitality expense is considered a bribe, it has to be established that the hospitality expense constitutes an improper benefit (in line with the definition of bribery as indicated in Section 1.2).

Whether a hospitality expense could be considered a bribe needs to be determined on a case-by-case basis, taking into account all the facts and circumstances.

Please note that most of the internal codes of conduct by which public officials are usually bound prohibit the acceptance of gifts with a value exceeding EUR50 and any payment for trips, travel, accommodation, entertainment, lunches or dinners.

2. Domestic bribery (private to private)

2.1 Legal framework

Bribery of non-public officials is regulated under Article 328*ter* of the Dutch Criminal Code.

---

[1] Please note that a legislative bill, which is presently under review, proposes to also cover local political parties.

2.2 Definition of private bribery

A private bribe, *inter alia*, refers to any pecuniary or non-pecuniary gift, promise (even if not realized) or service to someone other than a public official who is employed or acts as a mandatory, which is, contrary to the standards of good faith, concealed from that person's employer or principal.

The benefit must be offered/accepted in connection with what the non-public official – in the course of his or her employment or the execution of his or her mandate – has done or omitted, or will do or omit. The person who is bribed must have concealed the benefit from his or her employer/principal, and the person who bribes must reasonably assume that the benefit will be concealed from the non-public official's employer/principal.

2.3 Consequences of private bribery

(a) For the individuals involved

- Fines of up to EUR82,000 or imprisonment of up to four years
- Exclusion from certain professions
- Confiscation of illegally obtained assets/proceeds of the crime
- Publication of the judgment

(b) For the company / legal entity

- Fines of up to 10 percent of the annual turnover of the company if the fine of up to EUR82,000 is considered insufficient punishment
- Confiscation of illegally obtained assets/proceeds of the crime
- Publication of the judgment

2.4 Limitation applicable to hospitality expenses (gifts, travel, meals, entertainment, among others)

The Dutch Criminal Code does not establish quantitative or qualitative limitations on hospitality expenses. The relevant element of the offense is "[concealed] contrary to the standards of good faith." It should be decided whether the employee/mandatory was obliged to inform his employer/principal according to objective criteria. In case of doubt, the employee/mandatory should thus inform his or her employer/principal of any received hospitality expenses.

3. Corruption of foreign public officials / Corruption abroad

3.1 Legal framework

In the Dutch Criminal Code, no distinction is made between bribing national or foreign officials. Foreign public officials are equated with Dutch public officials in the Dutch Criminal Code for the purpose of Article 177, which penalizes active bribery (i.e., the bribing of public officials) and Article 363, which penalizes passive bribery (i.e., the public officials who are bribed).

In the case of corruption abroad, the following persons can be prosecuted in the Netherlands:

- A Dutch public official bribed abroad
- A person who is employed by an international institution that was established in the Netherlands and bribed abroad
- Anyone who bribed a Dutch person or Dutch public official abroad[2]
- A Dutch person/entity who bribed a Dutch or foreign public official (abroad)

---

[2] Under the condition that the offense is punishable in the country where the bribery took place.

- A Dutch public official or person, employed by an international institution that was established in the Netherlands, who violates Article 177 abroad[3]

A foreign public official (not employed by the Netherlands) who is bribed (abroad) by a Dutch person cannot be prosecuted in the Netherlands unless the public official is employed by an international institution established in the Netherlands.

3.2 Definition of corruption of foreign public officials

A public bribe refers to any pecuniary or non-pecuniary gift, promise (even if not realized), or service to a former, current or future public official, either directly or indirectly/through an intermediary, in order to induce him or her to commit any act, or refrain from acting, in the performance of his or her public duties, whether contrary or in accordance with his or her official duties.

Reference is also made to Section 1.2.

3.3 Definition of foreign public official

For the purpose of this crime, a foreign public official is any person with a public function who is employed by a foreign state or international institution. Reference is also made to Section 1.3.

3.4 Consequences of corruption of foreign public officials

(a) For the individuals involved

The Dutch Criminal Code establishes the same range of penalties for public officials and for individuals that bribe public officials.

(i) Fines of up to EUR82,000 or imprisonment up to six years

(ii) Exclusion from certain professions

---

[3] *Idem.*

(iii) Confiscation of illegally obtained assets/proceeds of the crime

(b) For the company/legal entity

(i) Fines of up to 10 percent of the annual turnover of the company if the fine of up to EUR82,000 is considered insufficient punishment

(ii) Confiscation of illegally obtained assets/proceeds of the crime

3.5 Limitation applicable to hospitality expenses (gifts, travel, meals, entertainment, among others)

The Dutch Criminal Code does not establish quantitative or qualitative limitations on hospitality expenses. In order to assess whether a hospitality expense is considered a bribe, it has to be established that the hospitality expense constitutes an improper benefit (in line with the definition of bribery as indicated in Section 1.2).

Establishing that a hospitality expense is a bribe needs to be determined on a case-by-case basis, taking into account all the facts and circumstances.

4. Facilitation payments

The Dutch Criminal Code does not specifically identify so-called facilitation payments. Having said that, facilitation payments are considered improper benefits and thereby, constitute bribery. Although illegal/punishable, facilitation payments to foreign public officials are, according to internal guidelines of the Dutch public prosecutor's office, not prosecuted in the Netherlands when the following conditions (derived from the OECD convention) are met:

- Small amounts (in absolute or relative terms) are concerned.
- The payment does not distort competition in any way.

- The payment has been provided at the initiative of the (foreign) official.
- Payments to lower level public officials are concerned.
- The payment is not concealed by the company and is reflected transparently in the company's financial accounts.

5. Compliance programs

5.1 Value of a compliance program in mitigating/eliminating the criminal liability of legal entities

Bribery may be attributed to a legal entity if the crime is committed in the sphere/spirit of the legal entity, which may be the case in the following circumstances:

- The act has been committed by someone employed by the legal entity.
- The act correspond to the usual course of business of the legal entity.
- The act has been useful in the course of business of the legal entity.
- The legal entity had power of disposal over the act and accepted the act (which is also the case if no due care has been exercised in order to prevent the act from happening).

The Dutch Criminal Code does not recognize a compliance program as an instruments to mitigate or eliminate the liability of legal entities. However, legal entities could potentially mitigate their exposure to corruption if they adopt an effective compliance program. In addition, legal entities may potentially escape attribution of the crime if they can prove that – by means of the compliance program – the legal entity exercised due care in order to prevent the act from happening and did not approve of the act.

5.2 Absence of a compliance program as a crime

The Dutch Criminal Code does not recognize the absence of a compliance program as a crime.

5.3 Elements of a compliance program

(a) Legal framework

The Dutch Criminal Code does not recognize nor regulate the elements of a compliance program.

(b) Recommended practice

Although there are no explicit legal provisions regarding compliance programs, the adoption of a compliance program is a recommended measure to limit a company's exposure to bribery.

6. Regulator with jurisdiction to prosecute corruption

A public prosecutor of the public prosecutor's office in Rotterdam has been appointed as the national corruption prosecutor. This specialized prosecutor offers assistance to other members of the public prosecution service in relation to the investigation and prosecution of corruption matters.

Poland

Radoslaw Nozykowski

Radoslaw Nozykowski assists in compliance matters, mostly for the technological and pharmaceutical companies He also handles various IP issues, including copyright law and IT law, unfair competition and privacy-related concerns.

radoslaw.nozykowski@bakermckenzie.com
Tel: +48 22 445 32 10

Wiktor Krzymowski

Wiktor Krzymowski is a member of Pharmaceuticals & Healthcare practice. He assists in compliance matters for pharmaceutical and medical companies, including the preparation of compliance procedures.

wiktor.krzymowski@bakermckenzie.com
Tel: +48 22 445 32 03

Baker & McKenzie Krzyzowski i Wspólnicy
Spólka Komandytowa
Rondo ONZ 1
00-124 Warsaw
Poland

1. Domestic bribery (private to public)

1.1 Legal framework

Bribery of public officials is regulated under the Polish Penal Code (PC), Articles 228-230a.

1.2 Definition of bribery

The PC distinguishes offering a bribe from accepting it in relation to public officials.

Bribery (Article 229 of the PC) consists of giving or promising to give financial or personal benefits to a person holding a public post (public post holder) in connection with this post.

Venality (Article 228 of the PC) refers to accepting or promising to accept financial or personal benefits by a person holding a public post in connection with holding this post.

Financial benefit is understood as the receipt of assets or the avoidance of losses or encumbrances on assets, and therefore, refers both to an increase in assets and a reduction in liabilities. Financial benefits are money, securities, items of value, performances and property rights (e.g., a donation, an entry in a will, the forgiveness of a debt and the waiver of enforcement of tax due).

Personal benefit should be understood as satisfying needs of a nature other than financial or those in which the intangible benefit is of a dominant nature (e.g., recommending someone for a position, promotion, the award of a distinction, or the withdrawal of a negative appraisal contained in the personal files).

1.3 Definition of public official

Article 115 Section 19 of the PC defines a public official as any public post holder, like a member of a body of a local government; a person employed in an organizational unit holding public funds, unless it only performs activities on contract; as well as any other person whose rights and duties in public activities are specified or recognized by the PC or an international agreement that is binding on the Republic of Poland, or is a listed public official.

The following are public officials under the PC (see Article 115 Section 13 of the PC):

- The president of the Republic of Poland
- A deputy, senator or counsellor
- A member of the European Parliament
- A judge, juror, prosecutor, official of a financial investigative authority or authority supervising the financial investigative authority, a notary, a bailiff, a court curator, a receiver, a court supervisor and administrator, a person adjudicating in disciplinary bodies operating in accordance with the PC

1.4 Consequences of bribery

(a) For the individuals involved

The PC establishes the same penalties for public officials as for individuals that corrupt public officials.

- Typical imprisonment from six months to eight years (In gross cases that are higher - e.g., a bigger bribe may result in up to 12 years of imprisonment; smaller bribe cases will net a fine of up to PLN1.08 million, up to one year of restricted liberty, or imprisonment of up to two years.)

(b) For the company / legal entity (a specific procedure may be initiated following the prosecution of the original perpetrator)

- A fine of between PLN1,000 and PLN5 million; however, not more than 3 percent of revenues for the financial year in which the offense was committed

- Forfeiture of the financial benefits or duty to return obtained benefits

- Prohibition for up to five years from:

  - advertising the company, company's services and manufactured or sold goods;

  - using grants, subventions or any other form of state aid;

  - using aid of international organizations that the Republic of Poland is part of; and

  - entering into contracts with the public sector.

- Publication of the court judgment in media

1.5 Political contributions

- Contributions to political parties are regulated under the Act on Political Parties of 27 June 1997.

- Political parties may receive financial contributions only from Polish citizens with a permanent place of residence in Poland. The limit of a contribution received from one person cannot exceed annually the ratio of the minimum monthly salary (for 2016, it is estimated to be PLN1,850[1]) multiplied by 15.

- Political parties may not receive financial contributions from legal entities.

- Politicians may not receive financial contributions at all.

---

[1] However, this provision has very unclear wording. Due to the State Election Commission, which controls the finance of political parties, this provision relates to the allowance of members of district election commissions (PLN380).

1.6 Limitation applicable to hospitality expenses (gifts, travel, meals, entertainment, among others)

Polish law does not establish quantitative or qualitative limitations on hospitality expenses. The line between a permissible gift and an impermissible bribe is neither precise nor easy to determine, and it should be assessed on a case-by-case basis.

However, to some extent, case law has established some guidance. A judgment of the Polish Supreme Court states that, "[o]ffering items that only symbolically express gratefulness of the benefactor and have money value not exceeding such symbolic level is not a financial benefit."

Furthermore, the Act on the Restrictions on Public Officials Conducting Business Activities provides additional guidance on that matter. According to that act, high-ranking government officials must disclose information on all gifts, the value of which exceeds 50 percent of the minimum monthly salary (for 2016, it is estimated to be PLN1,850) and hospitality received in the Register of Benefits.

To some extent, in order to determine the scope of admissible hospitality, the Code of Ethics of Civil Servants may be used as a guide. The said act defines civil servants as a special class of lower ranking Polish public officials with administrative, non-political functions, and establishes the following principles for the provision of hospitality: (i) civil servants are prohibited from accepting any financial or personal benefit from a person or entity engaged in official proceedings before the civil servant; and (ii) civil servants are prohibited from acting in a manner that may raise doubts as to whether they are acting in their own interests or those of the government of Poland.

2. Domestic bribery (private to private)

2.1 Legal framework

Private bribery (managerial bribery) is regulated under the PC, Article 296a.

2.2 Definition of private bribery

Bribery is defined as demanding, accepting or offering financial or personal benefits or a promise thereof, in exchange for abusing the rights granted to a manager or a person employed in any form by a company/entity, or for failing to fulfil an obligation for which he or she is responsible, and which leads to possible damage to this entity, an act of unfair competition, or inadmissible preferential act for a purchaser or customer of goods or services.

2.3 Consequences of private bribery

(a) For the individuals involved

- Typically, imprisonment from three months to five years (in smaller cases, a fine up to PLN1.08 million; restriction of liberty up to one year or imprisonment up to two years; if high damages are incurred, from six months to eight years)

(b) For the company / legal entity

- A fine of between PLN1,000 and PLN5 million; however, not more than 3 percent of revenues for the financial year in which the offense was committed
- Forfeiture of the financial benefits or duty to return obtained benefit
- Prohibition for up to five years from:
  - o advertising the company, company's services and manufactured or sold goods;

  - using grants, subventions or any other form of state aid;
  - using aid of international organizations that the Republic of Poland is part of; and
  - entering into contracts with the public sector.
- Publication of the court judgment in media

2.4 Limitation applicable to hospitality expenses (gifts, travel, meals, entertainment, among others)

Similar rules apply to hospitality acts of private persons and public officials. Any gifts should be reasonably proportionate to the occasion; otherwise, it may be deemed as corruption.

3. Corruption of foreign public officials

3.1 Legal framework

Polish law does not specifically regulate the corruption of foreign officials. Articles regarding the corruption of public post holders in general will apply.

3.2 Definition of corruption of public post holder

Polish law does not provide a definition of corruption of foreign public officials. The same rules apply as to bribery of public officials under the PC.

3.3 Definition of foreign public official

Polish law does not, *expressis verbis,* define a foreign public post holder. However, the definition of the public post holder may give some guidance in this regard.

3.4 Consequences of corruption of foreign public officials

(a) For the individuals involved

- Bribery: The same rules as to domestic bribery apply.
- Venality: Considering the fact that some of the foreign public officials may have immunity while representing their states in the Republic of Poland (e.g. diplomatic immunity), the PC does not apply to illegal actions performed by them, unless their country of origin waives immunity in particular situations.

(b) For the legal entity

- The same rules as to domestic bribery apply.

3.5 Limitation applicable to hospitality expenses (gifts, travel, meals, entertainment, among others)

The same rules apply to foreign public officials as to domestic regulations.

4. Facilitation payments

Polish law does not recognize any facilitation payments.

5. Compliance programs

5.1 Value of a compliance program in mitigating/eliminating the criminal liability of legal entities

The PC does not recognize a compliance program as an instrument to mitigate or eliminate the liability of legal entities before the crime of corruption has been committed. However, based on Article 5 Paragraph 2 of the Act on the Liability of Collective Entities for acts prohibited under the fine (LCE), it may be a defense in case of the entities' liability - the liability of the particular company may be established if the illegal act has been committed following the lack of due diligence in the internal organization of the company, which if done could have prevented the occurrence of the illegal act. The existence of a compliance program in the company does not automatically waive the liability of the collective entity, but under the provisions of LCE, this may be a factor that a court will take into consideration in deciding on the company's liability (i.e., a properly planned and executed compliance program may reduce the risk of liability).

5.2 Absence of a compliance program as a crime

The PC does not view the absence of a compliance program as a crime.

5.3 Elements of a compliance program

(a) Legal framework

The PC does not recognize nor regulate the elements of a compliance program. However, Article 5, Paragraph 2 of the LCE may be of some guidance (proper internal organization of the company).

(b) Recommended practice

In the absence of PC regulations, non-governmental organizations, as well as market practice recommend that legal entities adopt internal compliance programs (or structure an internal organization of the company in a similar way) as a strategy to mitigate and eliminate corruption, and to establish a line of defense in the case of court proceedings regarding the corruption made on behalf of the collective entity.

6. Regulator with jurisdiction to prosecute corruption

In addition to the police and the Public Prosecutor's Office or other law enforcement agencies dealing with specific areas (e.g., secret services), the Polish legal system has a specific regulator responsible for investigating corruption – The Central Anti-corruption Bureau (*Centralne Biuro Antykorupcyjne* or CBA). The CBA is equipped with tools to detect corruption among public officials and legal entities and to gather evidence for criminal cases. It does not, however, possess the power to prosecute defendants accused of corruption before courts, which is a role that is reserved for public prosecutors.

Russia

Alexander Bychkov

Alexander Bychkov is a partner in the Moscow office of Baker & McKenzie. He is the co-head of the Firm's CIS Tax Practice Group and head of the Firm's CIS customs practice, which includes professionals working in the Almaty, Baku, Kyiv, Moscow and St. Petersburg offices of the Firm. Alexander specializes in advising multinational clients on tax, customs, compliance and general commercial matters. In addition, he is a member of the Firm's Healthcare and Pharmaceuticals Practice Group.

alexander.bychkov@bakermckenzie.com
Tel: +7 495 787 2700

Natalia Tataru

Natalia Tataru is an associate in the Moscow office of Baker & McKenzie. She specializes in the areas of corporate law, mergers and acquisitions, as well as in corporate compliance, including internal and other corporate investigations, international M&A, and commercial work. Natalia's work includes advising on the structuring and conducting corporate and commercial compliance investigations in international transactions and in the activities of Russian companies.

natalia.tataru@bakermckenzie.com
Tel: +7 495 787 2700

Alexander Monin

Alexander Monin is a corporate/commercial partner at the Moscow office of Baker & McKenzie. On a regular basis, he advises clients on the compliance review of potential agents and distributors and on the introduction of corporate compliance and risk management programs in their Russian subsidiaries. He also conducts the training of Russian personnel (legal and non-legal) and generally consults international companies on all compliance-related aspects of doing business in Russia.

alexander.monin@bakermckenzie.com
Tel: +7 495 787 2700

Baker & McKenzie - CIS, Limited
White Gardens
9 Lesnaya Street
Moscow 125047
Russia

Key Practitioners

Paul Melling
Moscow
Tel: +7 (495) 787-2700
paul.melling@bakermckenzie.com

1. Domestic bribery (private to public)

1.1 Legal framework

Russian criminal law prohibits active and passive bribery of public officials.

1.2 Definition of bribery

A bribe is defined as money, securities, other property, or the illegal provision of services, or the provision of other property benefits to a public official (bribe taker) for the latter's acts or omissions in favor of the bribe giver or any parties that represent the bribe giver, if such acts or omissions fall within the range of the *ex-officio* powers of the public official or if such a public official can, by reason of his or her *ex officio* status, foster such acts or omissions, or for general patronage or connivance in service.

Aiding and abetting public bribery is a separate criminal offense. Aiding and abetting is defined as the physical giving of a bribe on the instructions of the person either giving or receiving a bribe, as well as any other assistance to either of these persons in reaching or executing an agreement between them to give and take a bribe. This also applies to offers or promises of assistance in public bribery regardless of the value of the bribe.

1.3 Definition of public official

Russian public officials are defined, in Article 285 of the Criminal Code, as persons who permanently or temporarily, pursuant to a specific authorization, perform the function of a representative of state power as well as persons who perform organizational or administrative functions in the state and municipal bodies, state or municipal establishments, as well as in the Russian military and other armed forces.

1.4 Consequences of bribery

(a) For the individuals involved

The sanctions under Article 291 of the Criminal Code vary, depending on (a) whether the person giving a bribe has acted alone or in conspiracy with others; (b) whether the bribe is given for the commission of a lawful or an unlawful act (or failure to act); and (c) the amount of the bribe.

The minimum sanction for a bribe not exceeding RUB25,000 (approximately USD312) is a fine of up to RUB500,000 (approximately USD6,250); or a salary or other income of the convicted person for a period of up to one year; or a fine from five to 30 times the amount of the bribe; or correctional labor for up to two years, with or without the prohibition from holding certain positions or engaging in certain professional activity for up to three years; or forced labor for up to three years; or imprisonment for up to two years, with or without a fine of five to 10 times the amount of the bribe. The maximum sanction for a bribe exceeding RUB1 million (approximately USD12,500) is a fine from 70 to 90 times the amount of the bribe, or imprisonment for seven to 12 years and a fine 70 times the amount of the bribe. A person who has given a bribe may be relieved of criminal liability if he or she actively aids in the detection and prosecution of the crime, or voluntarily reports to the criminal law enforcement authorities after the commission of the crime, or was solicited by a particular public official to give a bribe.

According to Article 104.1 of the Criminal Code, property obtained as a result of a criminal offense and any property into which such criminally obtained property has been subsequently transformed, as well as any proceeds from the use of such property, may be subject to confiscation.

The sanctions for aiding and abetting public bribery are similar to those for bribery.

(b) For the company / legal entity

In Russia, legal entities have no criminal liability. When a legal entity is held responsible for unlawful conduct, the entity is ordinarily subjected to administrative liability, such as administrative fines.

Article 19.28 of the Code of Administrative Offences provides for the administrative liability of a legal entity for the unlawful provision, offer or promise of anything of pecuniary value to a Russian public official for any actions or omissions to act in the interests of this legal entity.

The sanctions under Article 19.28 of the Code of Administrative Offences vary, depending on the amount of the unlawful remuneration, that is, the bribe. The minimum sanction for a bribe up to RUB1 million (approximately USD12,500) is a fine of up to three times the amount of the bribe, but not less than RUB1 million. The maximum sanction for a bribe over RUB25 million (approximately USD312,500) is a fine of up to 100 times the amount of the bribe, but not less than RUB100 million (approximately USD1.25 million). In all cases, the bribe or its equivalent value may be confiscated.

A legal entity may be held liable under Article 19.28 of the Code of Administrative Offences, irrespective of the liability of a particular individual involved in the giving of a bribe.

1.5 Political contributions

Contributions to political parties are regulated by Federal Law No. 95-FZ "On Political Parties" of 11 July 2001. In general terms, contributions to political parties from legal entities are allowed if they do not exceed RUB43.3 million (approximately USD541,250) per year from one legal entity. As a general rule, political parties are not entitled to receive any contributions from state authorities, foreign entities, individuals and non-commercial organizations that have received any funds from the abovementioned within a year prior to the assumed contribution to a political party.

1.6 Limitations applicable to hospitality expenses (gifts, travel, meals, entertainment, among others)

The applicable limitations on acts of hospitality generally do not depend on the type of hospitality, but rather on the status of the recipient and the general purpose of the hospitality. A general prohibition on accepting any hospitalities (gifts, loans, services, payment for entertainment, vacations and transportation expenses, among others) applies to state and municipal servants. At the same time, under Russian law, not every public official falls under the category of a state or a municipal servant, and each case requires a separate assessment.

2. Domestic bribery (private to private)

2.1 Legal framework

Russian criminal law prohibits active and passive commercial bribery.

2.2 Definition of private bribery

Article 204 of the Criminal Code defines private bribery (named in the legislation as "commercial bribery") as the unlawful provision of anything that has pecuniary value (including property rights and services, among others) to a person who performs managerial functions in a commercial or other organization for an act or omission in connection with such person's official position, in the interest of the provider.

Article 204 contains provisions on passive commercial bribery, that is, receipt by a person who performs managerial functions in a commercial or other organization of anything that has pecuniary value (including property rights, services, among others) for an act or omission in connection with such person's official position in the interests of the provider.

Moreover, the same conduct may be prosecuted under Article 201 of the Criminal Code, which prohibits abuse of authority, that is, the use by a person who performs managerial functions in a commercial or other organization of his authority, contrary to the lawful interests of this organization for the purpose of obtaining an advantage not only for himself but also for other persons, as well as for the purpose of causing damage to other persons.

A person who performs managerial functions, according to Article 201 of the Criminal Code, may be an individual executive officer or a person who is a member of a collective executive body or the board of directors. In addition to the top management, relevant persons include those who perform organizational or administrative functions, that is, manage at least some personnel or at least some property of the organization. As a practical matter, it should be noted that Article 204 of the Criminal Code also covers conspiracies to engage in commercial bribery, which expands the reach of this article beyond persons with managerial functions.

2.3 Consequences of private bribery

(a) For the individuals involved

The sanctions for active commercial bribery under Article 204 of the Criminal Code vary, depending on whether the person giving a commercial bribe has acted alone or is in conspiracy with others, as well as on whether the commercial bribe is given for the commission of a lawful or an unlawful act (or failure to act).

The minimum sanctions are a fine from 10 to 50 times the amount of the commercial bribe and prohibition on holding certain positions or engaging in certain professional activity for a period of up to two years, or limited freedom for a period of up to two years, or forced labor for a period of up to three years, or imprisonment for a period of up to three years. The maximum sanctions are a fine from 40 to 70 times the amount of the commercial bribe and prohibition from holding certain positions or engaging in certain professional activity for a period of up to three years, or forced labor for a period of up to four years, or an arrest for a period from three months to six months, or imprisonment for a period of up to six years.

The sanctions for passive commercial bribery under Article 204 of the Criminal Code vary depending on whether the person receiving a bribe has acted alone or in conspiracy with others, as well as on whether the commercial bribe is received for the commission of a lawful or an unlawful act (omission) and on whether there was extortion of the commercial bribe. The minimum sanctions are a fine from 15 to 70 times the amount of the commercial bribe and prohibition from holding certain positions or engaging in certain professional activity for a period of up to three years, or forced labor for a period of up to five years with or without prohibition from holding certain positions or engaging in certain professional activity for a period of up to three years, or imprisonment for a period of up to seven years and a fine of up to 40 times the amount of the commercial bribe. The maximum sanctions are a fine from 50 to 90 times the amount of the commercial bribe and prohibition from holding certain positions or engaging in certain professional activity for a period of up to three years, or imprisonment for a period of up to 12 years and a fine of up to 50 times the commercial bribe.

A person who has committed an offense of active commercial bribery covered by Article 204 of the Criminal Code may be relieved of criminal liability if he or she actively aided in detecting or prosecuting this offense, or the commercial bribe was extorted from him or her, or he or she voluntarily reported the commercial bribe to criminal law enforcement authorities.

(b) For the company / legal entity

In Russia, there is no criminal liability for legal entities. When a legal entity is held responsible for unlawful conduct, the entity is ordinarily subjected to administrative liability, such as administrative fines.

Article 19.28 of the Code of Administrative Offences provides for the administrative liability of a legal entity for the unlawful provision, offer or promise of anything of pecuniary value to an officer in a commercial company for any actions or omissions to act in the interests of this legal entity.

The sanctions under Article 19.28 of the Code of Administrative Offences vary, depending on the amount of the unlawful remuneration, that is, the bribe. The minimum sanction for a bribe of up to RUB1 million (approximately USD12,500) is a fine of up to three times the amount of the bribe, but not less than RUB1 million. The maximum sanction for a bribe over RUB25 million (approximately USD312,500) is a fine of up to 100 times the amount of the bribe, but not less that RUB100 million (approximately USD1.25 million). In all cases, the bribe or its equivalent value may be confiscated.

A legal entity may be held liable under Article 19.28 of the Code of Administrative Offences, irrespective of the liability of a particular individual involved in the giving of a bribe.

2.4 Limitations applicable to hospitality expenses (gifts, travel, meals, entertainment, among others)

Generally under Russian law, acts of hospitality as a means for the establishment and maintenance of business contacts and a favorable atmosphere of cooperation are not prohibited. The most important restrictions apply against corruption and similar activities that may qualify as a crime and/or administrative offense. In order to make a correct determination of applicable limitations and qualification of possible breaches of anti-corruption and other applicable legislation while providing acts of hospitality, it is essential to understand who the counterparty is and what the purpose of the act is.

3. Corruption of foreign public officials

3.1 Legal framework

Corruption of foreign public officials is prohibited pursuant to the Russian Criminal Code and the Code of Administrative Offences.

3.2 Definition of corruption of foreign public officials

Article 291 of the Criminal Code prohibits the provision of a bribe to foreign public officials and officials of public international organizations. This article also covers the provision of a bribe through intermediaries.

3.3 Definition of foreign public official

A foreign public official is defined in Article 290 of the Criminal Code as any person who is appointed or elected to an office in the legislative, executive, administrative or judicial body of a foreign state, including a public administration or enterprise. An official of a public international organization is an international civil servant or any person authorized by such an organization to act on its behalf.

3.4 Consequences of corruption of foreign public officials

(a) For the individuals involved

The sanctions under Article 291 of the Criminal Code vary, depending on (a) whether the person giving a bribe has acted alone or is in conspiracy with others; (b) whether the bribe is given for the commission of a lawful or an unlawful act (or failure to act); and (c) the amount of the bribe.

The minimum sanction for a bribe not exceeding RUB25,000 (approximately USD312) is a fine of up to RUB500,000 (approximately USD6,250); or a salary or other income of the convicted person for a period of up to one year; or a fine from five to 30 times the amount of the bribe; or correctional labor for up to two years, with or without the prohibition from holding certain positions or engaging in certain professional activity for up to three years; or forced labor for up to three years; or imprisonment for up to two years, with or without a fine of five to 10 times the amount of the bribe. The maximum sanction for a bribe exceeding RUB1 million (approximately USD12,500) is a fine from 70 to 90 times the amount of the bribe, or imprisonment for seven to 12 years and a fine 70 times the amount of the bribe.

A person who has given a bribe may be relieved of criminal liability if he or she actively aids with the detection and prosecution of the crime, or voluntarily reports to the criminal law enforcement authorities after the commission of the crime, or was solicited by a particular public official to give a bribe.

According to Article 104.1 of the Criminal Code, property obtained as a result of a criminal offense and any property into which such criminally obtained property has been subsequently transformed, as well as any proceeds from the use of such property may be subject to confiscation.

(b) For the company / legal entity

In Russia, legal entities have no criminal liability. When a legal entity is held responsible for unlawful conduct, the entity is ordinarily subjected to administrative liability, such as administrative fines.

Article 19.28 of the Code of Administrative Offences provides for the administrative liability of a legal entity for the unlawful provision, offer or promise of anything of pecuniary value to a foreign public official, or an official of a public international organization for any actions or omissions to act in the interest of this legal entity.

The sanctions under Article 19.28 of the Code of Administrative Offences vary, depending on the amount of the unlawful remuneration, that is, the bribe. The minimum sanction for a bribe up to RUB1 million (approximately USD12,500) is a fine of up to three times the amount of the bribe, but not less than RUB1 million. The maximum sanction for a bribe over RUB25 million (approximately USD312,500) is a fine of up to 100 times the amount of the bribe, but not less that RUB100 million (approximately USD1.25 million). In all cases, the bribe or its equivalent value may be confiscated.

A legal entity may be held liable under Article 19.28 of the Code of Administrative Offences, irrespective of the liability of a particular individual involved in the giving of a bribe.

3.5 Limitations applicable to hospitality expenses (gifts, travel, meals, entertainment, among others)

Generally under Russian law, acts of hospitality as a means to establish and maintain business contacts and a favorable atmosphere of cooperation are not prohibited. The most important restrictions apply against corruption and similar activities that may qualify as a crime and/or administrative offense. Thus, hospitalities are possible only insofar as they do not contain the constituent elements of the crime of bribery.

4. Facilitation payments

Russian law does not recognize facilitation payments, and in most cases, such payments could qualify as bribes, and thus, prohibited by law.

5. Compliance programs

5.1 Value of a compliance program to mitigate/eliminate the liability of legal entities

The requirement on companies to take enhanced measures to prevent corruption is contained in Federal Law No. 273 "On Combatting Corruption."

For legal entities and individuals in Russia, administrative liability is fault-based. The Code of Administrative Offences defines fault of a legal entity as a failure to take all measures within its power to comply with the code's requirements. Therefore, a legal entity may raise, as a defense, the measures it has taken to prevent bribery on its behalf. Since 2014, Russian courts have started to recognize and uphold this defense, thus discharging legal entities from liability if a strong compliance program was in place.

5.2 Absence of a compliance program as a crime

Although the absence of or material defects in the Russian entity's internal compliance program does not, *per se*, qualify as a crime under local law, the enforcement practice at the moment includes an increasing number of prosecutors' actions and court cases in connection with inspections of Russian entities on their compliance with the requirements of Federal Law No. 273 "On Combatting Corruption," specifically on measures taken by the companies to prevent corruption. Also, the absence of or material defects in the Russian entity's internal compliance program would constitute an aggravating circumstance in case of prosecution of the Russian entity or its officials for corrupt behavior.

5.3 Elements of a compliance program

Article 13.3 of Federal Law No. 273 "On Combatting Corruption" requires all organizations to develop and implement measures to prevent bribery and specifically recommends the following:

(a) Designating departments, as well as structural units and officers who will be responsible for the prevention of bribery and related offenses

(b) Cooperating with law enforcement authorities

(c) Developing and implementing standards and procedures designed to ensure ethical business conduct

(d) Adopting a code of ethics and professional conduct for all employees

(e) Determining the means for identifying, preventing and resolving conflicts of interest

(f) Preventing the creation and use of false and altered documents

Official guidance as to how the measures should be taken by the legal entities has been prepared by Russia's Ministry of Employment, in cooperation with several public associations, and released in November 2013. The comprehensive guidance includes clarifications of the legal frameworks in terms of Russian, international and foreign laws, as well as practical recommendations for implementing the requirements of the abovementioned article.

6. Regulator with jurisdiction to prosecute corruption

Russia's legal system does not have a specific regulator with exclusive responsibilities to prosecute corruption cases. Any public prosecutor could start a corruption investigation.

Saudi Arabia

Ayman Alawad

Ayman Alawad is actively assisting in general corporate and commercial matters in relation to listed companies, joint stock companies and limited liability companies, as well as in ongoing initial public offerings, including due diligence reviews and work on prospectuses. Prior to joining Legal Advisors, Ayman was a Safety and Environmental Compliance Advisor at Saudi Aramco.

ayman.alawad@bakermckenzie.com
Tel: +966 11 265 8900

Legal Advisors in Association with
Baker & McKenzie Limited
Olayan Complex
Tower II, 3rd Floor
Al Ahsa Street, Malaz
P.O. Box 4288
Riyadh 11491
Saudi Arabia

1. Domestic bribery (private to public)

1.1 Legal framework

Bribery of public officials in Saudi Arabia is prohibited by the Regulations for Combating Bribery, issued under Royal Decree M/36 dated 29/12/1412H, corresponding to 27/6/1992G (the "Bribery Regulations"). The Civil Service Regulations and the Military Officers Regulations also prohibit public servants and military officers from misusing their positions or using influence, including in connection with accepting bribes, and they may be disciplined or terminated for doing so. But unlike the Bribery Regulations, these regulations do not impose any penalties on anyone other than the public servants of officers.

1.2 Definition of bribery

For purposes of the Bribery Regulations, bribery generally means the request or acceptance, and the offer or making, of any promise or gift (defined as any profit or other advantage, tangible or intangible, regardless of what it is called) by or to a public official in order to cause him or her to perform or fail to perform his or her official duties (whether or not to act or the failure to act is lawful), or to pursue any matter with the government.

1.3 Definition of public official

The term "public official" is broadly defined to include the following:

(a) Persons working for the government or any public service whether on a permanent or temporary basis

(b) Arbitrators or experts appointed by the Saudi government or by any authority with judicial capacity

(c) Any person assigned to a specific mission by the Saudi government

(d) Directors and employees of any company or other business establishment who manage or maintain a public establishment or perform a public service, as well as directors and employees of joint stock companies or companies to which the government contributes capital or perform banking activities.

1.4 Consequences of bribery

Penalties under the Bribery Regulations include fines not exceeding SAR1 million or imprisonment for a period not exceeding 10 years or both. They may be imposed on either or both the person offering or making, and the person requesting or accepting a bribe. Pursuing matters with the government that are not within the official duties of the public official is punishable by either or both a fine not exceeding SAR200,000 and imprisonment for a period not exceeding two years. In both cases, the penalties will include the seizure of the bribe.

Companies and other firms, whether Saudi or foreign, are subject to fines of up to 10 times the value of the bribe and, significantly, may be blacklisted from bidding for or participating in government projects if it is proven that a director or an employee was involved in bribery for the benefit of the business entity.

1.5 Political contributions

There are no political parties in Saudi Arabia and public officials are appointed by either the government itself or by the king.

1.6 Limitation applicable to hospitality expenses (gifts, travel, meals, entertainment, among others)

There are no statutory exceptions for or limitations on "hospitality expenses" that exempt them from the definition of bribery. Each such expense must be evaluated on its own and with consideration to the surrounding facts in order to make a judgment on whether it is likely to be considered a bribe.

2. Domestic bribery (private to private)

2.1 Legal framework

The Bribery Regulations do not generally extend to promises or gifts as defined, requested or accepted, and offered or made among persons in the private sector, subject to the following exceptions. Although technically, in the private sector, the definition of "public servant" in the Bribery Regulations does include persons who work for joint stock companies and banks (whether or not they have any government ownership or other relationships with the government), a joint stock company being a reasonably common form of doing business in Saudi Arabia. In addition, the Bribery Regulations also extend to persons performing a "public service," presumably even if not employed by the government. These terms are not defined in the Bribery Regulations and may be interpreted very broadly (e.g., a person performing medical services could be categorized as a public servant even if performing services for a private hospital or clinic).

Other theories of liability may apply to render the participants in wholly private sector bribery, subject to either civil or even criminal exposure. For example, under the Islamic Law (the "*Shari'ah*"), the overriding law of Saudi Arabia, bribery is generally condemned and although whether civil or criminal penalties may be imposed in cases other than those involving public servants is a matter of some debate, some believe that they may be. Other Saudi regulations, such as the Labour, Competition and Procurement Regulations and the Health Professions Law, also contain possible bases to impose liability for private sector bribery, including on an aiding and abetting theory.

2.2 Definition of private bribery

The wide definition of the term "bribery" is as under the Bribery Regulations.

Under the *Shari'ah*, bribery is generally taken to mean the offer or payment of money or any benefit to a person with control over "public" interests in order to obtain entitlements or to stop others from same.

In the Health Professions Regulation, bribery means to request, accept or receive commissions or gratuities, or obtain any benefits in return for the promotion of, or commitment to prescribe certain preparations, or for directing patients to some particular hospital or laboratory or any other acts of similar nature.

2.3 Consequences of private bribery

Penalties that may result from private to private bribery, otherwise subject to the Bribery Regulations, are the same as described in Section 1.4.

Under the *Shari'ah*, the penalties may include fines, the seizure of the bribe or benefit, and the termination of the position held by the bribe taker.

2.4 Limitation applicable to hospitality expenses (gifts, travel, meals, entertainment, among others)

See Section 1.6, which also pertains under the *Shari'ah* and the other regulations cited.

3. Corruption of foreign public officials

There are no Saudi Arabian laws prohibiting or regulating the corruption of public officials of other countries.

4. Facilitation payments

There are no statutory exceptions for or limitations on" facilitation expenses" that exempt them from the definition of bribery, either public or private. Each such expense must be evaluated on its own and with consideration to the surrounding facts in order to judge whether it is likely to be considered a bribe.

5. Compliance programs

There are no compliance program defenses to liability that otherwise might be attached to acts of bribery in Saudi Arabia, although it is possible (though there is no jurisprudence on the issue as far as we are aware of), as an equitable matter, that a court might take into account the existence and operation in fact of such programs in considering the liability of or penalties to be assessed against, for example, a corporate body whose employee engaged in the act of bribery without authorization. The absence of such a compliance program is not in itself an offense, and Saudi law does not prescribe what elements must be part of a compliance program.

6. Regulator with jurisdiction to prosecute corruption

The Public Prosecutor of the Control and Investigation Board has power to prosecute bribery cases before the Board of Grievances, the Saudi court with jurisdiction over such matters, among many others. The investigation is generally carried out by the Administrative Investigation Office. In addition, Saudi Arabia has established the National Anti-Corruption Commission (also known as *Nazaha*) to investigate corruption allegations and follow up on prosecution as well as implement judgments made by the Board of Grievances.

South Africa

Morné van der Merwe

Morné van der Merwe is an M&A/corporate lawyer whose practice has developed a focus on mining transactions and other transactional and corporate work. He routinely assists clients in matters involving mergers and acquisitions, securities law, mining transactions, Black Economic Empowerment transactions, capital markets, corporate finance and structuring, leveraged and management buy-outs, and private equity transactions.

morne.vandermerwe@bakermckenzie.com
Tel: +27 11 911 4305

Gerhard Rudolph

Gerhard Rudolph has extensive experience advising on transactional matters and disputes in a broad range of legal areas, including banking, insurance, construction and engineering, mining and resources, information technology and insolvency, as well as general corporate and commercial issues.

gerhard.rudolph@bakermckenzie.com
Tel: +27 11 911 4370

Nikita Shaw

Nikita Shaw is an associate in the litigation department in Johannesburg and focuses her practice primarily in the corporate and commercial area. Nikita has extensive experience in local labor laws, human resource issues, employee investigations and disciplinary action, and resolving employee disputes.

nikita.shaw@bakermckenzie.com
Tel: +27 11 911 4376

Baker & McKenzie Johannesburg
1 Commerce Square
39 Rivonia Road, Sandhurst
Sandton.2196,
South Africa

1. Domestic bribery (private to public)

1.1 Legal framework

Bribery of public officials is primarily regulated under the Prevention and Combating of Corrupt Activities Act, 2004 (PCCAA), which criminalizes corruption and bribery. However, there are extensive legislations and regulations that deal with various industry-specific forms of corruption. These include the following:

- The Financial Intelligence Centre Act, 2001 (FICA), which is aimed at fighting financial crime such as money laundering, tax evasion and terrorist financing activities

- The Public Finance Management Act, 1999 (PFMA) and the Local Government: Municipal Finance Management Act, 2003 (MFMA), which regulate and monitor government spending to reduce wasteful and unauthorized spending of public funds, and seek to prevent corruption in the procurement process

- The Prevention of Organised Crime Act, 1988 (POCA), which was introduced to combat organized crime, (including money laundering and criminal gang activities), and provides for the preservation and forfeiture of property implicated in these offenses

- The Protected Disclosures Act, 2000, which provides protection to employees who disclose information relating to corrupt activities within the workplace, in both the private and public spheres

- The Criminal Procedure Act, 1977 (CPA), which provides for procedures relating to all crimes, including domestic bribery

- The Companies Act, 2008 (Companies Act), which seeks to provide protection for whistleblowers and to stop corrupt activities within companies through the practice of good corporate governance

- Various international agreements and conventions to which South Africa is a party, which oblige South Africa to address corruption and bribery in the public and private spheres

1.2 Definition of bribery

The concept of bribery in South Africa is referred to as "corruption" and is a crime that may be committed by both public officials and private individuals, as well as both public and private entities.

The PCCAA provides for a general offense of corruption, which is very broadly defined, as well as specific offenses in respect of corrupt activities relating to a range of specific persons and specific matters. We do not intend to belabor this article with the provisions relating to specified corrupt activities and will accordingly deal predominantly with the general offense of corruption.

In general, a person will commit corruption if he or she directly or indirectly accepts or offers to accept gratification from another person, or gives or agrees to give gratification to any other person for his or her benefit, or that of another, and such giving or receipt is done in order to induce the other party to act in an improper manner, in the performance of that individual's duties.

Gratification is also extremely broadly defined and includes, but is not limited to, money, donations and gifts, employment, avoidance of loss or liability and any other valuable consideration, or benefit of any kind.

The PCCAA has extraterritorial jurisdiction in certain circumstances. Even if the act alleged to constitute an offense was committed outside of South Africa, South African courts will have jurisdiction if the person to be charged is:

- a citizen of South Africa;
- ordinarily resident in South Africa;
- was arrested in the territory of South Africa;
- is a company incorporated or registered as such in South Africa; or
- any body of persons, corporate or unincorporated in South Africa.

1.3 Definition of public official

The position of public official in South Africa is referred to as a "public officer" and is defined in terms of the PCCAA as any person who is a member, an officer, an employee or a servant of a public body, and includes any person in the public service, any person receiving remuneration from public funds, or where a public body is a corporation, the person who is incorporated as such. This definition explicitly excludes members of the legislative and prosecuting authorities, as well as judicial officers.

1.4 Consequences of bribery

(a) For the individuals involved

The penalty provisions in the PCCAA differentiate between certain categories of offenses. The penalties in relation to the majority of the offenses (including the general offense of corruption) are the following:

- In the case of a sentence to be imposed by a High Court, a fine or imprisonment up to a period of imprisonment for life
- In the case of a sentence to be imposed by a regional court, a fine or imprisonment up to a period not exceeding 18 years
- In the case of a sentence to be imposed by a magistrate's court, a fine or imprisonment up to a period not exceeding five years

Other categories of offenses in terms of the PCCAA, such as the concealment of the offense of corruption and being an accessory to or after the offense of corruption, carry lesser penalties, namely:

- In the case of a sentence to be imposed by a High Court or regional court, a fine or imprisonment up to a period not exceeding 10 years
- In the case of a sentence to be imposed by a magistrate's court, a fine or imprisonment up to a period not exceeding three years

In addition to any fine a court may impose, as abovementioned, the court may further impose a fine equal to five times the value of the gratification involved in the offense.

Furthermore, the PCCAA provides for a register of entities and individuals convicted of acts of corruption relating to contracts and the procurement and withdrawal of tenders, with the consequence being that the national treasury may terminate any agreement and prevent such persons from doing business with the government for 10 years. The national treasury may also recover from the person or enterprise any damages incurred or sustained by the state as a result of the tender process or the conclusion of the agreement, or that the state may suffer by having to make less favorable arrangements afterwards.

Lastly, the proceeds of and assets instrumental in the commission of the offense of corruption may be confiscated and/or forfeited in terms of the POCA. Generally, the value of assets may be used to compensate victims of the crime involved, or forfeited to the state.

(b) For the company / legal entity

Both the general offense of corruption and the penalties previously identified apply equally to a company / legal entity that commits the crime of corruption.

(c) For the public official involved

The PFMA and MFMA provide for measures to deal with financial mismanagement (which may constitute corruption) in the context of procurement in the public sector. Any spending by political officials that falls outside of the regulatory framework, and which results in allegations of financial mismanagement, will lead to an investigation and a subsequent disciplinary hearing in accordance with the prescribed procedures. Furthermore, the codes of conduct for public officials, as provided for in various statutes such as the Public Service Act, 1994 and the Executive Members' Ethics Act, 1998, regulate the management of gifts and hospitality.

Regulations published under the Local Government: Municipal Systems Act, 2000, further seek to curb corruption in municipalities by banning a person dismissed for financial and related misconduct from being employed as a senior manager in any municipality for up to 10 years.

Most of the penalties for violations of the abovementioned legislative framework apply to employees of the public service and include termination of employment, criminal charges, and publishing the identity of the person and details of the contravention.

1.5 Political contributions

Public funding by the state to political parties represented in Parliament and in the provincial legislatures is regulated by the Public Funding of Represented Political Parties Act, 1997.

By contrast, private funding of political parties is almost entirely unregulated and disclosure is discretionary. Public opinion and recent case law on this issue is divided.

1.6 Limitation applicable to hospitality expenses (gifts, travel, meals, entertainment, among others)

In general terms, South African law does not prescribe any limitation on hospitality expenses; however, whether or not a hospitality expense is appropriate will depend on the reasons for the gift or entertainment and on the level of employment of the government official to whom it is offered.

Accordingly, public officials must ensure that they do not compromise the credibility or integrity of the supply chain management system and must not use their official positions to obtain gifts or benefits for themselves during the performance of their official duties, or accept any gifts or benefits when offered.

However, senior government employees may accept gifts that are offered as part of a formal exchange of gifts, or if the gifts are unsolicited or constitute a moderate act of hospitality, and they are satisfied that they will not, in any way, be compromised by such acceptance. Senior government employees, however, are required to disclose the following:

- Gifts and acts of hospitality from a source other than a family member with a value in excess of ZAR350
- Gifts from a single source that cumulatively exceed the value of ZAR350 in a 12-month period
- Hospitality intended as a gift in kind

2. Domestic bribery (private to private)

2.1 Legal framework

Private bribery is regulated by the PCCAA.

2.2 Definition of private bribery

Private bribery falls within the ambit of the general offense of corruption, as earlier set out.

2.3 Consequences of private bribery

The consequences of private bribery for the individual and/or for the company / legal entity committing the crime of corruption are as earlier set out. Please see Section 1.4.

2.4 Limitation applicable to hospitality expenses (gifts, travel, meals, entertainment, among others)

In general terms, South African law does not prescribe any limitation on hospitality expenses; however, whether or not a hospitality expense is appropriate will depend on the reasons for the gift or entertainment, and if the purpose of the hospitality expense was to induce the other party to act in an unauthorized manner. Accordingly, hospitality expenses in the private sector are not unlawful, *per se*, provided that the expenses are not given as a form of gratification for an unauthorized or improper inducement to do, or not to do, anything. In practice, most companies have their own internal hospitality expenses policy, which regulates the acceptance and offering of gifts.

3. Corruption of foreign public officials

3.1 Legal framework

Corruption of foreign public officials is regulated by the PCCAA. In addition, the Companies Act regulates dealings with foreign officials through a Social and Ethics Committee. Finally, certain foreign legislation has extraterritorial jurisdiction and can therefore be imposed on activities in South Africa that deal with foreign public officials.

3.2 Definition of corruption of foreign public officials

While corruption of foreign public officials falls within the ambit of the general offense of corruption, as earlier explained, the PCCAA also provides for specific offenses in respect of corrupt activities relating to foreign public officials.

Generally speaking, these provisions make it an offense for any person to directly or indirectly give or agree or offer to give any gratification to a foreign public official, whether for the benefit of that foreign public official or for the benefit of another person, in order to act, personally or by influencing another person to act, in an improper or unauthorized manner.

In this context, "to act" specifically includes using a foreign public official's or such other person's position to influence any acts or decisions of the foreign state or the public international organization concerned, or obtaining or retaining a contract, business or an advantage in the conduct of business of that foreign state or public international organization.

3.3 Definition of foreign public official

For purposes of this crime, a foreign public official means:

- any person holding a legislative, administrative or judicial office of a foreign state;

- any person performing public functions for a foreign state, including any person employed by a board, commission, corporation or other body or authority that performs a function on behalf of the foreign state; or
- an official or agent of a public international organization.

3.4 Consequences of corruption of foreign public officials

The consequences of corruption of foreign public officials for individuals and/or for the company/legal entity involved are as set out in Section 1.4.

3.5 Limitation applicable to hospitality expenses (gifts, travel, meals, entertainment, among others)

In general terms, South African law does not prescribe any limitation on hospitality expenses; however, whether or not a hospitality expense is appropriate will depend on the reasons for the gift or entertainment and on the level of employment of the government official to whom it is offered.

4. Facilitation payments

Facilitation payments (i.e., a financial payment to a public official made with the intention of expediting an administrative process) are not excluded from the ambit of the PCCAA. Accordingly, such payments would fall squarely within the definition of an unauthorized gratification, and as such, could amount to corruption.

5. Compliance programs

5.1 Value of a compliance program to mitigate/eliminate the criminal liability of legal entities

As a general proposition, South African legal entities may be held vicariously liable in terms of the CPA for the crimes committed by directors or servants, acting within the scope of their employment or authority, or while furthering the interests of the corporate body.

Furthermore, South African case law has held that knowledge of the acts of omissions by the corporation or its members is not a relevant consideration when determining criminal liability.

South African law does not specifically recognize compliance programs and as such, does not officially stipulate how such programs may mitigate liability.

However, the South African government has introduced requirements for certain companies (such as state-owned and public companies) to adopt the international recommendations on combating bribery, bribe solicitation and extortion, as contained in the Organisation for Economic Co-operation and Development guidelines for multinational enterprises. These requirements are contained in the Companies Act and, *inter alia*, provide for the establishment of a Social and Ethics Committee. A Social and Ethics Committee must be established by:

- every state-owned company;
- every listed public company; and
- any other company that has, in any two of the previous five years, had a public interest score of at least 500 points.

The public interest score of a company is calculated at the end of each financial year as the sum of the following:

- The number of points equal to the average number of employees of the company during the last financial year
- 1 point for every ZAR1 million (or portion thereof) in third-party liability of the company, at the financial year end
- 1 point for every ZAR1 million (or portion thereof) in turnover during the financial year

- 1 point for every individual (natural person) who, at the end of the financial year, is known by the company to directly or indirectly have a beneficial interest in any of the company's issued securities

The Social and Ethics Committee is tasked with a number of monitoring activities, including monitoring the company's activities in relation to good corporate citizenship, which includes the company's measures to address corruption.

While the implementation of a compliance program may not necessarily absolve a legal entity of vicarious liability, it may be considered mitigating if the company is able to show that it has taken all reasonable steps to prevent the commission of corruption.

5.2 Absence of a compliance program as a crime

South African law does not recognize the absence of a compliance program as a crime.

5.3 Elements of a compliance program

(a) Legal framework

South African law does not specifically recognize or regulate compliance programs.

(b) Recommended practice

It is recommended practice that companies establish a Social and Ethics Committee to initiate, monitor and implement a robust compliance program as a strategy to mitigate liability for crimes of corruption.

6. Regulator with jurisdiction to prosecute corruption

The primary law enforcement body in South Africa is the South African Police Services (SAPS), which is the first port of call for any person wanting to report a suspected act of corruption and open a criminal case. Within the SAPS is the Directorate for Priority Crime Investigations (colloquially known as the Hawks).

The National Prosecuting Authority (NPA), which is South Africa's centralized prosecuting authority, has the power to initiate criminal proceedings on behalf of the state. Within the NPA are the Specialized Commercial Crimes Unit, which has specialized commercial crime prosecutors and courts, and the Asset Forfeiture Unit, which recovers the proceeds of organized crime.

Other bodies utilized in investigating and prosecuting corruption are the following:

- The Public Protector, which accepts complaints of corruption that involve government departments, agencies or officials who violate their ethical codes or codes of conduct, as long as it is not a criminal case

- Auditor General, which audits all government departments and state institutions to oversee whether funds are being used for a proper purpose

- The Public Service Commission, which accepts complaints from individuals regarding maladministration, dishonesty, improper behavior or financial misconduct by government employees

- The Magistrates' Commission, which investigates complaints of corruption involving magistrates

- The Judicial Service Commission, which receives and investigates complaints of corruption involving judges

- The Independent Police Investigative Directorate, which investigates complaints of misconduct, including corruption, involving the SAPS and metro police services

- The Special Investigating Unit, which investigates corruption and maladministration in government

- The Multi-Agency Working Group, which was set up by the Minister of Finance to coordinate and investigate corruption related to supply chain management practices

- The Anti-Corruption Task Team, which fast tracks high priority corruption investigations and prosecutions and co-ordinates all government anti-corruption agencies and initiatives

- The Special Anti-Corruption Unit in the Department of Public Service and Administration, which focuses on the investigation and prosecution of disciplinary cases against senior public servants involved in corruption

Spain

Rafael Jimenez-Gusi

Rafael Jiménez-Gusi is a partner of the Corporate Group and co-chair of the Spanish Compliance Practice Group. He is also a member of the Firm's Compliance Steering Committee in EMEA. Rafael has more than 25 years of experience handling cross-border M&A transactions and company reorganizations. He serves as secretary of several Spanish corporations, where he regularly advises on corporate issues and compliance matters. He has advised companies in different sectors in their compliance policies and in risk analysis. He has organized and conducted numerous internal investigations involving allegations of corruption and company fraud.

rafael.jimenez-gusi@bakermckenzie.com
Tel: +34 93 206 08 20

Baker & McKenzie Barcelona S.L.P.
Avda. Diagonal, 652
Edif. D, 8th Floor
Barcelona 08034
Spain

Cecilia Pastor

Cecilia Pastor is a partner in the Corporate/Commercial Department of Baker & McKenzie's Madrid office. She is co-chair of the Spanish Compliance Practice Group, which includes practitioners from all areas of practice. Cecilia has worked extensively with clients in regulated sectors, especially in the healthcare sector. She regularly advises on compliance and has put in place a number of programs and training, primarily working with multinational companies. She has also led compliance audits and participated in cross-border compliance investigations and therefore has a grasp of the wider issues triggered by compliance-related issues.

cecilia.pastor@bakermckenzie.com
Tel: +34 91 230 4500

Baker & McKenzie Madrid S.L.P.
Paseo de la Castellana, 92
Madrid 28046
Spain

Diego Pol

Diego Pol is a senior associate of the Corporate Department of Baker & McKenzie's Barcelona office. He is a member of the Task Force of Global Compliance News, a compliance news platform moderated by Baker & McKenzie. He advises Spanish and foreign clients on acquisitions and investments in Spain, corporate compliance, anti-corruption laws, corporate criminal liability, exports of military and dual use items, and international sanctions. He regularly assists clients in internal investigations. He is a dual qualified lawyer, admitted both to the Barcelona Bar and the Florida Bar (USA).

diego.pol@bakermckenzie.com
Tel: +34 93 206 08 20

Baker & McKenzie Barcelona S.L.P.
Avda. Diagonal, 652
Edif. D, 8th Floor
Barcelona 08034
Spain

1. Domestic bribery (private to public)

1.1 Legal framework

The Spanish Criminal Code has seen significant amendments since 2010, when criminal liability of legal entities for bribery and other crimes was introduced.

The present overview of Spanish anti-bribery laws reflects the new amendment of the Spanish Criminal Code that entered into force on 1 July 2015.

Bribery of public officials (*cohecho*) is regulated under the Spanish Criminal Code, Sections 419 to 427.

1.2 Definition of bribery

Bribery can be committed by private individuals who try to corrupt a public official (active bribery) and by the corrupted public officials (passive bribery).

Bribery occurs whenever a public servant or authority receives or is offered a reward to: (1) carry out an act or omission breaching the duties required of his or her position; or (2) carry out any act relating to the performance of his or her duties. The offense can take the form of 'passive bribery,' where the initiative to commit the offense originates with the public official or authority (i.e., soliciting a bribe), or 'active bribery,' where the bribe is offered at the initiative of the individual paying it. To be punishable, it is necessary that such acts be committed maliciously, that is to say, intentionally.

1.3 Definition of public official

The Spanish Criminal Code has a broad definition of "public official" and "authority." Section 24 of the Criminal Code defines an 'authority' as one who, either himself or herself, or as a member of an agency, tribunal or collective body, has the power to give orders or who exercises his or her own jurisdiction. Meanwhile, a 'public official' is one who, either by operation of law or by appointment of the relevant authority, participates in the discharge of public duties.[1]

Additionally Section 427 of the Spanish Criminal Code expands the concept of public official to those public officials of the European Union or foreign countries (including elected officials and individuals carrying out public duties on behalf of an international organization or a public company of a foreign government).

Section 423 of the Spanish Criminal Code states that the offense of bribery can also be committed by juries, arbitrators, experts and 'any person participating in the performing of a public service.'

1.4 Consequences of bribery

(a) For individuals

The Spanish Criminal Code foresees the same penalties for corrupted public officials and for private individuals that corrupt public officials.

Passive bribery is regulated under Sections 419 to 423 of the Criminal Code. There are four different types of conduct that constitute passive bribery:

- Those that consist in carrying out an act or omission breaching the duties required of the public servant or authority's position (Section 419)

This is punishable by imprisonment for a period of three years to six years, a daily fine (from a minimum of EUR2 to EUR400) the amount of which will depend on the accused party's wealth and which may apply for 12 months to 24 months, and specific disqualification from holding public office or employment for a period of seven years to 12

[1] As Spanish courts have consistently held, the concept of public servant contained in the Criminal Code is only applicable for criminal law purposes, as is clear from Article 24, and that it is different from the term used in the administrative sphere.

years, in addition to the penalty for committing the act or omission breaching the required duties, if this constitutes a separate crime.

- Those that consist in carrying out an act relating to the performance of the public servant or authority's duties (Section 420)

This is punishable by imprisonment for a period of two years to four years, a daily fine the amount of which will depend on the accused party's assets and which may apply for 12 months to 24 months, and specific disqualification from holding public office or employment for a period of three years to seven years.

- Those that have as an intended purpose the reward of an act that has already been carried out (Section 421)

This is punishable by the same penalties referred to in the aforementioned Sections 419 and 420.

- The acceptance of a reward offered to an authority or public servant in view of his or her office or duty (Section 422), even if he or she is not asked to carry out any act

This is punishable by imprisonment for a period of six months to one year and specific disqualification from holding public office or employment for a period of one year to three years.

Active bribery is regulated under Sections 424 and 425 of the Criminal Code, and punishes a private individual for the commission of the following:

- The offer or delivery of a gift or remuneration of any kind to an authority or public servant (i) for the latter to perpetrate an act that is against the duties inherent in his or her office or an act inherent in his or her office; or (ii) to delay what he or she should carry out, or in consideration of his or her office or duty

- The delivery of a gift or remuneration following solicitation by the authority or public servant

The penalties imposed on private individuals who commit active bribery are the same as those imposed on the public servant or authority to whom the reward is offered (Articles 419 to 422 of the Criminal Code).

(b) For legal entities

- A daily fine the amount of which will depend on the legal entity's assets and which may apply from six months to five years (from a minimum of EUR30 to EUR5,000 per day), or up to five times the profit obtained, if such amount was higher
- Additionally, the court can impose one of the following discretionary penalties:
    - Dissolution of the legal entity
    - Suspension of its activities for up to five years
    - Closure of premises and establishments for up to five years
    - Temporary (up to 15 years) or indefinite prohibition to carry out the activities that have led to a crime
    - Prohibition (up to 15 years) to benefit from public subsidies, enter into contracts with the public sector, or benefit from tax and social security incentives or benefits
    - Judicial intervention for an unlimited time of all or part of the activities of the legal entity to protect general interest and employees

1.5 Political contributions

Contributions to political parties are currently regulated by Organic Law 8/2007 of July 4, 2007, on financing of political parties (*Ley Orgánica de Financiación de Partidos Políticos*) (as amended by Organic Law 5/2012). In general terms, contributions to political parties are allowed if they do not exceed EUR100,000 per year. Anonymous contributions are forbidden.

Additionally, political parties shall not accept or receive, directly or indirectly: (i) contributions from private companies (its affiliates or foundations) that provide services or perform works, under a contract in force, for the government, public bodies or companies with majority of public capital; nor (ii) contributions from private foundations, associations or other entities receiving grants from the government or whose budget is composed, in whole or in part, by direct or indirect public contributions.

The Spanish government has announced the adoption of stricter laws related to the financial control of political parties.

1.6 Limitation applicable to hospitality expenses (gifts, travel, meals, entertainment, among others)

Spanish courts have generally recognized that two key objective elements are necessary (apart from performing one of the abovementioned acts) for a finding of bribery, namely:

(a) the reward should not be socially acceptable in the sector in which the public servant performs his or her duties; and

(b) the value of the reward should be high enough to be able to influence the public servant's decision.

In addition, Spanish courts have consistently demanded the existence of a causal link between the delivery of the gift, hospitality or remuneration and the public office of the public servant. That is to say, the reason for the gift must be the status or condition of authority or public servant of the individual receiving the gift.

There is no legal guidance as to the value of any benefit and its capacity to influence a public servant's decision. Whether a hospitality expense could be considered bribery will need to be determined on a case-by-case basis, taking into account all the facts and circumstances surrounding the case and applying the two criteria referred to previously.

2. Domestic bribery (private to private)

2.1 Legal framework

Bribery of private entities or individuals is regulated under Section 286-*bis* of the Spanish Criminal Code. Such crime was introduced *ex novo* by amendment of the Criminal Code of December 2010,[2] fulfilling the mandate contained in Framework Decision 2003/568/JAI to prevent acts intended to corrupt company management in a similar way to those of bribery.

2.2 Definition of private bribery

As in the case of public bribery, the offense requires the act of offering, promising, giving, soliciting, accepting or receiving an unjustified benefit or advantage that, in this case, must be intended to secure preferential treatment in the acquisition or sale of goods or in hiring professional services, in breach of the recipient's obligations.

---

[2] Organic Law 5/2010, 22 June, which amends Organic Law 10/1995, 23 November, of the Criminal Code.

2.3 Consequences of private bribery

Section 286-*bis* of the Criminal Code punishes this conduct with the following penalties:

(a) For individuals

- Imprisonment (for six months to four years)
- A fine amounting from the value of the illicit benefit or advantage to three times the said value
- Disqualification from the right to carry out an industrial or commercial activity (from one year to six years)

(b) For legal entities

- Daily fine of up to five years (please see first bullet point of Section 1.4 (b))
- Publication of the court judgment in the corresponding official gazettes and, if the victims so request, in the general newspapers
- Dissolution of the legal entity
- Suspension of the activity of the legal entity for up to five years
- Close-down of the legal entity's facilities for up to five years
- Temporary (up to 15 years) or indefinite prohibition to carry out the activities that have made it possible for the crime to be committed
- Prohibition of up to 15 years to benefit from public aid, enter into contracts with the public sector, or benefit from tax and Social Security incentives or benefits

- Judicial intervention for an unlimited time of all or part of the activities of the legal entity to protect the interest of the general public and the employees of the legal entity in particular

2.4 Limitation applicable to hospitality expenses (gifts, travel, meals, entertainment, among others)

The Criminal Code does not establish quantitative nor qualitative limitations on hospitality expenses. Case law has established two criteria to determine whether a hospitality payment could be considered private bribery:

- The hospitality offered or received is not "socially acceptable."

- The hospitality offered or received could affect the judgment of the receiver.

Whether a hospitality expense could be considered bribery will need to be determined on a case-by-case basis, taking into account all the facts and circumstances surrounding the case and applying the two criteria referred to previously.

3. Corruption of foreign public officials

3.1 Legal framework

The regulation of domestic bribery (see Section 1 above) encompasses corruption of foreign public officials, since these are considered public officials as well for these purposes, pursuant to Section 427 of the Spanish Criminal Code.

Additionally, Section 286 *ter* of the Spanish Criminal Code sets out a specific offense of bribery of foreign public officials when committed with the objective of obtaining or retaining a contract or business, as well as any other competitive advantage in the context of international economic activities.

3.2 Definition of corruption of foreign public officials

See Section 1.2 above in relation to the general crime of corruption of public officials.

The offense of Section 286 *ter* of the Criminal Code requires the offer, promise or giving of any undue benefit or advantage to a public official so that the public official acts or omits to act in relation to the exercise of his or her public duties, to obtain or retain a contract or business, as well as any other competitive advantage in the context of international economic activities

3.3 Definition of foreign public official

See Section 1.3 above.

3.4 Consequences of corruption of foreign public officials

See Section 1.4 above in relation to the general crime of corruption of public officials.

In relation to the offense set out in Section 286 *ter* of the Spanish Criminal Code, the following may be imposed, unless the author has received a more severe punishment for the same conduct pursuant to another section of the Criminal Code:

(a) For individuals

- Three months' to six months' imprisonment
- A daily fine from three months to six months or, if the benefit obtained is higher than said fine, thrice the value of the benefit or advantage obtained
- Prohibition to contract with the public sector, disqualification from receiving public subsidies, contracting with public entities, obtaining tax or social security benefits and prohibition from participating in transactions of public importance for seven to 12 years

(b) For legal entities

- Same as in Section 2.3(b)

3.5 Limitation applicable to hospitality expenses (gifts, travel, meals, entertainment, among others)

The Criminal Code does not establish quantitative nor qualitative limitations on hospitality expenses. Case law has established two criteria to determine whether a hospitality payment could be considered a crime of corruption of a public official:

- The hospitality offered or received is not "socially acceptable."
- The hospitality offered or received could affect the judgment of the receiver.

Whether a hospitality expense could be considered bribery will need to be determined on a case-by-case basis, taking into account all the facts and circumstances surrounding the case and applying the two criteria referred to previously.

4. Facilitation payments

The Spanish Criminal Code does not recognize so-called facilitation payments, and consequently, quantitative or qualitative limitations as established by case law (see Section 3.5) should apply for this purpose.

As a matter of principle, however, cash payments to public officials are very likely to be considered as corruption payments since the first criteria (i.e., be considered "socially acceptable") will not be met.

5. Compliance programs

5.1 Value of a compliance program to mitigate/eliminate the criminal liability for legal entities

Compliance programs are regulated under Section 31 *bis* paragraph 2 of the Spanish Criminal Code. In accordance to such section, the effective adoption of an organization and management model implementing supervision and control measures capable of preventing offenses (the "Compliance Program") is expressly deemed to exempt liability. To benefit from such exemption of liability, the legal entity will need to prove the following:

- The directors have adopted and executed in an efficient manner a Compliance Program.
- The functioning and supervision of the Compliance Program have been bestowed to a body of the legal entity with independent powers of initiative and control, or which has legally entrusted with the power to supervise the internal controls of the entity.
- The individual authors have committed the criminal offense while fraudulently eluding the Compliance Program.
- There has been no omission or insufficient exercise of the supervision and control functions by the abovementioned body.

Additionally, Section 31 *quáter* considers as mitigating circumstance the adoption by the legal entity (once the offense has been committed) of one or more of the following actions:

- Confession to the criminal offense to the relevant authorities before any investigation is initiated
- Collaboration with the investigation by providing key evidence or information to solve the case

- Mitigation of damages caused as a consequence of the offense before the trial hearing takes place

- Implementation of a Compliance Program before the trial hearing takes place

5.2 Absence of a Compliance Program as a crime

The Spanish Criminal Code does not deem the absence of a Compliance Program itself as a crime of the directors of the entity.

5.3 Elements of a Compliance Program

(a) Legal framework

The Spanish Criminal Code defines the content of a Compliance Program that every legal entity must have to avoid criminal liability. A Compliance Program must:

- identify the activities in which the offenses to be prevented can happen (risk assessment);

- establish the protocols or procedures defining the legal entity's decision-making process and the execution of such decisions;

- implement adequate financial management models;

- impose the obligation to report potential risks and breaches to the body in charge of supervising compliance with the prevention model and its functioning;

- establish a disciplinary system to appropriately punish any breaches of the measures established by the model; and

- impose a periodic verification and, if necessary, amendment to the model when there have been significant violations of its provisions, or when organizational changes take place in the control structure or activity developed by the entity.

(b) Recommended practice

The adoption of a robust Compliance Program is the only valid defense to prevent criminal liability of the legal entity.

6. Regulator with jurisdiction to prosecute corruption

The Spanish legal system does not have a specific regulator with exclusive responsibilities to prosecute corruption. Any public prosecutor could request a judge to start a corruption investigation. However, the Spanish system has a group of public prosecutors that specializes in prosecuting corruption. In this sense, the Spanish government created an Anti-Corruption Prosecution Office, whose main purpose is to investigate and become party to all major cases related to financial offenses or any offense committed by public officials or authorities that constitutes bribery.

The Anti-Corruption Prosecutor's Office has been strengthened with the inclusion of real criminal investigation groups, including public officials, special police forces and other civil servants.

The judicial police units have also been strengthened, with their investigations carried out in criminal proceedings under the authority of a judge.

Sweden

Mattias Hedwall

Mattias Hedwall is head of Baker & McKenzie's Global Trade & Commerce Group. He specializes in trade and commerce and compliance, mergers and acquisitions, and franchising. His practice encompasses negotiating commercial transactions and agreements, handling international compliance programs and trade-related issues, privately negotiated transactions, and advising on mergers, reorganizations and investments. Mattias has more than two decades' legal experience. He joined Baker & McKenzie Stockholm in 1996. He has for many years been on the Stockholm office's board of directors and is currently the chairman of the board. He also heads the Stockholm Commercial Transactions and Projects Department. He represents and advises a number of prominent companies in industries such as manufacturing, transportation, retail, advertisement, travel and media.

mattias.hedwall@bakermckenzie.com
Tel: +46 8 566 177 33

Johan Strand

Johan Strand is an associate in the Firm's Stockholm Trade & Commerce Practice Group. He specializes in commercial agreements, anti-bribery and data privacy compliance. He has experience advising clients on developing and implementing specific compliance procedures and general compliance programs.

johan.strand@bakermckenzie.com
Tel: +46 8 566 177 41

Baker & McKenzie Advokatbyrå KB
P.O. Box 180
Vasagatan 7, Floor 8
Stockholm SE-101 23
Sweden

1. Domestic bribery (private to public)

1.1 Legal framework

In Swedish legislation, there is no distinction between bribery of public officials and private bribery. There is also no distinction between bribery of foreign or domestic public officials. However, the involvement of a public official will act as an aggravating circumstance and make it more likely that a benefit is deemed a bribe. Bribery is regulated under the Swedish Penal Code, Chapter 10, Section 5 a-e. There are also some ancillary legislation that could be applicable in relation to bribery issues, such as the Marketing Act (SFS 2008:486) and the Swedish Income Tax Act (SFS 1999:1229).

1.2 Definition of bribery

An employee or person performing an assignment who, for himself or another person, receives, accepts a promise of, or demands an improper benefit for the performance of the employment or assignment, may be deemed as taking a bribe.

A person who, on the other hand, gives, promises or offers an improper benefit in the cases referred to above may be viewed as giving a bribe.

A benefit does not necessarily have to be aimed at, give rise to or reward improper action, or be beneficial to the person who has given, promised or offered the benefit in order to be deemed improper. An improper benefit is a benefit that objectively has the potential to affect the performance of a task or be perceived as a reward for the performance of a task.

In addition to the offenses of taking and giving a bribe, trading in influence and negligent financing of bribery are also punishable offenses related to bribery. Trading in influence involves the act of taking or giving an improper benefit in order to influence a person's action or decision in the exercise of public authority or in public procurement. An individual acting on behalf of a company that provides money or assets used by a third party for the giving of a bribe may be found guilty of negligent financing of bribery.

1.3 Definition of public official

The Swedish Criminal Code contains no definition of public official since there is no specific offense for bribery of public officials. However, "employee or person performing an assignment" includes, *inter alia*, assignments based on election, appointment, duty and agreement.

1.4 Consequences of bribery

(a) For the individuals involved

The Swedish Penal Code establishes the same range of penalties for public officials as for individuals that bribe public officials. The penalties are the following:

- A fine (proportional to the income of the individual, limited to a maximum of SEK150,000) or up to two years of imprisonment
- If deemed as a gross crime, between six months and six years of imprisonment (The non-exhaustive lists of criteria to be considered include the position of the individual, the value of the benefits, whether the bribery has been part of systematic criminal activity or criminal activity of large proportions, or otherwise is of a particularly dangerous kind.)

(b) For the company / legal entity

- A fine between SEK5,000 and SEK10 million (This requires that the company has not done what can be reasonably expected to prevent the bribery, or that the bribery has been committed by an individual in a leading position or with special responsibility for supervision.)

1.5 Political contributions

Political parties must report to the Swedish public authority (*Kammarkollegiet*) contributions received, and such information must be made available to the public. This requirement follows from an act that entered into force on 1 April 2014 (*Lagen (2014:105) om insyn i finansiering av partier*). The act applies to parties that are taking part in elections for the Swedish Parliament or the European Parliament. The report shall also cover the contributions made to personal campaigns for persons elected as members of the Swedish or European parliament.

There are no limits on the amount of private contributions to political parties. Anonymous contributions are allowed but political parties that accept an anonymous contribution of a value greater than SEK22,150 (limit applies 2016) are not eligible to receive public funding.

1.6 Limitation applicable to hospitality expenses (gifts, travel, meals, entertainment, among others)

The Penal Code does not establish quantitative or qualitative limitations on hospitality expenses. In order to assess whether a hospitality expense is considered to be a bribe, the fact of the hospitality expense being an improper benefit has to be established. The meaning of improper benefit is further described in preparatory works of the Penal Code as a benefit that objectively has the potential to affect the performance of a task or be perceived as a reward for the performance of a task.

Whether a hospitality expense could be considered bribery will need to be determined on a case-by- case basis, taking into account all the facts and circumstances surrounding the case. The type of hospitality, the economic value and the position of the receiver are examples of these kinds of circumstances. Even though there is no separate legislation regarding bribery of public officials, hospitality given to public officials is more likely to be deemed improper due to the responsibility and trust associated with their position.

2. Domestic bribery (private to private)

2.1 Legal framework

In Swedish legislation, there is no distinction between bribery of public officials and private bribery. There is also no distinction between bribery of foreign or domestic public officials. However, the involvement of a public official will act as an aggravating circumstance and make it more likely that a benefit will be deemed a bribe. Bribery is regulated under the Swedish Penal Code, Chapter 10, Section 5 a-e. There are also some ancillary legislation that could be applicable in relation to bribery issues, such as the Marketing Act (SFS 2008:486) and the Swedish Income Tax Act (SFS 1999:1229).

2.2 Definition of private bribery

An employee or person performing an assignment who, for himself or herself or another person, receives, accepts a promise of, or demands an improper benefit for the performance of the employment or assignment, may be deemed as taking a bribe.

A person who, on the other hand, gives, promises or offers an improper benefit in the cases referred to above may be viewed as giving a bribe.

A benefit does not necessarily have to be aimed at, give rise to or reward improper action, or be beneficial to the person who has given, promised or offered the benefit in order to be deemed improper. An improper benefit is a benefit that objectively has the potential to affect the performance of a task or be perceived as a reward for the performance of a task.

In addition to the offenses of taking and giving a bribe, trading in influence and negligent financing of bribery are also punishable offenses related to bribery. Trading in influence involves the act of taking or giving an improper benefit in order to influence a person's action or decision in the exercise of public authority or in public procurement. An individual acting on behalf of a company that provides money or assets used by a third party for the giving of a bribe may be found guilty of negligent financing of bribery.

2.3 Consequences of private bribery

(a) For the individuals involved

- A fine (proportional to the income of the individual, limited to a maximum of SEK150,000) or up to two years of imprisonment
- If deemed as a gross crime, between six months and six years of imprisonment (The non-exhaustive lists of criteria to be considered include the position of the individual, the value of the benefits, whether the bribery has been part of systematic criminal activity or criminal activity of large proportions, or otherwise is of a particularly dangerous kind.)

(b) For the company / legal entity

- A fine between SEK5,000 and SEK10 million (This requires that the company has not done what can be reasonably expected to prevent the bribery or that the bribery has been committed by an individual in a leading position or with special responsibility for supervision.)

2.4 Limitation applicable to hospitality expenses (gifts, travel, meals, entertainment, among others)

The Penal Code does not establish quantitative or qualitative limitations on hospitality expenses. In order to assess whether a hospitality expense is considered to be a bribe, the fact of the hospitality expense being an improper benefit has to be established. The meaning of improper benefit is further described in the preparatory works of the Penal Code as a benefit that objectively has the potential to affect the performance of a task or be perceived as a reward for the performance of a task.

Whether a hospitality expense could be considered bribery will need to be determined on a case-by-case basis, taking into account all the facts and circumstances surrounding the case. The type of hospitality, the economic value and the position of the receiver are examples of these types of circumstances.

3. Corruption of foreign public officials

3.1 Legal framework

In Swedish legislation, there is no distinction between bribery of public officials and private bribery. There is also no distinction between bribery of foreign or domestic public officials. However, the involvement of a public official will act as an aggravating circumstance and make it more likely that a benefit is deemed a bribe. Bribery is regulated under the Swedish Penal Code, Chapter 10, Section 5 a-e. There are also some ancillary legislation that could be applicable in relation to bribery issues, such as the Marketing Act (SFS 2008:486) and the Swedish Income Tax Act (SFS 1999:1229).

3.2 Definition of corruption of foreign public officials

An employee or person performing an assignment who, for himself or herself or another person, receives, accepts a promise of, or demands an improper benefit for the performance of the employment or assignment, may be deemed as taking a bribe.

A person who gives, promises or offers an improper benefit in in the cases referred to above may be viewed as giving a bribe.

A benefit does not necessarily have to be aimed at, give rise to or reward improper action or be beneficial to the person who has given, promised or offered the benefit in order to be deemed improper. An improper benefit is a benefit that objectively has the potential to affect the performance of a task or be perceived as a reward for the performance of a task.

In addition to the offenses of taking and giving a bribe, trading in influence and negligent financing of bribery are also punishable offenses related to bribery. Trading in influence involves the act of taking or giving an improper benefit in order to influence a person's action or decision in the exercise of public authority or in public procurement. An individual acting on behalf of a company that provides money or assets used by a third party for the giving of a bribe may be found guilty of negligent financing of bribery.

3.3 Definition of foreign public official

The Swedish Criminal Code contains no definition of foreign public official since there is no specific offense for bribery of foreign public officials. The same rules apply to foreign and domestic public officials.

3.4 Consequences of corruption of foreign public officials

(a) For the individuals involved

The Swedish Penal Code establishes the same penalties for foreign public officials as for individuals that bribe foreign public officials. The penalties are the following:

- A fine (proportional to the income of the individual, limited to a maximum of SEK150,000) or up to two years of imprisonment
- If deemed as a gross crime, between six months and six years of imprisonment (The non-exhaustive lists of criteria to be considered include the position of the individual, the value of the benefits, whether the bribery has been part of systematic criminal activity or criminal activity of large proportions, or otherwise is of a particularly dangerous kind.)

(b) For the company / legal entity

- A fine between SEK5,000 and SEK10 million (This requires that the company has not done what can be reasonably expected to prevent the bribery or that the bribery has been committed by an individual in a leading position or with special responsibility for supervision.)

3.5 Limitation applicable to hospitality expenses (gifts, travel, meals, entertainment, among others)

The Penal Code does not establish quantitative or qualitative limitations on hospitality expenses. In order to assess whether a hospitality expense is considered to be a bribe, the fact of the hospitality expense being an improper benefit has to be established. The meaning of improper benefit is further described in preparatory works of the Penal Code as a benefit that objectively has the potential to affect the performance of a task or be perceived as a reward for the performance of a task.

Whether a hospitality expense could be considered bribery will need to be determined on a case-by- case basis, taking into account all the facts and circumstances surrounding the case. The type of hospitality, the economic value and the position of the receiver are examples of these types of circumstances. Even though there is no separate legislation regarding bribery of public officials, hospitality given to public officials are more likely to be deemed improper due to the responsibility and trust associated with their position.

4. Facilitation payments

The Penal Code does not recognize so-called facilitation payments. Facilitation payments are considered improper benefits and thereby constitute bribery. Cash payments to public officials may objectively be seen as improper due to the nature of the benefit (cash) and the position of the receiver (public official).

5. Compliance programs

5.1 Value of a compliance program in mitigating/eliminating the criminal liability of legal entities

The Swedish Penal Code does not specifically recognize compliance programs as instruments to mitigate or eliminate the liability of legal entities before the crime of corruption has been committed. However, legal entities could partly mitigate their criminal liability if they adopt an effective compliance program.

As described above, a company that is found not to have done what could be reasonably expected to prevent bribery may receive a corporate fine. By adopting a compliance program, a legal entity reduces the risk of not having done what can reasonably be expected to prevent bribery from taking place and thereby, the risk of receiving a corporate fine is reduced. However, a compliance program is not an effective defense if the bribery has been committed by individuals in leading positions or with special responsibility for supervision. If a corporate fine is issued, the existence of a compliance program may reduce the amount of the fine.

5.2 Absence of a compliance program as a crime

The Swedish Penal Code does not view the absence of a compliance program as a crime.

5.3 Elements of a compliance program

(a) Legal framework

The Swedish Penal Code does not recognize nor regulate the elements of a compliance program.

(b) Recommended practice

In the absence of explicit legal provisions regarding compliance programs, the adoption of a compliance program is a recommended measure that can mitigate criminal liability by contributing to the view that a company has done what can reasonably be expected to prevent bribery from taking place. Preventive actions taken as a part of a compliance program may also be taken into account in determining the corporate fine.

6. Regulator with jurisdiction to prosecute corruption

The Swedish Prosecution Authority has jurisdiction to prosecute corruption cases, which are processed and executed by prosecutors at the National Anti-Corruption Unit of the Prosecution Authority.

Switzerland

Markus Berni

Markus Berni's practice focuses on mergers and acquisitions, private equity and corporate restructurings. He advises clients on governance and compliance matters, and he is a contributor to the Partnership Against Corruption Initiative (PACI) of the World Economic Forum. Markus also advises clients in a broad range of commercial—often cross-border—transactions, including distribution structures, development and licensing agreements, integration and outsourcing projects, electronic commerce and telecommunications regulations.

markus.berni@bakermckenzie.com
Tel: +41 44 384 1281

Philippe Monnier

Philippe Monnier advises clients in commercial law and in general contract and corporate matters, including in particular anti-corruption and antitrust compliance. Beyond that, he represents clients before Swiss authorities and courts, as well as in national and international arbitration proceedings. Philippe is fluent in English, French and German.

philippe.monnier@bakermckenzie.com
Tel: +41 44 384 1367

Baker & McKenzie
Holbeinstrasse 30
8034 Zurich
Switzerland

Key Practitioners

Philippe Reich
Zurich
Tel: +41 44 384 13 82
philippe.reich@bakermckenzie.com

1. Domestic bribery (private to public)

1.1 Legal framework

Bribery of public officials is prohibited under the Swiss Criminal Code, Articles 322*ter* to 322*quater*.

1.2 Definition of bribery

The Swiss Criminal Code distinguishes between active bribery, which can be committed by anyone who tries to corrupt a public official (Swiss Criminal Code, Article 322*ter*), and the acceptance of bribes, which can be committed only by said officials (Swiss Criminal Code, Article 322*quater*).

Bribery consists of offering, promising or giving an advantage that is not due to the public official, or offering, promising or giving such an advantage to a third party, in order to cause that public official to carry out or to fail to carry out an act in connection with his or her official activity, which is contrary to his or her duty or dependent on his or her discretion.

Acceptance of bribes consists of demanding, securing the promise of or accepting an advantage that is not due to the public official for himself or herself or for a third party in order that he or she carries out or fails to carry out an act in connection with his or her official activity that is contrary to his or her duty or dependent on his or her discretion.

1.3 Definition of public official

The Swiss Criminal Code uses a broad definition of public official, which includes but is not limited to a member of a judicial or other authority; an officially appointed expert; an officially appointed translator or interpreter; and an arbitrator or a member of the armed forces. This concept may also include private individuals and employees of publicly owned companies, if such individuals exercise public functions.

1.4 Consequences of bribery

(a) For the individuals involved

The Swiss Criminal Code establishes the same penalties for individuals who actively bribe public officials as for the public officials who accept a bribe. The penalties include the following:

- Up to five years in jail
- Monetary penalty, calculated on a *per diem* basis, of up to 360 daily penalty units (a judge will determine the daily penalty, taking into account the financial strength of the individual, from CHF10 to CHF3,000 per day, and will multiply such amount by the number of days imposed)
- Up to five years of prohibition on exercising a profession
- Criminal forfeiture of objects and assets that were used, intended to be used or produced as a result of the offense

(b) For the company / legal entity

- Criminal fine of up to CHF5 million
- Criminal forfeiture of objects and assets that were used, intended to be used or produced as a result of the offense

1.5 Political contributions

Switzerland has not enacted any federal laws dealing with political contributions, thus leaving room for the cantons to regulate this issue. In most cantons, however, political parties are not required to disclose political donations and contributions. Even though the funding of political parties has been a subject of debate in Switzerland in the last few years, there is presently no consensus on whether or not and in what form such regulations could be adopted.

1.6 Limitation applicable to hospitality expenses (gifts, travel, meals, entertainment, among others)

The Swiss Criminal Code does not establish general quantitative or qualitative limitations on hospitality expenses. However, some of the relevant regulations for public officials contain explicit guidance and limitations on such expenses. For example, according to Article 93 of the Swiss Ordinance on Federal Public Employees, gifts and advantages for certain public officials are limited to those with a value of CHF200 or less.

Aside from such explicit rules, the question of whether a hospitality expense may be considered bribery within the meaning of the Swiss Criminal Code will need to be determined on a case-by-case basis, taking into account all the facts and circumstances surrounding the case.

2. Domestic bribery (private to private)

2.1 Legal framework

Private bribery is prohibited under Article 4a of the Swiss Act on Unfair Competition. Pursuant to an amendment of the Swiss Criminal Code passed in 2015 and expected to be enacted on 1 July 2016, private bribery will be prohibited under the Swiss Criminal Code, Articles 322*octies* to 322*novies*, rather than merely qualifying as an act of punishable unfair competition.

2.2 Definition of private bribery

The Swiss Criminal Code as amended in 2015 distinguishes between active private bribery (Swiss Criminal Code, Article 322*octies*), which can be committed by anyone who tries to bribe certain persons in the private sector, and the acceptance of bribes (Swiss Criminal Code, Article 322*novies*), which can only be committed by said persons in the private sector.

Private bribery entails offering, promising or giving an advantage that is not due to an employee, company member, mandatee or agent in the private sector in connection with his or her business-related duties and in exchange for an act or omission violating such duties or in exchange for a discretionary act or omission for the benefit of himself or herself or for the benefit of a third party.

Acceptance of a bribe in the private sector entails demanding, securing the promise of or accepting an advantage that is not due in connection with business-related duties as an employee, company member, mandatee or agent in the private sector and in exchange for an act or omission violating such duties or in exchange for a discretionary act or omission for the benefit of himself or herself or for the benefit of a third party.

2.3 Consequences of private bribery

(a) For the individuals involved

- Up to three years in jail (small cases, however, are being prosecuted only upon request of the affected person or legal entity)
- Monetary penalty, calculated on a *per diem* basis, of up to 360 daily penalty units (a judge will determine the daily penalty, taking into account the financial strength of the individual, from CHF10 to CHF3,000 per day, and will multiply such amount by the number of days imposed)
- Up to five years of prohibition on exercising a profession
- Criminal forfeiture of objects and assets that were used, intended to be used or produced as a result of the offense

(b) For the company / legal entity

- Criminal fine of up to CHF5 million

- Criminal forfeiture of objects and assets that were used, intended to be used or produced as a result of the offense

2.4 Limitation applicable to hospitality expenses (gifts, travel, meals, entertainment, among others)

Neither the Act on Unfair Competition nor the Swiss Criminal Code as amended establish general quantitative or qualitative limitations on hospitality expenses. In some industries, however, guidance on hospitality expenses can be found in the relevant industry standards or in documents relating to self-regulation. Aside from such explicit soft law rules, the Act on Unfair Competition and the Swiss Criminal Code as amended state that certain advantages that have been approved by the third party, as well as small advantages that are socially acceptable, will not fall under their scope (Swiss Act on Unfair Competition, Article 4a, Paragraph 2 and Swiss Criminal Code, Article 322*decies*). However, since there is thus far only very limited guidance on the exact scope of this exception, the question of whether a hospitality expense may be considered private bribery will in any case need to be determined on a case-by-case basis, taking into account all the facts and circumstances surrounding the case.

3. Bribery of foreign public officials

3.1 Legal framework

Bribery of foreign public officials is prohibited under the Swiss Criminal Code, Article 322*septies*.

3.2 Definition of bribery of foreign public officials

The Swiss Criminal Code distinguishes between active bribery, which can be committed by anyone who tries to corrupt a foreign public official (Swiss Criminal Code, Article 322*septies*, Paragraph 1), and the acceptance of bribes, which can be committed only by said officials (Swiss Criminal Code, Article 322*septies*, Paragraph 2).

Bribery of foreign officials entails offering, promising or giving an advantage that is not due to the foreign public official or the official of an international organization, or offering, promising or giving such an advantage to a third party, in order to cause that public official to carry out or to fail to carry out an act in connection with his or her official activity that is contrary to his or her duty or dependent on his or her discretion.

Acceptance of bribes by foreign public officials entails demanding, securing the promise of or accepting an advantage that is not due to the foreign public official or the public official of an international organization for himself or herself or for a third party in order that he or she carries out or fails to carry out an act in connection with his or her official activity that is contrary to his or her duty or dependent on his or her discretion.

3.3 Definition of foreign public official

The Swiss Criminal Code uses a broad definition of foreign public officials, which includes but is not limited to a member of a judicial or other authority; an officially appointed expert; an officially appointed translator or interpreter; and an arbitrator or a member of the armed forces of a foreign state or an international organization. This concept can also include private individuals and employees of publicly owned companies, if such individuals exercise public functions.

3.4 Consequences of corruption of foreign public officials

(a) For the individuals involved

The Swiss Criminal Code establishes the same penalties for individuals who actively bribe foreign public officials as for the public officials who accept a bribe. The penalties include the following:

- Up to five years in jail
- Monetary penalty, calculated on a per diem basis, of up to 360 daily penalty units (a judge will determine the daily penalty,

taking into account the financial strength of the individual, from CHF10 to CHF3,000 per day, and will multiply such amount by the number of days imposed)

- Up to five years of prohibition on exercising a profession
- Criminal forfeiture of objects and assets that were used, intended to be used or produced as a result of the offense

(b) For the company / legal entity

- Criminal fine of up to CHF5 million
- Criminal forfeiture of objects and assets that were used, intended to be used or produced as a result of the offense

3.5 Limitation applicable to hospitality expenses (gifts, travel, meals, entertainment, among others)

The Swiss Criminal Code does not establish general quantitative or qualitative limitations on hospitality expenses. Accordingly, the question of whether a hospitality expense may be considered bribery will need to be determined on a case-by-case basis, taking into account all the facts and circumstances surrounding the case. However, the Swiss Criminal Code as amended in 2015 does state that certain advantages that have been approved by the third party, as well as small advantages that are 'socially acceptable' will not fall under its scope (Swiss Criminal Code, Article 322*decies*).

4. Facilitation payments

The Swiss Criminal Code does not explicitly recognize so-called facilitation payments. No facilitation payment exception applies under Swiss law. Therefore, it is advisable to refrain from offering/accepting facilitation payments.

5. Compliance programs

5.1 Value of a compliance program in mitigating/eliminating the criminal liability of legal entities

Where a crime of corruption has been committed in a legal entity in the exercise of commercial activities, the Swiss Criminal Code in principle sets out two different types of criminal liability for the legal entity in question, namely: (i) a secondary criminal liability when it is not possible to attribute this act to any specific natural person due to the inadequate organization of the legal entity (Swiss Criminal Code, Article 102 Paragraph 1); and (ii) a primary or 'concurrent' criminal liability where the undertaking is responsible for failing to take all the 'reasonable organizational measures' that were required in order to prevent the offense, in which case the legal entity is penalized irrespective of the criminal liability of (and thus potentially in addition to) any natural persons (Swiss Criminal Code, Article 102 Paragraph 2). Accordingly, in cases involving concurrent criminal liability (which are most relevant in practice), an effective compliance program can in effect eliminate the criminal liability of the legal entity if the legal entity is deemed to have taken all reasonable organizational measures that were required in order to prevent the offense in question. Beyond that and in any case, an effective compliance program can at least mitigate the criminal liability of the legal entity in question.

5.2 Absence of a compliance program as a crime

If a crime of corruption is committed within a legal entity in the exercise of commercial activities and if such legal entity lacks adequate compliance procedures, the legal entity in question can, as a matter of Swiss law, become criminally liable irrespective of the criminal liability of any natural persons. Beyond that, Swiss authorities can be entitled to confiscate the proceeds connected with the act in question.

5.3 Elements of a compliance program

(a) Legal framework

The Swiss Criminal Code does not explicitly regulate the elements of a compliance program.

(b) Recommended practice

In the absence of case law, Swiss legal doctrine recommends that legal entities adopt a robust compliance program as a defense strategy to mitigate or exclude the legal entity's criminal liability for crimes of corruption.

6. Regulator with jurisdiction to prosecute corruption

Jurisdiction to prosecute corruption is set forth in the Swiss Code of Criminal Procedure, in particular in Article 23, Letter j.

According to this article, the Federal Prosecutor's Office shall have jurisdiction to prosecute all acts of corruption committed by Swiss federal public officials or committed against the Swiss federal government. The same applies for other acts of private to public bribery, if the offenses have to a substantial extent been committed abroad or if they have been committed in two or more cantons with no single canton being the clear focus of the criminal activity (Swiss Code of Criminal Procedure, Article 24 Paragraph 1).

Other cases are prosecuted by the cantonal prosecutor's offices. According to the general rule in Article 31 of the Swiss Code of Criminal Procedure, the place where the crime was committed will generally determine which cantonal authority has jurisdiction to prosecute.

Turkey

Birturk Aydin

Birturk Aydin focuses his practice on compliance issues and specializes in anti-corruption, trade sanctions and export controls. He has carried out on-the-ground due diligence reviews for clients, both as part of the M&A process and general internal compliance assessment, and he has worked with clients to design and implement their compliance programs, policies, procedures and risk assessments. Birturk also advises local and multinational clients, including property developers, real estate companies, property consultants, construction companies, real estate investment companies and manufacturing entities on real estate matters.

birturk.aydin@esin.av.tr
Tel: +90 212 376 64 45

Sertac Kokenek

Sertac Kokenek focuses his practices on corporate compliance and domestic and international mergers and acquisitions. He drafts and negotiates corporate transaction documents, including share purchase, asset purchase and merger agreements. In addition, he advises companies on general corporate and business law matters. Sertac also advises clients on data privacy, real estate, and trade and commerce issues.

sertac.kokenek@esin.av.tr
Tel: +90 212 376 64 90

Gokce Serez

Gokce Serez focuses her practice on corporate compliance, including corporate investigations, anti-bribery, anti-money laundering, anti-corruption, white-collar crimes, trade sanctions and export controls. In addition, she advises clients on corporate and business law matters, domestic and international mergers and acquisitions, real estate, and trade and commerce issues.

gokce.serez@esin.av.tr
Tel: +90 212 376 64 85

Baker & McKenzie Consultancy Services
Attorney Partnership
Ebulula Mardin Cad., Gül Sok. No. 2
Maya Park Tower 2, Akatlar-Beşiktaş
Istanbul 34335
Turkey

1. Domestic bribery (private to public)

1.1 Legal framework

Turkey does not have a general anti-corruption or bribery law. Other Turkish laws, however, contain provisions on anti-corruption – primarily the Turkish Criminal Code; the Law on Declaration of Property and Combating Bribery and Corruption; the Law on the Ethics Board for Public Officials; and the Regulation on the Civil Servants Ethical Principles and Application Procedures and Principles (the "Ethics Regulation").

Bribery of public officials is regulated under the Turkish Criminal Code No. 5237, Article 252.

1.2 Definition of bribery

A person receiving a bribe and a person providing a bribe are both held under the same prohibition.

Bribery may refer to, directly or through an intermediary, providing a benefit to a public officer or a third party indicated by the public officer for the performance or non-performance of an act relating to its duty. If the public official and the private individual agree on the bribe to be provided, the act is deemed bribery.

1.3 Definition of public official

The Turkish Criminal Code defines "public official" broadly as any person who participates in the conduct of public activities by way of appointment or election or otherwise, for a continuous, limited or temporary period of time.

Although state-owned company employees are not expressly defined as public officials under the Turkish Criminal Code, they are considered public officials as long as they participate in the conduct of public activities according to the Turkish Appellate Court. Employees of a publicly owned company also qualify as public officials under the Ethics Regulation.

1.4 Consequences of bribery

(a) For individuals

The Turkish Criminal Code applies the same penalties for public officials and for individuals who corrupt public officials. The penalties are as follows:

- Imprisonment of four years to 12 years (For persons who offer or promise to give bribes and public officials who request bribes, but are rejected by the counterparty, the term of imprisonment will be reduced by half.)
- Increased prison term if the person who receives, agrees on or requests a bribe is a judicial officer, arbitrator, court-appointed expert, notary public or sworn financial adviser
- Termination of an employment contract
- Prohibition from participating in public tenders and termination of public procurement agreement
- Security measures for individuals (e.g., prohibition on conducting public service, confiscation of bribe)

(b) For intermediaries

- According to the Turkish Criminal Code, intermediaries will be subject to the same penalties imposed on actual bribe makers and public officials, regardless of their position as such.

(c) For companies / legal entities

- Under Article 253 of the Turkish Criminal Code, legal entities that obtain a benefit by committing the offense of bribery are subject to security measures. Concordantly, Article 20 of the Turkish Criminal Code sets forth that "criminal sanctions may not be imposed upon legal entities." Under this article, private legal entities may only be subject to the following security measures as specified in Article 60 of the Turkish Criminal Code:

- Revocation of license/permit if: (a) a private legal entity abuses its authority, arising out of a license/permit granted to it by a public entity; and (b) the legal entity's governing bodies or representatives participated in the actions of such entity; if so, the court may revoke the legal entity's license/permit.

- Confiscation of property or material interests; if the conditions of confiscation specified under the Turkish Criminal Code are satisfied, the court may confiscate the property or material interests connected to the offense/crime.

- Prohibition from participating in public tenders and termination of public procurement agreement

- Administrative fines

1.5 Political contributions

Contributions to political parties are regulated by the Political Parties Law No. 2820.

In general terms, except for the real persons and legal entities listed in the Political Parties Law (e.g., publicly owned companies), real persons and legal entities can donate to a political party, in cash or in kind, up to approximately TRY37,105 (the amount for 2016) within a year. Political parties are prohibited from receiving donations from foreign states, international organizations, foreign real persons and legal entities.

1.6 Limitation applicable to hospitality expenses (gifts, travel, meals, entertainment, among others)

The Turkish Criminal Code establishes no limitation on hospitality expenses. However, according to the Ethics Regulation, public officials may not accept any gift and cannot benefit for themselves, their relatives, real or legal third parties, directly or through an agent, from real or legal persons with a business, service or beneficial relationship related to their task.

According to the Ethics Regulation, gift is defined as "any kind of goods and benefits having an economic value or not, accepted directly or indirectly, which have an impact or may have an impact on the objectivity, performance, decision or fulfilment of the task of a public officer." The decisive element is that "the benefit has or may have an impact on the objectivity, performance, decision or fulfilment of the task of a public officer."

Moreover, the Ethics Regulation sets out in detail what kind of gifts and benefits are within the scope of the gift prohibition, including but not limited to: any welcome, farewell and congratulatory gifts; and scholarships, trips, *gratis* accommodation and gift vouchers received from entities with which the relevant public body has a business, service or interest. The Ethics Regulation also sets out in detail the kinds of gifts and benefits that are not within the scope of the gift prohibition, which include but are not limited to: books, magazines, articles, cassettes, calendars, CDs or similar materials, as well as souvenir-type gifts distributed at public conferences, symposia, forums, panels, meals, receptions or similar activities.

The Law on the Public Officials Ethics Board refers to discipline provisions to which the public officials are subject for contraventions.

The Ethics Regulation imposes no quantitative limitation on hospitality expenses.

2. Domestic bribery (private to private)

2.1 Legal framework

Turkish anti-corruption laws do not prohibit a private person from receiving or being provided with an advantage that is tendered or accepted by another private person. However, there is an exception for representatives of: professional organizations with the character of a public institution; companies incorporated through (i) the participation of governmental institutions and organizations or through (ii) professional organizations with the character of a public institution; foundations that operate under the supervision of the same; associations that work for the benefit of the public; cooperatives; and public companies.

2.2 Definition of private bribery

Private bribery entails, directly or through an intermediary, providing, offering or promising a benefit to representatives of: professional organizations with the character of a public institution; companies incorporated through the participation of governmental institutions and organizations or through professional organizations with the character of a public institution; foundations that operate under the supervision of the same; and associations that work for the benefit of the public, cooperatives or public companies; as well as requesting or accepting a benefit by such person; acting as an intermediary for these; or providing a benefit to a third party referring to such a relationship for the performance or non-performance of an act relating to its duty, regardless of his or her role as a public official.

2.3 Consequences of private bribery

The consequences of public bribery also apply to private bribery.

2.4 Limitation applicable to hospitality expenses (gifts, travel, meals, entertainment, among others)

The Turkish Criminal Code and the Ethics Regulation do not regulate hospitality expenses made by private persons to private persons.

3. Corruption of foreign public officials

3.1 Legal framework

Bribery of foreign public officials is regulated under the Turkish Criminal Code, Article 252.

3.2 Definition of corruption of foreign public officials

The Turkish Criminal Code does not provide a separate definition for bribing foreign public officials. The abovementioned public bribery definition also applies to bribing foreign public officials.

3.3 Definition of foreign public official

The Turkish Criminal Code does not provide a separate definition for foreign public officials. However, Article 252 also applies to the following persons:

(a) Public officials elected or appointed in a foreign state

(b) Judges, jurymen or other officials performing a duty in international or supranational courts or in foreign states' courts

(c) International or supranational parliament members

(d) Persons performing a public service for a foreign state, including public institutions or public organizations

(e) Citizens or foreign arbitrators assigned within the framework of an arbitration

(f) Officials or representatives of international or supranational organizations established based on an international agreement

3.4 Consequences of bribery of foreign public officials

The consequences of public bribery also apply to bribing foreign public officials.

3.5 Limitation applicable to hospitality expenses (gifts, travel, meals, entertainment, among others)

The Turkish Criminal Code and the Ethics Regulation do not regulate hospitality expenses made by private persons to foreign public officials.

4. Facilitation payments

The Turkish Criminal Code does not recognize so-called facilitation payments. Facilitation payments are payments made to accelerate or secure the performance of routine public acts. Without a clear court precedent, facilitation payments may fall within the scope of bribery.

5. Compliance programs

5.1 Value of a compliance program in mitigating/eliminating the criminal liability of legal entities

The Turkish Criminal Code does not specifically recognize compliance programs as instruments to mitigate or eliminate the liability of legal entities. Adopting a compliance program is, nevertheless, recommended for companies in order to establish a compliance culture and ensure the compliance of employees in minimizing any liability risk.

5.2 Absence of a compliance program as a crime

N/A

5.3 Elements of a compliance program

(a) Legal framework

N/A

(b) Recommended practice

N/A

6. Regulator with jurisdiction to prosecute corruption

The Turkish legal system has no specific regulator with the exclusive responsibility to prosecute corruption cases. Public prosecutors are, however, eligible to prosecute such cases.

Ukraine

Ihor Siusel

Ihor Siusel advises and represents local and foreign clients in commercial, real estate, construction, corporate, IP, tax, customs, labor, insurance, loan, maritime, aviation, telecommunications, product liability and bankruptcy disputes, including complex cross-border disputes. He serves clients from a number of industries, including mining, oil and gas, steel production, food production, publishing, ship building, telecommunications, pharmaceuticals, IT, construction, transport, agriculture, distribution and retail, insurance, and banking and finance.

ihor.siusel@bakermckenzie.com
Tel: +380 44 590 0101

Mariana Marchuk

Mariana Marchuk advises Ukrainian and foreign clients on labor and migration law, focusing on employee compensation, executive transfers, data protection, and employee privacy. She is also experienced in dispute resolution and internal investigations, compliance and anti-corruption, international trade and commerce, consumer protection, mergers and acquisitions, information technology, and in matters concerning the pharmaceutical sector.

mariana.marchuk@bakermckenzie.com
Tel: +380 44 590 0101

Baker & McKenzie - CIS, Limited
Renaissance Business Center
24 Vorovskoho St.
Kyiv 01054
Ukraine

1. Domestic bribery (private to public)

1.1 Legal framework

Bribery of public officials is regulated under the Criminal Code of Ukraine (Chapter XVII) and the Law of Ukraine "On Prevention of Corruption" of 2014. On 1 September 2014, Chapter XIV-1 of the Criminal Code of Ukraine, which provides for the criminal liability of private legal entities for corrupt practices, became effective.

1.2 Definition of bribery

Ukrainian legislation employs the term "unlawful benefit" rather than "bribery." Thus, according to the applicable rules, an unlawful benefit may include funds or other assets, benefits, privileges, services or non-material assets that are promised, proposed, provided or received with no legal grounds.

This crime (i.e., proposition or provision of the unlawful benefit) can be committed both by public officials and by private individuals who try to corrupt or has corrupted a public official.

1.3 Definition of public official

The Criminal Code of Ukraine has a broad definition of public official, and includes any individual who exercises public managerial functions on behalf of the state. Under the Law of Ukraine "On Prevention of Corruption," this concept includes not only public servants, but also municipal officers, managers of public companies, notaries, auditors, experts, judges of domestic arbitration tribunals or other persons who offer public services.

1.4 Consequences of bribery

(a) For the individuals involved in giving unlawful benefits (bribes)

The Criminal Code of Ukraine establishes the penalties for public officials as well as for individuals who corrupt public officials. Depending on the particular facts and possible aggravating circumstances (if any) of a given situation, the penalties on the persons bribing the officials are the following:

- Penalty of up to EUR566[1]
- Up to four years of limited freedom
- Up to 10 years of imprisonment
- Confiscation of property

The penalties on the officials accepting illegal benefits are the following:

- Penalty up to EUR8,500
- Up to three years of disqualification form taking certain positions
- Up to 12 years of imprisonment
- Confiscation of property

[1] All figures have been calculated according to the official exchange rate of the euro / Ukrainian hryvna of the National Bank of Ukraine as of 1 March 2016.

(b) However, since 1 September 2014, the Criminal Code of Ukraine (as amended) has provided for the criminal liability of private legal entities for corrupt practices. The penalties are as follows:

- Imposition of penalties of twice the benefit received by the entity or approximately EUR2,833 to EUR42,5000
- Liquidation of the legal entity
- Confiscation of property (additional measure)

1.5 Political contributions

Contributions to political parties are regulated in detail by relevant Ukrainian legislation since 2015. Specifically, contributions cannot be made by certain persons (including foreigners or companies the ultimate beneficiaries of which are foreigners). A legal entity may not contribute more than EUR41,333 within one calendar year to one recipient. Individuals can make contributions for up to EUR20,667 per year to one and the same recipient. Contributions can be made in the form of money, goods, services or any non-material benefit (e.g., intellectual property or free labor of volunteers).

1.6 Limitation applicable to hospitality expenses (gifts, travel, meals, entertainment, among others)

Ukrainian legislation does not provide for the separate and specific regulation of hospitalities (including, but not limited to, travels, hosted meals and entertainment, among others) that may be lawfully offered to public officials. At the same time, the Law of Ukraine, "On Prevention of Corruption" establishes limitations regarding the value of the allowed gifts that may be presented to public officials.

In particular, Ukrainian legal rules prohibit public officials from receiving any gifts except those corresponding with generally recognized hospitality and within expressly allowed limits. The value of a gift (donation) may not exceed the statutory minimum monthly salary, established as of the date of its receipt. Within a calendar year, an official is not allowed to receive gifts from one source with a value of more than one statutory subsistence allowance for a working person legally applicable as of 1 January of the relevant year. Presently, the value of gifts per occasion should not exceed the equivalent of EUR51 at the current exchange rate, and the total value of such gifts (donations) from one source within a calendar year should not exceed the equivalent of EUR92 at the current exchange rate.

Any gift (donation) made for the purpose of influencing, in any manner, the performance by the public official of his or her duties (e.g., performance or non-performance of any actions), or offered by a subordinated person, is prohibited, even if the value of such gift (donation) is small.

2. Domestic bribery (private to private)

2.1 Legal framework

Private bribery is regulated under the Criminal Code of Ukraine (Chapter XVII) and the Law of Ukraine "On Prevention of Corruption." On 1 September 2014, the Criminal Code of Ukraine has included Chapter XIV-1, which provides for criminal liability of private legal entities for corrupt practices.

2.2 Definition of private bribery

For private bribery, Ukrainian legislation also operates with the term "unlawful benefit" rather than "bribery." Thus, according to applicable rules, unlawful benefit may include funds or other assets, benefits, privileges, services and non-material assets that are promised, proposed, provided or received with no legal grounds.

This crime (i.e., proposition, promise, acceptance or provision of the unlawful benefit) can be committed both by public officials and by private individuals who try to corrupt or have corrupted an official of a private company.

2.3 Consequences of private bribery

(a) For individuals involved in giving unlawful benefits (bribes)

The Criminal Code of Ukraine establishes penalty that may amount to approximately EUR397, in addition to confiscation of the unlawful benefit. Also, the bribe-giver may be imprisoned for up to four years.

The corporate officer to whom the unlawful benefit has been given or who has accepted such offer, can be imprisoned for up to seven years and be subjected to confiscation of the unlawful benefit, of other property, and be prohibited to occupy certain positions for up to three years.

(b) Since 1 September 2014, the Criminal Code of Ukraine has provided for the criminal liability of private legal entities for corrupt practices. The penalties are as follows:

- Imposition of penalties of twice the benefit received by the entity, or, if the benefit cannot be determined, a fine in the range of between EUR2,833 to EUR42,500
- Liquidation of the legal entity
- Confiscation of assets (auxiliary to liquidation)

2.4 Limitation applicable to hospitality expenses (gifts, travel, meals, entertainment, among others)

Applicable Ukrainian legislation does not provide for a separate and specific regulation of hospitalities (including, but not limited to, travels, hosted meals and entertainment) that may be legally offered to officials of private companies. However, when offering such hospitalities, it is strongly recommended that they ensure that their activities conform with generally recognized reasonability and modesty to avoid the potential treatment of such hospitality as "unlawful benefit," as provided by the Criminal Code of Ukraine.

3. Corruption of foreign public officials

3.1 Legal framework

Corruption of foreign public officials is regulated under the Criminal Code of Ukraine (Chapter XVII) and the Law of Ukraine "On Prevention of Corruption." Since 1 September 2014, the Criminal Code of Ukraine has provided for the criminal liability of private legal entities for corrupt practices.

3.2 Definition of corruption of foreign public officials

For corruption of foreign public officials, Ukrainian legislation also operates with the term "unlawful benefit" rather than "bribery." Thus, according to the applicable rules, unlawful benefit may include funds or other assets, benefits, privileges, services and non-material assets that are promised, proposed, offered, provided or received with no legal grounds.

3.3 Definition of foreign public official

For the purpose of bribery, a foreign public official may refer to any of the following:

- A person who has a legislative, administrative or judicial function in a foreign country
- A judge of an international (alternative) commercial arbitration tribunal
- An official of a public international organization and members of an international parliamentary assembly, among others

3.4 Consequences of corruption of foreign public officials

Corruption of foreign public officials is regulated under the provisions of the Criminal Code of Ukraine applicable to the domestic corruption of public officials. For more details, please see Section 1.3.

3.5 Limitation applicable to hospitality expenses (gifts, travel, meals, entertainment, among others)

Applicable Ukrainian legislation does not provide for a separate and specific regulation of hospitalities (including, but not limited to, travels, hosted meals and entertainments among others) that may be legally offered to foreign public officials. However, when offering such hospitalities, it is strongly recommended that they ensure that their activities conform with generally recognized reasonability and modesty to avoid the potential treatment of such hospitality as "unlawful benefit," as provided by the Criminal Code of Ukraine.

4. Facilitation payments

The Ukrainian Criminal Code does not recognize so-called facilitation payments. Any payment made with the intention/purpose to influence the actions of the recipient, even if the recipient will not exceed or abuse his or her powers, is illegal.

Therefore, cash payments to public officials are very likely to be considered as corruption payments, even if they fall within the value limits described in Section 2 (for permitted gifts).

5. Compliance programs

5.1 Value of a compliance program in mitigating/eliminating the criminal liability of legal entities

The Ukrainian Criminal Code does not specifically recognize a compliance program as an instrument to eliminate the liability of legal entities. The existence of a compliance program, *per se*, does not preclude criminal investigation or sanctions against a legal entity. However, at the time of determining the punishment for the legal entity, the existence and evidence of concrete steps for the implementation and enforcement of a compliance program shall be viewed as a mitigating factor by the presiding judge and may help to lower the amount of the imposed fine.

As of 1 September 2014, Ukrainian legal entities may be criminally liable for the crime of corruption committed by their employees or other authorized persons (e.g., those acting on the basis of agreement or other agents). It is irrelevant whether such a person was able to commit the corruption crime because the directors or officers of the legal entity have not exercised "due control" over him or her. Consequently, the value of the compliance programs is not only in that it is a mitigating circumstance for punishment, but also in that proper awareness and training among employees and other authorized persons should decrease the likelihood of a corruption event taking place.

5.2 Absence of a compliance program as a crime

The Ukrainian Criminal Code does not view the absence of a compliance program as a crime.

5.3 Elements of a compliance program

(a) Legal framework

The Ukrainian Law on Prevention of Corruption lists the elements of a compliance program.

(b) Recommended practice

It is recommend that legal entities adopt a robust compliance program as a defense strategy to prevent the occurrence of and to mitigate liability for crimes of corruption committed by the legal entity's employees or other authorized persons. For legal entities that are going to take part in government tenders for over UAH20 million (about EUR666,667 at the current exchange rate), existence of an anti-bribery program and of an Authorized Anti-Bribery Officer is mandatory.

6. Regulator with jurisdiction to prosecute corruption

The Ukrainian legal system includes the National Anti-Corruption Bureau, which is authorized to criminally prosecute corruption cases among highly positioned officials. The State Security Service, the Prosecutor's Office and some other authorities are authorized to start a criminal investigation for corruption, depending on who the suspect is (individual, legal entity, state official, an international organization, etc.).

United Arab Emirates

Borys Dackiw

Borys Dackiw has been a partner at Baker & McKenzie since 1995. In 2008, Borys was appointed managing partner of the Gulf offices (including Abu Dhabi, Doha, Riyadh and Bahrain), coordinating the opening of the Abu Dhabi and Doha offices and the merger in the UAE with Habib Al Mulla in July 2013. Borys specializes in mergers and acquisitions (including privatizations), compliance and general corporate and commercial law.

borys.dackiw@bakermckenzie.com
Tel: +971 4 423 0072

Hani Naja

Hani Naja's practice focuses on mergers and acquisitions as well as corporate establishments and restructuring both in the UAE and Qatar. His experience also covers general commercial contracts and advice on corporate governance, compliance and anti-corruption. Hani has gained substantive experience advising governmental authorities on developing their internal structures and on drafting legislations. He is trilingual and is positioned to practice in English, French and Arabic.

hani.naja@bakermckenzie.com
Tel: +971 2 696 1200

Sabaa Alyanai

Sabaa Alyanai is part of the corporate and commercial team at Baker & McKenzie and splits her time between Abu Dhabi and Dubai. She supports clients with advice on corporate and commercial matters, including employment, telecommunications, corporate governance, licensing and data privacy. Sabaa is fluent in English and Arabic.

sabaa.alyanai@bakermckenzie.com
Tel: +971 4 423 0064

Baker & McKenzie LLP - Abu Dhabi
Level 8, Al Sila Tower
Abu Dhabi Global Market Square
Al Maryah Island
P.O. Box 44980
Abu Dhabi
United Arab Emirates

1. Domestic bribery (private to public)

1.1 Legal framework

At present, the United Arab Emirates (UAE) has no comprehensive anti-corruption legislation. Specific provisions dealing with anti-corruption and bribery (directly or indirectly) are, however, included in a number of federal and local laws, including the UAE Federal Law No. 3 of 1987 (the 'Penal Code'); the UAE Federal Law No. 21 of 2001 concerning Civil Service; the Dubai Government Human Resources Management Law No. 27 of 2006; and the Abu Dhabi Law No. 1 of 2006 concerning Civil Service in the Emirate of Abu Dhabi (the last three laws are collectively referred to as the "Civil Service Laws").

1.2 Definition of bribery

The definition of bribery can be culled from several articles in UAE legislation, notably the Penal Code. Under the provisions of the Penal Code, bribery would be anything that confers a benefit on a public or private sector employee, as the case may be, with the intent to influence such employee to act in a way that violates the duties assigned to his or her function, or to commit or abstain from doing an act.

1.3 Definition of public official

With regard to the definition of a public official, Article 5 of the Penal Code provides that: "Shall be considered a public official under this Law:

1. Anyone charged to do the works of the main authority and the people in the ministries and governmental departments

2. Members of the armed forces

3. Heads of the legislative councils and the consultancy [councils] and municipality [councils] and their members

4. Any person delegated by a public authority to perform a specific job within the limits of the assigned job

5. Heads of the administrative councils and its members and its directors and all personnel working in the public bodies and establishments

6. Heads of the administrative councils and its members and its directors and all personnel working in public associations and establishments with public benefits

Shall also be considered, under this Law, as entrusted with a public service, any individual who does not belong to any of the categories mentioned in the preceding clauses and who performs a job relating to public service by virtue of a mandate given to him by a public officer who is authorized to do so according to the laws and regulations, provided that said individual shall be considered as a public officer only within the limits of the job assigned to him."

1.4 Consequences of bribery

(a) For the individuals involved

Depending on the severity of the crime, any public official who is found guilty of accepting a bribe would be subject to a fine equivalent to the benefit accepted by them (provided the fine is not less than AED1,000); confiscation of the actual benefit accepted; and depending on the circumstances of each case, imprisonment ranging from five years to a maximum of 10 years. In addition, individuals who are found guilty of accepting a bribe in exchange for exerting their influence over a public official would be subject to a fine not exceeding AED10,000 and imprisonment of up to one year.

Individuals who offer a bribe to a public official or to an individual who is in a position to exert influence over a public official would be subject to a fine equivalent to the benefit they offered as a bribe (provided the fine is not less than AED1,000), or confiscation of the actual benefit offered and imprisonment not exceeding five years.

Similar penalties would apply to any individual who facilitates a bribe between the offeror and the recipient.

(b) For the company / legal entity

Entities may also be held liable to the extent that their "inaction," either when aware or unaware of the bribery activities, resulted in the facilitation of the bribery in question. The UAE Commercial Companies Law specifically holds top officials and employees liable for any violation under the law and, in general, holds all companies, regardless of their structure, criminally liable together with their representatives if they violate any of the said provisions.

In addition, there are many other provisions within various UAE laws, such as Federal Law No. 4 of 2000 Concerning the Emirates Securities and Commodities Authority and Market, which subject entities and their representatives to criminal liability. Also, civil liability under Civil Transaction Law No. 5 of 1985 discusses the vicarious liability of the employer in this regard.

Despite the provisions discussed earlier, in practice, courts review cases on a case-by- case basis and penalize the liable employee/entity accordingly. In this regard, the Public Prosecutor employs wide discretion, which can lead to inconsistency in enforcement and penalties imposed.

1.5 Political contributions

There are no political parties in the UAE and public officials are appointed by either the government itself or by the rulers of each emirate (as the case may be).

1.6 Limitation applicable to hospitality expenses (gifts, travel, meals, entertainment, among others)

There is no statutory benchmark for business courtesies in the UAE. However, when offering business courtesies to public officials, the following factors should be considered carefully:

(i) The value of such business courtesies

(ii) The frequency with which they are offered

(iii) The intention behind offering them

(iv) The relevance of such gifts/hospitalities to both the recipient and the offeror

Business courtesies benefiting the recipient exclusively are more likely to be considered improper. On the other hand, a business courtesy that is connected with the company's core business and the function of the relevant official, such as provision of relevant training, is likely to be considered as acceptable. So, by way of example, if provided in connection with a demonstration or training program, paid travel expenses unless excessive in value, would unlikely be considered improper. Similarly, paying the fees to attend a third-party conference would not likely be considered improper if connected with the functions of the relevant official (although in such cases, we would ordinarily recommend that the invitation to attend be addressed through the competent organizational unit at the relevant ministry or government agency). Meals, if provided as basic sustenance during a business meeting and unless excessive in value, would unlikely be considered improper.

Promotional items bearing the emblem or logo of the company would be more justifiable than unbranded items, provided that such items offered are not excessive in value. On the other hand, entertainment (golfing, concert, sporting events, among others) is less likely to be acceptable, as this would be difficult to justify as being connected with the functions of the relevant official.

In any event, it should be noted that it is preferable for any invitation to participate in an event that includes payment of business courtesies to not be addressed to the official benefiting from such courtesies but to his or her manager/supervisor/team head who will appoint a direct beneficiary or provide approval.

According to the Civil Service Laws, the acceptance, taking, offering and requesting of bribes is prohibited. Under these laws, government employees should not accept any gifts (as opposed to bribes) unless they are symbolic advertising or promotional gifts bearing the name and emblem of the entity presenting them, and each ministry must define the organizational unit allowed to accept gifts on its behalf in accordance with its regulations and standards.

Finally, pursuant to the Code of Professional Conduct and Ethics for Public Servants (Cabinet Resolution No. 15 of 2010), a public servant (or any relative up to the fourth degree) may not accept any gifts, hospitalities or services from any person if it results in any obligation; if it has a direct or indirect effect on the public servant's objectivity in implementing his or her duties; if it might affect his or her decisions; or if it might make him or her subject to obligations in consideration of what he or she accepted.

2. Domestic bribery (private to private)

2.1 Legal framework

As stated previously, the UAE has no comprehensive anti-corruption legislation. Specific provisions dealing with anti-corruption and bribery (directly or indirectly) in the private sector are mainly found in the Penal Code.

2.2 Definition of private bribery

In relation to acts of bribery committed by individuals in the context of the private sector, Article 236 *bis* of the Penal Code states that only the individual who accepts a bribe, in exchange for committing or omitting an act in violation of the duties of his or her position would be guilty of an offense under the Penal Code. The recipient, in this instance, is defined by the Penal Code as any member of the board of directors of any private company, institution, cooperative association or public benefit association, as well as any manager or employee in any of these.

2.3 Consequences of private bribery

(a) For the individuals involved

Individuals who accept bribes in the private sector would be subject to a fine equivalent to the benefit accepted by them (provided the fine is not less than AED1,000), confiscation of the actual benefit accepted, and imprisonment not exceeding five years.

Even though the UAE authorities have, as yet, not taken any firm steps towards addressing corrupt practices in the private sector, the Penal Code does allow them to prosecute individuals suspected of such practices. That being said, it is conceivable that the authorities may very well, in the future, expand the provisions and application of Article 236 *bis* of the Penal Code to facilitate the prosecution of bribery in the private sector such that the offeror and facilitator of a bribe would also be guilty of an offense.

(b) For the company / legal entity

Entities can also be held liable to the extent that their "inaction," either when aware or unaware of the bribery activities, resulted in the facilitation of the bribery in question. The UAE Commercial Companies Law specifically holds top officials and employees liable for any violation under the law and, in general, holds all companies, regardless of their structure, criminally liable together with their representatives if they violate any of the said provisions.

In addition, there are many other provisions within various UAE laws, such as Federal Law No. 4 of 2000 Concerning the Emirates Securities and Commodities Authority and Market, which subject entities and their representatives to criminal liability. Also, civil liability under Civil Transaction Law No. 5 of 1985 discusses the vicarious liability of the employer in this regard.

Despite the provisions discussed earlier, in practice, courts review cases on a case-by-case basis and penalize the liable employee/entity accordingly. In this regard, the Public Prosecutor employs wide discretion, which can lead to inconsistency in enforcement and penalties imposed.

2.4 Limitation applicable to hospitality expenses (gifts, travel, meals, entertainment, among others)

See Section 1.5.

3. Corruption of foreign public officials

There are no UAE laws prohibiting or regulating the corruption of public officials of other countries. The UAE did, however, ratify the United Nations Convention against Corruption and does abide by its rules, although it did not produce separate legislations to complement the said convention.

4. Facilitation payments

There are no statutory exceptions for or limitations on “facilitation expenses” that exempt them from the definition of bribery, either public or private. Each such expense must be evaluated on its own and with consideration to the surrounding facts in order to determine whether it is likely to be considered a bribe.

5. Compliance programs

5.1 Value of a compliance program to mitigate/eliminate the criminal liability of legal entities

UAE laws do not regulate compliance programs.

5.2 Absence of compliance program as a crime

N/A

5.3 Elements of a compliance program

(a) Legal framework

UAE laws do not regulate compliance programs.

(b) Recommended practice

Despite the lack of heavy regulation in relation to the requirement/method that will be used in implementing compliance programs, many international, national and governmental authorities implement a transparent compliance program. This is the case largely because the benefits of having a compliance program system outweigh the risks associated with not adopting one. In many corporations and governmental entities, it is a core policy and part of a wider corporate governance program. Such provisions convey transparency, enabling governmental authorities, companies and senior officers in organizations to have a clear picture of what is going on within the respective entity. Such programs are also commonly used as a preventive mechanism within governmental or corporate structures to combat wrongdoing internally in order to avoid situations from happening, in addition to allowing them to be in a position to report and expose such wrongdoing.

6. Regulator with jurisdiction to prosecute corruption

The Public Prosecutor has the power to prosecute bribery cases before the UAE courts, with jurisdiction over such matters, among many others.

United Kingdom

Joanna Ludlam

Joanna is a partner in the Dispute Resolution team in the Firm's London office, where she developed her practice in the areas of commercial litigation and administrative and public law. Joanna co-leads the London office's Compliance & Investigations Practice Group, as well as chairing the steering committee of the Firm's European Compliance & Investigations Practice.

In addition to her active commercial litigation practice, Joanna regularly counsels on public law, media and defamation law, and reputation and crisis management. She also handles all manner of global compliance investigations, both internal and regulatory, and is seasoned in providing crisis management advice. Joanna also has extensive experience in managing large scale and high-profile corporate disputes.

joanna.ludlam@bakermckenzie.com
Tel: + 44 207 919 1822

Andrew Matheson

Andrew is an associate in Baker & McKenzie's Business Crime Unit in London. Alongside his work in commercial and banking litigation, Andrew has particular experience in managing corporate investigations in the finance sector, both from regulatory law and from competition law perspectives. He has advised on a range of matters, including anti-corruption compliance, compliance program development and anti-corruption due diligence. Andrew has also advised clients who have been the victim of corporate fraud.

andrew.matheson@bakermckenzie.com
Tel: +442079191079

London
Baker & McKenzie LLP
100 New Bridge Street
London EC4V 6JA
England

Key Practitioners

Sunny Mann
London
Tel: +442079191397
sunny.mann@bakermckenzie.com

Jonathan Peddie
London
Tel: +442079191222
jonathan.peddie@Bakermckenzie.com

1. Domestic bribery (private to public)

1.1 Legal framework

The Bribery Act 2010 provides for a general offense of bribery, which criminalizes both the receipt and payment of bribes. There is no distinction between bribes paid in the private sector and those paid in the public sector.

1.2 Definition of bribery

UK anti-bribery legislation does not distinguish between bribes paid to a public official and those paid in the private sector. See Paragraph 2.2.

1.3 Definition of public official

Per Paragraph 1.1, UK anti-corruption legislation does not distinguish between bribes paid to a public official and those paid in the private sector.

1.4 Consequences of bribery for individuals involved and companies/legal entities

UK anti-bribery legislation does not distinguish between bribes paid to a public official and those paid to those in the private sector. See Paragraph 2.3.

1.5 Political contributions

The Bribery Act does not include any specific provisions in relation to political contributions, although the general offenses of giving or receiving a bribe may be applicable. See Paragraph 2.2.

1.6 Limitation applicable to hospitality expenses (gifts, travel, meals, entertainment, among others)

Corporate hospitality will only amount to one of the general offenses if there is improper conduct on the part of the person bribing or being bribed. If the act of hospitality is routine and inexpensive, it is unlikely to amount to a breach of an expectation of good faith, impartiality or trust.

The UK government has confirmed that legislation should not be used to penalize legitimate and proportionate hospitality, including in respect of foreign public officials, but its view is that hospitality is also an issue best considered by prosecutors rather than by Parliament.

2. Domestic bribery (private to private)

2.1 Legal framework

The Bribery Act 2010 provides for a general offense of bribery, which criminalizes both the receipt and payment of bribes. There is no distinction between bribes paid in the private sector and those paid in the public sector.

2.2 Definition of bribery

A bribe is paid where a person receives, offers or gives a bribe either (i) intending that, as a consequence, a function should be performed "improperly"; or (ii) where the bribe is or amounts to a reward for "improper" performance.

The Bribery Act provides three examples of when a function would be deemed to have been carried out "improperly":

(a) The person performing it is expected to perform the function or activity in good faith, but does not.

(b) The person performing it is expected to perform it impartially, but does not.

(c) The person is in a position of trust, but breaches that trust.

The types of functions that are covered by the Bribery Act are as follows:

(a) Functions of a public nature

(b) Activities connected with a business

(c) Activities performed in the course of a person's employment

(d) An activity performed by or on behalf of a body of persons

A corporate or commercial organization will also commit an offense under Section 7 of the Bribery Act, where a person "associated with" it bribes another person, intending to obtain or retain business for the organization or to obtain or retain an advantage in the conduct of business for the organization. This is a strict liability offense that can be committed in the UK or overseas. Note the following:

(a) A person will be "associated with" the company for these purposes, where the person acts on an organization's behalf. This could include an employee, agent or subsidiary of the organization. Contractors, suppliers, joint venture entities and joint venture partners may also be associated persons.

(b) While there is a rebuttable presumption that an employee acts on behalf of his or her organization, an individual's association will be determined by reference to all relevant circumstances, not merely the relationship between the individual and the organization.

(c) It is a defense for an organization to prove that it had "adequate procedures" in place to prevent the bribery. See Section 5 for further details.

2.3 Consequences of private bribery for individuals involved companies/legal entities

(a) An individual convicted of committing any of the general bribery offenses may:

 (i) be imprisoned for a term of up to 10 years; and/or

 (ii) be subject to an unlimited fine.

(b) A company or partnership that commits any of the general bribery offenses will be liable on conviction on indictment, to an unlimited fine, and to automatic and perpetual debarment from competing for public contracts.

(c) Note that a conviction under Section 7 of the Bribery Act will attract discretionary rather than mandatory disbarment from competing for public contracts. Where an organization has been convicted of a bribery offense, senior officers of the organization who have consented to or connived in the conduct can also be convicted of the offense concerned.

(d) In addition, the Serious Fraud Office (SFO) will be able to use its civil recovery powers to recover property obtained through the unlawful conduct without resorting to prosecution.

2.4 Limitation applicable to hospitality expenses (gifts, travel, meals, entertainment, among others)

Corporate hospitality will only amount to one of the general bribery offenses if there is improper conduct on the part of the person bribing or being bribed. If the hospitality is routine and inexpensive, it is unlikely to amount to a breach of an expectation of good faith, impartiality or trust.

The government has confirmed that the legislation should not be used to penalize legitimate and proportionate hospitality, including in respect of foreign public officials, but its view is that hospitality is also an issue best considered by prosecutors rather than by Parliament.

3. Corruption of foreign public officials

3.1 Legal framework

The Bribery Act includes a specific offense of "bribery of foreign public officials" (FPOs).

3.2 Definition of corruption of foreign public officials

Broadly, an offense will be committed where a person directly or through a third party offers, promises, or gives a financial or other advantage to an FPO in his capacity as an FPO (or to a third party at the FPO's request) and intends to obtain or retain business or a business advantage.

The offense is not committed where the FPO is either permitted or required by the written law applicable to the FPO to be influenced in his or her capacity as an FPO. Effectively, this is only likely to provide protection in the very limited circumstances where a written law explicitly permits or requires the payment to the FPO.

A company or another commercial organization will also commit an offense where a person "associated with" it bribes an FPO, intending to obtain or retain business for the organization or to obtain or retain an advantage in the conduct of business for the organization. This is a strict liability offense that can be committed in the UK or overseas. Note the following:

(a) A person will be "associated with" the company for these purposes where the person acts on an organization's behalf. This could include an employee, agent or subsidiary of the organization. Contractors, suppliers, joint venture entities and joint venture partners may also be associated persons.

(b) While there is a rebuttable presumption that an employee acts on behalf of his or her organization, an individual's association will be determined by reference to all relevant circumstances, not merely the relationship between the individual and the organization.

(c) It is a defense for an organization to prove that it had "adequate procedures" in place to prevent the bribery. See Section 5.

3.3 Definition of foreign public official

For the purposes of the Bribery Act, an FPO includes an individual who: holds a legislative, administrative or judicial position of any kind; exercises a public function for or on behalf of a country or territory outside the UK or for any public agency or public enterprise of that country or territory; or is an official or agent of a public international organization.

Foreign political parties or candidates for foreign political office are not considered FPOs.

3.4 Consequences of corruption of foreign public officials

(a) For the individuals involved

An individual convicted of bribing a foreign public official may be imprisoned for a term of up to 10 years and/or be subject to an unlimited fine.

(b) For a company/legal entity

A company or partnership that is found to have bribed an FPO will be liable on conviction on indictment, to an unlimited fine and to automatic and perpetual debarment from competing for public contracts.

Where an organization has been convicted of a bribery offense, senior officers of the organization who have consented to or connived in the conduct can also be convicted of the offense concerned.

In addition, the SFO will be able to use its civil recovery powers to recover property obtained by the unlawful conduct without resorting to prosecution.

3.5 Limitation applicable to hospitality expenses (gifts, travel, meals, entertainment, among others)

Corporate hospitality will only amount to one of the general offenses if there is improper conduct on the part of the person bribing. If the hospitality is routine and inexpensive, it is unlikely to amount to a breach of an expectation of good faith, impartiality or trust.

The government has confirmed that the legislation should not be used to penalize legitimate and proportionate hospitality, including in respect of foreign public officials, but its view is that hospitality is also an issue best considered by prosecutors rather than by Parliament.

However, there is some risk that corporate hospitality may trigger the specific offense of bribing an FPO if the provider of the hospitality: (a) intends to influence the official in his or her capacity as foreign public official; and (b) intends to obtain or retain business or a business advantage, and the official is neither permitted nor required to be influenced under the local written law.

4. Facilitation payments

A facilitation payment refers to the practice of paying a small sum of money to a public official as a way of ensuring that they perform their routine, non-discretionary duties, either promptly or at all.

Facilitation payments are illegal under the Bribery Act. Nevertheless, the UK government has recognized "the problems that commercial organizations face in some parts of the world and in certain sectors." Although the UK's Joint Committee has recommended that there be guidance as to the circumstances in which facilitation payments will be prosecuted, the government has made it clear that this should be policed by prosecutorial discretion exercised in the public interest, leaving the position uncertain. Even if prosecutions do not take place, the continuing illegality of facilitation payments causes issues from a money laundering point of view.

5. Compliance programs

5.1 Value of a compliance program in mitigating/eliminating the criminal liability of companies

It is a defense to the corporate offense under Section 7 of the Bribery Act (identified in Paragraphs 2.2 and 3.2) for an organization to prove, on the balance of probabilities, that it had "adequate procedures" in place to prevent persons associated with it from engaging in bribery.

The UK Ministry of Justice has issued guidance on procedures that commercial organizations can put into place to prevent persons associated with them from bribing. See Paragraph 5.3.

It is worth noting that the UK government has published draft legislation that provides for a new corporate criminal offense of failure to prevent the facilitation of tax evasion. Similar to the corporate bribery offense, this new offense would be subject to a defense of having "reasonable procedures" in place to prevent the criminal facilitation of tax evasion. The legislation is likely to be implemented before the end of 2016.

The UK government has also suggested introducing corporate offenses for failing to prevent other economic crimes such as fraud, money laundering and false accounting.

5.2 Absence of a compliance program as a criminal offense

The failure of a corporate entity to implement a compliance program is not an offense under the Bribery Act. However, there is significant value in corporates having a robust anti-bribery program in place to protect against corporate liability, as explained in Paragraphs 2.2 and 3.2.

5.3 Elements of a compliance program

The Ministry of Justice's guidance is not prescriptive as to the nature of systems and procedures that firms should implement in order to meet the "adequate procedures" standard necessary to provide a defense against the Section 7 corporate offense. A one-size-fits-all approach is simply not possible. However, the guidance highlights six principles of bribery prevention that an organization's officers should consider when drafting an anti-bribery compliance program:

(a) Proportionate procedures

An organization's internal procedures to prevent bribery by persons associated with it ought to be proportionate to the bribery risks it faces and to the nature, scale and complexity of the organization's activities.

(b) Top-level commitment

The management of an organization (i.e., directors, owners or any other equivalent body or person) ought to be committed to preventing bribery by persons associated with it. The management should endorse a culture in which bribery is never acceptable.

(c) Risk assessment

An organization should consider the nature and extent of its exposure to potential risks of bribery on its behalf by persons associated with it. Its assessment ought to be "periodic, informed and documented."

(d) Due diligence

An organization must implement due diligence procedures, applying a proportionate approach, in respect of persons who perform or will perform services for or on its behalf.

(e) Communication (including training)

An organization should seek to ensure that its anti-bribery policies are understood throughout the organization via internal and external communication and, if appropriate, training.

(f) Monitoring and Review

An organization needs to periodically monitor and review its anti-bribery procedures.

6. Regulator with jurisdiction to prosecute corruption

The SFO is the main prosecutor with the responsibility for enforcing the Bribery Act. Broadly speaking, when determining whether to commence a prosecution (against corporates or individuals), the SFO will consider both the evidential case against the suspect and whether a prosecution would be in the public interest.

Latin America

Argentina

Vanina Caniza

Vanina Caniza advises clients on transactional, general commercial and compliance matters. She has conducted several compliance investigations and has trained Argentine subsidiaries of global companies in compliance matters. She focuses her practice on the life sciences and healthcare industry and has extensive experience on regulatory law and specialized knowledge of legal issues related to the pharmaceutical and healthcare industry.

vanina.caniza@bakermckenzie.com
Tel: +54 11 4310 2226

Fernando Goldaracena

Fernando Goldaracena currently gives advice on corporate crimes, anticorruption and compliance matters, antitrust law matters, criminal tax evasion, currency exchange regime, anti-money laundering law, and economic and financial criminal offenses (new white collar crimes). He is a former federal court clerk, currently a member of the Buenos Aires office's Compliance Group and has conducted several investigations as well as trainings of local subsidiaries of multinational companies.

fernando.goldaracena@bakermckenzie.com

Tel: +54 11 4310 2216

Baker & McKenzie SC
Avenida Leandro N. Alem 1110, Piso 13
C1001AAT Buenos Aires
Argentina

1. Domestic bribery (private to public)

1.1 Legal framework

The Argentine Criminal Code applies to any public officer and to any individual who engages in corrupt practices with public officers. The Argentine Criminal Code defines the offenses of domestic bribery (active, passive and improper lobbying), corruption and transnational bribery (other local laws to consider are Public Employment Law, the Ethics on Public Office Law, and the Code of Ethics of Public Office).

1.2 Definition of bribery

Bribery can be committed by both public officials and private individuals.

The Argentine Criminal Code prohibits government officials from receiving or accepting money or other benefits/gifts in order to do or not to do something related to their duties (active bribery); and further prohibits any individual from personally, or through an intermediary, giving or offering any gift to a public officer (passive bribery).

1.3 Definition of public official

Article 77 of the Argentine Criminal Code defines "Public/Government Official" broadly, and includes those who are temporarily or permanently involved in the exercise of public functions either by election or by appointment of a competent authority, including: individuals (elected or appointed) who hold legislative, administrative, military or judicial positions of any kind; senior managers, officers and government appointees of any government-owned or government-controlled commercial enterprise; employees of any governmental regulatory agency, exchange or listing authority; and individuals who exercise a public function for or on behalf of any national, local or municipal public agency (e.g., public health agencies).

1.4 Consequences of bribery

(a) For the individuals involved

Depending on the type of criminal offense (described), sanctions imposed by the Argentine Criminal Code are imprisonment from one to six to 12 years, including, if applicable, special disqualification for life.

(b) For the company / legal entity

The Argentine Criminal Code does not provide for corporate liability for bribery acts.

1.5 Political contributions

Section 16 of the Political Party Financing Law No. 26,215 (the "Law") provides that political parties may receive contributions/donations that shall not exceed 1 percent of the permitted expenses when the contribution/donation is performed by an entity, and 2 percent of the permitted expenses when the contribution/donation is performed by an individual. Please note that to calculate such amounts, other legal limits should be considered.

Section 15 of the Law expressly prohibits donations performed by individuals or legal entities that do not have an established domicile in Argentina. If this provision is not complied with, a fine could be imposed. Additionally, the Law provides certain specific restrictions on the financing of electoral campaign. The Law further expressly prohibits private entities (but not individuals) from giving donations or contributions during electoral campaigns.

1.6 Limitation applicable to hospitality expenses (gifts, travel, meals, entertainment, among others)

Argentine laws do not offer direct guidance when it comes to gifts, benefits or meals and other invitations to public officers. However, and as a general rule, no gifts (except those of nominal value) should be offered to public officers. Considering the above legal provisions, the mere giving of something of value to a public officer could qualify as a crime under Argentine law, even if nothing is requested or offered in return.

2. Domestic bribery (private to private)

2.1 Legal framework

The Argentine Criminal Code does not provide for a comprehensive description of conducts to sanction acts of corruption in the private sector, as it does not specifically regulate private corruption. However, there are certain specific conducts that may be considered similar to domestic private corruption, such as fraud, concealment, embezzlement and wrongful administration carried out by individuals.

Further examples include punishment provided under Section 173, paragraph 7 of the Argentine Criminal Code, which provides sanctions of imprisonment for any person who, vested with the management, administration or care of goods or pecuniary interests belonging to another person and, with the purpose of obtaining an unlawful gain for himself or a third party, damages such interests or makes excessive expenses to the detriment of the represented person.

2.2 Definition of private bribery

See Section 2.1.

2.3 Consequences of private bribery

(a) For the individuals involved

See Section 2.1.

(b) For the company / legal entity

See Section 2.1.

2.4 Limitation applicable to hospitality expenses (gifts, travel, meals, entertainment, among others)

Argentine laws do not offer direct guidance when it comes to gifts, benefits or meals and other invitations to public officers. However, and as a general rule, no gifts (except those of nominal value) should be offered to public officers. Considering the above legal provisions, the mere giving of something of value to a public officer could qualify as a crime under Argentine law, even if nothing is requested or offered in return.

3. Corruption of foreign public officials

3.1 Legal framework

The Argentine Criminal Code

3.2 Definition of corruption of foreign public officials

Section 258 "b" of the Argentine Criminal Code was incorporated in 2003 and was extracted from Article VIII of the United Nations Convention Against Corruption. It provides that any person who offers or gives a public officer from a foreign state or from an international public organization money or other benefits for the purpose of having such officer do or refrain from doing an act related to his office or to use the influence derived from the office he holds in an economic, financial or commercial transaction, shall be punished.

3.3 Definition of foreign public official

The definition of public/government officer is the same as for the offenses mentioned above. The definition is broad and it covers those who are temporarily or permanently involved in the exercise of public functions either by election or by appointment of another state or who are part of an international public organization.

3.4 Consequences of corruption of foreign public officials

(a) For the individuals involved

Imprisonment of up to six years and special disqualification for life in respect of the exercise of any public office

(b) For the legal entity

See 1.4 (b).

3.5 Limitation applicable to hospitality expenses (gifts, travel, meals, entertainment, among others)

Argentine laws do not offer direct guidance when it comes to gifts, benefits or meals and other invitations to public officers. However, and as a general rule, no gifts (except those of nominal value) should be offered to public officers. Considering the above legal provisions, the mere giving of something of value to a public officer could qualify as a crime under Argentine law, even if nothing is requested or offered in return.

4. Facilitation payments

Facilitation payments are not permitted under Argentine law. Therefore, any such payments will be considered illegal and subject to the same provisions as the ones indicated in Section 1 (domestic bribery).

5. Compliance programs

5.1 Value of a compliance program to mitigate/eliminate criminal liability for companies

There is no criminal liability for corporations for corruption misconducts[1] under the Argentine Criminal Code. Therefore, compliance programs do not have any influence regarding corporate

---

[1] There are certain sections of the Argentine Criminal Code that provide for corporations' liability for money laundering and other related offenses.

criminal liability. There are bills at the National Congress for the amendment to the Argentine Criminal Code that make reference to compliance programs through a new concept of corporate criminal liability, although they have not been approved yet.

5.2 Absence of a compliance program as a criminal offense.

See 5.1.

5.3 Elements of a compliance program.

The elements of any compliance program should follow the structure of US/UK compliance programs.

6. Regulator with jurisdiction to prosecute corruption

While the Argentine Anti-corruption Office aims at developing and coordinating programs to combat corruption, the actual enforcement is in the hands of criminal federal courts.

Brazil

Bruno Maeda

Bruno Carneiro Maeda joined the Firm in 2002 and is a member of its Compliance Group. His activities include assistance in FCPA and internal investigation cases; adaptation and implementation of global corporate policies to the local practices and law; assistance in preventive compliance audits; and review of contracts from the perspective of risk management related to compliance with anti-corruption policies and law.

bruno.maeda@trenchrossi.com
Tel: +55 11 3048 6838

Esther Flesch

Esther Miriam Flesch is the head of the Brazilian Compliance Group. She has significant experience in anti-corruption and FCPA-related projects, including internal investigations, cooperation with US colleagues for DOJ disclosures, and dealing with crisis upon local management arrests and indictment. Esther also has significant experience in preventive practice related to the FCPA, such as due diligence of third parties and implementation of compliance programs.

esther.flesch@trenchrossi.com
Tel: +55 11 3048 6940

Erica Sarubbi

Erica Sellin Sarubbi joined the Firm in 2010. Her practice includes internal investigations and assistance in cases of potential violation of anti-corruption laws including the FCPA, review and assistance in the implementation of global compliance programs, review of internal policies and codes of conduct, elaboration and review of compliance training materials, and review of contracts from the perspective of risk management related to compliance with anti-corruption laws.

erica.sarubbi@trenchrossi.com
Tel: +55 11 3048 6796

Carlos Ayres

Carlos Ayres joined the firm in 2008. His practice focuses on anticorruption and compliance issues, internal and independent corporate investigations in Latin America, Europe, Africa and United States, including some that were responsible to subpoenas by the DOJ, SEC and other enforcement agencies, review of compliance programs, and anti-corruption due diligence of third parties and in the context of corporate and commercial transactions.

carlos.ayres@trenchrossi.com
Tel: +55 11 3048 6885

1. Domestic bribery (private to public)

1.1 Legal framework

Individuals and legal entities can be liable for bribery of public officials in Brazil.

Bribery of public officials is regulated under the Brazilian Criminal Code (Decree Law n. 2.848), Article 333. Only individuals are criminally liable for bribery in Brazil. The Brazilian Anti-Bribery Law (Law 12.846/2013) establishes judicial and administrative sanctions for legal entities. The Brazilian Anti-Bribery law not only covers acts of corruption, but also prohibits acts against national and foreign public administration, such as fraud in public tenders.

1.2 Definition of bribery

The Brazilian Criminal Code sets forth the crime of Active Bribery, which is defined as the crime to offer or promise undue advantage to a public official, in order to influence him or her to perform, hide or delay an official act within the scope of his or her duties.

According to the Brazilian Anti-Bribery Law, it is prohibited to promise, offer or give, directly or indirectly, an undue advantage to a national or foreign public official, or a third person related to them.

1.3 Definition of public official

As set forth in Article 327 of the Brazilian Criminal Code, a "government official" is described as any person who, even on a temporary basis or without remuneration, renders services in governmental agencies or entities, and carries out a public function, job or office.

1.4 Consequences of bribery

(a) For the individuals involved

Under the Brazilian Criminal Code, individuals who commit acts of corruption can be subject to penalties of a fine and up to 12 years of imprisonment.

(b) For the company / legal entity

Under the Brazilian Anti-Corruption Law, legal entities can be subject to administrative and judicial penalties.

- Administrative: (i) Fine of 0.1 percent to 20 percent of the gross revenue in the last year prior to the start of the administrative proceedings; if such criteria cannot be used, the fine will range from BRL6,000 to BRL60 million; and (ii) publication of the condemnatory decision

- Judicial: (i) Prohibition from receiving incentives, subsidies, grants, donations or loans from public agencies or entities and from public financial institutions or institutions controlled by the government, for up to five years; (ii) loss of assets, rights or valuables representing the advantage or profit, directly or indirectly, obtained from the wrongdoing; (iii) partial suspension or interdiction of the legal entity's activities; and (iv) compulsory dissolution of the legal entity

1.5 Political contributions

According to Law No. 9,504/97, Individuals can make political contributions, in an amount that does not exceed 10 percent of the person's gross income. Law No. 9,504/97 also allowed companies to make contributions to candidates or political parties in an amount of up to 2 percent of the company's gross revenue in the year prior to the election, but this provision was revoked by Law 13.165/2015. Companies are no longer permitted to make political contributions.

1.6 Limitation applicable to hospitality expenses (gifts, travel, meals, entertainment, among others)

Brazilian legislation does not establish a limit on hospitality expenses given to government officials, and there is no minimum or maximum amount allowed by local laws. There is however, a Code of Conduct for the High Level Administration, which contains a set of guidelines and ethical principles to be observed by some government officials. This code is only applicable to government officials and is not applicable to private entities, but it is useful in setting out specific parameters to assess the appropriateness of conduct towards a public official regarding gifts, hospitalities and entertainment. According to the code of conduct, government officials must refrain from accepting presents or other benefits when the offeror is any individual or company that: (i) is subject to the regulatory jurisdiction of the agency for which the government official works; (ii) has any personal, professional or corporate interest with the government official; (iii) maintains a business relationship with the agency to which the official provides services; or (iv) represents third parties that have interests with the agency in which the official is employed.

The code of conduct also establishes that government officials may accept small free gifts, given for advertisement or for celebration of events of historical and cultural nature. The commercial value of the free gift cannot exceed BRL100 per year, from the same company, on an annual basis. Moreover, its distribution must be generalized (i.e., it should not be exclusively targeted to a specific public official), and the gift must not be offered more than once every 12 months to the same government official.

2. Domestic bribery (private to private)

2.1 Legal framework

Private bribery is not regulated by Brazilian legislation.

2.2 Definition of private bribery

Private bribery is not regulated by Brazilian legislation.

2.3 Consequences of private bribery

Private bribery is not regulated by Brazilian legislation.

2.4 Limitation applicable to hospitality expenses (gifts, travel, meals, entertainment, among others)

Brazilian Legislation does not establish limits to hospitality expenses between private parties.

3. Corruption of foreign public officials

3.1 Legal framework

Individuals and legal entities can be liable for bribery of foreign public officials in Brazil.

Bribery of foreign public officials is regulated under the Brazilian Criminal Code (Decree Law n. 2.848), Article 337-B for individuals, and in the Brazilian Anti-Corruption Law (Law 12.846/2013) for legal entities. The Brazilian Anti-Bribery law not only covers acts of corruption, but also prohibits acts against national and foreign public administration, such as fraud in public tenders.

3.2 Definition of corruption of foreign public officials

Under the Brazilian Criminal Code, which sets forth the crime of Active Bribery in International Commercial Transaction, it is a crime for an individual to offer or promise undue advantage to a foreign public official, or to a third party, in order to influence him to perform, hide or delay an official act related to an international commercial transaction.

Under the Brazilian Anti-Bribery Law, it is forbidden to promise, offer or give, directly or indirectly, an undue advantage to a national or foreign public official, or a third person related to them.

3.3 Definition of foreign public official

Foreign public officials are those who, even transitorily and without compensation, hold a public position, job or office in government agencies and entities, or in diplomatic representations of a foreign country, as well as in legal entities controlled, directly or indirectly, by the government of a foreign country or in international public organizations.

Public agencies and entities, diplomatic representations of a foreign country, of any government level or sphere, and legal entities controlled, directly or indirectly, by the government of a foreign country, as well as international public organizations, are considered foreign public administration, according to Law 12.846/13.

3.4 Consequences of Corruption of foreign public officials

(a) For the individuals involved

Under the Brazilian Criminal Code, individuals who commit acts of corruption in international commercial transactions can be subject to penalties of a fine and up to eight years of imprisonment.

(b) For the company / legal entity

Under the Brazilian Anti-Bribery Law, legal entities can be subject to administrative and judicial penalties.

- <u>Administrative</u>: (i) Fine of 0.1 percent to 20 percent of the gross revenue in the last year prior to the start of the administrative proceedings; if such criteria cannot be used, the fine will range from BRL6,000 to BRL60 million; and (ii) publication of the condemnatory decision

- <u>Judicial</u>: (i) Prohibition from receiving incentives, subsidies, grants, donations or loans from public agencies or entities and from public financial institutions or institutions controlled by the government, for up to five years; (ii) loss of assets, rights or valuables representing the advantage or profit, directly or indirectly, obtained from the wrongdoing; (iii) partial suspension or interdiction of the legal entity's activities; and (iv) compulsory dissolution of the legal entity

3.5 Limitation applicable to hospitality expenses (gifts, travel, meals, entertainment, among others)

Brazilian legislation does not establish a limit on hospitality expenses given to government officials, and there is not a minimum amount allowed. Any amount can be considered corrupt, depending on the context.

4. Facilitation payments

Under Brazilian legislation, facilitation payments are prohibited.

5. Compliance programs

5.1 Value of a compliance program to mitigate/eliminate the criminal liability for legal entities

The existence of a compliance program does not eliminate judicial or administrative liability for legal entities. However, it can mitigate sanctions that legal entities can be subject to. According to the Brazilian Anti-Bribery Law, "the existence of internal mechanisms and procedures of integrity, audit and incentive for the reporting of irregularities, as well as the effective enforcement of codes of ethics and of conduct within the scope of the legal entity" will be taken into consideration when applying sanctions.

5.2 Absence of a compliance program as a crime

The Brazilian legislation does not establish that the absence of a compliance program is a crime or a violation of any laws.

5.3 Elements of compliance program

(a) Legal framework

On 19 March 2015, the Federal Executive Branch issued Decree n. 8,420/15 ("Decree"), which provides regulation for the Brazilian Anti-Bribery Law. Among the several items regulated in the decree are the parameters for the evaluation of a compliance program.

Article 42 of the Decree sets forth that compliance programs will be evaluated according to the following parameters:

I. Commitment of the legal entity's senior management, including board members, proven by their clear and unequivocal support to the program

II. Standards of conduct, code of ethics, policies, and integrity procedures that are applied to all employees and administrators, regardless of their position or role

III. Standards of conduct, code of ethics and integrity policies that are extended, when necessary, to third parties such as suppliers, service providers, intermediaries and other associates

IV. Periodic training on the integrity program

V. Periodic analysis of risks in order to implement necessary adjustments to the integrity program

VI. Accounting records that precisely and completely reflect the transactions of the legal entity

VII. Internal controls that assure that reports and financial statements of the legal entity are readily prepared and credible

VIII. Specific procedures to prevent frauds and illicit acts within the tender process, on the execution of administrative contracts or on any interaction with the public sector, even if intermediated by third parties, such as the payment of taxes, subjection to inspections, or obtainment of authorizations, licenses, permits and certificates

IX. Independence, in structure and authority, of the internal department that is responsible for enforcing the integrity program and monitoring its compliance

X. Channels to report irregularities, openly and broadly disseminated among employees and third parties, and mechanisms to protect good-faith whistleblowers

XI. Disciplinary measures enforced against those found to have violated the integrity program

XII. Procedures that assure the immediate suspension of irregularities or detected infractions and the timely remediation of the damages caused

XIII. Proper due diligence conducted prior to engaging third parties and, depending on the circumstances, the monitoring of third parties such as suppliers, service providers, intermediaries, and other associates

XIV. Verification, during a merger, acquisition or other corporate restructuring, of the occurrence of irregularities or illicit acts, or the existence of vulnerabilities in the legal entities involved

XV. Continuous monitoring of the integrity program to ensure it remains effective at preventing, detecting and otherwise addressing the wrongful acts set forth in Article 5 of the Anticorruption Law

XVI. Transparency surrounding donations to candidates and political parties made by the legal entity

(b) Recommended practice

It is recommended that companies create, maintain and update mechanisms and procedures to prevent, detect and correct prohibited acts. Having an effective compliance program allows companies to decide about the convenience of making voluntary disclosures to enforcement authorities, as well as to obtain credit in case of possible wrongdoing.

Compliance programs should be implemented and revised on a regular basis, considering the evaluation of key risk factors related to the company and varying according to the company's size, amount and nature of commercial operations; location where their activities take place; and risk perception. However, the mere creation and revision of a compliance program is not sufficient. It is important to disseminate and apply such programs throughout the company, as well as to third parties and business partners. It is very important to provide periodic training to employees and also to third parties. The Decree also establishes that companies should make their reporting channels available to such third parties. This will also be a factor to be taken into consideration for the evaluation of the compliance program, as set forth in the Decree.

It is also important to note that the Brazilian Anti-Bribery Law, unlike other anti-corruption legislation, does not only cover acts of corruption, but also other acts against public administration, mainly related to public tender procedures and public contracts. For that reason, it is important for companies to take this into consideration when structuring or reviewing their compliance program, even if they already have a compliance program with focus on corruption matters.

6. Regulator with jurisdiction to prosecute corruption

If the crime of corruption is committed by individuals, the state police, the federal police, and the state and federal public prosecutor office are the authorities who can prosecute corruption.

Under the Brazilian Anti-Corruption Law, for legal entities who commit acts of corruption, the highest authorities of each entity of the executive, legislative and judiciary powers, and the Office of the Federal Comptroller General are the authorities who can prosecute acts of corruption and apply administrative sanctions. The federal government, the states, the federal district, the municipalities and the public prosecutor office are the authorities who can prosecute acts of corruption and apply civil sanctions.

Chile

Leon Larrain

Leon Larraín leads the Corporate M&A group of the Santiago office. His practice includes corporate, mergers and acquisitions, banking and finance, real estate and securities. He graduated from the University of Chile Law School (Licensee in Juridical and Social Sciences, LL.B.) and was admitted to the Chilean bar in 1980. He also took a course on tax law at the University of Chile Law School in 1985-1986. Leon graduated from the Harvard Law School where he attended an International Tax Program (ITP) in 1989-1990, as well as Harvard Negotiation Workshop (PIL) in 1997. Leon was a consultant with the Harvard Institute for International Development (HIID) for tax reform in Bolivia in 1991, and customs reform in Perú in 1991-1992. He was also Chilean correspondent for Tax Notes International. Additionally, he is a conciliator at the Center for Settlement of International Investment Disputes (ICSID) in Washington, D.C., having been appointed by the Chilean government.

leon.larrain@bakermckenzie.com
Tel: +56 2 2367 7041

Sebastian Doren

Sebastian Doren advises local and multinational clients on criminal litigation. He specifically handles cases dealing with fraud against his clients and the financial/banking system, as well as anti-counterfeiting. He also helps client companies set their compliance programs and perform internal investigations. Much of his practice proceedings have been against Chilean Customs and administrative offices.

sebastian.doren@bakermckenzie.com
Tel: +56 2 2367 7065

Baker & McKenzie Ltda.
Nueva Tajamar 481
Torre Norte, Piso 21
Las Condes, Santiago
Chile

1. Domestic bribery (private to public)

1.1 Legal framework

Bribery of public officials (*cohecho*) is regulated under the Chilean Criminal Code, Articles 248 to 251 ter.

1.2 Definition of bribery

The Chilean Criminal Code sanctions any public official who:

- requests or agrees to receive fees greater than those applicable to the office he holds, or an economic benefit in his or her or a third party's benefit, in consideration for performing or having performed an act within the purview of his or her office;

- requests or accepts an economic benefit for his or her own or a third party's benefit, in consideration for refraining or having refrained from performing an act pertaining to his or her position, or for the execution of an action in contravention of his or her statutory duties; or

- requests or accepts to receive an economic benefit, for his or her own or a third party's benefit, in order to commit certain other special public official crimes (i.e., embezzlement, crimes against individuals' constitutional rights, etc.).

<u>Any person</u> who offers or agrees to offer an economic benefit to a public official who performs any of the abovementioned actions is also punished under criminal law.

1.3 Definition of public official

Article 260 the Chilean Criminal Code defines "public official" for criminal purposes in Chile:

Whoever holds a position or a public duty, either in the Central Administration or in semi fiscal, municipal, autonomous institutions or companies or in organisms created by the state or state dependent, even if they are not appointed by the Chilean president (*Presidente de la Republica)* and even if they do not receive a state salary, qualifies as public official.

A functional concept of public official is established (as understood by the Supreme Court in its decision in 1958) that covers numerous situations not contemplated by the strict application of the Administrative Statute.

1.4 Consequences of bribery

The maximum penalty for domestic bribery is imprisonment of up to three years and a fine from 0.5 to three times the amount of the benefit requested or accepted.

Temporary or permanent disqualification from holding public posts is also possible.

For the company / legal entity

- Dissolution of the legal entity or cancelation of its legal capacity
- Temporary or permanent prohibition from executing acts and agreements with state institutions
- Partial or complete loss of fiscal benefits, together with the complete prohibition to receive said benefits during a specific period
- Fines for the treasury's benefit
- Ancillary Penalties – The law establishes that the following ancillary penalties may be applied in addition to those previously detailed: publication of an abstract of the ruling in the Official Gazette or in another newspaper that is published nationwide; confiscation of any products derived from the

crime, as well as confiscation of other assets, objects, documents and instruments pertaining to the same; and, in those cases in which the felony involves making an investment that exceeds the legal entity's income, the deposit of a sum equivalent to such investment in an account held by the treasury.

1.5 Political contributions

Political contributions are regulated under Law 19.884. In the case of an opened election process, there are thresholds depending on the authority being elected.

Foreign persons or entities cannot make political contributions.

1.6 Limitation applicable to hospitality expenses (gifts, travel, meals, entertainment, among others)

Neither law nor regulations establish a specific monetary threshold.

Article 64 N°5 Law 18,575 expressly states that actions that consist of "requesting," "making someone promise" or "accepting" gifts, advantages or privileges of whichever nature, either for themselves or for third parties, especially contravene the Public Integrity Principle.

It also states that official and protocol gifts, as well as gifts recognized by custom as courtesy and expressions of politeness, are exempted from the prohibition.

Examples of gifts recognized by customs as courtesy and expressions of politeness are not set out by the law. Still, some regulations clarify their scope to some extent. For instance, the Guide of Transparency and Honesty of the State Administration, issued by the General Secretariat Ministry of the Presidency last January 2008 (the "Guide"), has explained the prohibition of Article 64 N°5 stating that it is an ample prohibition that not only covers the material dispense of a gift but that also extends to any kind of advantages, such as discounts to acquire a product; scholarships for the public official or his or her family members; paid invitations (events, banquets, travels, etc.); and receptions or special treatments (e.g., discounts more beneficial than those granted to the general public). The Guide summarizes the concept by stating that it embraces whatever could compromise the public official's spirit to benefit the one promising or handing the gift or favor. The Guide also stipulates that receiving or requesting economic advantages as those described may be deemed beyond an administrative infringement and be considered a bribery criminal offense.

2. Domestic bribery (private to private)

As opposed to other jurisdictions, Chilean criminal law does not contemplate a criminal offense description regarding advantages granted to private sector business associates in the context of contractual negotiations. Thus, in principle, we believe that such conduct remains currently unpunished from a strict criminal law perspective in Chile. (On 30 January 2007, the United Nations Convention against Corruption was published in the Official Gazette. Pursuant to its Article 21, bribery in the private sector could be dealt with in the future.)

Nonetheless, such a conduct could be deemed as an unlawful competition practice, where Law N° 20.169, published in the Official Gazette of 16 February 2007, in its Article 3, broadly defines an unlawful competition act as any conduct contrary to bona fide or fair customs that by illicit means aims toward deviation of the customers from a market agent (see Article 3 of Law 20,169). Should a third party feel affected by an unlawful competition act pursuant to the law, it could file a claim before a civil court to request the termination or prohibition of the act or the conclusion of the effects produced by the act, and possibly seek compensatory damages. In certain cases, a fine could also be applied.

Another alternative would be that a party deemed affected by the conduct could seek an indemnification pursuant to the general regulations of extra contractual liability pursuant to the Chilean Civil Code.

3. Corruption of foreign public officials

3.1 Legal framework

Corruption of foreign public officials is regulated under the Chilean Criminal Code, Article 251 *bis*.

3.2 Definition of corruption of foreign public officials

It is a criminal offense to:

- offer, promise or give an economic or other benefit to a foreign public official, for such public official or a third party's benefit, in order for the foreign public official to act or refrain from acting, for the purpose of obtaining or retaining for him or herself or for another party any business or unfair advantage in the course of international business transactions;

- offer, promise or give such a benefit to a foreign public official as consideration for past performance of such an action or omission; and

- consenting or agreeing to give or provide such a benefit.

3.3 Definition of foreign public official

Pursuant to the Chilean Criminal Code, Article 251 ter., a foreign public official is a person who:

- holds a parliamentary, administrative or judicial position in a foreign state, whether appointed or elected;

- performs public duties or functions for a foreign state, whether in a public entity or a state-owned company; or

- is an official or agent of a public international organization.

3.4 Consequences of corruption of foreign public officials

The maximum penalty is imprisonment of up to five years and a fine from one to two times the amount of the benefit requested or accepted; if the benefit is not of economic nature, a fine of up to 1,000 UTM (approximately USD65,000 at the current exchange rate).

3.5 Limitation applicable to hospitality expenses (gifts, travel, meals, entertainment, among others)

There is no limitation established in the law.

4. Facilitation payments

The Criminal Code does not make any reference to so-called facilitation payments.

However, facilitation payments are not allowed, and would likely be considered domestic bribery.

5. Compliance programs

5.1 Value of a compliance program to mitigate/eliminate the criminal liability for legal entities

Pursuant to Law 20.393 published in the Official Gazette on 2 December 2009, and which "Establishes Criminal Liability for legal entities arising from certain felonies of money laundering, terrorism financing and bribery of public officials," the existence of a compliance program, named in the law as "Crime Prevention Model," may serve to eliminate or mitigate the criminal liability for legal entities.

5.2 Absence of a compliance program as a crime

The absence of a crime prevention model may give rise to criminal liability for a legal entity as such program is one of the concurrent requirements for legal entities. Indeed, the legal offense corresponds to what legal doctrine defines as "organizational flaws" imputation forms.

5.3 Elements of compliance program

Article 4 of Law 20.393 sets forth a minimum legal standard for a prevention model, which, besides the appointment of a prevention supervisor, shall at the very least contain the following elements:

- Identification of the entity's activities or processes, whether regular or sporadic, within the context of which the risk of the felonies mentioned in Article 1 (money laundering, terrorism financing and bribery) being perpetrated is either created or increased

- Establishment of specific protocols, rules and procedures that allow the individuals who take part in specific activities and processes to program and execute tasks or labors, in a manner that prevents the perpetration of crimes

- Identification of the management and audit procedures of financial resources that allow the entity to prevent their use in the crimes described by the law

- Existence of internal administrative penalties, as well as of other procedures to report and prosecute the financial liability of the parties that breach the crime prevention system

6. Regulator with jurisdiction to prosecute corruption

The Chilean legal system does not have a specific regulator with exclusive responsibilities to prosecute corruption. Any public prosecutor could start a corruption investigation. However, the Chilean system has a Specialized Anti-Corruption Unit that assesses public prosecutors in the legal, financial and accounting areas.

Colombia

Carolina Pardo

Carolina Pardo advises clients on general compliance matters related to transactional, general commercial and regulatory matters. She has conducted several compliance investigations and has trained subsidiaries of global companies in Colombia, Peru and Central America on competition, anti-corruption, data protection and regulatory matters. She has participated as speaker in Colombia and abroad in events related to these matters. She has actively advised and represented national and multinational clients in investigations and in the implementation of internal procedures to comply with the applicable regulations on anti-corruption, competition, data protection, consumer regulation and compliance matters in general. She was part of the panel of experts that assisted the Colombian government in the design of the leniency program on competition matters. She has also coordinated and prepared submissions containing input from industry group members to the Colombian authorities regarding their consumer protection, competition and data protection initiatives.

carolina.pardo@bakermckenzie.com
Tel: +57 1 634 1559

Bibiana Cala

Bibiana Cala is an associate in Baker & McKenzie's Bogota office. She has worked in criminal litigation for more than 11 years and has served as an adviser to the Vice-Minister of Justice in Colombia. Her main areas of practice are economic criminal law, criminal litigation, and intellectual property.

bibiana.cala@bakermckenzie.com
Tel: + 57 1 634 1565

Baker & McKenzie S.A.S.
Avenue 82 No. 10-62 6th Floor
Bogota
Colombia

1. Domestic bribery (private to public)

1.1 Legal framework

The Colombian Criminal Code applies to any public officer and to any individual who engages in corrupt practices with public officers. Furthermore, in July 2011, the Colombian Congress approved the Anti-Bribery Statute in an effort to reinforce the prevention, investigation and penalty mechanisms against private and public corruption. With this enactment, various provisions contained in the Criminal Code, the Public Procurement Statute, the Health Law and the Disciplinary Statute were amended, imposing more drastic measures to companies and individuals that commit corruption-related crimes. More recently, Colombian Congress approved an amendment to this statute to enhance the application of anti-corruption laws to legal entities and regarding their liability for transnational bribery.

The Colombian Criminal Code defines the offenses of domestic bribery (proper, improper and by giving or offering), corruption and transnational bribery.

1.2 Definition of bribery

Bribery can be committed both by public officials and by private individuals.

The Colombian Criminal Code prohibits government officials from requesting, receiving or accepting money or any other benefits/gifts, or from accepting promises of benefits, for their own benefit or for the benefit of a third party to undertake their duties (improper bribery) or to delay or omit something related to their duties or to carry out an action that contravenes their official duties (proper bribery).

The Colombian Criminal Code further prohibits any individual from giving or offering money or other illegal profit (bribery by giving or offering) to a public servant for his or her benefit or that of a third party to: (i) unduly influence the performance of duties that the public servant must comply with; (ii) to influence the servant to delay or omit the performance of his or her duties; or (iii) to unduly influence the public servant to carry out an action that contravenes his or her official duties.

1.3 Definition of public official

Article 20 of the Colombian Criminal Code defines, for the purpose of criminal law, public servers as all the members of public corporations and employees of the state and of all of its decentralized (by territory or services) entities. Furthermore, public servers are all members of the public force; officers of private entities that perform permanent or transitory public functions,; functionaries and employees of the Central Bank (*Banco de la Republica*); members of the Citizens National Commission for the Fight against Corruption; and persons that administer resources enshrined in Article 123 of the Constitution.

1.4 Consequences of bribery

(a) For the individuals involved

Depending on the type of criminal offense (as previously described), sanctions imposed by the Colombian Criminal Code are imprisonment from six years to 12 years; fines ranging from 66 to 150 minimum monthly legal wages (i.e., from approximately USD13,000 to approximately USD30,000 at rates applicable as of the date of edition of this publication); and, if applicable, incapacity from exercising public rights and functions from six years to 12 years.

(b) For the company / legal entity

The Colombian Criminal Code provides for corporate liability for bribery acts, and hence would be responsible for compensating all the damages caused by a crime.

In addition to these, companies may be subject to the following:

(i) Fines

Companies found guilty of incurring in or benefiting from corruption can be subject to fines imposed by the Superintendence of Companies of up to 200,000 times the value of the minimum monthly legal wages (i.e., approximately USD40 million at rates applicable as of the date of edition of this publication).

(ii) Debarment on their ability to contract with the government

Companies and individuals seeking state contracts can be debarred from public procurement contracting if the companies or individuals have committed crimes against the public administration (i.e., bribery or other corrupt actions or omissions) or have been sentenced for crimes related with the promotion, financing and affiliation with illegal groups, crimes against humanity, drug trafficking in Colombia or abroad, and transnational bribery.

This debarment applies not only to companies in which its shareholders are those who have committed the aforementioned crimes, but also to its parent companies and subordinates, with the exception of open stock corporations. The duration of the term of debarment was increased from five years to 20 years.

(iii) Debarment on their ability to contract with the government for those who finance political campaigns

Companies or individuals that have financed political campaigns for presidential, gubernatorial or mayoral elections with contributions that exceed 2.5 percent of the maximum amounts permitted by law, may not enter into contracts with government entities, even those decentralized, of the respective administrative level for which the candidate was elected and for the period for which the candidate was elected.

This prohibition also applies to existing companies or companies that are to be incorporated (other than open stock corporations) where its legal representatives or any of its shareholders have directly or indirectly financed said political campaigns.

(iv) Liability of statutory auditors

The Anti-Bribery Statute included an additional circumstance that would result in the cancelation of the registration as a public accountant. According to the statute, the professional license of a public accountant shall be canceled when, acting as a statutory auditor, the accountant does not report before the competent prosecutor or disciplinary authorities corruption acts that he or she becomes aware of while carrying out his or her duties.

1.5 Political contributions

Article 14 of Law 130 of 1994 establishes that political parties, movements and candidates may not receive from entities and individuals, six months prior the election, economic contributions or donations exceeding the amounts fixed by the National Electoral Council. Regarding donations made by entities, Law 130 of 1994 requires that the donation be approved by no less than of 50 percent plus one of the members of the board of directors, or the general assembly of shareholders or the board of trustees.

Regarding presidential campaigns, Law 996 of 2005 establishes that 20 percent of expenditures of a presidential campaign may be financed by individuals, taking into account that these campaigns cannot receive single contributions from individuals for amounts greater than 2 percent of the top fixed amount of the campaign. Regarding the contributions of entities to presidential campaigns, the Constitutional Court declared that these were not in accordance with the constitution.

1.6 Limitation applicable to hospitality expenses (gifts, travel, meals, entertainment, among others)

In principle, Colombian regulations prohibit private and public parties from offering or giving something of value to any Colombian government agency or officials as this may trigger a violation of anti-bribery rules, even in the absence of corrupt intent.

However, Supreme Court Rulings have indicated that there may be situations in which private parties could extend very moderate and reasonable invitations to certain public officials, since those moderate invitations do not have the potential of influencing the officer to whom the invitation is extended.

It is advisable to extend these invitations only in cases in which there is no pending decision from said public officials, and the invitation is made with a very clear purpose. Offering or granting any lavish or luxurious hospitality to Colombian public officers should be avoided at all times.

In general, Colombian regulation does not have specific mandatory procedures that can be followed in order to determine whether a sponsorship or hospitality offered or extended to a government's agency or its officials is appropriate or not. A good reference in determining the value of the invitations is the regulation that the Colombian government publishes on a yearly basis, containing the capped values that the public servants will receive as per diems when travelling on official matters.

2. Domestic bribery (private to private)

2.1 Legal framework

The Anti-Bribery Statute added to the Colombian Criminal Code the crime of private corruption. Furthermore, there are certain provisions in the Colombian Criminal Code that provide for punishment whenever certain specific conducts such as disloyal administration, insider trading and bid rigging in procurement contracting are carried out by individuals.

2.2 Definition of private bribery

Private bribery may be committed by any individual who directly or indirectly offers or grants to directors, administrators, employees or consultants of any company, association or non-profit corporation, gifts or any unjustified rewards, for his or her own benefit or for the benefit of a third party, in detriment of the company, association or non-profit corporation.

It may be also committed by the directors, administrators, employees or consultants of any company, association or non-profit corporation that, directly or indirectly, receive, request or accept gifts or any unjustified reward, in detriment of said company, association or non-profit corporation.

2.3 Consequences of private bribery

(a) For the individuals involved

For the individual and the directors, administrators, employees or consultants, the Criminal Code imposes a sanction of imprisonment from four to eight years, and fines that may reach 1,000 minimum monthly legal wages (i.e., approximately USD200,000 at current rates). When the conduct results in economic damage to the company, association or non-profit corporation, the sanction will be imprisonment for six years to 10 years.

(b) For the company / legal entity

A company / legal entity could be responsible for compensating the damages caused by the crime.

2.4 Limitation applicable to hospitality expenses (gifts, travel, meals, entertainment, among others)

See Section 1.6.

3. Corruption of foreign public officials

3.1 Legal framework

The Colombian Criminal Code, in its recently amended Article 433, proscribes the crime of transnational bribery. Additionally, Colombia ratified the OECD Convention on Combating Bribery of Foreign Public Officials in International Business Transactions.

3.2 Definition of corruption of foreign public officials

Transnational bribery is any action preformed by any individual or legal persons acting through one or more employees, contractors, managers or partners, or those of any subordinate entity, to directly or indirectly give, offer, or promise to a foreign public official bribes in the form of money, benefit, profit or something of value in exchange for the foreign public official's undertaking, omitting, or delaying any act related to the exercise of his or her functions with the purpose to retain or obtain business.

3.3 Definition of foreign public official

In line with the definition of the OECD Convention on Combating Bribery of Foreign Public Officials in International Business Transactions, Law 1778 defines a foreign public official as any person who occupies a legislative, administrative or judicial position in a foreign country, either by election or by appointment; any person that exercises public functions for a foreign country, such as in a public dependency or in a public enterprise; and any other functionary or representative of a public international organization.

3.4 Consequences of corruption of foreign public officials

(a) For the individuals involved

Imprisonment from nine years to 15 years and fines from 650 to 50,000 minimum monthly legal wages (i.e., approximately USD130,000 to USD10 million at rates current as of the edition date)

(b) For the legal entity

Corporate liability for bribery acts, could trigger fines of up to USD40 million and debarment from participating in any public procurement for up to 20 years

3.5 Limitation applicable to hospitality expenses (gifts, travel, meals, entertainment, among others)

See Section 1.6.

4. Facilitation payments

Facilitation payments are not permitted under Colombian law. Therefore, any such payments will be considered illegal and subject to the same provisions as the ones indicated in Section 1 (domestic bribery).

5. Compliance Programs

5.1 Value of a compliance program to mitigate/eliminate criminal liability for companies

With the enactment of Law 1778 in February 2016, Congress introduced the concept of mitigation of criminal liability of legal entities for implementing adequate compliance programs. According to the new law, the Superintendence of Companies can impose on legal entities the obligation to adopt and implement compliance programs that are adequate and comprehensive.

5.2 Absence of a compliance program as a criminal offense

There are no express reference in the law regarding the liability of companies for not having a compliance program. However, if such programs are imposed by the Superintendence of Companies, there could be adverse administrative consequences against the entity and its responsible officers for not adopting them.

5.3 Elements of a compliance program

The elements of any compliance program should include the framework established in Colombian Criminal Code, the Anti-Bribery Statute, the Public Procurement Statute, the Health Law and the Disciplinary Statute, in addition to international standards that are applicable, such as the ones encompassed in the OECD Convention on Combating Bribery of Foreign Public Officials in International Business Transactions.

There have been some initiatives to enact guides for compliance programs, such as the Anti-Bribery Guide for Enterprises, launched by the Bogotá Chamber of Commerce. This guide includes certain parameters for the establishment of compliance and anti-bribery ethics programs.

6. Regulator with jurisdiction to prosecute corruption

While the Transparency and Anti-bribery Observatory is in charge of developing and coordinating programs for enhancing transparency in Colombia, the criminal authorities (i.e., the General Prosecutor as well as the local prosecutors are in charge of the actual enforcement of the Criminal Code. The Superintendence of Companies is the authority in charge of imposing administrative sanctions and monetary fines against entities for their corporate liability in acts or omissions of public bribery.

Mexico

Reynaldo Vizcarra-Mendez

Reynaldo Vizcarra is the national administrative partner for Baker & McKenzie's five offices in Mexico. He has led numerous internal investigations for multinational clients and regularly advises on day-to-day compliance and anti-corruption matters. He also practices in corporate law matters, including mergers and acquisitions and the preparation, supervision and implementation of agreements. Reynaldo's extensive experience includes working on the privatization processes of ports, airports, as well as telecommunications and insurance companies. He has also served as adviser and board member to several multinational companies. In addition to his practice, Reynaldo regularly lectures on foreign investments in Mexico and on various issues related to the Acquisitions, Leasing and Public Sector Services Law; privatization; and bidding processes, among others.

reynaldo.vizcarra-mendez@bakermckenzie.com
Tel: +52 55 5279 2908

Jonathan Adams

Jonathan Adams is the national coordinator for Mexico of the Firm's Compliance practice. He focuses a majority of his practice on compliance matters for numerous multinational clients from the pharmaceutical and other technology-focused industries, as well as clients with significant government sales in Latin America. For these clients, he has handled numerous sensitive and high-impact internal compliance investigations and anti-corruption matters. This work has also included risk assessments based on local documentation, which is often a hotspot for corrupt propositions and/or payments. He also frequently assists clients with their investments and transactions in Central America (Costa Rica, Honduras, Guatemala, Nicaragua and El Salvador). He is admitted to practice in Arizona, Illinois and Mexico.

jonathan.adams@bakermckenzie.com
Tel: +52 55 5351 4128

Baker & McKenzie Abogados, S.C.
Edificio Virreyes - Piso 12
Pedregal 24

Lomas Virreyes / Col. Molino del Rey
Mexico

1. Domestic bribery (private to public)

1.1 Legal framework

Bribery of public officials (*cohecho*) is regulated under the Mexican Federal Criminal Code, Article 222. State criminal codes have similar definitions.

1.2 Definition of bribery

Bribery can be committed both by public servants who solicit or receive a bribe and by private individuals who offer or pay to corrupt a public servant.

> The public servant who, directly or indirectly, solicits or receives unduly for the public servant or another person, money or any other gift, or accepts a promise, to do or refrain from doing any just or unjust act in relation to the public servant's functions, and
>
> Whoever spontaneously gives or offers money or any other gift to any of the persons described in the foregoing paragraph, to cause any public servant to do or refrain from doing any just or unjust act related to the public servant's function.

1.3 Definition of public official

The Mexican Federal Criminal Code has a broad definition of public servant, and it includes any individual that has an employment, position or charge of any type in the central Public Federal Administration, Mexico City, decentralized organisms, government majority-owned companies, organizations or entities that have been assimilated to these, public trusts, autonomous Constitutional organs, Federal Congress, or Federal Judicial or Mexico City Judicial, or that handle federal economic resources. The provisions also apply to state governors, local legislatures and magistrates in local tribunals.

1.4 Consequences of bribery

(a) For the individuals involved

The Mexican Federal Criminal Code establishes the same penalties for public officials as for individuals that corrupt public officials. The penalties are the following:

- Up to 14 years in jail
- A fine of up to approximately USD3,700[1]
- Removal from public office, if applicable
- Up to 14 years of prohibition from exercising public functions

(b) For legal entities

The Mexican Federal Criminal Code does not directly establish criminal liability for legal entities. If it can be shown that the legal entity was used as an instrumentality for the commission of a crime and that it benefitted from such crime, the suspension of operations or dissolution of the entity can be ordered if the judge deems it necessary for public safety.[2] This provision has been in Mexican law for many decades but is not commonly used by courts.

The Criminal Code for Mexico City (formerly known as the Federal District) recently implemented criminal liability for corporate entities. The element of intent is imputed to the company if it can be shown that an individual who acted on the company's behalf had the requisite intent.[3] Penalties can be based on daily company profits commensurate with the prison time to which an individual would have been sentenced for the same crime, with 920 days of profits to be assessed for each year of prison sentence.[4] This legislative innovation

---

[1] All US dollar amounts are calculated using a MXN19 to USD1 exchange rate.
[2] Mexican Federal Criminal Code, Art. 11.
[3] Criminal Code for the Mexico City, Art. 27bis.
[4] Criminal Code for Mexico City, Art. 38bis.

could be a model for the federal level in the implementation of the recent constitutional amendments on anti-corruption.

For activities that are analogous to criminal bribery, there are also administrative sanctions in the public procurement context for individuals as well as companies.[5] The penalties are as follows:

(a) For individuals

- Fines of up to approximately USD275,000, or 35 percent of the value of the contract, whichever is greater
- Debarment for up to eight years

(b) For companies

- Up to approximately USD7.3 million, or 35 percent of the value of the contract, whichever is greater
- Debarment for up to 10 years

1.5 Political contributions

Foreign persons may not participate in politics in Mexico.[6] Parties and independent candidates must disclose all income by source (which must be legal) and all expenditures. Strict spending limits apply to campaigns.[7]

1.6 Limitation applicable to hospitality expenses (gifts, travel, meals, entertainment, among others)

The Federal Criminal Code does not establish quantitative or qualitative limitations on hospitality expenses. Whether a hospitality expense could be considered bribery will need to be determined on a

---

[5] Federal Law to Prevent Corruption in Public Procurement (2012).
[6] Article 33, Political Constitution of the United Mexican States.
[7] General Law on Electoral Institutions and Procedures (2014).

case-by-case basis, taking into account all the facts and circumstances surrounding the case.

2. Domestic bribery (private to private)

2.1 Legal framework

Domestic bribery is not specifically proscribed by Mexican law, although an employee who receives a bribe from a third party would potentially be liable for fraud or theft, and for justified termination of employment.

2.2 Limitation applicable to hospitality expenses (gifts, travel, meals, entertainment, among others)

The Federal Criminal Code does not establish quantitative or qualitative limitations on hospitality expenses. Rather, the determination of whether a gift or hospitality would fall under the definition of bribery would depend upon the intent of the individual providing it.

3. Corruption of foreign public officials

3.1 Legal framework

Corruption of foreign public officials is regulated under the Mexican Federal Criminal Code, Article 222 *bis*.

3.2 Definition of corruption of foreign public officials

Corruption of a foreign public official is defined as purposefully giving, directly or indirectly, anything of value to a foreign public official, in order to influence him or her to act or refrain from acting in relation to functions inherent to his or her position, for the purpose of obtaining or retaining an undue business advantage.

3.3 Definition of foreign public official

The law defines a foreign public official as any person holding public employment, commission, or office in the legislative, executive or judicial branch, or in any public entity, including state-owned companies, of a foreign state, and any official of an international organization.

3.4 Consequences of Corruption of foreign public officials

(a) For the individuals involved

- Up to 14 years' imprisonment
- Fines of up to approximately USD3,700
- Up to eight years of prohibition of contracting with any federal public authority

(b) For the legal entity

- Fines of up to USD3,700
- Dissolution of the legal entity
- Up to eight years of prohibition of contracting with any federal public authority

For activities that are analogous to criminal bribery of foreign public officials, there are also administrative sanctions in the public procurement context for individuals as well as companies.[8] The penalties are as follows:

(a) For individuals

- Fines of up to approximately USD275,000, or 35 percent of the value of the contract, whichever is greater
- Debarment for up to eight years

---

[8] Federal Law to Prevent Corruption in Public Procurement (2012).

(b) For companies

- Fines of up to approximately USD7.3 million, or 35 percent of the value of the contract, whichever is greater
- Debarment for up to 10 years

3.5 Limitation applicable to hospitality expenses (gifts, travel, meals, entertainment, among others)

The Criminal Code establishes neither quantitative nor qualitative limitations on hospitality expenses. Rather, the determination of whether a gift or hospitality would fall under the definition of bribery would depend upon the intent of the individual providing it.

4. Facilitation payments

The Federal Criminal Code does not recognize the concept of facilitation payments.

5. Compliance programs

5.1 Value of a compliance program to mitigate/eliminate the criminal liability for legal entities

The Mexican Federal Criminal Code does not recognize a compliance program as an instrument to mitigate or eliminate liability for the crime of corruption. As discussed above, liability for entities is a tenuous concept, much in disuse. However, the recently updated Criminal Code of Mexico City provides that a compliance program may be an attenuating factor in assigning criminal liability to the company.[9]

5.2 Absence of a compliance program as a crime

Neither the Mexican Federal Criminal Code nor the newly updated Criminal Code of Mexico City recognizes the absence of having a compliance program as a crime.

---

[9] Criminal Code of Mexico City, Art. 27quintus(c).

5.3 Elements of Compliance program

(a) Legal framework

The Mexican Federal Criminal Code does not recognize or regulate the elements of a compliance program. The Criminal Code of Mexico City does not contain detail on the characteristics of the program that would be an attenuating factor in determining criminal liability.

(b) Recommended practice

In the absence of relevant legal provisions, knowledgeable Mexican legal counsel recommend that legal entities adopt a robust compliance program as a defense strategy to prevent criminal liability for its employees and reputational damage for itself.

6. Regulator with jurisdiction to prosecute corruption

Mexican law establishes the Secretary of Public Administration to investigate, punish administratively and recommend prosecution of corruption. Any public prosecutor may begin a corruption investigation and indict a suspect. In 2014, the Attorney General of Mexico created a special prosecutor's office to handle corruption matters.

Peru

Teresa Tovar

Teresa Tovar focuses her practice on the areas of antitrust and competition, consumer protection, unfair competition, advertising and promotions, and market access. She regularly represents clients during administrative proceedings before the competition agency and other corresponding Peruvian authorities. She also advises clients on the application of regulatory framework on public transportation infrastructure and telecommunications. Teresa has also been advising several companies on conducting data privacy and compliance projects.

teresa.tovar@bakermckenzie.com
Tel: +51 1 618 8500 x552

1. Domestic bribery (private to public)

1.1 Legal framework

The Peruvian laws and regulations that establish the principles, guidelines and penalties applicable to bribery of public officials are as follows:

- Peruvian Criminal Code – Legislative Decree N° 635. Articles 393 to 398

- Law that regulates the liability of legal entities for the crime of active foreign bribery – Law No. 30424. This law was published on 21 April 2016, and will be effective on 1 July 2017.

- Supreme Decree that defines and establishes the national mandatory policies for state entities – Supreme Decree No. 027-2007-PCM

- National Anti-Corruption Plan

- Law that regulates lobbying in the Public Administration – Law No. 28024, and its complementary norm approved by Supreme Decree No. 099-2003-PCM

- Law of the Ethics Code in the Public Function – Law No. 27815

- Law of Civil Service – Law N° 30057, and its complementary norm Supreme Decree N° 040-2014-PCM

1.2 Definition of bribery

Peruvian anti-corruption laws distinguish between passive bribery and active bribery.

Passive bribery is the act of requesting, accepting or receiving donations, promises or any type of advantages performed by a public official, to carry out or omit an act in violation of his or her obligations, or without violating his obligations. This constitutes a crime that will be sanctioned with imprisonment, as well as disqualification from future public service.

Active bribery is the act of offering, giving or promising to a public official a donation, promise, benefit or advantage, to persuade him or her to perform or omit acts in violation of his or her obligations, or without violating them.

1.3 Definition of public official

According to the Peruvian Criminal Code, a public official is (Article 425):

a) any person who is part of the public administrative career;

b) any person who has been appointed for a political or confidence public position, even if publicly elected;

c) any person who, regardless of the labor regime applicable, has a labor or contractual relationship of any nature with governmental organisms or entities, including state-owned companies;

d) an administrator or custodian of assets attached by a court, even if such assets belong to private entities or persons;

e) a member of the military or police forces;

f) any person who performs functions in the name of the state; or

g) any other person considered to be a public official pursuant to the Peruvian Constitution or the law.

1.4 Consequences of bribery

According to the Peruvian Criminal Code, the penalties that could be imposed for committing the conducts aforementioned are (Article 393 to 401-B):

- For companies[1]

  (i) Placement under judicial supervision and intervention for a maximum period of two years

  (ii) Permanent closure of the establishment

  (iii) Temporary closure of the establishment for up to five years

  (iv) Dissolution and liquidation of the company

  (v) Suspension of activities for a maximum period of two years

  (vi) Prohibition from engaging in any commercial activities similar to those of which the offense was committed

- For private individuals

---

[1] Under Peruvian Criminal Law, legal entities are not criminally liable. The consequences mentioned are not sanctions, but they are considered as "accessory measures" applicable to legal entities. However, the recently published Law No. 30424 establishes the legal entity's autonomous - from the criminal liability of the individual - criminal liability for the commission of the crime of active foreign bribery. The measures that the Criminal Judge can impose on the legal entities for the commission of this crime are the following: (i) fine, up to six times the benefit obtained or expected to be obtained; (ii) suspension of activities of the legal entity; (iii) temporary or definitive prohibition from conducting activities of the same kind; (iv) suspension from entering into contract with the government; (v) cancellation of licenses/authorizations; (vi) temporary or definitive closure of premises; and (vii) dissolution of the legal entity.

Up to eight years of imprisonment depending on the type of bribery committed, as well as secondary penalties such as prohibition from carrying on the professional or social activity in the exercise or the context of which the offense was committed and prohibition from being elected or designated for a public office for up to five years; in certain cases, a monetary fine could also be applied.

- For public officers

Up to 15 years of imprisonment, depending on the type of bribery committed, and secondary penalties such as destitution from office and prohibition from being elected or designated for a public office for up to five years; in certain cases, a monetary fine could also be applied.

1.5 Political contributions

The Political Parties Law (Law No. 28094) states that financial contributions to political parties cannot exceed 60 Tax Units per year (approximately PEN237,000 or USD68,000).

Political parties are forbidden from receiving contributions from the following entities:

a) Any governmental body or state-owned company

b) Religious institutions

c) Foreign political parties or foreign governmental agencies, except when the contributions are assigned for education, training and research.

Political candidates are not allowed to personally receive contributions. Any contribution must be made directly to the political party.

1.6 Limitation applicable to hospitality expenses (gifts, travel, meals, entertainment, among others)

According to Peruvian anti-corruption legislation, any payment made in favor of a public officer (even if it is a small amount required for a routine activity), a gift or hospitality could be considered as bribery if no prior formal request has been filed and no formal approval has been issued by the corresponding public agency.

Pursuant to Articles 393 to 401-B of the Peruvian Criminal Code, a gift or hospitality could be considered as bribery, depending on the circumstances and time on which it is granted. In this regard, "concealed bribery" will be considered as effective bribery if there is an obvious disproportion between the reason for the gift or hospitality (for example, the birthday of the official) and the value of the gift (for example, a new car).

The courts will also consider the behavior of the public officials as an element to analyze the commission of "concealed bribery." This means determining whether –as consequence of the gift or hospitality given– the official performs an act under his or her direct functional competence benefiting the person or company who delivered the gift or hospitality (for example, grant an authorization or award a tender).

2. Domestic bribery (private to private)

2.1 Legal framework

The Peruvian Criminal Code does not sanction the bribery or benefit received from or given to an officer, director or executive of a private company or business entity. Nevertheless, pursuant to Section 3 of Article 425 of the Peruvian Criminal Code, officers, directors or executives of state-owned companies are considered as public officials; therefore, the sanctions mentioned in Section 1.4 are applicable.

Regarding private citizens, the Peruvian Criminal Code does not sanction the bribery or benefit received from or given to a private citizen that: (i) has no relation with public service; (ii) has no relation with state-owned companies; or (iii) is not executing public-related activities (for example, an arbitrator or expert appraiser).

2.2 Definition of private bribery

There is no definition of private bribery under Peruvian laws.

2.3 Consequences of private bribery

As mentioned in Section 2.1, private bribery is not sanctioned under Peruvian laws.

2.4 Limitation applicable to hospitality expenses (gifts, travel, meals, entertainment, among others)

N/A

3. Corruption of foreign public officials

3.1 Legal framework

The basic Peruvian laws and regulations that establish the principles, guidelines and penalties applicable to corruption of foreign public officials (from the active and passive standpoint) are the following:

- United Nations Convention Against Corruption
- Inter-American Convention Against Corruption
- The Peruvian Criminal Code (Legislative Decree N° 635) Articles 393-A and 397-A
- Law that regulates the liability of legal entities for the crime of active foreign bribery - Law No. 30424.[2]

[2] This law was published on 21 April 2016 and will be effective on 1 July 2017.

3.2 Definition of corruption of foreign public officials

The Peruvian Criminal Code also distinguishes between active and passive bribery when it regulates the corruption of foreign public officials.

Passive bribery is the act of requesting, accepting or receiving donations, promises or any type of advantages performed by a foreign public officer or any officer of an international organization, to carry out or omit an act in violation of his or her obligations, or without violating them, in order to obtain or maintain a business or another undue advantage in the development of economic and commercial international activities.

Active bribery is the act of offering, giving or promising to any foreign public officer or any officer of an international organization, a donation, promise, benefit or advantage, to persuade them to perform or omit acts in violation of his or her obligations, or without violating them, in order to obtain or maintain a business or another undue advantage in the development of economic and commercial international activities.

3.3 Definition of foreign public official

Pursuant to Article 2 (b) of the United Nations Convention Against Corruption, a foreign public official is: any person holding a legislative, executive, administrative or judicial office of a foreign country, whether appointed or elected; and any person exercising a public function for a foreign country, including for a public agency or public enterprise.

3.4 Consequences of corruption of foreign public officials

The sanctions described in Section 1.4 are also applicable for the corruption of foreign public officials.

3.5 Limitation applicable to hospitality expenses (gifts, travel, meals, entertainment, among others)

Please see Section 1.6.

4. Facilitation payments

In general terms, Peruvian anti-corruption law criminalizes both receiving a bribe (passive bribery) and giving a bribe (active bribery). In this regard, there are no exceptions in relation to the kind of benefit given/received, so facilitation payments are generally not acceptable.

5. Compliance programs

5.1 Value of a compliance program to mitigate/eliminate the criminal liability for legal entities

According to Law 30424, a legal entity will not be liable for active foreign bribery offenses if it has voluntarily implemented a "Prevention Model" prior to the commission of the offense. If a legal entity implements a "Prevention Model" (compliance program) after the offense is committed, it will be considered as a mitigating factor.[3]

5.2 Absence of a compliance program as a crime

The Peruvian Criminal Code does not recognize the absence of having a compliance program as a crime.

5.3 Elements of a compliance program

Law 30424 establishes that the elements that a compliance program[4] must have for a legal entity to receive full exemption from liability in case of active foreign bribery offenses are as follows:

- A person or body responsible for Internal Prevention Audit

[3] See footnote 2.

[4] The Regulations are yet to be enacted - probably on July 2016 - and would define the characteristics of these elements.

- Adoption of preventive measures:
    - To identify activities and proceedings that increase the risks of the crime being committed
    - To have specific processes to program and execute crime-prevention tasks
    - To audit financial resources to prevent their use in the commission of the crime
    - To have internal systems for whistleblowing, whistleblower protection, prosecution and sanctions for employees
- A mechanism for internal diffusion and oversight

6. Regulator with jurisdiction to prosecute corruption

The Peruvian legal system does not have a specific and centralized regulator with exclusive responsibilities to prosecute corruption. The National Police Department, the attorney general's office and the enforcing government agencies such as the Ministry of Justice are entities with this power. In addition, the General Comptroller of the Republic has the faculty to issue dispositions and regulate proceedings against administrative corruption, and pursuant to Law N° 29976, an Anti-Corruption High Level Commission was created in order to oversee governmental anti-corruption efforts and strategies.

Venezuela

Maria Fernanda Zajia

Maria Fernanda Zajía has more than 20 years of experience providing extensive legal advice on municipal tax, regulatory matters and corporate compliance. She counsels local and foreign businesses on public bids, exchange control procedures, consumer protection issues, anti-corruption issues and training, and pharmaceutical regulation. She has participated in many of the most complex and significant forceful acquisition measures in Venezuela, and has assisted clients in designing and implementing tailored action plans to protect their investments and to implement preventive actions to improve the legal condition of companies in the case of eventual expropriations. She also assists clients in the legal analysis of governmental authorizations and approvals for the validity of agreements with Venezuelan government agencies and corporations.

mariafernanda.zajia@bakermckenzie.com
Tel: +58 212 276 5159

Jesus Davila

Jesus Davila joined the Firm in 2002 and became partner in 2009. Recognized as a leading lawyer in Venezuela by Chamber Latin America and IFLR1000, Mr. Davila has helped clients structure and execute corporate transactions for almost a decade. He frequently advises clients on compliance matters. He also has a strong track record providing insightful advice on corporate and commercial matters related to the areas of antitrust and competition, foreign investment and technology transfer, IT/Communications, and trade and commerce.

jesus.davila@bakermckenzie.com
Tel: +58 (212) 276 5243

Ignacio Duque

Ignacio Duque focuses on administrative and regulatory matters, with emphasis on pharmaceutical, public contracts and consumer protection regulations. He also has experience in anti-corruption and compliance practices.

ignacio.duque@bakermckenzie.com
Tel: +58 2122765278

Baker & McKenzie SC
Centro Bancaribe, Intersección
Av. Principal de Las Mercedes
con inicio de Calle París
Urbanización Las Mercedes
Caracas 1060
Venezuela

1. Domestic bribery (private to public)

1.1 Legal framework

Bribery of public officials is regulated under the Law against Corruption, published in the Official Gazette No. 6.155 dated 19 November 2014 (the "Anticorruption Law"), which partially amended the Anticorruption Law published in the Official Gazette No. 5.637 of 7 April 2003.

1.2 Definition of bribery

According to the Anticorruption Law, there are different types of bribery:

(a) Concussion (qualified extortion) – This crime is committed when a public official, abusing his or her functions, induces someone to give or promise, to him or her or to another person, a sum of money or any other undue benefit or gift.

(b) Improper passive corruption (bribe) – This crime is committed when a public official, as a result of a certain act related to his or her functions, receives or accepts a promise, for him or her or for others, of retribution or other benefits not due to him or her. The person giving or promising the retribution or benefit shall also be subject to criminal liability.

(c) Proper passive corruption (bribe) – This crime is committed when a public official, with the purpose of delaying or omitting an act corresponding to his or her functions or performing an act contrary to his or her functions, receives or accepts money, a promise or other benefits, directly or indirectly. In this case, the penalties corresponding to this crime will also be imposed on: (i) the person who receives the money, promise or other benefits on account of the public official, if any; and (ii) the person who gave or promised the money or other benefits.

(d) The crime of proper passive corruption shall be aggravated in the following circumstances:

  (i) When the object of the act of corruption is to confer public employment, subsidies, pensions or honors or to cause the public official to agree to sign contracts related to the administration to which the official belongs

  (ii) When the object of the act of corruption is to favor or cause any harm or damage to any of the parties in an administrative, criminal, civil or any other kind of procedure or lawsuit

  (iii) When the act of corruption is committed by a judge who renders a judgment of deprivation of freedom exceeding six months

(e) Inducement to corruption – This crime is committed by a person who, without achieving his or her objective, insists on persuading or inducing a public official to commit any of the crimes of corruption.

(f) Agreement with contractors – This crime is committed when a public official who participates by reasons of his or her position in the entering into of an agreement or other transaction, negotiates with the interested parties or intermediaries for a specific result to ensue, or uses any maneuver or ruse for this purpose. The person with whom the official agrees to give or promise the wrongful money, benefits or gifts will also be subject to criminal liability.

1.3 Definition of public official

Article 3 of the Anticorruption Law establishes that the following persons qualify as public officials:

(a) Those invested with public functions, permanently or transitorily, remunerated or *ad honorem*, whether by election, appointment or contract granted by competent authorities, serving at: agencies of the republic; of the states, territories and federal dependencies; districts, metropolitan districts or municipalities; national, state, district and municipal autonomous institutes; public universities; the Central Bank of Venezuela; or of any entities that exercise public powers

(b) Directors and administrators of civil and commercial companies, foundations, civil associations and other institutions created with public funds or managed by any of the persons mentioned in Article 4 of the Anticorruption Law, or when the aggregate of contributions in a year, from one or several of these persons, represents 50 percent or more of its budget or net worth; and the directors appointed to represent such bodies and entities, even if the participation of the Venezuelan government is less than 50 percent of the capital or net worth of such civil and commercial companies, foundations, civil associations or institutions

For purposes of the Anticorruption Law, directors and administrators are persons who:

a. perform functions such as direction, management, supervision, control or audit;

b. participate with the right to speak and vote in committees for procurement, bidding, contracts, business, donations or of any other nature, whose actions could jeopardize public assets; who manage or are custodians of warehouses, workshops or deposits, and in general, decide upon the receipt, provision and delivery of personal property to the entity or agency for consumption;

c. are responsible for transactions using the entity's or agency's funds deposited in bank accounts;

d. represent the entity or agency having the authority to confer obligations on the agency;

e. can make commitments on behalf of the entity or agency or authorize the pertinent payments; and

f. adopt measures having an impact on individuals' sphere of rights or obligations, or on the powers and duties of the state.

The provisions of the Anticorruption Law apply to the persons abovementioned even when they perform their duties or carry out their activities outside the territory of Venezuela.

(c) Any other person in the cases provided for in the Anticorruption Law

Additionally, Article 2 of the Anticorruption Law states that all individuals and legal entities, public and private, public officials, communes, communal councils, socio-productive associations and base organizations of the popular power, as well as any other forms of popular organizations, are subject to the application of the Anticorruption Law when managing public funds.

1.4 Consequences of bribery

(a) For the individuals involved

- Concussion – Two years to six years of imprisonment and a monetary fine of up to 50 percent of the value of the thing given or promised

- Improper passive corruption – One year to four years of imprisonment, monetary fine of up to 50 percent of the value of the thing given or promised, and confiscation of the money or objects given

- Proper passive corruption – Three years to seven years of imprisonment, monetary fine of up to 50 percent of the value of the thing given or promised, and confiscation of the money or objects given

- Inducement to corruption – Six months to two years of imprisonment in the case of inducement to improper passive corruption; in the case of inducement to the crime of proper passive corruption, the penalties established for such crime, but reduced in half

- Agreement with contractors – Two years to five years of imprisonment; if the purpose of the crime was to obtain money, gifts or wrongful profits given or offered to the official or to a third party, imprisonment from two years to six years and a monetary fine of up to 100 percent of the benefit given or promised

(b) For the company / legal entity

If the commission of a crime is established by a court of law, legal entities may be subject to monetary fines, confiscation of profits and prohibition from entering into contracts with the public sector. Furthermore, under the Law against Organized Crime and Terrorism Financing, corruption and other crimes against the public patrimony shall be deemed to constitute organized crime (which is subject to harsher penalties) when: (i) they are committed by one person acting on behalf of a company or an association, if the means to commit the crime are technological or cybernetic, or by electronic, digital or computer means, or are related to any other product using scientific knowledge; and (ii) they are committed by three or more persons associated for a certain time with the intent to commit crimes.

1.5 Political contributions

According to Article 24.4 of the Law on Political Parties, Public Reunions and Manifestations, published in the Official Gazette No. 6.013 dated 23 December 2010, political parties are obliged not to accept donations or subsidies from: governmental entities, whether autonomous or not; foreign companies or those with headquarters abroad; concessionaries of public works or services; and foreign states or foreign political organizations.

1.6 Limitation applicable to hospitality expenses (gifts, travel, meals, entertainment, among others)

There is no specific regulation regarding hospitality expenses. However, under the Anticorruption Law, public officials may not receive or accept gifts or any benefits in order to do or not to do an act.

Meals or receptions are acceptable as long as there is no connection between the meal/reception and the duties and obligations of the government official with regard to the host's business. A meal or reception that is reasonable in cost and provided as a courtesy without corrupt intent is not likely to be considered by a Venezuelan judge as an unlawful acceptance of a benefit. Venezuelan law does not establish a specific value limit for meals offered to a public official for such offer to be considered an act of corruption.

Gifts, on the other hand, are not acceptable, except gifts of nominal value customarily given during traditional celebrations, such as Christmas and New Year's Eve (e.g., a bottle of wine, a box of chocolates or candies). Offering of cash or any other gift should be avoided. There is no legal provision in Venezuela imposing gift value limits.

2. Domestic bribery (private to private)

2.1 Legal framework

Private bribery is regulated, in similar terms, under the Anticorruption Law and the Organic Law on Fair Prices, published in the Official Gazette No. 40.787 dated 12 November 2015 (the "Fair Price Law").

2.2 Definition of private bribery

This crime is committed when a person, either directly or through a mediator, promises, offers or grants directors, administrators, employees or collaborators of companies, partnerships, associations, foundations or organizations, any kind of benefit or advantage in exchange for favors or benefits either for himself or herself or for another person vis-à-vis others, thus failing to perform his or her obligations with regard to the acquisition or sale of goods or the provision of services.

Likewise, the directors, administrators, employees or collaborators who personally, or through third parties receive, accept or request such benefit or advantage, will also be subject to criminal liability.

2.3 Consequences of private bribery

(a) For the individuals involved – Two years to six years of imprisonment

(b) For the company / legal entity – Suspension from the Sole Register of Persons that Engage in Economic Activities (RUPDAE)

2.4 Limitation applicable to hospitality expenses (gifts, travel, meals, entertainment, among others)

There is no specific regulation regarding hospitality expenses.

3. Corruption of foreign public officials

3.1 Legal framework

Bribery of foreign public officials is regulated under the Anticorruption Law.

3.2 Definition of corruption of foreign public officials

Anyone who personally, or through third parties, promises, offers or conveys to a public official of a foreign state, directly or indirectly, any object of commercial value or other benefits, favors, promises or advantages, in exchange for an action or omission from the foreign official while exercising his or her public functions related to a commercial, economic or any other kind of transaction, commits this type of crime.

3.3 Definition of foreign public official

There is no specific definition of foreign public official in Venezuelan legislation.

3.4 Consequences of corruption of foreign public officials

(a) For the individuals involved – Six years to 12 years of imprisonment

(b) For the legal entity – They may be subject to monetary fines and confiscation. Furthermore, depending on the case, legal entities may be subject to civil, administrative or criminal liability under the Law against Organized Crime and Terrorism Financing if it is deemed that the crime was perpetrated by an organized crime group.

3.5 Limitation applicable to hospitality expenses (gifts, travel, meals, entertainment, among others)

There is no specific regulation regarding hospitality expenses.

4. Facilitation payments

Venezuelan law does not recognize so called facilitation payments. Under the Anticorruption Law, public officials may not receive or accept gifts or any benefits in order to do or not to do an act.

5. Compliance programs

5.1 Value of a compliance program to mitigate/eliminate the criminal liability for legal entities

The Anticorruption Law does not specifically recognize compliance programs as instruments to mitigate or eliminate liability for legal entities before the crime of corruption has been committed. However, legal entities could mitigate their criminal liability if they can prove that they had exercised over their employees due control by means of a robust compliance program.

5.2 Absence of a compliance program as a crime

The Anticorruption Law does not recognize the absence of having a compliance program as a crime.

5.3 Elements of compliance program

(a) Legal framework

The Anticorruption Law does not recognize or regulate the elements of a compliance program. However, certain rules on compliance programs are established in the Organic Law against Organized Crime and Terrorism Financing for regulated entities such as banks and insurance companies, brokerage firms, bingos and casinos, hotels, businesses and tourism centers authorized to conduct foreign exchange operations; foundations, civic associations and other nonprofit organizations; political parties; and public notaries, among others.

(b) Recommended practice

Legal entities should adopt a robust compliance program as a defense strategy to mitigate, or in the case of crimes of corruption committed by the legal entity's employees, exclude the legal entity's criminal liability for crimes of corruption.

6. Regulator with jurisdiction to prosecute corruption

In Venezuela corruption is prosecuted by the Comptroller General's Office, the Public Prosecutor's Office and the National Anti-Corruption Body. The latter was created in 2014 with the mission to plan, organize and execute the necessary preventative, investigative and operative actions against corruption.

North America

Canada

Peter MacKay

Peter MacKay PC, QC (Privy Council and Queen's Counsel) is a partner in the Baker & McKenzie Toronto office. Prior to joining the Firm, Peter served in the Parliament of Canada for over 18 years and in a ministerial post in the Canadian government for nine years since the Conservative Party formed a government in 2006. Most recently, he served as Canada's Attorney General and Minister of Justice, a position to which he was appointed in 2013. Prior to this post, Peter served as the Minister of National Defence for six years and held joint cabinet positions as Minister of Foreign Affairs and Minister for the Atlantic Canada Opportunities Agency for 18 months. His practice focuses on government enforcement proceedings and compliance matters, and he provides strategic advice to Canadian companies doing business globally and international companies doing business in Canada.

Peter is also a member of the Compliance and Government Investigations practice group.

peter.mackay@bakermckenzie.com
Tel: +1 416 865 6889

Lisa Douglas

Lisa Douglas is counsel in the International Commercial practice group. She focuses on commercial law and regulatory compliance, including information governance, financial services regulatory advice, anti-money laundering compliance, as well as on the regulatory aspects of public procurement that involve lobbying and anti-corruption compliance. Her commercial practice covers contracting, sales and distribution relationships and consumer protection, particularly from an e-commerce perspective.

lisa.douglas@bakermckenzie.com
Tel: +1 416 865 6972

Christopher Burkett

Chris Burkett is a senior associate. His practice is focused on dispute resolution, internal investigations, compliance program development and related litigation. He has appeared on behalf of his clients before a variety of tribunals, at all levels of trial court, and the Court of Appeal for Ontario. In addition, he has conducted internal investigations of compliance issues for multinational corporations and their subsidiaries across multiple international jurisdictions, including Canada, the United States, the United Kingdom, Russia, India, Europe, and South America. He has previously worked alongside the compliance team in our London office.

christopher.burkett@bakermckenzie.com
Tel: +44 2 0791 91847

Baker & McKenzie LLP
Barristers & Solicitors
Brookfield Place
Bay/Wellington Tower
181 Bay Street, Suite 2100
Toronto, Ontario M5J 2T3
Canada

1. Domestic bribery (private to public)

1.1 Legal framework

Canada's domestic anti-bribery provisions are part of the Criminal Code, RSC 1985, c C-46. Sections 119 through 125 of the Criminal Code create a number of bribery, corruption and "influence peddling" offences that capture the payment of bribes, benefits and advantages to domestic public officials in Canada. All advantages granted to Canadian public officials are illegal if made in violation of the Criminal Code of Canada.

1.2 Definition of bribery

Section 121 of the Criminal Code makes it an offence to: (i) directly or indirectly give or offer to give to an official a loan, reward, advantage or benefit of any kind as consideration for cooperation, assistance, exercise of influence, or an act or omission in connection with the transaction of business or any matter of business relating to the government, or a claim against the government, or any benefit that the government is authorized to bestow; (ii) have dealings of any kind with the government, pay a commission or reward to or confer an advantage or benefit of any kind on an employee or official of the government with respect to those dealings, unless the head of the branch of government has consented in writing; or (iii) give or offer to an official a reward, advantage or benefit of any kind as consideration for cooperation, assistance, exercise of influence or an act or omission in connection with the transaction of business with or any matter of business relating to the government, or a claim against the government, or any benefit that the government is entitled to bestow, or the appointment of any person to an office.

1.3 Definition of public official

For purposes of the Criminal Code provisions, "official" means a person who holds an office or is appointed or elected to discharge a public duty. "Office" includes an office or appointment under the government, a civil or military commission, and a position or employment in a public department. "Government" means the government of Canada, the government of a province of Canada, or Her Majesty in right of Canada or a province. Accordingly, the definition of "official" in this context is broad enough to include those who hold an office with government-controlled enterprises.

1.4 Consequences of bribery

Under the anti-bribery provisions of the Criminal Code, potential penalties include fines in an unlimited amount and imprisonment for up to 14 years. Officials and employees can be convicted personally and companies can be liable as parties to offences committed by "senior officers." The actions of middle managers are sufficient to make a company criminally liable in appropriate circumstances.

A company may be liable for the acts of agents and contractors in two different ways:

i. First, the company may be aware that an agent is about to pay a bribe and fail to take all reasonable measures to stop the agent.

ii. Secondly, if an agent or contractor is delegated management of an important aspect of the company's activities, the agent may become part of the class of senior officers who bind the company in criminal law, even where the executives of the company are unaware that the agent is offside.

There is no limitation period for prosecution.

1.5 Political contributions

Contribution to political parties and candidates is regulated under federal and provincial law, with relatively low annual contribution limits as well as certain prohibitions on contributions by corporations, trade unions, associations and groups.

1.6 Limitation applicable to hospitality expenses (gifts, travel, meals, entertainment, among others)

It is acceptable to offer gifts, hospitality and other benefits to public officials if it is done outside the context of contractual negotiations and in accordance with all applicable conflict of interest laws and related codes of conduct. There is some uncertainty with respect to a precise ceiling beyond which gifts and hospitality would be considered unacceptable, because the relevant laws and codes do not define any dollar limits. Much will depend on the context. Generally, however, gifts, hospitality or other benefits arising out of activities associated with the performance of a public official's duties may be acceptable if such gifts, hospitality or other benefits are within the bounds of propriety, a normal expression of courtesy, or within the normal standards of hospitality; are not such as to bring suspicion on the recipient's objectivity and impartiality; and would not compromise the integrity of the government.

Note that the total value of all gifts, hospitality or other benefits received by a federal public official in Canada may be reportable by the public official, through the filing of a public declaration maintained in a public registry, if such value goes above a certain threshold (e.g., CAD200 from any one source in a 12-month period).

2. Domestic bribery (private to private)

2.1 Legal framework

Canada's anti-bribery laws generally apply to public officials and not to private sector transactions.

2.2 Definition of private bribery

Section 426 of the Criminal Code, however, establishes the offence of corruptly giving "secret commissions" in the context of agency relationships, and the general law of fraud applies more broadly to any business relationship. For example, it is illegal if an agent is paid a commission for referring business to a company and this is not disclosed to the agent's principal.

2.3 Consequences of private bribery

Although of more limited application, violation of the foregoing prohibition against "secret commission" or criminal fraud can result in penalties similar to those previously outlined in respect of domestic bribery (private to public).

2.4 Limitation applicable to hospitality expenses (gifts, travel, meals, entertainment, among others)

Given the lack of a bribery law applicable to commercial bribery (i.e., not involving public or government interests), there are no restrictions or guidelines in connection with hospitality in this context.

3. Corruption of foreign public officials

3.1 Legal framework

The *Corruption of Foreign Public Officials Act*, SC 1998, c 34 (CFPOA) applies to corrupt practices in relation to foreign public officials. It applies to Canadian citizens, permanent residents of Canada, companies and other organizations incorporated or formed in Canada, and to persons anywhere in the world whose acts or omissions have a "real and substantial connection" to Canada. In addition to the corruption offences, the CFPOA also includes a "books and records" offence, which requires that all transactions and expenditures be adequately and accurately identified in the books and records.

3.2 Definition of corruption of foreign public officials

It is an offence, in order to obtain or retain an advantage in the course of business, to directly or indirectly give, offer or agree to give or offer a loan, reward, advantage or benefit of any kind to a foreign public official or to any person for the benefit of a foreign public official:

(a) as consideration for an act or omission by the official in connection with the performance of the official's duties or functions; or

(b) to induce the official to use his or her position to influence any acts or decisions of the foreign state or public international organization for which the official performs duties or functions.

3.3 Definition of foreign public official

"Foreign public official" means:

(a) a person who holds a legislative, administrative or judicial position in a foreign state;

(b) a person who performs public duties or functions for a foreign state, including a person employed by a board, commission, corporation or other body or authority that is established to perform a duty or function on behalf of the foreign state, or is performing such a duty or function; and

(c) an official or agent of a public international organization that is formed by two or more states or governments, or by two or more such public international organizations.

Note that the definition does not include members of political parties that are not in power (i.e., opposition parties) but caution should be exercised in this scenario.

It is not necessary to prove that a bribe was actually paid to a foreign official to establish a violation of the CFPOA; it is sufficient for the party to believe that a bribe was being paid to such an official. The concept of conspiracy applies in relation to CFPOA offences. Where there is a conspiracy, the prosecution need not prove the identity of the recipient of a proposed bribe as this could put foreign nationals at risk.

Furthermore, the doctrine of wilful blindness applies to the level of intent required, and imputes knowledge to an accused whose suspicion is aroused to the point where he or she sees the need for further inquiries, but deliberately chooses not to make those inquiries.

3.4 Consequences of corruption of foreign public officials

Under the CFPOA, potential penalties include fines in an unlimited amount and imprisonment for up to 14 years. Officials and employees can be convicted personally and companies can be liable as parties to offences committed by "senior officers." The actions of middle managers are sufficient to make a company criminally liable in appropriate circumstances.

A company may be liable for the acts of agents and contractors in two different ways:

i. First, the company may be aware that an agent is about to pay a bribe and fail to take all reasonable measures to stop the agent.

ii. Secondly, if an agent or contractor is delegated management of an important aspect of the company's activities, the agent may become part of the class of senior officers who bind the company in criminal law, even where the executives of the company are unaware that the agent is offside.

There is no limitation period for prosecution.

3.5 Limitation applicable to hospitality expenses (gifts, travel, meals, entertainment, among others)

The CFPOA contains an exemption for reasonable promotional expenses. To be exempt, the payment or benefit made to cover reasonable expenses must be made in good faith and be directly related to the promotion, demonstration or explanation of the products or services of the business, and not in furtherance of any personal interest.

4. Facilitation payments

Facilitation or "grease" payments are illegal under Canada's Criminal Code in relation to Canadian (domestic) public officials.

The CFPOA currently includes an exception for facilitation payments (e.g., payments made for acts of a routine nature such as the issuance of a permit or the processing of official documents). However, amendments to the CFPOA provide for the elimination of the exception for facilitation payments to foreign public officials at a later date (yet to be determined).

5. Compliance programs

5.1 Value of a compliance program to mitigate/eliminate criminal liability for companies

It is important to have a robust compliance program in place to help mitigate criminal liability involving internal policies; the screening of agents and contractors; and the ongoing training of employees, agents and contractors in compliance policies and procedures.

5.2 Absence of a compliance program as a criminal offence

Failure by a company to institute a compliance program is not, in and of itself, a criminal offence. For a corporation to attract criminal liability in Canada, a "senior officer" must have had the intent at least in part to benefit the corporation, and that: (i) the senior officer, acting within the scope of his or her authority, was himself a party to the offence (section 22.2(1)(*a*) of the Criminal Code); (ii) the senior officer had the required *mens rea* for the offence, was acting within the scope of his or her authority, and directed the work of other "representatives" (including employees, agents or contractors) of the corporation to perform the *actus reus* of the offence (section 22.2(1)(*b*)); or (iii) knowing that a representative of the corporation is or is about to be a party to the offence, the senior officer fails to take "all reasonable measures to stop them from being a party to the offence" (section 22.2(1)(*c*)). Section 2 of the Criminal Code defines "senior officer" broadly and is not limited to individuals appointed by the board of directors. Specifically, a senior officer is defined as a director, chief executive officer, chief financial officer, partner, employee, member, agent or contractor "who plays an important role in the establishment of a corporation's policies or is responsible for managing an important aspect of the corporation's activities."

Canadian law is unsettled as to the meaning of the phrase "all reasonable measures" and, in particular, the nature and the extent of the burden that that provision may (as a matter of statutory construction and constitutional law) impose on corporations, through their "senior officers," to stop or prevent fault-based criminal conduct, including bribery, in order to avoid liability in circumstances where such officers are not themselves parties to the offence.

If a compliance program falls within the definition of "all reasonable measures," it may qualify as a defense in those sectors that are under the supervision of senior officers. However, such a program will not be a defense at the senior officer level, but will serve in mitigation of sentence only.

As a practical matter, as previously noted, it is good practice for all companies operating in Canada to ensure they have implemented a robust anti-bribery compliance program.

5.3 Elements of a compliance program

- Proportionate Procedures: The one-size-fits-all solution is rejected in favor of a tailor made approach.

- Top Level Commitment: This requires that senior officers specifically address bribery risks.

- Risk Assessment: External risks (such as country risk and sector risk) must be evaluated along with internal risks (such as poor training, cultures that promote excessive risk-taking and poor financial controls).

- Due Diligence: Commercial organizations should put in place due diligence procedures that adequately inform the application of proportionate measures designed to prevent persons associated with them from bribing on their behalf.

- Communication (including training): Communication is not only done from the top, but should include the creation of a confidential means to report bribery conduct.

- Monitoring and Review: Methods may include staff surveys, testing and verification of procedures by outside parties and certified compliance by multilateral bodies.

6. Regulator with jurisdiction to prosecute corruption

The Criminal Code and the CFPOA are administered by the federal Department of Justice while the Anti-Corruption Unit of the Royal Canadian Mounted Police (RCMP) investigates corruption and lays charges.

USA

Trevor McFadden

Trevor McFadden focuses on international white-collar criminal matters, including FCPA investigations, anti-money laundering and Bank Secrecy Act issues, and FATCA and criminal tax guidance for foreign financial institutions. He has been extensively involved in advising multiple Swiss banks regarding the US Department of Justice's recent Program for Non-Prosecution Agreements for Swiss Banks. His prior experience as Counsel to the US Deputy Attorney General and as an Assistant US Attorney gives him the ability to identify areas of corporate risk and advise clients on successful resolutions to internal and criminal investigations.

trevor.mcfadden@bakermckenzie.com
Tel: +1 202 835 1869

Crystal Jezierski

Crystal Jezierski focuses on corporate compliance and investigations. She works with legal departments and compliance officers to advise them on compliance trends and government expectations, the design and implementation of global compliance programs, compliance program remediation in the course of government enforcement actions, global compliance risk assessments, compliance training, and conducting internal investigations.

crystal.jezierski@bakermckenzie.com
Tel: +1 202 835 6168

Maria McMahon

Maria McMahon has extensive experience in corporate transactions — including mergers and acquisitions, foreign direct investment, joint ventures, corporate governance, hostile takeover defense — and complex disputes. She also focuses on emerging markets, particularly Russia and the former Soviet Union. Maria has represented oil and gas, freight forwarding and defense companies.

maria.mcmahon@bakermckenzie.com
Tel: +1 202 452 7058

John Kosmidis

John Kosmidis focuses on criminal litigation, securities litigation and anti-corruption. He assists clients in a broad range of dispute resolution matters — including internal investigations, white-collar criminal defense, governmental investigations, civil class actions and related derivative litigation. He has represented clients before the US Department of Justice, the Securities and Exchange Commission and the New York Attorney General. He has handled federal class action lawsuits and cases before the Delaware Court of Chancery. John has also advised on patent infringement actions and real estate disputes and has contributed to all phases of the litigation process.

john.kosmidis@bakermckenzie.com
Tel: +1 202 835 6142

Andrew Okhotin

Andrew Okhotin concentrates his practice on assisting clients with anti-corruption compliance matters, with an emphasis on internal investigations, international transactions, dispute resolution, and compliance-related due diligence on acquisition targets and potential partners. He has an in-depth understanding of compliance-related matters in emerging markets, particularly in Russia and the former Soviet Union.

andrew.okhotin@bakermckenzie.com
Tel: +1 202 835 6113

Jean-Paul Theroux

Jean-Paul Theroux assists clients with a range of dispute resolution and corporate compliance matters, including domestic civil litigation and internal investigations related to the FCPA and other trade and economic sanctions.

jean-paul.theroux@bakermckenzie.com
Tel: +1 202 835 6194

Joan Meyer

Joan Meyer counsels on best practices for compliance with US and international legal requirements and regulations, and advises senior management and corporate audit committees on the formulation, conduct and consequences of enforcement inquiries, including the development of appropriate defenses, disclosures, disciplinary actions and compliance policies. Joan chairs the North America Compliance and Investigations Practice Group, and co-chairs the Firm's US-Mexico Cross-Border Initiative, which sponsors a cross-border team of compliance specialists who advise and conduct internal investigations for international companies doing business in Latin America. She has advised and worked with companies in the manufacturing, life sciences, mining and extraction, financial services, transportation and logistics sectors, to conduct global risk assessments, develop and implement compliance programs, create remediation plans, and develop emergency/crisis management strategies.

joan.meyer@bakermckenzie.com
Tel: +1 202 835 6119

Baker & McKenzie LLP
815 Connecticut Avenue, N.W.
Washington, District of Columbia 20006
United States

Key Practitioners

Thomas Doyle
Chicago
Tel: +1 312 861 8866
thomas.doyle@bakermckenzie.com

David Hackett
Chicago
Tel: +1 312 861 6640
david.hackett@bakermckenzie.com

Robert Kent
Chicago
Tel: +1 312 861 8077
robert.kent@bakermckenzie.com

Jerome Tomas
Chicago
Tel: +1 312 861 8616
jerome.tomas@bakermckenzie.com

Peter Tomczak
Chicago
Tel: +1 312 861 8030
peter.tomczak@bakermckenzie.com

Lawrence Finder
Houston
Tel: +1 713-427-5030
lawrence.finder@Bakermckenzie.com

William Devaney
New York
Tel: +1 212 626 4337
william.devaney@bakermckenzie.com

John McKenzie
San Francisco
Tel: +(415) 576-3033
john.mckenzie@bakermckenzie.com

Robert Tarun
San Francisco
Tel: +(415) 591-3220
robert.tarun@bakermckenzie.com

Maurice Bellan
Washington, DC
Tel: +1 202 452 7057
maurice.bellan@bakermckenzie.com

Richard Dean
Washington, DC
Tel: +1 202 452 7009
richard.dean@bakermckenzie.com

Reagan Demas
Washington, DC
Tel: +1 202 835 1886
reagan.demas@bakermckenzie.com

Janet Kim
Washington, DC
Tel: +1 202 835 1653
janet.k.kim@bakermckenzie.com

Brian Whisler
Washington, DC
Tel: +1 202 452 7019
brian.whisler@bakermckenzie.com

1. Domestic bribery (private to public)

1.1 Legal framework

Multiple federal statutes in the United States prohibit bribery of federal officials in specific contexts, but the most important statute that most directly criminalizes federal public corruption is 18 U.S.C. § 201. Section 201 has two main subparts: Section 201(b) criminalizes the payment, offer and receipt of bribes, and § 201(c) prohibits the payment, offer and receipt of illegal "gratuity." Violations of § 201(b) are punished more severely than violations of the anti-gratuities provision. Other federal and state statutes prohibit bribery of state and local government officials.

1.2 Definition of bribery

(a) Section 201(b)—Bribery

Section 201(b) proscribes the giving and receiving bribes. As to the giver, § 201(b) requires the prosecution to show that something of value was corruptly given, offered or promised, directly or indirectly, to a public official. As to the recipient, it requires the prosecution to show that something of value was corruptly demanded, sought, received, accepted, or agreed to be received or accepted by a public official. The intent required for the giver is the intent "to influence any official act," whereas the intent required for the recipient is the intent to be "influenced in the performance of any official act."

(b) Section 201(c)—Illegal Gratuity

Section 201(c) deals with illegal official "gratuity." As to the giver, § 201(c) requires the prosecution to show that something of value was given, offered or promised to a public official. As to the recipient, it requires a showing that something of value was demanded, sought, received, accepted, or agreed to be received or accepted by a public official. Under § 201(c), the unlawful gratuity must be "for or because of any official act performed or to be performed by such public official."

A key difference between the bribery and illegal gratuity sections is that bribery requires a specific intent "to influence" a particular official act (in the case of the giver), or "to be influenced" in an official act (in the case of the recipient); however, illegal gratuity only requires that the unlawful gift be given or received "for or because of" any official act. Unlike illegal gratuity, which may be forward or backward looking at a past or future official act, bribery requires a specific intent to give or receive something of value in exchange for a future official act—in other words, a specific *quid pro quo* or direct nexus between the value given and a particular future act.

The bribery and gratuity offenses under § 201 do not require that an unlawful gift actually be paid, or even that the object of the unlawful gift be attainable. Section 201 prohibits conduct as soon as an offer (in the case of the giver) or an acceptance (in the case of the recipient) has occurred.

1.3 Definition of public official

Section 201 proscribes bribes and gratuities given or offered to, or received or requested by a "public official." The term "public official" is defined to include any:

> Member of Congress, Delegate, or Resident Commissioner, either before or after such official has qualified, or an officer or employee or person acting for or on behalf of the United States, or any department, agency or branch of Government thereof, including the District of Columbia, in any official function, under or by authority of any such department, agency, or branch of Government, or a juror. 18 U.S.C. § 201(a)(1).

The prohibitions of § 201 apply not only to current public officials, but also to any "person who has been selected to be a public official." In other words, the statute extends to "any person who has been nominated or appointed to be a public official, or [who] has been officially informed that such person will be so nominated or appointed." 18 U.S.C. § 201(a)(2).

The definition also establishes that § 201 is primarily focused on federal, rather than state or local public officials—although the US Supreme Court has held that § 201 may be used to prosecute corruption of state and local officials, and even private individuals, who administer federal programs and occupy "a position of public trust with official federal responsibilities." *Dixson v. United States*, 465 U.S. 482, 496 (1984).

The definition of public official under § 201 precludes the statute's use against purely private commercial bribery.

1.4 Consequences of bribery

As previously described, both the giving or offering, and the receiving of a bribe and gratuity are proscribed under § 201.

Section 201(b) (bribery) is punishable by up to 15 years' imprisonment, a fine of USD250,000 (USD500,000 for organizations) or up to three times the value of the bribe, whichever is greater, and disqualification from holding any federal office.

Section 201(c) (illegal gratuity) is punishable by up to two years' imprisonment and a fine of USD250,000 (USD500,000 for organizations).

1.5 Political contributions

Political contributions are not prohibited under § 201. Such contributions, being to an extent protected by the U.S. Constitution, are generally permissible in the United States so long as they are made in conformity with the federal and states campaign finance laws and regulations applicable to political donations (for example, federal laws that impose limitations on how much individuals and organizations can donate to campaigns and political parties). Payments made as a *quid pro quo* for an official act would still be illegal, despite having been made as a campaign contribution.

1.6 Limitations applicable to hospitality expenses (gifts, travel, meals, entertainment, among others)

Section 201 does not expressly prohibit hospitality expenses, such as for gifts, meals or entertainment, incurred for public officials. However, such expenditures may constitute "things of value" that, if given or received in order "to influence" any official act (bribery) or "for or because of" any official act (gratuity) may form the basis of criminal liability under § 201.

Under both the bribery and gratuity provisions of § 201, a "thing of value" is defined broadly, and it includes anything that has commercial value or subjective value to the recipient. Thus, the term encompasses not only cash, but also meals, travel, entertainment, other "in kind" gifts that have commercial value, and even gifts that have purely subjective value to the recipient. Often the key issue in determining whether such activities were permissible is whether the giver or the recipient acted with corrupt intent.

Further, although § 201 does not expressly prohibit hospitality expenses, other laws and regulations enacted at the federal, state and local government levels do limit how such expenditures may be provided to and accepted by public officials. For example, members of Congress are subject to regulations that govern their travel and receipt of gifts—the Rules of the House of Representatives and the Standing Rules of the Senate.

2. Domestic bribery (private to private)

2.1 Legal framework

Both the US Department of Justice (DOJ) and the Securities and Exchange Commission (SEC) are authorized to punish domestic bribery. The DOJ has used state laws, in combination with federal laws, such as the Travel Act, 18 U.S.C. § 1952, and wire fraud statutes, 18 U.S.C. §§ 1341, 1343 and 1346, to criminally prosecute commercial bribes. The SEC can civilly punish domestic bribes that violate the SEC's books and records and internal controls provisions (the "accounting provisions" – Sections 13(b)(2)(A) and 13(b)(2)(B) of the Exchange Act). Additionally, for instances of willful violation of the accounting provisions, the SEC can refer the case to the DOJ for criminal prosecution.

2.2 Definition of bribery

2.2.1 *The Travel Act*

The Travel Act is a federal statute that prohibits travel in interstate commerce and the use of the mails with the intent to distribute the proceeds of any unlawful activity or to promote, manage, establish or carry on any unlawful activity, including violations of the FCPA or state bribery laws.

As of 2015, commercial bribery is illegal in 36 US states, and its definition in respective state statutes varies. Some states, such as California, focus on the actions of the recipient of the bribe[1]; however, others, including most notably New York, criminalize the actions of both the recipient of, and the person offering, the bribe.[2]

In general, commercial bribery has been treated under state laws as a breach of a fiduciary duty and defined as:

- Giving or offering to give, directly or indirectly, anything of apparent present or prospective value to any private agent, employee, or fiduciary, without the knowledge and consent of the principal or employer, with the intent to influence such agent's, employee's, or fiduciary's action in relation to the principal's or employer's affairs.[3]

---

[1] California Penal Code § 641.3.
[2] NY Penal Code, Article 180.
[3] Mississippi Code § 97-9-10.

2.2.2 *Mail and wire fraud statutes and the accounting provisions*

The federal mail and wire fraud statutes, 18 U.S.C. §§ 1341, 1343 and 1346, prohibit the use of mail and interstate wire communications to execute a "scheme or artifice to defraud" or deprive another of money or property, including the intangible right of "honest services." In *Skilling v. United States*, the US Supreme Court held that honest-services theory of fraud includes bribes and kickbacks paid to employees of private firms, but not more generalized efforts to defraud a company's shareholders.[4] Thus, the use of mail and wire communication in connection with commercial bribery can subject respective persons to prosecution for mail and wire fraud.

2.2.3 Accounting Provisions of the FCPA

In addition, under the FCPA's accounting provisions, the SEC may pursue claims against publicly traded companies for commercial bribery in the domestic context. As held by the Court in *SEC v. FalconStor*,[5] the FCPA's accounting provisions, which require publicly traded companies to keep accurate books and records and maintain adequate internal controls, also apply to domestic transactions. For both willful and non-willful violations of the accounting provisions, the SEC can pursue both individuals and issuers of registered securities or issuers that are required to file annual or other periodic reports with the SEC. These issuers include any entity whose securities trade on a United States exchange.

2.3 Consequences of bribery

The consequences of commercial bribery conduct vary by the prosecuting entity and the statute under which the bribe is punished. The SEC can only assess civil monetary fines, and any criminal charges, which can lead to both fines and jail time, must be brought by the DOJ at the federal level.

---

[4] Skilling v. United States, 561 U.S. 358 (2010).
[5] SEC v. FalconStor Software, Inc., Civil Action No. CV 12-3200 (E.D.N.Y. June 27, 2012).

Under the Travel Act, the mail and wire fraud statutes, and willful violations of the accounting provisions of the FCPA, the DOJ can criminally punish the giver and recipient of a private bribe, those who are willfully involved in creating misleading books and records, and related corporate entities. For individuals, the punishment can include both incarceration and fines. Corporate entities, both public and private, can be punished under either an agency theory or *respondeat superior* and assessed with fines and other impositions. US law provides for broad corporate responsibility for the actions of its directors, agents, officers and employees. Corporate entities can be held responsible for the misconduct of employees or agents, even if senior management was uninvolved in or even unaware of the misconduct.

2.3.1 Travel Act (DOJ)

(a) Individuals

- Imprisonment for not more than: i) five years if the individual distributed the bribe or facilitated it; or ii) 20 years if the individual committed any crime of violence to further the bribe, with life imprisonment possible if the violent crime caused death
- Not more than twice the gross gain from the bribe or not more than USD250,000, whichever is greater

(b) Entities

- Not more than twice the gross gain from the bribe or not more than USD500,000, whichever is greater

2.3.2 Mail or Wire Fraud (DOJ)

(a) Individuals

- Imprisonment of not more than 20 years
- Not more than twice the gross gain from the bribe or not more than USD250,000, whichever is greater

(b) Entities

- Not more than twice the gross gain from the bribe or not more than USD500,000, whichever is greater

2.3.4 Willful Accounting Violations (FCPA - DOJ)

(a) Individuals

- Imprisonment of not more than 20 years
- Not more than twice the gross gain from the bribe or not more than USD5 million, whichever is greater.

(b) Entities

- Not more than twice the gross gain from the bribe or not more than USD25 million, whichever is greater

2.3.5 Non-Willful Accounting Violations (FCPA - SEC)

(a) Individuals

- Not more than the gross gain of the bribe or USD7,500 to USD150,000, based on the egregiousness of the violation, whichever is greater

(b) Entities

- Not more than the gross gain of the bribe or USD75,000 to USD725,000, based on the egregiousness of the violation, whichever is greater

2.4 Limitations applicable to hospitality expenses (gifts, travel, meals, entertainment, among others)

There are no specific federal statutory limitations on hospitality expenses provided to private parties, and the provision of non-lavish meals, entertainment and gifts will likely not lead to prosecution. Hospitality expenses that are provided as a *quid pro quo* intended to influence government officials, on the other hand, may expose the giver and recipient to criminal liability.

In general, the hallmarks of proper hospitality expenses are those: (a) given openly and transparently, properly recorded in the giver's books and records; (b) provided only to reflect esteem; and (c) permitted under local state law.

3. Corruption of foreign public officials

3.1 Legal framework

The corruption of foreign public officials is primarily prohibited under the Foreign Corrupt Practices Act of 1977, as amended, 15 U.S.C. §§ 78dd-1, *et seq.* (the "FCPA"). The FCPA comprises anti-bribery and accounting provisions. In general, the FCPA's anti-bribery provision prohibits offering to pay, paying, promising to pay, or authorizing the payment of money or anything of value to a foreign official in order to influence any act or decision of the foreign official in his official capacity or to secure any other improper advantage in order to retain or obtain business. In addition, the FCPA's accounting provisions require companies whose securities are listed in the United States to: (a) make and keep books and records that accurately and fairly reflect the transactions of the corporation; and (b) devise and maintain an adequate system of internal accounting controls.[6]

The DOJ and SEC are very aggressive about prosecuting individuals and entities that engage in foreign corruption, including individuals and entities with limited connections to the United States. Recent activity by the DOJ – such as the issuance in 2015 of the memorandum regarding "Individual Accountability for Corporate Wrongdoing" issued by Deputy Attorney General Sally Yates (commonly referred to as the "Yates Memorandum") emphasizing the need for individual prosecutions – suggests that the DOJ will be further intensifying its focus on individual liability for corruption violations and other compliance failures in the upcoming years. Under the Yates Memorandum, companies seeking cooperation credit from the Justice Department must provide all relevant information regarding the individuals responsible for the corporate misconduct.

On 5 April 2016, the DOJ announced the FCPA Pilot Program. The Pilot Program is intended to impart more concrete guidance and policy information on the benefits for companies in making voluntary self-disclosures to the DOJ of their own potentially corrupt conduct in FCPA cases. The Pilot Program is applicable to organizations that voluntarily self-disclose or cooperate in FCPA matters during the next year. The Pilot Program will be re-evaluated and may be made permanent after this initial trial period.

The Pilot Program provides credit in FCPA matters "above and beyond any fine reduction provided for under the [United States] Sentencing Guidelines." That credit may affect the type of disposition, the reduction in fine, or the determination of the need for a monitor. More specifically, the Pilot Program provides for the possibility of a

---

[6] Conduct that violates the FCPA may also violate other statutes or regulations. Moreover, payments to foreign government officials and intermediaries may violate these other laws even if all of the elements of an FCPA violation are not present. The US government has relied upon the Travel Act, anti-money laundering statutes, mail and wire fraud statutes, and other certification, reporting, and tax regulations to prosecute individuals and entities involved in foreign corruption.

declination or a 50 percent reduction off the bottom end of the Sentencing Guidelines fine range for companies that voluntarily self-disclose, fully cooperate, and engage in timely and appropriate remediation.

However, "to receive this additional credit under the pilot program, organizations must meet the standards described [in the Pilot Program], which are more exacting than those required under the Sentencing Guidelines." For example, the Pilot Program requires: self-disclosure on a timely basis of all facts relevant to the wrongdoing at issue, including all facts related to involvement in the criminal activity by the corporation's officers, employees and agents; proactive rather than reactive cooperation; and disclosure of the locations in which overseas documents were found and to identify the individuals who found them. To the extent consistent with the attorney-client privilege, the Pilot Program also requires that all relevant facts gathered during an internal investigation be attributed to specific sources. For companies that earn cooperation and remediation credit but do not voluntarily self-disclose, the Pilot Program provides for a maximum 25 percent reduction off the bottom of the Sentencing Guidelines fine range.

3.2 Definition of corruption of foreign public official

Bribery provisions of the FCPA

As previously stated, the FCPA prohibits US "issuers" -- meaning those companies with a class of securities registered pursuant to section 12 or that are required to file reports under section 15(d) of Securities Exchange Act of 1934 -- and any officer, director, employee, or agent or any stockholder thereof acting on behalf of such issuer, as well as US individuals (citizen or resident), and companies incorporated or having their principal place of business in the United States, and certain non-US entities and individuals from:

a) *Making a payment, offer or promise (or the authorization of a payment, offer or promise) of*

b) *Anything of value* - This is defined broadly and has no minimum value, threshold or materiality, and includes, though not limited to, the following:

- Cash or the equivalent (including gift cards)
- Travel, meals, lodging, shopping, lavish entertainment expenses or hospitality
- Benefits and favors (e.g., special access to a government agency)
- Performing services that would otherwise have to be paid for or purchased
- Contracts or other business opportunities awarded to a company in which a public official has an ownership or other beneficial interest
- Employment or consultancy opportunities
- Charitable donations
- Political contributions
- Medical, educational or living expenses

c) *Directly or indirectly, "knowing" that some or all of the payment will be paid* – knowledge under the statute can be established when a person is aware that there is a high probability that a bribe is occurring. Actual knowledge need not be proved.

d) *To a "Foreign Public Official"* – as defined in the succeeding section

e) *Corruptly*: To induce an official to misuse his or her public position to improperly direct business to a company or individual. There must be an "evil motive" or purpose/intent to wrongfully influence the recipient to "misuse" his or her official position to wrongfully direct, obtain or retain business. "Willful blindness" is not a defense to liability under the statute.

f) *For the purpose of obtaining or retaining business*. This includes the following:

- Payments made to obtain a specific contract or piece of business

- Payments made to secure *any* other business advantage, including reductions in taxes, duties or fees, favorable treatment for or avoidance of customs duties, securing grants of or exemptions from otherwise applicable permits or licensing requirements, etc.

Affirmative defenses to the Anti-Bribery Provisions of the FCPA

- Payment is lawful under the written laws and regulations of the country.

- Payment is a reasonable and bona fide expenditure directly related to: (a) the promotion of products or services; or (b) the execution of a contract with a foreign government or agency.

- The foreign public official who receives the unlawful payment is not usually exposed to criminal liability under the FCPA. However, the DOJ has occasionally prosecuted foreign public officials who receive unlawful payments under other anti-corruption statutes.

3.3 Definition of foreign public official

A "Foreign Public Official" is any officer or employee of a foreign government or any department, agency or instrumentality thereof, or of a public international organization, or any person acting in an official capacity for or on behalf of any such government or department, agency or instrumentality, or for or on behalf of any such public international organization.

The definition of a Foreign Public Official is very broad and encompasses any officer or employee of: any government entity (e.g., mayor, governor, legislator), any department, instrumentality, or agency of a government, any political party, any person acting in any official capacity for such organization, candidates for political office, etc. Importantly, employees of foreign state-owned enterprises (SOEs) are also considered Foreign Public Officials for the purposes of the FCPA.

3.4 Consequences of corruption of foreign public officials

(a) For the individuals involved

- Violation of the anti-bribery provisions of the FCPA can be punished by a fine of up to USD250,000 and imprisonment of up to five years for each violation.

- Violation of the internal control provisions of FCPA can be punished by a fine of up to USD5 million and imprisonment of up to 20 years.

(b) For the legal entity

- Violation of the FCPA anti-bribery provisions can be punished by a fine of up to USD2 million per violation.

- Violation of the FCPA internal control provisions can be punished by a fine of up to USD25 million per violation.

(c) In addition to the above-described criminal penalties, the SEC can assess additional civil penalties and require disgorgement of ill-gotten gains. These penalties can run into the hundreds of millions of dollars.

Despite the higher statutory maximum penalties for violations of the internal control provisions, in practice, violations of the anti-bribery provisions are usually perceived to be more egregious and are punished accordingly.

3.5 Limitations applicable to hospitality expenses (travel, gifts, meals, entertainment, among others)

Hospitality expenses – including meals, travel, lodging, entertainment and modest gifts – may give rise to liability under the FCPA. Reasonable expenses include expenses directly related to the promotion or demonstration of products or services, or the execution or performance of a contract with a foreign government or its agency. Lavish hospitalities, repeated instances of meals and entertainment, and a lack of transparency surrounding a gift can be viewed as improper payments under the FCPA.

4. Facilitation payments

The FCPA's anti-bribery provision contains a narrow exception for facilitation payments made in furtherance of routine governmental action. Also known as "grease payments," facilitation payments are made to expedite non-discretionary acts by a government official. Facilitation payments differ from standard bribes because they are made to secure goods or services, such as the issuance of a license, visa, police protection, or power and water supply, to which the payment maker is already entitled. In contrast, typical bribes are paid to influence the outcome of a governmental decision over which a public official can exercise his or her discretion. Routine governmental action does not include a decision to award new business or any acts that would constitute misuse of an official's office.

The practical value of the exception, however, is quite limited. US enforcement authorities are highly skeptical of facilitation payments and have often pursued anti-bribery charges against defendants who claim the exception. Furthermore, to avoid violating the FCPA's accounting provisions, parties who intend to invoke the exception must accurately record their payments (e.g., listing them as "facilitation payments") on their books and records, thereby exposing them to liability in other jurisdictions where such payments are not permitted. As a result, reliance on the facilitation payment exception is not advisable. Very few defendants have successfully invoked the exception to avoid liability under the FCPA.

5. Compliance program

5.1 Value of a compliance program to mitigate/eliminate criminal liability for companies

The implementation and effectiveness of a company's compliance program plays a significant role in mitigating, or possibly even avoiding, corporate criminal liability under US Sentencing Guidelines (USSG or the "Guidelines") and the DOJ's Principles of Federal Prosecution of Business Organizations (the "Principles"), and now the FCPA Pilot Program. In 1991, the US Sentencing Commission (the "Commission") promulgated sentencing guidelines for business organizations, which instructed federal judges to impose significant monetary penalties on companies convicted of criminal offenses. Despite a 2005 US Supreme Court ruling concluding that judges are not bound by the Guidelines when imposing sentences, they remain the primary framework for resolving criminal corporate enforcement actions and imposing related fines and are, thus, highly informative for anticipating the consequences of a US anti-bribery enforcement action against a company. As with all sentencing guidelines, the Commission identified factors that would increase or reduce an organization's culpability. Among these factors is the "existence of an effective compliance and ethics program" at the time of the offense. (*See* USSG §8C2.5(f).) Section §8B2.1 of the Guidelines details the seven components of what it views as an effective compliance program. These seven elements are described by the Commission as the minimum requirements for establishing a compliance program that promotes an organizational culture of ethical conduct. Thus, they direct companies, at a minimum, to:

1. establish standards and procedures to prevent and detect criminal conduct;

2. ensure that leaders understand and oversee the compliance program in order to verify its effectiveness and the adequacy of support for the program and that specific individuals are vested with the authority and responsibility to implement the program;

3. use reasonable efforts to deny leadership positions to people who have engaged in illegal activities or other misconduct;

4. periodically communicate the standards and procedures of the compliance program to employees, and conduct effective training programs;

5. monitor and audit employee conduct, evaluate the effectiveness of the compliance program, and maintain reporting mechanisms for employees who become aware of misconduct;

6. provide incentives for employees to perform in accordance with the compliance program, and impose disciplinary measures against personnel who engage in criminal conduct; and

7. respond quickly to allegations of criminal conduct and modify aspects of the compliance program, if necessary.

An amendment gave corporations an incentive to create a direct line of communication between compliance personnel and the board of directors. In particular, it provides that if compliance personnel have "express authority" to communicate with the board about potential criminal misconduct "promptly," as well as the status of the compliance program at least annually, a corporation found guilty of wrongdoing may still receive credit for having an effective compliance program even if high level personnel were involved. (*See* USSG Commentary to §8C2.5(f); Application Note 11.)

Additional guidance on US law enforcement's expectations for an effective compliance program can be found in the DOJ's "Principles." First issued in 1999, and now codified in the US Attorneys Manual, these principles serve as a guide for federal prosecutors when deciding whether to criminally charge a corporation for the misconduct of its employees. The fifth of these factors instructs prosecutors to consider whether the company attempted to prevent the wrongdoing through a well-designed and pre-existing compliance program. Under the Principles, prosecutors are counseled to determine whether a company's compliance program is "merely a 'paper program'" or a program "designed, implemented, reviewed and revised, as appropriate in an effective manner." When read together, the USSG and the Principles provide guidance on compliance program minimum standards to which companies subject to US legal and regulatory jurisdiction should adhere.

In November 2012, when the DOJ and SEC jointly released "A Resource Guide to the US Foreign Corrupt Practices Act" (the "Guidance"), which addresses a variety of topics related to the agencies' enforcement of the FCPA. Significantly, it also provides direction on the "hallmarks" of an effective anti-corruption compliance program and the best practices that the DOJ and the SEC expect companies to put in place when addressing their anti-corruption risks. The Guidance instructs companies that when assessing an anti-corruption compliance program, the agencies ask three key questions: (1) Is the program well designed?; (2) Is it applied in good faith?; and (3) Does it work? This third criterion is now a critical part of the DOJ and SEC's assessment of whether to reward a company for its compliance program, and companies are now expected to provide tangible proof in response to this question.

Significantly, in November 2015 the DOJ appointed a new DOJ compliance consultant who will evaluate the existence and effectiveness of compliance programs for companies under FCPA investigations.

5.2 Absence of a compliance program as a criminal offense

As previously described, the presence of an effective compliance program can be a powerful mitigating factor in the prosecution calculus, and the absence of a compliance program may be an aggravating factor in an anti-corruption prosecution. There is no general criminal statute requiring corporations to have an anti-corruption compliance program, although certain regulated industries may have specific statutory compliance program requirements (*e.g.*, the Bank Secrecy Act requires financial institutions to develop and implement anti-money laundering compliance programs).

5.3 Elements of a compliance program

Five elements of an effective compliance program

When viewed together, the abovementioned pronouncements from US enforcement authorities on corporate compliance program expectations all touch upon a set of key issues that can be boiled down to five essential elements: leadership, risk assessment, standards and controls, training and communication, and oversight. These five elements serve as the organizing principles for the way Baker & McKenzie counsels our clients in the area of corporate compliance and can be practically and effectively applied to any compliance area. If a company's compliance program effectively covers these five elements, in addition to meeting US compliance program expectations, it will likely meet the wide variety of law enforcement expectations around the world.

- Leadership. A successful compliance program must consist of well-articulated internal policies and procedures and be built on a solid foundation of ethics endorsed by the board of directors. This includes having a high-ranking compliance officer in place who is provided adequate authority and resources to manage the program on a day-to-day basis. The compliance officer must also have the ear of the board of directors and report to the board at least annually.

- Risk Assessment. A company should annually evaluate its risks, including the degree to which company employees conduct business with government officials, its use of third-party agents and intermediaries, the regulatory enforcement of the regions where it operates, and the impact of recent business developments such as new joint ventures, corporate affiliations, or expansion into markets that could create additional risk.

- Standards and Controls. In addition to a code of business conduct, companies should have detailed written policies and clear procedures and protocols for ensuring those policies are implemented.

- Training and Communication. Keys to effective training programs include live, annual training for high-risk personnel; tailoring programs to each country where a company operates; and frequent updates to programs that demonstrate an understanding of evolving trends and new legislation. The manner in which the company communicates the importance of its program, internally and externally, will also be an important consideration.

- Monitoring, Auditing, Testing and Response. In order to ensure that a corporate compliance program is not "merely a 'paper program'" enforcement authorities expect companies to monitor, audit, and test their compliance programs to verify their effectiveness and prove to enforcement authorities that the program does, indeed, work.

6. Regulator with jurisdiction to prosecute corruption

The DOJ is the primary prosecutorial body with authority to prosecute corruption. Within the DOJ, a specialized FCPA Unit of the Fraud Section handles many foreign corruption cases, and the Public Integrity Section handles domestic corruption cases. Each of the 93 US Attorneys Offices also has authority to bring federal criminal charges regarding corruption with a nexus to their district, and the SEC has broad civil authority to address civil violations of the FCPA involving publicly listed companies. Finally, state and local prosecutors can bring criminal charges for violations of state anti-corruption laws.

Baker & McKenzie AP Offices

Office phone numbers and addresses change from time to time. Please refer to www.bakermckenzie.com for current contact information.

Australia

Brisbane
Baker & McKenzie
Level 8
175 Eagle Street
Brisbane QLD 4000
Australia
Tel +61 7 3069 6200
Fax: +61 7 3069 6201

Melbourne
Baker & McKenzie
Level 19
181 William Street
Melbourne VIC 3000
Australia
Tel: +61 3 9617 4200
Fax: +61 3 9614 2103

Sydney
Baker & McKenzie
Level 27, A.M.P. Centre
50 Bridge Street
Sydney, NSW 2000
Australia
Tel: +61 2 9225 0200
Fax: +61 2 9225 1595

China

Beijing
Baker & McKenzie LLP - Beijing
Representative Office
Suite 3401, China World Office 2
China World Trade Center
1 Jianguomenwai Dajie
Beijing 100004, PRC
China
Tel: +86 10 6535 3800
Fax: +86 10 6505 2309

Hong Kong - SAR
Baker & McKenzie
14th Floor, Hutchison House
10 Harcourt Road, Central
Hong Kong, SAR
China
Tel: +852 2846 1888
Fax: +852 2845 0476

Shanghai
Baker & McKenzie
Unit 1601, Jin Mao Tower
88 Century Avenue, Pudong
Shanghai 200121, PRC
China
Tel: +86 21 6105 8558
Fax: +86 21 5047 0020

Indonesia
Jakarta
Hadiputranto, Hadinoto & Partners
The Indonesia Stock Exchange Building
Tower II, 21st Floor
Sudirman Central Business District
Jl. Jendral Sudirman Kav. 52-53
Jakarta 12190
Indonesia
Tel: +62 21 2960 8888
Fax: +62 21 2960 8999

Japan
Tokyo
Baker & McKenzie (Gaikokuho Joint Enterprise)
Ark Hills Sengokuyama Mori Tower, 28th Floor
1-9-10 Roppongi, Minato-ku
Tokyo 106-0032
Japan
Tel: +81 3 6271 9900
Fax: +81 3 5549 7720

Malaysia
Kuala Lumpur
Wong & Partners
Level 21, The Gardens South Tower
Mid Valley City
Lingkaran Syed Putra
Kuala Lumpur 59200
Malaysia
Tel: +60 3 2298 7888
Fax: +60 3 2282 2669

Myanmar
Yangon
Baker & McKenzie Yangon
1203 12th Floor Sakura Tower
339 Bogyoke Aung San Road
Kyauktada Township
Yangon
Myanmar
Tel: +95 1 255 056
Fax: +95 1 255 057

Philippines
Manila
Quisumbing Torres
12th Floor, Net One Center
26th Street corner 3rd Avenue
Crescent Park West
Bonifacio Global City
Taguig City 1634
Philippines
Tel: +63 2 819 4700
Fax: +63 2 816 0080, 728 7777

Singapore
Baker & McKenzie.Wong & Leow
8 Marina Boulevard
#05-01 Marina Bay Financial Centre Tower 1
Singapore 018981
Singapore
Tel: +65 6338 1888
Fax: +65 6337 5100

South Korea
Seoul
Baker & McKenzie LLP Foreign Legal Consultant Office
17/F, Two IFC
10 Gukjegeumyung-ro
Yeongdeungpo-gu
Seoul 150-945
Korea
Tel: +82 2 6137 6800
Fax: +82 2 6137 9433

Taiwan
Taipei
Baker & McKenzie
15/F, 168 Dunhua North Road
Taipei 10548,
Taiwan
Tel: +886 2 2712 6151
Fax: +886 2 2712 8292

Thailand
Bangkok
Baker & McKenzie Limited
25th Floor, Abdulrahim Place
990 Rama IV Road
Bangkok 10500
Thailand
Tel: +66 2636 2000
Fax: +66 2636 2111

Vietnam
Hanoi
Baker & McKenzie (Vietnam) Ltd.
(Hanoi Branch Office)
Unit 1001, 10th floor,
Indochina Plaza Hanoi
241 Xuan Thuy Street,
Cau Giay District
Hanoi 10000
Vietnam
Tel: +84 4 3825 1428
Fax: +84 4 3825 1432

Ho Chi Minh City
Baker & McKenzie (Vietnam) Ltd. (HCMC)
12th Floor, Saigon Tower
29 Le Duan Blvd.
District 1
Ho Chi Minh City
Vietnam
Tel: +84 8 3 829 5585
Fax: +84 8 3 829 5618

Baker & McKenzie EMEA Offices

Office phone numbers and addresses change from time to time. Please refer to www.bakermckenzie.com for current contact information.

Austria
Vienna
Diwok Hermann Petsche
Rechtsanwälte LLP & Co KG
Schottenring 25
1010 Vienna
Austria
Tel: +43 1 24 250
Fax: +43 1 24 250 600

Azerbaijan
Baku
Baker & McKenzie - CIS, Limited
The Landmark Building
90A Nizami Street
Baku AZ1010
Azerbaijan
Tel: +994 12 497 18 01
Fax: +994 12 497 18 05

Bahrain
Manama
Baker & McKenzie Limited
18th Floor, West Tower
Bahrain Financial Harbour
PO Box 11981, Manama
Kingdom of Bahrain
Tel: +973 1710 2000
Fax: +973 1710 2020

Belgium
Antwerp
Baker & McKenzie CVBA/SCRL
Meir 24
2000 Antwerp
Belgium
Tel: +32 3 213 40 40
Fax: +32 3 213 40 45

Brussels
Baker & McKenzie CVBA/SCRL
Louizalaan 149 Avenue Louise
Eleventh Floor
Brussels 1050
Belgium
Tel: +32 2 639 36 11
Fax: +32 2 639 36 99

Czech Republic
Prague
Baker & McKenzie s.r.o.,
advokátní kancelář
Klimentská 46
110 02 Prague 1
Czech Republic
Tel: +420 236 045 001
Fax: +420 236 045 055

Egypt

Cairo

Baker & McKenzie
(Helmy, Hamza & Partners)
Nile City Building, North Tower
21st Floor 2005C, Cornich El Nil
Ramlet Beaulac
Cairo
Egypt
Tel: +20 2 2461 9301
Fax: +20 2 2461 9302

France

Paris

Baker & McKenzie SCP
1 rue Paul Baudry
75008 Paris
France
Tel: +33 1 4417 5300
Fax: +33 1 4417 4575

Germany

Berlin

Baker & McKenzie Partnerschaft von Rechtsanwälten, Wirtschaftsprüfern und Steuerberatern mbB
Friedrichstraße 88/Unter den Linden
10117 Berlin
Germany
Tel: +49 30 2200281 0
Fax: +49 30 2200281 199

Dusseldorf

Baker & McKenzie Partnerschaft von Rechtsanwälten, Wirtschaftsprüfern und Steuerberatern mbB
Neuer Zollhof 2
40221 Dusseldorf
Germany
Tel: +49 211 31 11 6 0
Fax: +49 211 31 11 6 199

Frankfurt

Baker & McKenzie Partnerschaft von Rechtsanwälten, Wirtschaftsprüfern und Steuerberatern mbB
Bethmannstrasse 50-54
60311 Frankfurt/Main
Germany
Tel: +49 69 29 90 8 0
Fax: +49 69 29 90 8 108

Munich

Baker & McKenzie Partnerschaft von Rechtsanwälten, Wirtschaftsprüfern und Steuerberatern mbB
Theatinerstrasse 23
80333 Munich
Germany
Tel: +49 89 55 23 8 0
Fax: +49 89 55 23 8 199

Hungary
Budapest
Kajtár Takács Hegymegi-Barakonyi Baker & McKenzie
Ügyvédi Iroda
Dorottya utca 6.
1051 Budapest
Hungary
Tel: +36 1 302 3330
Fax: +36 1 302 3331

Italy
Milan
Studio Professionale Associato a Baker & McKenzie
Piazza Meda, 3
Milan 20121
Italy
Tel: +39 02 76231 1
Fax: +39 02 76231 620

Rome
Studio Professionale Associato a Baker & McKenzie
Viale di Villa Massimo, 57
Rome 00161
Italy
Tel: +39 06 44 06 31
Fax: +39 06 4406 3306

Kazakhstan
Almaty
Baker & McKenzie - CIS, Limited
Samal Towers, 8th Floor.
97 Zholdasbekov Street
Almaty Samal-2, 050051
Kazakhstan
Tel: +7 727 330 05 00
Fax: +7 727 258 40 00

Luxembourg
Baker & McKenzie
10 - 12 Boulevard Roosevelt
2450 Luxembourg
Luxembourg
Tel: +352 26 18 44 1
Fax: + 352 26 18 44 99

Morocco
Casablanca
Baker & McKenzie Maroc SARL
Ghandi Mall - Immeuble 9
Boulevard Ghandi
20380 Casablanca
Morocco
Tel: +212 522 77 95 95
Fax: +212 522 77 95 96

The Netherlands
Amsterdam
Baker & McKenzie Amsterdam N.V.
Claude Debussylaan 54
1082 MD Amsterdam
P.O. Box 2720
1000 CS Amsterdam
The Netherlands
Tel: +31 20 551 7555
Fax: +31 20 626 7949

Poland
Warsaw
Baker & McKenzie Krzyzowski i Wspólnicy Spólka Komandytowa
Rondo ONZ 1
Warsaw 00-124
Poland
Tel: +48 22 445 3100
Fax: +48 22 445 3200

Qatar
Doha
Baker & McKenzie LLP
Al Fardan Office Tower
8th Floor
Al Funduq 61
Doha, PO Box 31316
Qatar
Tel: +974 4410 1817
Fax: +974 4410 1500

Russia
Moscow
Baker & McKenzie - CIS, Limited
White Gardens
9 Lesnaya Street
Moscow 125047
Russia
Tel: +7 495 787 2700
Fax: +7 495 787 2701

St. Petersburg
Baker & McKenzie - CIS, Limited
BolloevCenter, 2nd Floor
4A Grivtsova Lane
St. Petersburg 190000
Russia
Tel: +7 812 303 9000
Fax: +7 812 325 6013

Saudi Arabia
Jeddah
Legal Advisors in Association with Baker & McKenzie Limited
Bin Sulaiman Center, 6th Floor, Office No. 606
Prince Sultan Street and Rawdah Street Intersection
Al-Khalidiyah District
P.O. Box 128224
Jeddah 21362
Saudi Arabia
Tel: + 966 12 606 6200
Fax: + 966 12 692 8001

Riyadh
Legal Advisors in Association with Baker & McKenzie Limited
Olayan Complex
Tower II, 3rd Floor
Al Ahsa Street, Malaz
P.O. Box 4288
Riyadh 11491
Saudi Arabia
Tel: +966 11 265 8900
Fax: +966 11 265 8999

South Africa
Johannesburg
Baker & McKenzie Johannesburg
4 Sandown Valley Crescent
Sandton, 2196
Johannesburg
South Africa
Tel: +27 11 911 4300
Fax: +27 11 784 2855

Spain
Barcelona
Baker & McKenzie Barcelona S.L.P.
Avda. Diagonal, 652
Edif. D, 8th floor
Barcelona 08034
Spain
Tel: +34 93 206 0820
Fax: +34 93 205 4959

Madrid
Baker & McKenzie Madrid S.L.P.
Paseo de la Castellana 92
Madrid 28046
Spain
Tel: +34 91 230 4500
Fax: +34 91 391 5145; 391 5149

Sweden
Stockholm
Baker & McKenzie Advokatbyrå KB
P.O. Box 180
Vasagatan 7, Floor 8
Stockholm SE-101 23
Sweden
Tel: +46 8 5661 7700
Fax: +46 8 5661 7799

Switzerland
Geneva
Baker & McKenzie Geneva
Rue Pedro-Meylan 5
Geneva 1208
Switzerland
Tel: +41 22 707 9800
Fax: +41 22 707 9801

Zurich
Baker & McKenzie
Holbeinstrasse 30
Zurich 8034
Switzerland
Tel: +41 44 384 14 14
Fax: +41 44 384 12 84

Turkey
Istanbul
Baker & McKenzie Consultancy Services Attorney Partnership
Ebulula Mardin Cad., Gül Sok. No. 2
Maya Park Tower 2, Akatlar-Beşiktaş
Istanbul 34335
Turkey
Tel: + 90 212 339 8100
Fax: + 90 212 339 8181

Ukraine
Kyiv
Baker & McKenzie - CIS, Limited
Renaissance Business Center
24 Bulvarno-Kudriavska (Vorovskoho) Street
Kyiv 01054
Ukraine
Tel: +380 44 590 0101
Fax: +380 44 590 0110

United Arab Emirates
Abu Dhabi
Baker & McKenzie LLP - Abu Dhabi
Level 8, Al Sila Tower
Abu Dhabi Global Market Square
Al Maryah Island
P.O. Box 44980
Abu Dhabi
United Arab Emirates
Tel: +971 2 696 1200
Fax: +971 2 676 6477

Dubai
Baker & McKenzie Habib Al Mulla
Level 14, O14 Tower
Al Abraj Street, Business Bay,
P.O. Box 2268
Dubai
United Arab Emirates
Tel: +971 4 423 0000
Fax: +971 4 447 9777

Level 3, Tower 1
Al Fattan Currency House, DIFC
P.O. Box 2268
Dubai
United Arab Emirates
Tel: +971 4 423 0005
Fax: +971 4 447 9777

United Kingdom
Belfast
Baker & McKenzie LLP
City Quays One
7 Clarendon Road
Belfast BT1 3BG
United Kingdom
Tel: +44 28 9555 5000

London
Baker & McKenzie LLP
100 New Bridge Street
London EC4V 6JA
United Kingdom
Tel: +44 20 7919 1000
Fax: +44 20 7919 1999

Baker & McKenzie LA Offices

Office phone numbers and addresses change from time to time. Please refer to www.bakermckenzie.com for current contact information.

Argentina
Buenos Aires
Baker & McKenzie SC
Avenida Leandro N. Alem 1110, Piso 13
Buenos Aires C1001AAT
Argentina
Tel: +54 11 4310 2200
Fax: +54 11 4310 2299

Brazil
Brasilia
Trench, Rossi e Watanabe Advogados
SAF/S, Quadra 2, Lote 04, Sala 203
Brasília - DF - Brasil - CEP 70070-600
Brazil
Tel: +55 61 2102 5000
Fax: +55 61 3323 3312

Porto Alegre
Trench, Rossi e Watanabe Advogados
Av. Borges de Medeiros, 2233 - 4° andar
Porto Alegre - RS - Brasil - CEP 90110-150
Brazil
Tel: +55 51 3220 0900
Fax: +55 51 3220 0901

Rio de Janeiro
Trench, Rossi e Watanabe Advogados
Av. Rio Branco, 1 - 19° andar - Ed. RB1 - Setor B
Rio de Janeiro - RJ - Brasil - CEP 20090-003
Brazil
Tel: +55 21 2206 4900
Fax: +55 21 2206 4949

Sao Paulo
Trench, Rossi e Watanabe Advogados
Rua Arq. Olavo Redig de Campos,
105 – 31° andar - Ed. EZ Towers Torre A - 04711-904
São Paulo
Brazil
Tel: +55 11 3048 6800
Fax: +55 11 5506 3455

Chile

Santiago
Baker & McKenzie Ltda.
Avenida Andrés Bello 2457
Piso 19, Providencia
Santiago
Chile
Tel: +56 2 2367 7000
Fax: +56 2 2362 9876

Colombia

Bogota
Baker & McKenzie S.A.S.
Avenue 82 No. 10-62 6th Floor
Bogota
Colombia
Tel: +57 1 634 1500 / 644 9595
Fax: +57 1 376 2211

Mexico

Guadalajara
Baker & McKenzie Abogados, S.C.
Av. Paseo Royal Country 4596
Torre Cube 2, 16th Floor
Fracc. Puerta de Hierro
Zapopan, Jalisco 45116
México
Tel: +52 33 3848 5300
Fax: +52 33 3848 5399

Juarez
Baker & McKenzie Abogados, S.C.
P.O. Box 9338 El Paso, TX 79995
P.T. de la República 3304, Piso 1
Juarez, Chihuahua 32330
México
Tel: +52 656 629 1300
Fax: +52 656 629 1399

Mexico City
Baker & McKenzie, S.C.
Edificio Virreyes
Pedregal 24, piso 12
Lomas Virreyes / Col. Molino del Rey
Ciudad de México 11040
México
Tel: +52 55 5279 2900
Fax: +52 55 5279 2999

Monterrey
Baker & McKenzie Abogados, S.C.
Oficinas en el Parque
Torre Baker & McKenzie Piso 10
Blvd. Antonio L. Rodríguez 1884 Pte.
Monterrey, N.L. 64650
Mexico
Tel: +52 81 8399 1300
Fax: +52 81 8399 1399

Tijuana
Baker & McKenzie Abogados, S.C.
Blvd. Agua Caliente 10611, Piso 1, Tijuana, B.C. 22420
México
Tel: +52 664 633 4300
Fax: +52 664 633 4399

Peru
Lima
Estudio Echecopar
Av. De la Floresta 497
Piso 5 San Borja
Lima 41
Peru
Tel: +51 1 618 8500
Fax: +51 1 372 7171 / 372 7374

Venezuela
Caracas
Baker & McKenzie SC
Centro Bancaribe, Intersección Avenida Principal de Las Mercedes con inicio de Calle París, Urbanización Las Mercedes
Caracas 1060
Venezuela
Tel: +58 212 276 5111
Fax: +58 212 993 0818; 993 9049

Valencia
Baker & McKenzie SC
Urbanización La Alegria
Postal Address: P.O. Box 1155
Valencia Estado Carabobo
Venezuela
Tel: +58 241 824 8711
Fax: +58 241 824 6166

Baker & McKenzie NA Offices

Office phone numbers and addresses change from time to time. Please refer to www.bakermckenzie.com for current contact information.

Canada

Toronto
Baker & McKenzie LLP
Barristers & Solicitors
Brookfield Place
Bay/Wellington Tower
181 Bay Street, Suite 2100
Toronto, Ontario M5J 2T3
Canada
Tel: +1 416 863 1221
Fax: +1 416 863 6275

United States

Chicago
Baker & McKenzie LLP
300 East Randolph Street,
Suite 5000
Chicago, Illinois 60601
United States
Tel: +1 312 861 8000
Fax: +1 312 861 2899

Dallas
Baker & McKenzie LLP
2300 Trammell Crow Center
2001 Ross Avenue
Dallas, Texas 75201
United States
Tel: +1 214 978 3000
Fax: +1 214 978 3099

Houston
Baker & McKenzie LLP
700 Louisiana, Suite 3000
Houston, Texas 77002
United States
Tel: +1 713 427 5000
Fax: +1 713 427 5099

Miami
Baker & McKenzie LLP
Sabadell Financial Center
1111 Brickell Avenue
Suite 1700
Miami, Florida 33131
United States
Tel: +1 305 789 8900
Fax: +1 305 789 8953

New York
Baker & McKenzie LLP
452 Fifth Avenue
New York, New York 10018
United States
Tel: +1 212 626 4100
Fax: +1 212 310 1600

Palo Alto
Baker & McKenzie LLP
660 Hansen Way
Palo Alto, California 94304
United States
Tel: +1 650 856 2400
Fax: +1 650 856 9299

San Francisco
Baker & McKenzie LLP
Two Embarcadero Center,
11th Floor
San Francisco, California 94111
United States
Tel: +1 415 576 3000
Fax: +1 415 576 3099

Washington, DC
Baker & McKenzie LLP
815 Connecticut Avenue, N.W.
Washington, District of Columbia
20006
United States
Tel: +1 202 452 7000
Fax: +1 202 452 7074

Correspondent Law Firm - South Korea

SHIN & KIM
8th Floor, State Tower Namsan
100 Toegye-ro, Jung-gu
Seoul 100-052, South Korea
Tel: +82 2 316 4085
Mobile: +82 10 5451 0819